THE HOLLY CLEGG
Trim & Terrific™
COOKBOOK

THE HOLLY CLEGG
Trim & Terrific™
COOKBOOK

by Holly Clegg

RUNNING PRESS

PHILADELPHIA · LONDON

9   8   7   6   5   4

Digit on the right indicates the number of this printing

Library of Congress Cataloging-in-Publication Number 2002100477

ISBN 0-7624-1334-4

Cover photograph by David Humphreys
Food styling by Danielle Chapman
Cover and interior design by Alicia Freile
Edited by Melissa Wagner
Typography: Baskerville, Stone Sans, and Garamond

This book may be ordered by mail from the publisher.
Please include $2.50 for postage and handling.
But try your bookstore first!

Running Press Book Publishers
125 South Twenty-second Street
Philadelphia, Pennsylvania 19103-4399

Visit us on the web!
www.runningpress.com

Dishes pictured on cover:
Front cover: Shrimp Tacos with Tropical Salsa, page 306
Back cover, top: Mandarin Chicken Salad, page 148
Back cover, bottom: Sweet Potato Cheesecake, page 424

Also by Holly Clegg*:

A TRIM & TERRIFIC™ LOUISIANA KITCHEN: SOUTHERN CUISINE

MEALS ON THE MOVE: RUSH HOUR RECIPES

EATING WELL THROUGH CANCER: EASY RECIPES & RECOMMENDATIONS
DURING AND AFTER TREATMENT

* To order these books by Holly Clegg, call 1-800-88HOLLY
or visit her website at www.hollyclegg.com

TABLE OF CONTENTS

Acknowledgments 8

Introduction 10

Appetizers 13

Breads, Muffins, and Brunch 51

Soups and Stews 85

Salads 121

Vegetables 163

Poultry 209

Meat 242

Seafood 283

Pasta 321

Cookies and Cakes 363

Desserts and Pies 411

Just for Kids 455

Reference 483

Suggested Menus 485

Stock Your Pantry 490

Back to Basics 492

Tips and Tricks 497

Cooking Terms 500

Index 503

ACKNOWLEDGMENTS

To my children, you are the absolute best and make me so proud to be your mother. My son, Todd, attending Wharton at the University of Pennsylvania, a caring son with our special phone calls that keep me smiling, and now my advisor. My daughter, Courtney, attending George Washington University in journalism, who is my soul mate, my cooking companion, and my love. Haley, my fourteen-year-old, my precious baby with my treasured hugs, who is lots of fun in and out of the kitchen; and Robert, my stepson, who is a great taster and great son. To Flappy and Elvis, my two daschunds, who sometimes are more company that I want in my office. And most important, my husband, Mike, who makes everything worthwhile because we can share it together. Your support is unconditional and we still have fun after twenty-three years.

To my incredible mother and father, Ruth and Jerry, who I love dearly and, who are still interested in every word I say every time I call. Thank you for encouraging me to reach for the stars and for sharing my passions with me. I am a lucky, spoiled daughter. Mae Mae, my invaluable in-town mother and #1 babysitter, a job no one else could match. There is never a time you aren't there for me with a caring hand. NaNa and Papa, so important in my life for so many years, and Aunt Garney, you keep us smiling. My sister, Ilene, my sidekick, confidant, critic, and most importantly, my daily phone call. Pam, my Clegg-sis, my fashion consultant–I love our fun times together. All my other family, Berkowitz and Cleggs: Bart, Jim, Michael, and Kim, Cannon and Cindy, Chuck and Barbara, thanks for listening and supporting my cookbooks throughout the years.

To my longtime friends, you know who you are, as I said, I am not getting new ones . . . Francine and Doll, Louann and Ronnie, Gail and Lew, Mary and Rob, Bev, Karen, Louise, Lynell, Melanie, Cliffords, Sligars, and Mocklers, for fun, friendship, and always food. My college friends Lila, Sherri, Jolie, Les, Jo, Missy, and all those I visit throughout my travels–I am still cooking! To Gerald, the best coauthor anyone could ask for, and I promise to still work hard on our cancer cookbook. Fort Worth friends, it began many years ago with you. Baton Rouge, you have put me on the national map with your wonderful local support.

Thanks to Al (my mentor and dear friend), Diane (other advisor), and Nancy, Danielle, and Moria of Diane Allen & Associates, who I lean on continuously. Thanks to the Louisiana Sweet Potato Commission for having me all these years as national spokesperson for Louisiana Yams, a role I enjoy so much. To Elizabeth and Kate at Campbell's Soup Inc., I love the opportunity of doing spokesperson media for you and Pace Salsas–you are the best! Dublin & Associates, you do an outstanding job, you're great friends, and you are so creative!

To the people who helped me get my manuscript together. Marlene, who typed all my recipes faster than I could proof them—you had unbelievable devotion to this project. Tammi Hancock of Hancock Nutrition, for a terrific job with the nutritional analysis and for keeping me on my toes. David Humphreys, for your expertise in the cover photography, and Danielle, for pulling it all together. Kendall, my office assistant, for always doing whatever needed to be done. Thanks to Freddie Strange at Wimmer, who has shared my cookbook career with me for many years in so many stages.

I want to especially thank Buz Teacher and Running Press for giving me the opportunity to do this new cookbook with all my favorite recipes. Carlo DeVito, for making that phone call with such enthusiasm and zest. Melissa Wagner, for being a soft-spoken, talented editor who is supportive with wonderful ideas and direction. You understood my passion for this project. Thank you for putting your heart into this book, too. To Ali, who was so creative and insightful that she turned my vision of this book into reality. Outstanding job with the design and putting up with all my suggestions! To Jennifer, for her commitment, patience in listening to all my excited thoughts, and continuous effort to make our book the best!

Last but not least, a big thank you to all my Trim & Terrific™ supporters through the years. I treasure all the stories about how my books have made a difference in your kitchen and life. I can't wait until everyone has the opportunity to cook from this book!

INTRODUCTION

"I'm always in a rush and I don't want to eat bland-tasting diet food!"

If these words sound familiar, you have opened the right book. I am the author of the Trim & Terrific™ cookbook series known for "user-friendly" healthier recipes. My cooking philosophy is simple, and my approach to cooking is mainstream. All the recipes in this book are designed to get you out of the kitchen in thirty minutes with a healthy meal everyone will savor. I hate diets and food that tastes like cardboard—my love of good food has been the driving force behind my recipe creations. My expertise is in showing today's busy person how to create menus that include favorite and classic recipes prepared with eating in mind. It *is* possible to make good food choices and to practice good food habits every day.

With my goal and philosophy in mind, I am thrilled to offer my new book, *The Holly Clegg Trim & Terrific Cookbook,* as the cooking solution for the everyday person. This book contains your favorite recipes, answers frequently asked culinary questions, contains a dictionary of cooking terms and ingredients, and presents menus for all occasions, each with a nutritional analysis and diabetic exchange. This book is a wonderful resource of recipes and information for every healthy kitchen.

The Holly Clegg Trim & Terrific Cookbook is a compilation of more than 500 recipes, including all my favorites. You will see favorites from the past, updated versions of familiar recipes, and newly developed dishes to spark your taste buds. Today's trends of bold flavors and ethnic ingredients are represented in recipes throughout the book.

I am also thrilled to include a special "Just for Kids" section with creative food ideas and easy recipes for beginning cooks. As a mother of three, I feel it is important for children to spend time in the kitchen. Cooking is a valuable experience that teaches children to follow directions, read in sequence, practice math with measurements, and follow through to a finished product. All ages will enjoy the simple, tasty recipes in this section. In fact, some of these recipes are family favorites that we prepare time and time again.

Cooking need not be a chore if you have easy-to-follow recipes, a prepared pantry, and a basic knowledge of cooking terms. Therefore, I have devoted the last section of my book to relieving kitchen stress by including information on how to stock a pantry, cooking techniques, tips, kitchen vocabulary, and menu planning ideas. This book includes recipes for occasions ranging from everyday home cooking to effortless entertaining, and the menus will guide you through any occasion. Throughout the book, sidebars provide helpful hints and additional information.

Each recipe in the book has a nutritional analysis, and my goal was to keep the percentage of overall calories from fat at less than 30 percent; many of the recipes have much lower percentages. I do feel that a certain amount of fat is necessary, as fat means flavor. I never want to sacrifice flavor in my recipe development, yet we must be aware of the type of fat consumed. I have tried to balance the amount of fat included in each recipe with reasonable portion sizes so the end result is not a microscopic portion of distasteful food. Instead, the recipes in this book are palate-pleasing, with satisfying portions. The nutritional analysis of each recipe is based on the larger portion size listed. Even those recipes slightly higher in fat are healthier versions of classic recipes.

I have always felt it extremely important to include the diabetic exchanges with each recipe. Please note that some of the recipes, particularly some of the desserts, may not be appropriate for some diabetic diets at the portion size listed. As in other books, a person must follow his or her doctor's recommendations.

I have tested all the recipes in my kitchen. Many nights, my family benefited, as there was always an abundance of food, sometimes several entrées and desserts. Most importantly, these are quick-cooking, healthy recipes made with familiar ingredients. Good nutrition is important, and using this book, you can easily maintain good nutrition for your family. Having a well-stocked kitchen, learning to use herbs and spices to infuse flavor, and using lower fat substitutes can make a difference in healthier meal preparation.

Whether you are preparing comfort food for your family or fine meals to impress guests, all the recipes in this book are healthier, delicious, and, of course, easy. Consider this book your guide to everyday cooking for busy lifestyle. Let's hit the kitchen and start cooking!

Holly B. Clegg

A Guide to Symbols:

 vegetarian recipe

freezer-friendly recipe

Roasted Red Bell Pepper Dip 15

Spinach Dip 16

Black Bean Dip 16

Guacamole 17

Wasabi Guacamole 18

Tex-Mex Dip 18

Appetizers

Corn Dip 19

Shrimp Rémoulade 19

Shrimp, Avocado, and Artichoke 20

Shrimp Spread 21

Shrimp Cocktail Spread 22

Shrimp Southwestern Pizza Dip 23

Zesty Cucumber Dip 24

Hummus 24

Salsa with Tortilla Chips 25

Fiesta Salsa 26

Fruit Dip 26

Sweet Cheese Ball 27

Spinach Artichoke Dip 28

Oyster Rockefeller Dip 29

Crawfish Dip 30

Black-Eyed Pea Dip 31

Sweet-and-Spicy Chicken Strips 31

Caponata 32

Hamburger Dip 33

Mexican Bean Dip 33

Marinated Shrimp 34

Marinated Crab Fingers 35

Crabmeat Mold 35

Caviar Mold 36

Salmon Mousse with Dill Sauce 37

Cold Poached Salmon with Dill Dijon Sauce 38

Smoked Salmon Tortilla Pinwheels 39

Tortilla Shrimp Bites 39

Seafood-Stuffed Mushrooms 40

Portabello Mushrooms Stuffed with Goat Cheese and Roasted Red Peppers 41

Spinach Balls with Jezebel Sauce 42

Mini Taco Cups 43

Artichoke Bites 44

Artichoke Dip 44

Artichoke Squares 45

Hearty Stuffed Artichokes 46

Glazed Brie 47

Artichoke and Red Pepper Pizza 48

Spinach-and-Cheese Tortilla Pizza 49

Asparagus and Brie Pizza 50

Roasted Red Bell Pepper Dip

Simple to make, this creamy red dip goes great with veggies or pita crisps. For pizzazz, serve in hollowed-out red or green bell peppers.

1 (10-ounce) jar roasted
  red peppers, drained
1 tablespoon olive oil
1 (16-ounce) container
  reduced-fat cottage
  cheese
½ teaspoon minced garlic
1 tablespoon lemon juice
Dash hot pepper sauce
Salt and pepper to taste

MAKES 3 CUPS OR 12¼ CUP SERVINGS

Place the peppers, oil, cottage cheese, garlic, lemon juice, hot pepper sauce, and salt and pepper to taste in food processor; blend until very smooth.

Nutritional information per serving

Calories 34, Protein (g) 5, Carbohydrate (g) 2,
Fat (g) trace, Calories from Fat (%) 10, Saturated Fat (g) 0,
Dietary Fiber (g) 0, Cholesterol (mg) 2, Sodium (mg) 248
Diabetic Exchanges: 1 very lean meat

QUICK TIP

To roast a red pepper: Slice the pepper in half; core and seed. Brush with olive oil. Broil until soft, about 20 minutes, turning once. Place the pepper halves in a paper bag and let steam for 10 minutes to loosen the skin. Remove the skin with a paring knife.

🥕 Spinach Dip

The ultimate spinach dip, this tastes great with crackers or fresh veggies.

1 (10-ounce) package frozen chopped spinach, thawed and squeezed dry
½ cup light mayonnaise
1 cup nonfat plain yogurt
1 teaspoon seasoned salt
½ teaspoon dried dill weed leaves
Juice of ½ lemon
½ cup chopped parsley
½ cup chopped green onion (scallion)

MAKES 12 (¼-CUP) SERVINGS

Blend the spinach with the mayonnaise, yogurt, seasoned salt, dill weed, lemon juice, parsley, and green onion. Refrigerate. This dip is best when made a day ahead.

Nutritional information per serving

Calories 54, Protein (g) 2, Carbohydrate (g) 4, Fat (g) 3, Calories from Fat (%) 56, Saturated Fat (g) 1, Dietary Fiber (g) 1, Cholesterol (mg) 4, Sodium (mg) 231
Diabetic Exchanges: *1 vegetable, 0.5 fat*

🥕 Black Bean Dip

This nutritious dip full of fiber and protein will be popular with guests. The sour cream and green onion slices are the ideal complement to the snappy dip.

1 medium onion, chopped
1 (15-ounce) can black beans, rinsed and drained (slightly chopped)
1 cup salsa
1 cup shredded reduced-fat Cheddar cheese, divided
⅓ cup fat-free sour cream
½ cup sliced green onions (scallions)

MAKES 9 (¼-CUP) SERVINGS

In a medium saucepan coated with nonstick cooking spray, sauté the onion until tender. Add the black beans, salsa, and ⅔ cup cheese, cooking over low heat until the cheese is melted. Pour into a serving dish; sprinkle with the remaining ⅓ cup cheese, the sour cream, and the green onion slices. Serve with chips.

Nutritional information per serving

Calories 90, Protein (g) 6, Carbohydrate (g) 11, Fat (g) 2, Calories from Fat (%) 23, Saturated Fat (g) 2, Dietary Fiber (g) 3, Cholesterol (mg) 7, Sodium (mg) 392
Diabetic Exchanges: *1 very lean meat, 0.5 starch*

🥕 Guacamole

Avocado is made up of monounsaturated fat, so enjoy this favorite without guilt. This is my most requested recipe for classic guacamole.

1 large avocado, peeled, pitted, and mashed
Salt and pepper to taste
1 clove garlic, minced
¼ teaspoon chili powder
1 teaspoon lemon juice
2 teaspoons minced onion
¼ cup nonfat plain yogurt

MAKES 8 (3-TABLESPOON) SERVINGS

Put the mashed avocado in a small bowl, and season with the salt, pepper, garlic, chili powder, and lemon juice. Stir in the onion. Cover with the yogurt to keep the mixture from darkening. Refrigerate until serving. Just before serving, stir well.

Nutritional information per serving
Calories 56, Protein (g) 1, Carbohydrate (g) 3,
Fat (g) 5, Calories from Fat (%) 72, Saturated Fat (g) 1,
Dietary Fiber (g) 2, Cholesterol (mg) 0, Sodium (mg) 10
Diabetic Exchanges: 1 fat

QUICK TIP

To pit and peel an avocado, hold the avocado in one hand. Run a sharp knife lengthwise around the avocado, turning only the avocado, not the knife. Twist the two halves apart. Using the edge of your knife, make a quick downward stroke into the pit, twist, and remove it. Cut each avocado half lengthwise in two, and then peel away the skin.

Wasabi Guacamole

The Asian trend influences a classic guacamole. This palate-pleasing dip can be served with seared tuna or grilled fish. Wasabi can be found in jars or in powdered form in the sushi area of grocery stores.

2 cups mashed avocado
⅓ cup finely diced red
   onion
2 tablespoons finely diced,
   seeded serrano pepper
2 tablespoons lime juice
2 teaspoons prepared
   wasabi
Salt to taste

MAKES 10 TO 12 SERVINGS

In a large bowl, mix together the avocado, onion, pepper, lime juice, wasabi, and salt. Serve with chips, veggies, or as a condiment.

Nutritional information per serving
Calories 65, Protein (g) 1, Carbohydrate (g) 4,
Fat (g) 6, Calories from Fat (%) 74, Saturated Fat (g) 1,
Dietary Fiber (g) 2, Cholesterol (mg) 0, Sodium (mg) 7
***Diabetic Exchanges:** 1 vegetable, 1 fat*

Tex-Mex Dip

A most popular and addictive spread that feeds a crowd, this recipe is easily doubled and is an attention grabber at any party.

1 cup fat-free sour cream
½ cup low fat mayonnaise
1 (1¼-ounce) package
   taco seasoning mix
1 (16-ounce) can fat-free
   refried beans
1 large tomato, chopped
1 bunch green onions
   (scallions), chopped
1 (3½-ounce) can pitted
   ripe olives, drained
   and coarsely chopped
1 cup shredded
   reduced-fat sharp
   Cheddar cheese

MAKES 15 TO 20 SERVINGS

In a small bowl, combine the sour cream, mayonnaise, and taco seasoning.

To assemble, spread the refried beans on a large shallow serving plate; then spread the sour cream–taco mixture over the beans. Sprinkle with the tomato, green onions, and olives. Top with the shredded Cheddar cheese. Refrigerate until serving.

Nutritional information per serving
Calories 83, Protein (g) 4, Carbohydrate (g) 9,
Fat (g) 4, Calories from Fat (%) 39, Saturated Fat (g) 1,
Dietary Fiber (g) 1, Cholesterol (mg) 5, Sodium (mg) 389
***Diabetic Exchanges:** 0.5 very lean meat, 0.5 starch, 0.5 fat*

Corn Dip

These simple ingredients create a dip that always gets tons of compliments and recipe requests.

2 (11-ounce) cans
  Mexi-corn, drained
1 (4-ounce) can chopped
  green chilies, drained
1 (4-ounce) can chopped
  jalapeño peppers,
  drained
5 green onions (scallions),
  sliced
1 cup shredded reduced-
  fat Cheddar cheese
1 cup fat-free sour cream

MAKES 16 (¼-CUP) SERVINGS

In a large bowl, mix together the Mexi-corn, green chilies, jalapeño peppers, green onions, cheese, and sour cream. Refrigerate until serving.

Nutritional information per serving
Calories 64, Protein (g) 4, Carbohydrate (g) 9,
Fat (g) 1, Calories from Fat (%) 19, Saturated Fat (g) 1,
Dietary Fiber (g) 1, Cholesterol (mg) 4, Sodium (mg) 359
Diabetic Exchanges: 0.5 very lean meat, 0.5 starch

Shrimp Rémoulade

Serve on a bed of lettuce as a light meal or with crackers as a dip. There's an abundance of flavor in every bite of this very popular, tasty sauce.

2 pounds peeled cooked
  shrimp
¼ cup light mayonnaise
2 tablespoons horseradish
2 tablespoons grainy,
  deli style, or country
  Dijon mustard
2 tablespoons Dijon
  mustard
1 tablespoon lemon juice
⅓ cup chopped fresh
  parsley
1 bunch green onions
  (scallions), sliced
Salt and pepper to taste

MAKES 8 (¼-CUP) SERVINGS

Place the shrimp in a large bowl.

In a small bowl, mix together the mayonnaise, horseradish, grainy mustard, Dijon mustard, lemon juice, parsley, and green onions. Season with salt and pepper to taste, and mix with the shrimp. Refrigerate until serving.

Nutritional information per serving
Calories 148, Protein (g) 24, Carbohydrate (g) 2,
Fat (g) 4, Calories from Fat (%) 24, Saturated Fat (g) 1,
Dietary Fiber (g) 1, Cholesterol (mg) 224, Sodium (mg) 483
Diabetic Exchanges: 3.5 very lean meat

Shrimp, Avocado, and Artichoke

This might be my most requested recipe. Served in a glass bowl, it continually steals the show. You can substitute crawfish tails for the shrimp, or as my sister does, make it without seafood. For an appetizer spread or a light lunch, this is a show-stopping recipe.

1 pound peeled medium
   shrimp
1 tablespoon margarine
Salt and pepper to taste
2 tablespoons lemon juice
2 (14-ounce) cans
   quartered artichoke
   hearts, drained
2 avocados, peeled,
   pitted, and cubed
3 tablespoons capers,
   drained
2 bunches green onions
   (scallions), sliced
½ cup grainy mustard
¼ cup ketchup

MAKES 16 SERVINGS

In a small pan, sauté the shrimp in the margarine until done. Season to taste. Remove from heat and stir in the lemon juice. Refrigerate for 15 minutes or until chilled.

In a bowl, combine the artichoke hearts, avocado, capers, green onion, and cooled shrimp.

In a small bowl, mix together the mustard and ketchup, and carefully toss with the shrimp mixture. Refrigerate until serving.

Nutritional information per serving
Calories 86, Protein (g) 6, Carbohydrate (g) 6,
Fat (g) 5, Calories from Fat (%) 48, Saturated Fat (g) 1,
Dietary Fiber (g) 2, Cholesterol (mg) 40, Sodium (mg) 36
Diabetic Exchanges: *0.5 very lean meat, 1 vegetable, 1 fat*

QUICK TIP

To speed up ripening avocados, place in a brown paper bag overnight, or cook at medium power in the microwave for 30 seconds. Let sit for 10 minutes before using.

Shrimp Spread

For unexpected company or a quick dip, throw this recipe together. Also great for stuffing celery or tomatoes, this spread is wonderful with crackers.

1 pound cooked peeled
   shrimp
1 (8-ounce) package
   reduced-fat cream
   cheese, softened
¼ cup light mayonnaise
1 bunch green onions
   (scallions), thinly sliced
1 tablespoon chopped
   parsley
1 tablespoon lemon juice
1 teaspoon
   Worcestershire sauce
¼ teaspoon hot pepper
   sauce
Salt and pepper to taste

MAKES 16 SERVINGS

Chop the shrimp coarsely; set aside.

In a bowl, combine the cream cheese, mayonnaise, green onions, parsley, lemon juice, Worcestershire sauce, hot pepper sauce, salt, and pepper, mixing well. Add the shrimp, and serve. Keep in the refrigerator.

Nutritional information per serving
Calories 78, Protein (g) 8, Carbohydrate (g) 1,
Fat (g) 5, Calories from Fat (%) 54, Saturated Fat (g) 2,
Dietary Fiber (g) 0, Cholesterol (mg) 67, Sodium (mg) 159
Diabetic Exchanges: *1 very lean meat, 1 fat*

Shrimp Cocktail Spread

The name "shrimp cocktail" is always a head turner, and this dip combines all the cocktail parts into one zesty spread. It is ideal for a gathering—make ahead and refrigerate until ready to serve. The colorful presentation is a holiday favorite.

2 (8-ounce) packages fat-free cream cheese, softened

1 tablespoon Worcestershire sauce

½ teaspoon minced garlic

½ teaspoon hot pepper sauce

1 (12-ounce) bottle cocktail sauce

½ cup sliced green onions (scallions)

2 cups cooked, peeled small shrimp

2 tablespoons minced parsley

MAKES 8 (¼-CUP) SERVINGS

In a large bowl, blend the cream cheese, Worcestershire sauce, garlic, and hot pepper sauce until creamy. Spread on the bottom of a 9-inch serving plate. Cover the cream cheese mixture with the cocktail sauce, and sprinkle with the green onions, shrimp, and parsley. Refrigerate until ready to serve.

Nutritional information per serving

Calories 122, Protein (g) 15, Carbohydrate (g) 13, Fat (g) 1, Calories from Fat (%) 5, Saturated Fat (g) 0, Dietary Fiber (g) 1, Cholesterol (mg) 60, Sodium (mg) 877
Diabetic Exchanges: *2 very lean meat, 1 other carbohydrate*

QUICK TIP

To sneak soy protein into your recipes, use half cream cheese and half silken tofu.

Shrimp Southwestern Pizza Dip

Southwestern-flavored shrimp and seasonings are the key ingredients in this attractive, layered, crowd-pleasing dip. For the black bean dip, you can always use two cans of black beans, drained and mashed with a little salsa.

1 pound small peeled shrimp
1 teaspoon chili powder
1 teaspoon ground cumin
1 (16-ounce) jar black bean dip
½ (8-ounce) package fat-free cream cheese
½ cup fat-free sour cream
1 (1¼-ounce) package taco seasoning mix
1 (16-ounce) jar chunky salsa
½ cup sliced green onions (scallions)
1 cup shredded reduced-fat Monterey Jack cheese or Cheddar cheese or mixture

MAKES 10 TO 12 SERVINGS

In a medium skillet coated with nonstick cooking spray, cook the shrimp until done. Drain and mix with the chili powder and cumin.

Spread the black bean dip to cover the bottom of a 10-inch platter.

In a small bowl, mix together the cream cheese, sour cream, and taco seasoning mix until creamy. Carefully spread the cream cheese mixture over the bean layer. Cover with the chunky salsa. Sprinkle with the cooked shrimp, green onions, and shredded cheese. Refrigerate until serving.

Nutritional information per serving
Calories 153, Protein (g) 13, Carbohydrate (g) 13, Fat (g) 4, Calories from Fat (%) 27, Saturated Fat (g) 2, Dietary Fiber (g) 2, Cholesterol (mg) 66, Sodium (mg) 746
Diabetic Exchanges: *1.5 lean meat, 1 starch*

🥕 Zesty Cucumber Dip

This simple dip amazes me with the number of compliments I get every time I prepare it. Sometimes I substitute diced avocado for the cucumber—fabulous!

1 cup nonfat plain yogurt
1 (.7-ounce) package
  Italian dressing mix
1 tomato, seeded and
  chopped
½ cucumber, seeded,
  peeled, and chopped
3 green onions (scallions),
  chopped
1 tablespoon lemon juice

MAKES 16 (2-TABLESPOON) SERVINGS

In a medium bowl, mix together the yogurt and dressing mix until well combined. Stir in the tomato, cucumber, green onions, and lemon juice. Refrigerate until ready to serve. Serve with chips.

Nutritional information per serving

Calories 16, Protein (g) 1, Carbohydrate (g) 3, Fat (g) 0, Calories from Fat (%) 0, Saturated Fat (g) 0, Dietary Fiber (g) 0, Cholesterol (mg) 0, Sodium (mg) 144
Diabetic Exchanges: *Free*

🥕 Hummus

Serve this simply prepared and full-flavored Greek dip with toasted pita.

2 (15-ounce) cans
  garbanzo beans,
  rinsed and drained
1 teaspoon minced garlic
1 tablespoon tamari
¼ cup lemon juice
1 tablespoon sesame oil
Salt and cayenne to taste

MAKES 8 (¼-CUP) SERVINGS

Place the garbanzo beans, garlic, tamari, lemon juice, sesame oil, salt, and cayenne in a food processor or blender and purée. Serve as a dip or sauce.

Nutritional information per serving

Calories 112, Protein (g) 5, Carbohydrate (g) 16, Fat (g) 3, Calories from Fat (%) 24, Saturated Fat (g) 0, Dietary Fiber (g) 4, Cholesterol (mg) 0, Sodium (mg) 420
Diabetic Exchanges: *0.5 very lean meat, 1 starch*

FOOD FACT

Hummus is a classic Middle Eastern spread made with ground garbanzo beans (chickpeas). Garbanzo beans provide healthy soluble fiber, complex carbohydrates, protein, potassium, iron, and zinc.

Salsa with Tortilla Chips

I can't tell you how many times I've made this quick salsa to rave reviews. No one believes it when I tell them I've used canned tomatoes.

3 green onions (scallions), chopped

2 cloves garlic, minced

1 (28-ounce) can chopped tomatoes, drained

2 tablespoons finely chopped jalapeño pepper

¼ cup chopped fresh cilantro

1 teaspoon dried oregano leaves

¼ teaspoon ground cumin

MAKES 2 CUPS

In a small bowl, combine the green onion, garlic, tomatoes, jalapeño pepper, cilantro, oregano, and cumin. Serve with homemade Tortilla Chips (see recipe below) or as a topping for chicken or fish.

QUICK TIP

Cilantro has a distinctive flavor and is available year-round in grocery stores. Choose bunches that have bright, even-colored leaves with no sign of wilting. Store in a plastic bag up to 1 week.

Tortilla Chips

12 (6- to 8-inch) whole wheat or white flour tortillas

Water

These make a great snack. For a variation, sprinkle with your favorite seasonings.

MAKES 12 SERVINGS

Preheat the oven to 425°F.

Brush each tortilla with water. Cut each tortilla into eight wedges, and place on a baking sheet coated with nonstick cooking spray. Bake for 3 minutes, turn, and continue baking 3 minutes longer, or until crisp. Repeat until all the tortillas have been baked.

Nutritional information per serving
Calories 111, Protein (g) 3, Carbohydrate (g) 20, Fat (g) 2, Calories from Fat (%) 16, Saturated Fat (g) 1, Dietary Fiber (g) 2, Cholesterol (mg) 0, Sodium (mg) 224
Diabetic Exchanges: *1 starch, 1 vegetable*

Fiesta Salsa

A blast of colors that created a favorite in my home, and it takes only minutes to prepare. My family requests this salsa so often, and there's never any left. Perfect to serve on holidays.

2 avocados, peeled, pitted, and chopped
2 cups cherry tomatoes, halved
1 cup frozen corn kernels, thawed
1 (4-ounce) can chopped green chilies, drained
1 bunch green onions (scallions), sliced
3 tablespoons lime juice
½ teaspoon sugar
Salt and pepper to taste

MAKES 14 (¼-CUP) SERVINGS

In a large bowl, carefully toss together the avocados, tomatoes, corn, green chilies, green onions, lime juice, sugar, salt, and pepper.

Nutritional information per serving
Calories 67, Protein (g) 1, Carbohydrate (g) 7, Fat (g) 5, Calories from Fat (%) 55, Saturated Fat (g) 1, Dietary Fiber (g) 2, Cholesterol (mg) 0, Sodium (mg) 19
Diabetic Exchanges: *1.5 vegetable, 1 fat*

FOOD FACT

To prevent discoloration and enhance the flavor of leftover avocado, simply mash the remaining flesh and combine it with lemon or lime juice in a ratio of a ½ teaspoon per half mashed avocado. Cover with plastic wrap and refrigerate for up to two days.

Fruit Dip

All ages will grab fresh fruit to dunk into this fabulous dip with a burst of orange and an abundance of flavor.

2 (8-ounce) cartons nonfat lemon yogurt
¼ cup blanched almonds, chopped and toasted
1 teaspoon grated orange rind
2 tablespoons orange liqueur or orange juice

MAKES 8 (¼-CUP) SERVINGS

In a small bowl, combine the yogurt, almonds, orange rind, and orange liqueur, and mix well. Refrigerate at least 1 hour before serving to blend the flavors.

Nutritional information per serving
Calories 84, Protein (g) 4, Carbohydrate (g) 12, Fat (g) 2, Calories from Fat (%) 18, Saturated Fat (g) 0, Dietary Fiber (g) 0, Cholesterol (mg) 1, Sodium (mg) 40
Diabetic Exchanges: *1 skim milk*

Sweet Cheese Ball

The seasoned cream cheese mixed with the dried fruit makes this an unforgettable cheese ball. Serve with sweet crackers, gingersnaps, or apple slices. This makes a big ball, so divide in half if you desire. It freezes well.

1 (8-ounce) package fat-free cream cheese, softened

1 (8-ounce) package reduced-fat cream cheese, softened

1 teaspoon seasoned salt

2 tablespoons finely chopped onion

1 cup shredded reduced-fat Cheddar cheese

1 cup chopped dates

1 cup golden raisins

1 cup dried cranberries

½ cup chopped pecans, toasted

MAKES 32 (2-TABLESPOON) SERVINGS

In a large bowl, mix together both the cream cheeses, the seasoned salt, and the onion. Stir in the Cheddar cheese, dates, raisins, cranberries, and pecans, mixing well. Mold into a ball, and refrigerate until serving.

Nutritional information per serving
Calories 89, Protein (g) 3, Carbohydrate (g) 12, Fat (g) 4, Calories from Fat (%) 35, Saturated Fat (g) 2, Dietary Fiber (g) 1, Cholesterol (mg) 8, Sodium (mg) 131
Diabetic Exchanges: 1 fruit, 1 fat

QUICK TIP

For a variation, use dried cherries or other dried fruits in the cheeseball.

Spinach Artichoke Dip

Spinach artichoke dip tops every person's list of favorites, and this wonderful, easy-to-prepare version won't add to your waistline.

½ teaspoon minced garlic

1 onion, chopped

2 tablespoons all-purpose flour

1 (12-ounce) can evaporated skimmed milk

2 (10-ounce) boxes frozen chopped spinach, thawed and squeezed dry

4 ounces reduced-fat Monterey Jack cheese, cubed

1 (14-ounce) can quartered artichoke hearts, drained

Salt and pepper to taste

Dash Worcestershire sauce

MAKES 10 SERVINGS

In a pot coated with nonstick cooking spray, sauté the garlic and onion until very tender. Add the flour. Gradually stir in the milk, heating until thickened. Add the spinach and cheese, stirring until the cheese is melted. Stir in the artichoke hearts. Season with the salt, pepper, and Worcestershire sauce to taste. Serve hot.

Nutritional information per serving

Calories 97, Protein (g) 9, Carbohydrate (g) 11, Fat (g) 2, Calories from Fat (%) 21, Saturated Fat (g) 1, Dietary Fiber (g) 2, Cholesterol (mg) 7, Sodium (mg) 228
Diabetic Exchanges: *0.5 very lean meat, 0.5 skim milk, 1 vegetable*

QUICK TIP

Don't go buy a specific lower fat mayonnaise for a recipe; use what you have in the refrigerator.

❄ Oyster Rockefeller Dip

This recipe has been the hit of many evenings. Mixing the oysters into the spinach mixture means you don't have to worry about the fuss of oyster shells. Serve with toasted bread points or crackers.

2 (10-ounce) packages chopped spinach

3 dozen oysters, drained (reserve liquid)

1 bunch parsley

1 bunch green onions (scallions), cut into 1-inch pieces

4 stalks celery, cut into pieces

4 tablespoons margarine

3 tablespoons Worcestershire sauce

½ cup Italian bread crumbs

2 tablespoons lemon juice

1 tablespoon anchovy paste, optional

¼ cup grated Parmesan cheese

½ cup evaporated skimmed milk

¼ cup oyster liquid

3 tablespoons anisette or Pernod, optional

MAKES 14 (¼-CUP) SERVINGS

Cook the spinach according to package directions; drain very well and set aside.

Broil the oysters on a baking sheet coated with nonstick cooking spray until the oysters begin to curl. Cut into bite-size pieces; set aside.

Place the parsley, green onions, and celery in a food processor, and blend until puréed. In a large pot coated with nonstick cooking spray, melt the margarine, and sauté the puréed mixture until the veggies are very tender. Add the cooked spinach, stirring until mixed. Stir in the Worcestershire sauce, bread crumbs, lemon juice, anchovy paste, Parmesan cheese, skimmed milk, and oyster liquid, stirring until heated. Add the anisette and chopped oysters, mixing well. Serve hot.

Nutritional information per serving
Calories 100, Protein (g) 5, Carbohydrate (g) 10,
Fat (g) 5, Calories from Fat (%) 42, Saturated Fat (g) 1,
Dietary Fiber (g) 2, Cholesterol (mg) 11, Sodium (mg) 260
Diabetic Exchanges: *0.5 very lean meat, 0.5 starch, 1 fat*

❋ Crawfish Dip

A fabulous choice when crawfish is in season. Serve with melba rounds. If there is ever any extra, serve over rice or patty shells for another meal.

¼ cup margarine
¼ cup all-purpose flour
½ teaspoon minced garlic
1 bunch green onions
   (scallions), chopped
1 small onion, chopped
1 (10¾-ounce) can 98%
   fat-free cream of
   mushroom soup
1 (10-ounce) can
   diced tomatoes
   and green chilies
1 teaspoon
   Worcestershire sauce
Salt and pepper to taste
1 pound crawfish tails,
   rinsed and drained

MAKES 16 (¼-CUP) SERVINGS

In a pot, melt the margarine, and add the flour, mixing well. Add the garlic, green onions, and onion, sautéing over medium heat until tender, stirring constantly to prevent sticking. Add the mushroom soup and the chopped tomatoes and green chilies; mix well. Season with the salt and pepper to taste. Gently stir in the crawfish tails. Cook over medium heat until dip is thoroughly heated, about 3 minutes. Serve hot.

Nutritional information per serving

Calories 74, Protein (g) 5, Carbohydrate (g) 5, Fat (g) 4, Calories from Fat (%) 45, Saturated Fat (g) 1, Dietary Fiber (g) 1, Cholesterol (mg) 38, Sodium (mg) 263
Diabetic Exchanges: *1 lean meat, 1 vegetable*

FOOD FACT

When crawfish tails are packaged in a sealed bag, they are already cooked and just need to be reheated.

Black-Eyed Pea Dip

Black-eyed peas are a Southern favorite believed to bring good luck in the coming year when served and eaten on New Year's Day. Prepare this recipe as a dip with chips or as a veggie side to make your family feel lucky any time of year.

1 onion, chopped
⅓ cup chopped green
  bell pepper
1 tablespoon chopped
  jalapeño peppers
2 (15-ounce) cans black-
  eyed peas, drained
3 tablespoons all-purpose
  flour
1 (10-ounce) can diced
  tomatoes and green
  chilies
4 ounces reduced-fat
  Monterey Jack cheese,
  shredded

MAKES 20 (¼-CUP) SERVINGS

In a pot coated with nonstick cooking spray, sauté the onion, green pepper, and jalapeño over medium-low heat until tender, about 5 minutes. Add the black-eyed peas, and stir in the flour. Gradually add the tomatoes and chilies and the cheese, stirring until melted and heated thoroughly. Serve hot.

Nutritional information per serving

Calories 57, Protein (g) 4, Carbohydrate (g) 8, Fat (g) 1, Calories from Fat (%) 17, Saturated Fat (g) 1, Dietary Fiber (g) 1, Cholesterol (mg) 3, Sodium (mg) 177
Diabetic Exchanges: *0.5 very lean meat, 0.5 starch*

Sweet-and-Spicy Chicken Strips

These sweet-and-spicy glazed strips make an easy dinner dish or great pickups as appetizers.

1 cup picante sauce
¼ cup honey
½ teaspoon ground
  ginger
1½ pounds skinless,
  boneless chicken
  breasts, cut into strips

MAKES 24 SERVINGS

Preheat the oven to 400°F.

In a medium bowl, mix the picante sauce, honey, and ginger. Toss the chicken strips with the picante sauce mixture. Place in a foil-lined shallow baking pan. Bake for 40 to 50 minutes, or until glazed and done, turning and brushing often with sauce during the last 30 minutes. Serve.

Nutritional information per serving

Calories 45, Protein (g) 7, Carbohydrate (g) 4, Fat (g) trace, Calories from Fat (%) 7, Saturated Fat (g) 0, Dietary Fiber (g) 0, Cholesterol (mg) 16, Sodium (mg) 89
Diabetic Exchanges: *1 very lean meat*

 Caponata

Keep covered for several days in the refrigerator. Serve at room temperature with pita chips.
This recipe can be halved if you don't want to prepare this much.

2 medium eggplants
2 onions, chopped
1½ cups thickly sliced
   celery
2 green bell peppers,
   seeded and cut into
   1-inch chunks
2 garlic cloves, minced
⅓ cup red wine vinegar
2 (14½-ounce) cans
   Italian stewed tomatoes
   with their juice
2 tablespoons sugar
2 tablespoons dried
   basil leaves
3 tablespoons tomato
   paste
½ cup chopped parsley
1 teaspoon pepper
¼ cup sliced stuffed
   green olives

MAKES 48 (¼-CUP) SERVINGS

Cut the unpeeled eggplants into 1-inch cubes. Heat a large pot coated with nonstick cooking spray over medium-low heat, and add the eggplant and onion, sautéing until lightly golden. Add the celery, green pepper, garlic, vinegar, tomatoes, sugar, basil, tomato paste, parsley, pepper, and green olives to the pot, and stir gently but thoroughly. Simmer, covered, for 30 minutes, stirring occasionally. Remove the lid, and simmer about 10 minutes more, or until thick. Cool and refrigerate. Serve chilled or at room temperature.

Nutritional information per serving
Calories 20, Protein (g) 1, Carbohydrate (g) 5,
Fat (g) 0, Calories from Fat (%) 8, Saturated Fat (g) 0,
Dietary Fiber (g) 1, Cholesterol (mg) 0, Sodium (mg) 71
Diabetic Exchanges: *1 vegetable*

❄ Hamburger Dip

The men always gravitate to this easy, five-ingredient, hearty and satisfying dip. During football season, this recipe is requested often in my house and my son in college even called for the recipe. Serve with chips.

1 pound ground sirloin
1 onion, chopped
½ pound mushrooms, sliced
1 (16-ounce) jar salsa
1 (8-ounce) package reduced-fat Monterey Jack cheese, cut into chunks

MAKES 20 (¼-CUP) SERVINGS

Coat a heavy, medium-sized pot with nonstick cooking spray, and cook the sirloin, onion, and mushroom over medium heat for 5 to 7 minutes until the meat is well browned. Drain off excess liquid. Add the salsa and cheese, stirring over medium heat until the cheese is melted. Serve hot.

Nutritional information per serving

Calories 72, Protein (g) 8, Carbohydrate (g) 2,
Fat (g) 3, Calories from Fat (%) 41, Saturated Fat (g) 2,
Dietary Fiber (g) 0, Cholesterol (mg) 18, Sodium (mg) 190
Diabetic Exchanges: *1 lean meat*

✎ ❄ Mexican Bean Dip

Serve with chips, or roll up in a tortilla as a bean burrito for dinner.

½ cup chopped onion
1 tablespoon margarine
1 (16-ounce) can fat-free refried beans
½ cup shredded reduced-fat Cheddar cheese
1 (11-ounce) can Mexi-corn, drained
½ teaspoon minced garlic
3 tablespoons taco sauce
1 bunch green onions (scallions), sliced

MAKES 10 (¼-CUP) SERVINGS

In a medium pot, sauté the chopped onion in the margarine over medium heat until tender. Stir in the beans, cheese, and corn, stirring until the cheese is melted. Add the garlic and taco sauce. Pour into a serving bowl or chafing dish. Top with the green onion slices. Serve warm.

Nutritional information per serving

Calories 88, Protein (g) 5, Carbohydrate (g) 12,
Fat (g) 2, Calories from Fat (%) 22, Saturated Fat (g) 1,
Dietary Fiber (g) 3, Cholesterol (mg) 3, Sodium (mg) 377
Diabetic Exchanges: *0.5 very lean meat, 1 starch*

Marinated Shrimp

Make the night before and serve in a glass bowl with frilled toothpicks for a spectacular-tasting appetizer and a dramatic presentation.

¼ cup olive oil

½ teaspoon minced garlic

1 tablespoon dry mustard

½ cup lemon juice

Salt and pepper to taste

1 tablespoon red wine vinegar

1 bay leaf

Dash cayenne pepper

2 tablespoons chopped fresh parsley

1 small red onion, thinly sliced

2 tablespoons capers, drained

2 pounds cooked shrimp, peeled

MAKES 10 SERVINGS

In a bowl, combine the oil, garlic, dry mustard, lemon juice, salt, pepper, vinegar, bay leaf, and cayenne pepper; mix well. Stir in the parsley, red onion, and capers. Add the shrimp, tossing until well coated. Refrigerate for 2 hours or overnight. Drain the marinade, remove the bay leaf, and serve the shrimp with the onion, parsley, and capers.

Nutritional information per serving

Calories 94, Protein (g) 19, Carbohydrate (g) 1,
Fat (g) 1, Calories from Fat (%) 10, Saturated Fat (g) 0,
Dietary Fiber (g) 0, Cholesterol (mg) 177, Sodium (mg) 255
Diabetic Exchanges: *3 very lean meat*

QUICK TIP

Most grocery stores and seafood markets sell small, cooked shrimp. If you can't find them, saute small shrimp in a skillet coated with non-stick cooking spray and salt and pepper.

Marinated Crab Fingers

A timesaving make-ahead recipe that allows these flavors to blend. The outstanding marinade makes this dish extra special.

½ cup balsamic vinegar
¼ cup Worcestershire sauce
2 tablespoons olive oil
¼ cup lemon juice
2 tablespoons minced garlic
½ teaspoon pepper
1 teaspoon dried basil leaves
1 teaspoon sugar
2 pounds crab fingers

MAKES 16 SERVINGS

In a large bowl, mix the vinegar, Worcestershire sauce, olive oil, lemon juice, garlic, pepper, basil, and sugar. Add the crab fingers. Refrigerate for several hours or overnight. Lay the mixture on leaf lettuce to serve.

Nutritional information per serving

Calories 71, Protein (g) 14, Carbohydrate (g) 1,
Fat (g) 1, Calories from Fat (%) 9, Saturated Fat (g) 0,
Dietary Fiber (g) 0, Cholesterol (mg) 61, Sodium (mg) 58
Diabetic Exchanges: *2 very lean meat*

Crabmeat Mold

Whenever I entertain, this recipe is a definite as long as I have access to crabmeat. To cut the cost, sometimes I mix in 1 pound cooked small shrimp instead of 1 pound white crabmeat. For my family, when we splurge, I simply serve the mixture in a bowl and we all have a big smile.

½ cup light mayonnaise
1 bunch green onions (scallions), chopped
¼ cup finely chopped onion
1 tablespoon lemon juice
1 tablespoon Worcestershire sauce
Dash hot pepper sauce
Salt and pepper to taste
2 pounds lump crabmeat
1 pound white crabmeat

MAKES 25 SERVINGS FOR A COCKTAIL PARTY

In a large bowl, combine the mayonnaise, green onions, onion, lemon juice, Worcestershire sauce, hot sauce, salt, and pepper. Pick through the crabmeat and remove any shells; then carefully fold in the crabmeat. Transfer to a 6-cup mold coated with nonstick cooking spray. Refrigerate until served.

Nutritional information per serving

Calories 80, Protein (g) 11, Carbohydrate (g) 1,
Fat (g) 3, Calories from Fat (%) 39, Saturated Fat (g) 1,
Dietary Fiber (g) 0, Cholesterol (mg) 55, Sodium (mg) 205
Diabetic Exchanges: *1.5 very lean meat*

Caviar Mold

A great way to serve caviar to a crowd, this mold also makes the perfect brunch hors d'oeuvre *served with miniature rye bread slices or crackers.*

1 package unflavored
   gelatin
¼ cup water
2 hard-cooked eggs,
   chopped
4 hard-cooked eggs,
   whites only, chopped
1 (8-ounce) container
   French onion dip
⅓ cup light mayonnaise
¼ cup finely chopped
   onion
1 tablespoon
   Worcestershire sauce
3 tablespoons lemon
   juice
⅛ teaspoon cayenne
   pepper
½ teaspoon hot
   pepper sauce
1 (4-ounce) jar lumpfish
   black caviar

MAKES 15 TO 20 SERVINGS

Stir the gelatin into ¼ cup water; then place in a pan of hot water, stirring until dissolved. Gently mix in the chopped eggs and egg whites, French onion dip, mayonnaise, onion, Worcestershire sauce, lemon juice, cayenne pepper, and hot pepper sauce.

Strain the caviar in a strainer until the water runs clear, and drain well. Add to the gelatin mixture, pour into a 1-quart mold coated with nonstick cooking spray, and refrigerate two hours or until congealed.

Nutritional information per serving
Calories 37, Protein (g) 2, Carbohydrate (g) 1,
Fat (g) 3, Calories from Fat (%) 64, Saturated Fat (g) 1,
Dietary Fiber (g) 0, Cholesterol (mg) 40, Sodium (mg) 127
Diabetic Exchanges: *0.5 fat*

FOOD FACT

Beluga is the most prized caviar, followed by osetra and sevruga. Other popular and more affordable caviars include whitefish, lumpfish, and red caviar.

Salmon Mousse with Dill Sauce

This is an old standby party recipe when you want to serve a mold. The Dill Sauce makes it really special. Serve with crackers.

2 envelopes unflavored
  gelatin
¼ cup cold water
½ cup boiling water
½ cup nonfat plain yogurt
1 tablespoon lemon juice
1 tablespoon grated onion
½ teaspoon hot pepper
  sauce
½ teaspoon paprika
Salt and pepper to taste
1 (14.75-ounce) can red
  salmon, drained, skin
  discarded, and bones
  picked
2 tablespoons capers,
  drained
½ cup evaporated
  skimmed milk, chilled
Dill Sauce (recipe follows)

MAKES 10 SERVINGS

In a small bowl, soften the gelatin in the cold water. Add the boiling water, and stir until the gelatin is dissolved; cool. Add the yogurt, lemon juice, onion, hot pepper sauce, paprika, salt, and pepper; mix well. Refrigerate until the mixture is the consistency of unbeaten egg whites. Add the salmon and capers, mixing well.

In a chilled mixing bowl, beat the cold evaporated milk at high speed until stiff peaks form. Fold into the salmon mixture. Pour into a 6-cup mold coated with nonstick cooking spray. Refrigerate two hours or until congealed. Unmold and cover with Dill Sauce (see recipe below), or serve the Dill Sauce on the side in a bowl.

FOOD FACT

Salmon is a good source of heart-healthy omega 3 fatty acids and high-quality protein.

Dill Sauce

1 cup nonfat plain yogurt
¼ teaspoon sugar
2 tablespoons lemon juice
1 tablespoon grated onion
Salt and pepper to taste
1 tablespoon dried dill
  weed leaves
½ cup grated, peeled,
  and seeded cucumber

In a small bowl, mix the yogurt, sugar, lemon juice, onion, salt, pepper, dill weed, and cucumber together. Stir and refrigerate.

Nutritional information per serving
Calories 104, Protein (g) 13, Carbohydrate (g) 5,
Fat (g) 3, Calories from Fat (%) 28, Saturated Fat (g) 1,
Dietary Fiber (g) 0, Cholesterol (mg) 20, Sodium (mg) 324
***Diabetic Exchanges:** 1 lean meat, 0.5 skim milk*

Cold Poached Salmon with Dill Dijon Sauce

For an appetizer, for dinner—it will be a winner anytime. The Dill Dijon Sauce is so good you could eat it with a spoon. I serve it with other fish dishes as well.

2 cups water

1 cup dry white wine

1 carrot, diced

1 stalk celery, chopped

1 onion, sliced

½ tablespoon black peppercorns

1 (2-pound) fresh salmon fillet

Dill Dijon Sauce (recipe follows)

Dill Dijon Sauce

1 cup nonfat plain yogurt

1½ tablespoons white vinegar

1½ tablespoons Dijon mustard

3 tablespoons light brown sugar

2 teaspoons dried dill weed leaves

MAKES 10 SERVINGS

In a large poacher or pan, combine water, wine, carrot, celery, onion, and peppercorns. Bring to a boil. Lower heat, cover, and cook for 15 minutes. Add the salmon fillet. Cover and cook over low heat until the salmon is done, approximately 15 to 20 minutes. Cool the salmon in its stock.

When cool, remove the salmon from its stock and remove the skin from the salmon; chill for several hours or overnight. Serve with Dill Dijon Sauce (see recipe below).

In a small bowl, mix the yogurt, vinegar, mustard, brown sugar, and dill weed together. Refrigerate before serving; it's best if refrigerated overnight.

Nutritional information per serving
Calories 164, Protein (g) 20, Carbohydrate (g) 11,
Fat (g) 3, Calories from Fat (%) 18, Saturated Fat (g) 1,
Dietary Fiber (g) 1, Cholesterol (mg) 48, Sodium (mg) 146
Diabetic Exchanges: *2.5 very lean meat, 0.5 starch*

Smoked Salmon Tortilla Pinwheels

For an outstanding presentation, arrange these pinwheels cut-side up on a serving platter.

1 (5-ounce) package reduced-fat garlic-and-herb spreadable cheese

1 (8-ounce) package reduced-fat cream cheese, softened

¼ cup chopped red onion

¼ cup capers, drained

1 tablespoon lemon juice

4 ounces smoked salmon

8 (6- to 8-inch) tortillas

MAKES 4 TO 5 DOZEN PINWHEELS

Cut salmon into pieces. In a mixing bowl, blend together both cheeses until creamy. Stir in the red onion, capers, lemon juice, and smoked salmon. Divide and spread the filling to cover each tortilla; then roll up jelly-roll style. Place seam down on a tray, and secure each roll with a toothpick. Refrigerate until well chilled. Cut each roll into pinwheels about $3/8$-inch thick. Serve with toothpicks.

Nutritional information per 2 pieces

Calories 57, Protein (g) 3, Carbohydrate (g) 6, Fat (g) 3, Calories from Fat (%) 42, Saturated Fat (g) 2, Dietary Fiber (g) 0, Cholesterol (mg) 9, Sodium (mg) 233
Diabetic Exchanges: 0.5 starch, 0.5 fat

❄ Tortilla Shrimp Bites

Serve with salsa for a great party food. Make ahead and freeze, if desired, in zipper-lock bags.

1 (8-ounce) package reduced-fat cream cheese, softened

2 tablespoons light mayonnaise

½ cup chopped green onion (scallions)

1 (4-ounce) can chopped green chilies, drained

½ teaspoon chili powder

½ teaspoon garlic powder

Salt and pepper to taste

½ cup coarsely chopped cooked, peeled shrimp

10 (6- to 8-inch) tortillas

Salsa

MAKES 25 (2-PIECE) SERVINGS

In a medium bowl, blend the cream cheese and mayonnaise. Add the green onion, chilies, chili powder, garlic powder, salt, pepper, and shrimp, mixing well. Place about $1/8$ cup of the filling on one end of a tortilla and roll up, jelly roll style. Place the rolled tortillas, seam side down, on a tray or baking sheet. Refrigerate until ready to serve, up to several days. Cut each tortilla into 5 pieces before serving. Serve with salsa.

Nutritional information per serving

Calories 65, Protein (g) 2, Carbohydrate (g) 8, Fat (g) 2, Calories from Fat (%) 34, Saturated Fat (g) 1, Dietary Fiber (g) 1, Cholesterol (mg) 11, Sodium (mg) 176
Diabetic Exchanges: 0.5 starch, 0.5 fat

Seafood-Stuffed Mushrooms

I admit that stuffed mushrooms are time consuming. However, you can make them ahead and refrigerate until ready to cook and serve. Use crawfish or shrimp for the seafood.

36 fresh medium
   mushrooms
1 onion, chopped
½ bunch green onions
   (scallions), chopped
¼ cup chopped green
   bell pepper
1 cup bread crumbs
½ teaspoon white pepper
¼ teaspoon cayenne
   pepper, optional
½ teaspoon garlic powder
Salt and pepper to taste
1 pound crawfish tails,
   rinsed and drained, or
   cooked shrimp
2 tablespoons olive oil
1 tablespoon sherry

MAKES 36 MUSHROOMS

Preheat the oven to 350°F.

Wash the mushrooms and remove the stems; chop the stems, and set aside the mushrooms and the stems.

In a large skillet coated with nonstick cooking spray, sauté the onion, green onions, green bell pepper, and mushroom stems until tender. Add the bread crumbs, white pepper, cayenne pepper, garlic powder, salt, pepper, and crawfish tails. Mix together and cook over low heat for 5 minutes, stirring occasionally. Add the olive oil and sherry, and remove from heat.

Place the mushrooms in a metal colander over a pot of boiling water. Cover with a lid. Cook the mushrooms for about 5 minutes. Remove from heat and submerge in ice water. Drain and lay on baking sheet coated with nonstick cooking spray. Stuff the mushrooms with the filling; then bake at 350°F for 15 minutes or until heated.

Nutritional information per serving
Calories 36, Protein (g) 3, Carbohydrate (g) 3,
Fat (g) 1, Calories from Fat (%) 27, Saturated Fat (g) 0,
Dietary Fiber (g) 0, Cholesterol (mg) 7, Sodium (mg) 38
Diabetic Exchanges: *1 vegetable*

Portabello Mushrooms Stuffed with Goat Cheese and Roasted Red Peppers

The rich, hearty flavor of portabello combined with goat cheese and roasted peppers makes this a trendy, tasteful choice. Cut in fourths for pickups, or serve whole as a first course.

2 ounces goat cheese, softened

4 large portabello mushroom caps

1 (10-ounce) jar roasted red bell peppers, drained

1 tablespoon olive oil

Salt and freshly ground pepper to taste

MAKES 16 SERVINGS

Preheat the oven to 350°F.

Place the mushrooms on a baking sheet that has been lined with foil or coated with nonstick cooking spray. Spread ¼ of the goat cheese on top of each mushroom cap. Cover the cheese with a layer of roasted red peppers. Drizzle the top of the mushrooms with olive oil, and season with salt and freshly ground pepper. Roast for 15 minutes, or until the cheese begins to melt, cut into fourths and serve immediately.

Nutritional information per serving

Calories 32, Protein (g) 1, Carbohydrate (g) 2, Fat (g) 2, Calories from Fat (%) 60, Saturated Fat (g) 1, Dietary Fiber (g) 0, Cholesterol (mg) 4, Sodium (mg) 84
Diabetic Exchanges: *0.5 fat*

QUICK TIP

Roasted red peppers in jars are a quick, convenient, and sometimes even cheaper substitution for roasting fresh red peppers.

🥕 ❄️ Spinach Balls with Jezebel Sauce

You can freeze the spinach balls on a baking sheet before cooking. When frozen, transfer them to zipper-lock bags and store in the freezer. Take them directly from the freezer to bake in the oven. I've made these spinach balls for years, and they are always popular in the Jezebel Sauce, which adds a real bite.

2 (10-ounce) packages frozen chopped spinach, cooked and well drained

2 cups herb bread stuffing mix

1 cup finely chopped onion

½ cup grated Romano cheese

1½ teaspoons garlic powder

1 teaspoon dried thyme leaves

⅛ teaspoon pepper

2 eggs

4 egg whites

Jezebel Sauce (recipe follows)

MAKES 48 BALLS

Preheat the oven to 350°F.

In a large bowl, combine the spinach, stuffing mix, onion, cheese, garlic powder, thyme, pepper, eggs, and egg whites; mix well. Form into ¾-inch balls, and place on a baking sheet coated with nonstick cooking spray; bake for 20 minutes. Serve with Jezebel Sauce (see recipe below).

QUICK TIP

Jezebel Sauce is also great served over reduced-fat cream cheese on crackers.

Jezebel Sauce

½ cup apricot preserves

1 (10-ounce) jar apple jelly

2 tablespoons dry mustard

2 tablespoons prepared horseradish

1 teaspoon pepper

MAKES 2 CUPS SAUCE

In a small bowl, mix together the apricot preserves, apple jelly, dry mustard, horseradish, and pepper.

Nutritional information per 1 ball and 2 teaspoons sauce
Calories 51, Protein (g) 2, Carbohydrate (g) 9,
Fat (g) 1, Calories from Fat (%) 14, Saturated Fat (g) 0,
Dietary Fiber (g) 1, Cholesterol (mg) 10, Sodium (mg) 68
Diabetic Exchanges: *0.5 other carbohydrate*

Mini Taco Cups

The perfect pickup or snack for all ages, these cups are simple to make. The chipotle salsa gives the meat a smoky flavor.

24 won ton wrappers
1 pound ground sirloin
1 teaspoon ground cumin
1 teaspoon chili powder
⅔ cup chipotle salsa,
    divided in half
1 cup shredded reduced-
    fat Cheddar cheese

MAKES 24 SERVINGS

Preheat the oven to 425°F.

Press the won ton wrappers into mini-muffin cups coated with nonstick cooking spray.

Cook the meat in a skillet until browned; then drain off excess liquid. Stir in the cumin, chili powder, and ⅓ cup salsa. Spoon the beef mixture into the won ton cups.

Top with the remaining salsa and the cheese. Bake about 8 minutes, or until the won tons are golden brown. Serve immediately with additional salsa, if desired.

Nutritional information per serving
Calories 61, Protein (g) 6, Carbohydrate (g) 5,
Fat (g) 2, Calories from Fat (%) 28, Saturated Fat (g) 1,
Dietary Fiber (g) 0, Cholesterol (mg) 13, Sodium (mg) 78
Diabetic Exchanges: *1 very lean meat, 0.5 starch*

QUICK TIP

Make these shells ahead of time, and fill them with your favorite dip for an interesting serving presentation. Place each square in a mini-muffin pan coated with nonstick cooking spray. Bake at 350ºF for 10 minutes, or until light brown. Cool and store in zipper-lock bags.

🥕 Artichoke Bites

Quick to make, and everyone grabs for these delicious bites! Make ahead and refrigerate until ready to bake.

2 (14-ounce) cans
  artichoke hearts,
  drained and finely
  chopped
1 (4-ounce) can chopped
  green chilies
½ cup grated Parmesan
  cheese
¼ cup light mayonnaise
¼ cup Dijon mustard
1 (.65-ounce) package
  cheese garlic or Italian
  dressing mix
Dash hot pepper sauce
6 English muffins,
  cut in half

MAKES 48 BITES

Preheat the oven to 350°F.

In a small bowl, combine the artichoke hearts, green chilies, Parmesan cheese, mayonnaise, Dijon mustard, dressing mix, and hot pepper sauce, mixing well. Divide the mixture on top of each of the split muffin halves, and place on a baking sheet. Bake for 30 minutes, or until lightly browned. Cut each half into four pieces, and serve immediately.

Nutritional information per 2 pieces

Calories 64, Protein (g) 2, Carbohydrate (g) 9,
Fat (g) 2, Calories from Fat (%) 25, Saturated Fat (g) 1,
Dietary Fiber (g) 1, Cholesterol (mg) 3, Sodium (mg) 362
Diabetic Exchanges: *0.5 starch*

🥕 Artichoke Dip

This incredibly simple dip will satisfy even the most sophisticated taste bud, as I always get asked for the recipe. Serve with veggies or crackers.

½ cup fat-free sour cream
½ cup light mayonnaise
1 (.7-ounce) package
  cheesy Italian or Italian
  dressing mix
1 (14-ounce) can
  artichoke hearts,
  drained and finely
  chopped

MAKES 12 (2-TABLESPOON) SERVINGS

In a medium bowl, mix the sour cream, mayonnaise, Italian dressing mix, and artichoke hearts together. Refrigerate until serving.

Nutritional information per serving

Calories 57, Protein (g) 1, Carbohydrate (g) 6,
Fat (g) 3, Calories from Fat (%) 52, Saturated Fat (g) 1,
Dietary Fiber (g) 0, Cholesterol (mg) 4, Sodium (mg) 26
Diabetic Exchanges: *0.5 starch, 0.5 fat*

Artichoke Squares

These tasty squares can be served hot, at room temperature, or even out of the refrigerator—just cover when reheating. For a snack or an hors d'oeuvre, *Artichoke Squares will become a favorite standby.*

1 cup chopped onion

1 cup chopped
   red bell pepper

1 cup chopped green
   bell pepper

1 cup sliced mushrooms

1 teaspoon minced garlic

2 (14-ounce) cans
   artichoke hearts,
   drained, rinsed, and
   chopped

3 egg whites,
   slightly beaten

2 eggs, slightly beaten

1 teaspoon dried
   oregano leaves

1 teaspoon dried
   basil leaves

¼ teaspoon cayenne
   pepper

½ cup Italian bread
   crumbs

¾ cup shredded reduced-
   fat sharp Cheddar
   cheese

¼ cup grated Parmesan
   cheese

MAKES 30 SQUARES

Preheat the oven to 350°F.

   In a medium pan coated with nonstick cooking spray, sauté the onion, red pepper, green pepper, mushroom, and garlic over medium heat until the vegetables are tender. Transfer the sautéed vegetables into a large bowl, and add the chopped artichokes, egg whites, eggs, oregano, basil, cayenne pepper, bread crumbs, Cheddar cheese, and Parmesan cheese, stirring until well combined. Pour the mixture into a 2-quart oblong dish coated with nonstick cooking spray. Bake for 30 minutes, or until the mixture is set and the top is light brown. Cut into squares before serving. Serve immediately.

Nutritional information per serving

Calories 37, Protein (g) 3, Carbohydrate (g) 4,
Fat (g) 1, Calories from Fat (%) 28, Saturated Fat (g) 1,
Dietary Fiber (g) 1, Cholesterol (mg) 16, Sodium (mg) 119
Diabetic Exchanges: *1 vegetable*

Hearty Stuffed Artichokes

It takes a little effort to prepare this incredibly tasty recipe. My kids didn't believe I made these myself, as they look and taste like fancy restaurant quality—but better, I think you'll agree.

1 onion, chopped

1 teaspoon minced garlic

1 pound ground sirloin

1½ cups Italian bread crumbs

¼ cup grated Romano cheese

2 teaspoons dried basil leaves

2 tablespoons lemon juice

¼ cup olive oil

3 whole artichokes

Sliced lemons, optional

FOOD FACT

Artichokes offer a health-protective substance called silymarin, which may play a role in cancer prevention.

MAKES 9 TO 12 SERVINGS

In a large pan, sauté the onion, garlic, and sirloin until the meat is browned. Drain any excess fat; remove from heat. Add the bread crumbs, cheese, basil, lemon juice, and olive oil, mixing well. Set aside.

Trim the stems off the artichokes with a sharp knife. With scissors, snip off the pointed tops of the leaves. Holding the artichokes firmly with one hand, turn them leaves down and pound them on a flat surface to force open the leaves. Turn them leaves up, and rinse quickly under cold running water. Shake to remove excess moisture. With your fingers, open the leaves more to make room for the stuffing. Stuff the reserved mixture into the spaces inside the open leaves. Top each artichoke with sliced lemon if desired.

Place the artichokes in a large pot with 1 inch lightly salted water. Bring to a boil; lower heat, cover, and cook about 1 hour, or until leaves pull off easily and are tender on the inside. Watch to be sure there is always water in the pot, and add more water as needed. Serve immediately.

Nutritional information per serving
Calories 168, Protein (g) 11, Carbohydrate (g) 16,
Fat (g) 7, Calories from Fat (%) 37, Saturated Fat (g) 2,
Dietary Fiber (g) 3, Cholesterol (mg) 22, Sodium (mg) 290
***Diabetic Exchanges:** 1 very lean meat, 1 starch, 1 fat*

🥕 Glazed Brie

Time for a splurge with this recipe I just had to include. Serve with seasonable fruit to help justify this unbelievable experience. The nuts, brown sugar, and coffee liqueur make quite a topping. Remember to watch the size of your portions with ingredients like these.

¼ cup walnuts or pecans, chopped

¼ cup coffee liqueur

3 tablespoons light brown sugar

½ teaspoon vanilla extract

1 (14-ounce) round Brie cheese

Assorted crackers

Assorted sliced fruit (apples, pears)

MAKES 20 SERVINGS

Preheat the oven to 325°F.

In a small saucepan, sauté the walnuts until golden brown, about 3 minutes, stirring. Stir in the liqueur, brown sugar, and vanilla, cooking until the brown sugar is melted; set aside. Watch carefully, as it cooks quickly.

Remove the top rind of the Brie. Place the Brie in a shallow baking dish. Top with the walnut mixture. Bake for 8 to 10 minutes, or until the Brie is soft and heated through. Serve immediately with assorted crackers and fruit slices.

Nutritional information per serving
Calories 96, Protein (g) 4, Carbohydrate (g) 4,
Fat (g) 6, Calories from Fat (%) 60, Saturated Fat (g) 4,
Dietary Fiber (g) 0, Cholesterol (mg) 20, Sodium (mg) 126
Diabetic Exchanges: *0.5 high-fat meat, 0.5 other carbohydrate, 0.5 fat*

FOOD FACT

Brie is a cream-colored, buttery-soft cheese that should be perfectly ripe for the best flavor—it oozes at the peak of ripeness. Brie from France is considered the best.

Artichoke and Red Pepper Pizza

Start with a prepared crust and add these gourmet ingredients for a real winner.
Also makes a good light lunch.

1 (10-ounce) can
   refrigerated pizza
   crust dough
5 cloves garlic
2 tablespoons olive oil
2 red bell peppers,
   seeded and cut
   into ¼-inch strips
1 teaspoon dried
   basil leaves
1 (2.5-ounce) jar sliced
   mushrooms, drained
1 (14-ounce) can
   artichoke hearts,
   drained and chopped
1½ cups shredded part-
   skim Mozzarella cheese

MAKES 12 SLICES

Preheat the oven to 425°F.

Coat a 12-inch pizza pan with nonstick cooking spray. Unroll the dough and place in the prepared pan, starting at the center and pressing out with your hands. Bake for 5 to 8 minutes, or until light golden brown.

In a food processor, mince the garlic and add the olive oil, blending well. Spread the garlic mixture over the partially baked crust.

In a medium skillet coated with nonstick cooking spray, sauté the red pepper strips until crisp-tender, about 5 minutes. Layer the pepper strips, basil, mushroom slices, and artichokes over the garlic mixture; top with the cheese. Bake for 10 minutes, or until the crust is golden brown and the cheese is melted. Cut into small slices before serving.

Nutritional information per serving
Calories 134, Protein (g) 6, Carbohydrate (g) 15,
Fat (g) 5, Calories from Fat (%) 36, Saturated Fat (g) 2,
Dietary Fiber (g) 1, Cholesterol (mg) 8, Sodium (mg) 304
Diabetic Exchanges: *0.5 lean meat, 1 starch, 0.5 fat*

QUICK TIP

Rub a halved garlic clove on top of the pizza crust to add lots of flavor with little effort.

Spinach-and-Cheese Tortilla Pizza

This makes a great pickup, or serve a single tortilla for lunch with a bowl of soup or salad. Keep the ingredients available for a special quickie treat.

2 large (10-inch) flour tortillas

2 tablespoons fat-free sour cream

1 (10-ounce) package frozen chopped spinach, thawed and squeezed dry

1 large tomato, chopped

Salt and pepper to taste

½ cup shredded reduced-fat Monterey Jack cheese

¼ cup thinly sliced green onion (scallion)

MAKES 12 SLICES

Preheat the oven to 450°F.

Place the tortillas on a baking sheet coated with nonstick cooking spray. Bake for 3 minutes, or until golden brown. Remove from the oven, and reduce the temperature to 350°F.

Spread the sour cream evenly over the tortillas. Top each with the spinach, tomato, salt, and pepper to taste. Next, sprinkle evenly with the Monterey Jack cheese. Bake for 5 minutes more, or until the cheese is melted. Sprinkle with the green onion. Cut each tortilla into four slices, and serve immediately.

Nutritional information per serving

Calories 65, Protein (g) 3, Carbohydrate (g) 9, Fat (g) 2, Calories from Fat (%) 25, Saturated Fat (g) 1, Dietary Fiber (g) 1, Cholesterol (mg) 3, Sodium (mg) 108
Diabetic Exchanges: *0.5 starch*

Asparagus and Brie Pizza

Brie cheese and asparagus team up to create a pizza of simple elegance. Substitute broccoli or your favorite veggie for asparagus, if desired.

12 thin asparagus spears, tips only

1 red bell pepper, seeded and thinly sliced, or 1 roasted red bell pepper, cut into strips

1 teaspoon minced garlic

1 (10-ounce) can refrigerated pizza crust dough, or 1 (16-ounce) Boboli prepared crust

½ teaspoon dried basil leaves

½ teaspoon dried oregano leaves

Salt and pepper to taste

3½ ounces Brie cheese, rind removed, thinly sliced

MAKES 12 SLICES

Preheat the oven to 425°F.

Fill a small saucepan with water, and bring to a boil. Cook the asparagus tips in the boiling water until tender, about 4 minutes. Drain and set aside.

Heat a skillet coated with nonstick cooking spray over medium heat, and sauté the red pepper until tender, about 4 minutes. Stir in the garlic.

Coat a 12-inch pizza pan with nonstick cooking spray. Unroll the dough and place in the prepared pan, starting at the center and pressing out with your hands. Bake for 5 minutes. Remove from heat, and sprinkle the crust with the basil, oregano, salt, and pepper; then evenly distribute the red pepper, Brie, and asparagus over the crust. Bake for 8 to 10 minutes more. Slice and serve immediately.

Nutritional information per serving

Calories 96, Protein (g) 4, Carbohydrate (g) 13, Fat (g) 3, Calories from Fat (%) 30, Saturated Fat (g) 1, Dietary Fiber (g) 1, Cholesterol (mg) 8, Sodium (mg) 210
Diabetic Exchanges: *1 starch, 0.5 fat*

QUICK TIP

When buying asparagus, examine the tips for signs of freshness, as they are the part most likely to break or spoil.

Try snapping off the bottom of each stalk instead of cutting. The stalk will usually separate right where the woody part ends.

Beer Bread 53

Herbed French Bread 54

Italian Puffs 55

Biscuits 56

Mexican Brunch Biscuit Bake 56

Herbed Biscuits 57

Breads, Muffins, and Brunch

Pull-Apart Biscuit Bake 57

Yam Biscuits 58

Cranberry Orange Scones 59

Lemon Berry Bread 60

Cranberry Orange Bread 61

Easy Cranberry Yam Bread 62

Banana Cranberry Bread 63

Zucchini Bread 64

Mango Bread 65

Apricot Bread 66

Butterscotch Banana Bread 67

Chocolate Zucchini Bread 68

Cinnamon Crescents 69

Cranberry Pineapple Muffins 70

Chunky Whole Wheat Apple Muffins 71

Lemon Raspberry Muffins 72

Tropical Muffins 73

Surprise Corn Bread 73

Cheesy Corn Muffins 74

Bran Muffins 74

Bread Pudding Florentine 75

Crabmeat Egg Casserole 76

Egg and Green Chile Casserole 77

Tex-Mex Eggs 78

Steak Creole with Cheese Grits 79

Quick Cheese Grits 80

Hot Fruit Casserole 81

Basic Pancakes 82

Baked French Toast 82

Cereal Mixture 83

Snack Mix 83

Granola 84

Beer Bread

The smell of yeast bread fills the kitchen, yet this homemade bread with a yeasty taste is effortless to make.

3 cups self-rising flour

⅓ cup sugar

1 (12-ounce) can light beer (room temperature)

2 tablespoons margarine, melted

MAKES 16 SLICES

Preheat the oven to 350°F. Coat a 9 x 5 x 3-inch loaf pan with nonstick cooking spray.

In a large bowl, combine the flour, sugar, beer, and margarine, mixing until just moistened. Pour the batter into the loaf pan. Bake for 50 minutes, or until golden brown. Serve warm.

Nutritional information per serving

Calories 110, Protein (g) 2, Carbohydrate (g) 21, Fat (g) 1, Calories from Fat (%) 11, Saturated Fat (g) 0, Dietary Fiber (g) 0, Cholesterol (mg) 0, Sodium (mg) 287
Diabetic Exchanges: *1.5 starch*

QUICK TIP

If you prefer a whole wheat version of this bread, use the following ingredients, but follow the same cooking instructions listed above.

2 cups self-rising flour

1 cup whole wheat flour

4 tablespoons honey

1 teaspoon baking powder

1 (12-ounce) can light beer (room temperature)

2 tablespoons margarine, melted

Herbed French Bread

So easy, and this takes French bread to a new level of taste.

3 tablespoons margarine, melted

1 teaspoon finely chopped parsley

½ teaspoon Worcestershire sauce

¼ teaspoon dried oregano leaves

¼ teaspoon dried basil leaves

¼ teaspoon garlic powder

1 (8-ounce) loaf French bread, split in half lengthwise

MAKES 6 TO 8 SERVINGS

Preheat the oven to 350°F.

In a small bowl, combine the margarine, parsley, Worcestershire sauce, oregano, basil, and garlic powder, stirring well. Lightly brush each half of the bread with the margarine mixture. Wrap in foil and bake for 10 minutes, or until the bread is crispy on the outside. Slice and serve.

Nutritional information per serving

Calories 117, Protein (g) 3, Carbohydrate (g) 15, Fat (g) 5, Calories from Fat (%) 40, Saturated Fat (g) 1, Dietary Fiber (g) 1, Cholesterol (mg) 0, Sodium (mg) 226
Diabetic Exchanges: *1 starch, 1 fat*

QUICK TIP

If your bread is:
Tough and heavy—too much flour or mixing
Peaked and smooth tops—too much mixing
Uneven texture with holes or tunnels—too much mixing
Dark crust and center not done—oven too hot

Italian Puffs

This simple recipe will be the hit of the entire meal. My kids love these melt-in-your-mouth rolls and will even make them for me. Make ahead, refrigerate, and pop in the oven later. For lower fat or if desired, just leave out the Cheddar cheese. They'll still melt in your mouth.

1 (8-ounce) can reduced-
    fat crescent dinner rolls
3 ounces reduced-fat
    Cheddar cheese, cut
    into ¾-inch cubes
2 tablespoons fat-free
    Italian dressing
3 tablespoons sesame
    seeds
3 tablespoons grated
    Parmesan cheese

MAKES 8 PUFFS

Preheat the oven to 375°F.

Separate the crescent dough into eight triangles. Place a cheese cube on the wide end of each triangle. Fold both corners on the wide side over the cheese, and roll to the opposite point, completely covering the cheese, sealing well.

In a small bowl, pour the dressing. On a small plate, combine the sesame seeds and Parmesan cheese. Dip each roll in the dressing, and then roll in the sesame seed/cheese mixture. Place the rolls on a baking sheet coated with nonstick cooking spray. Bake for 12 to 15 minutes, or until the rolls are golden. Serve immediately.

Nutritional information per serving

Calories 166, Protein (g) 7, Carbohydrate (g) 13,
Fat (g) 9, Calories from Fat (%) 51, Saturated Fat (g) 3,
Dietary Fiber (g) 0, Cholesterol (mg) 8, Sodium (mg) 400
Diabetic Exchanges: 0.5 lean meat, 1 starch, 1 fat

 Biscuits

Here's a great recipe when you have the urge for homemade biscuits. Best served hot.

1 cup all-purpose flour

1½ teaspoons baking
powder

⅛ teaspoon baking soda

⅛ teaspoon salt

2 tablespoons margarine

½ cup nonfat plain
yogurt

1 teaspoon honey

MAKES 8 SERVINGS

Preheat the oven to 425°F.

In a medium bowl, combine the flour, baking powder, baking soda, and salt; cut in the margarine with a pastry blender or fork until the mixture resembles coarse meal. Add the yogurt and honey, stirring just until the dry ingredients are moistened.

Turn the dough onto a floured surface and knead four times. Roll the dough to ½-inch thickness; cut with a cutter about 2½ inches wide. Place on an ungreased baking sheet. Bake for 10 minutes, or until golden. Serve hot.

Nutritional information per serving

Calories 94, Protein (g) 3, Carbohydrate (g) 14, Fat (g) 3, Calories from Fat (%) 29, Saturated Fat (g) 1, Dietary Fiber (g) 0, Cholesterol (mg) 0, Sodium (mg) 193
Diabetic Exchanges: *1 starch, 0.5 fat*

🥕❄ Mexican Brunch Biscuit Bake

This recipe is perfect for an eggless breakfast, a great snack, or a terrific bread with dinner.

1 (12-ounce) can
buttermilk biscuits
(10 count)

1 (6-ounce) can
buttermilk biscuits
(5 count)

1 (16-ounce) jar chunky
salsa

1 bunch green onions
(scallions), chopped

1 cup shredded reduced-
fat Monterey Jack cheese

MAKES 8 TO 10 SERVINGS

Preheat the oven to 350°F. Coat a 13 x 9 x 2-inch baking pan with nonstick cooking spray.

Separate the biscuits, and cut each into quarters. In a large mixing bowl, toss the biscuits with the salsa, green onions, and cheese. Transfer the mixture into the prepared pan. Bake, uncovered, for 30 minutes, or until the middle is fully cooked. Serve hot from the oven.

Nutritional information per serving

Calories 150, Protein (g) 6, Carbohydrate (g) 21, Fat (g) 3, Calories from Fat (%) 22, Saturated Fat (g) 1, Dietary Fiber (g) 1, Cholesterol (mg) 6, Sodium (mg) 643
Diabetic Exchanges: *0.5 lean meat, 1.5 starch*

🥕 ❄️ Herbed Biscuits

Hard to believe these incredible herby rolls begin with packaged biscuit dough. Prepare ahead, refrigerate covered, and bring up to room temperature before baking.

3 tablespoons margarine

1 (10-ounce) can refrigerated biscuits

2 cloves garlic, minced

1 teaspoon dried basil leaves

½ teaspoon dried oregano leaves

2 tablespoons grated Parmesan cheese

1 tablespoon sesame seeds

1 tablespoon chopped parsley

MAKES 4 TO 6 SERVINGS

Preheat the oven to 400°F.

Melt the margarine in a 9-inch round pan in the oven. Separate the biscuits, and cut each into four pieces. Stir the garlic, basil, oregano, cheese, sesame seeds, and parsley into the margarine in the pan. Arrange the pieces of biscuits next to one another in the margarine. Bake for 15 minutes, or until the tops are brown. Immediately invert the biscuits onto a platter and serve.

Nutritional information per serving

Calories 183, Protein (g) 4, Carbohydrate (g) 22, Fat (g) 9, Calories from Fat (%) 42, Saturated Fat (g) 1, Dietary Fiber (g) 1, Cholesterol (mg) 2, Sodium (mg) 505 **Diabetic Exchanges:** *1.5 starch, 1.5 fat*

🥕 ❄️ Pull-Apart Biscuit Bake

There's little time involved in this dish that's sure to be a family favorite.

2 tablespoons margarine, melted

1½ teaspoons dried dill weed leaves

1½ teaspoons poppy seeds

⅓ cup grated Parmesan cheese

2 (10-ounce) cans refrigerated buttermilk biscuits

MAKES 6 TO 8 SERVINGS

Preheat the oven to 400°F. Pour the melted margarine into a 9-inch round pan coated with nonstick cooking spray.

In a zipper-lock plastic bag, combine the dill weed, poppy seeds, and Parmesan cheese. Cut each biscuit into two pieces; add the biscuit pieces to the bag, and shake to coat. Arrange the coated biscuit pieces in the prepared pan; sprinkle with any remaining mixture. Bake for 15 minutes, or until golden. Serve hot.

Nutritional information per serving

Calories 214, Protein (g) 6, Carbohydrate (g) 33, Fat (g) 7, Calories from Fat (%) 28, Saturated Fat (g) 1, Dietary Fiber (g) 1, Cholesterol (mg) 3, Sodium (mg) 709 **Diabetic Exchanges:** *2 starch, 1 fat*

Yam Biscuits

Whip up these nutritious and delicious biscuits with pantry ingredients. Make different sizes of biscuits to match their intended use. I've served these at parties with a meat tray.

1 (15-ounce) can sweet
　　potatoes (yams),
　　drained and mashed
4 cups biscuit baking mix
½ teaspoon ground
　　cinnamon
¾ cup skim milk
3 tablespoons margarine,
　　softened

MAKES 20 TO 24 BISCUITS

Preheat the oven to 450°F.

　　In a mixing bowl, mix the mashed yams with the baking mix and cinnamon. Add the milk and margarine to the mixture, stirring until blended. Roll on a floured surface to 1-inch thickness. Cut with a 2-inch cutter or glass, and place on an ungreased baking sheet. Bake for 10 to 12 minutes, or until golden brown. Serve hot.

Nutritional information per serving
Calories 115, Protein (g) 2, Carbohydrate (g) 17,
Fat (g) 4, Calories from Fat (%) 35, Saturated Fat (g) 1,
Dietary Fiber (g) 1, Cholesterol (mg) 0, Sodium (mg) 286
Diabetic Exchanges: *1 starch, 1 fat*

QUICK TIP

For a savory biscuit, delete the cinnamon and add 1 tablespoon chopped parsley and 1 teaspoon seasoning salt or seasoning mix.

Cranberry Orange Scones

There's no need to pick up scones at a coffee store when in no time at all you can whip these up for a quick, wonderful morning treat.

2 cups all-purpose flour

¼ cup sugar

2 teaspoons baking powder

½ teaspoon baking soda

1 teaspoon grated orange rind

3 tablespoons chilled margarine, cut into small pieces

1 cup nonfat plain yogurt

⅓ cup dried cranberries

MAKES 10 SCONES

Preheat the oven to 400°F.

In a large bowl, combine the flour, sugar, baking powder, baking soda, and orange rind; cut in the margarine with a pastry blender until the mixture resembles coarse meal. Add the yogurt to the dry ingredients, stirring just until the ingredients are mixed. Stir in the cranberries. The dough will be sticky.

Turn the dough onto a floured surface and knead with floured hands several times, or until rolling consistency. Roll dough into a circle about 8 inches in diameter, and cut into rounds with a 2-inch biscuit cutter or glass. Place on a baking sheet, and bake for 15 minutes, or until golden brown.

Nutritional information per serving

Calories 167, Protein (g) 4, Carbohydrate (g) 29, Fat (g) 4, Calories from Fat (%) 20, Saturated Fat (g) 1, Dietary Fiber (g) 1, Cholesterol (mg) 0, Sodium (mg) 220
Diabetic Exchanges: *1.5 starch, 0.5 fruit, 0.5 fat*

Lemon Berry Bread

When blueberries aren't available, leave them out for a luscious lemon bread. The lemon syrup soaks through the bread, enhancing the flavor, and making this bread a lemon lover's favorite.

⅓ cup canola oil

⅔ cup plus ½ cup sugar, divided

2 tablespoons lemon extract

1 egg

2 egg whites

1 ½ cups all-purpose flour

1 teaspoon baking powder

½ cup skim milk

1 cup fresh blueberries

2 tablespoons grated lemon rind

½ cup lemon juice

MAKES 16 SERVINGS

Preheat the oven to 350°F. Coat a 9 x 5 x 3-inch loaf pan with nonstick cooking spray.

In a large bowl, mix the oil, ⅔ cup sugar, lemon extract, egg, and egg whites. In a separate, small bowl, combine the flour with the baking powder. Add the flour mixture to the sugar mixture alternately with the milk, stirring just until blended. Fold in the blueberries and lemon rind. Pour the batter into the prepared pan. Bake for 40 to 50 minutes, or until a wooden toothpick inserted in the center comes out clean.

Immediately poke holes at 1-inch intervals on the top of the bread. In a small saucepan over medium heat or in a microwave oven, combine the remaining ½ cup sugar and the lemon juice, heating until the sugar is dissolved. Pour over the bread. Cool, and slice to serve.

Nutritional information per serving

Calories 161, Protein (g) 2, Carbohydrate (g) 26, Fat (g) 5, Calories from Fat (%) 28, Saturated Fat (g) 0, Dietary Fiber (g) 1, Cholesterol (mg) 13, Sodium (mg) 46
Diabetic Exchanges: *1.5 starch, 0.5 other carbohydrate, 1 fat*

QUICK TIP

If you have frozen—instead of fresh—blueberries, do not thaw before using, or the berries will become too mushy.

❄ Cranberry Orange Bread

A great holiday bread! Dried cranberries may be substituted for fresh, and throw in some toasted pecans, if desired. It freezes well, so it makes a good gift.

2 cups all-purpose flour
1½ teaspoons baking powder
½ teaspoon baking soda
1 cup sugar
¼ cup canola oil
¾ cup orange juice
1 egg, beaten
1 tablespoon grated orange rind
½ teaspoon almond extract
1½ cups cranberries, coarsely chopped

MAKES 16 SLICES

Preheat the oven to 350°F. Coat a 9 x 5 x 3-inch loaf pan with nonstick cooking spray.

In a large bowl, combine the flour, baking powder, baking soda, and sugar in a bowl. In a separate, small bowl, combine the oil, orange juice, egg, orange rind, and almond extract. Add the orange juice mixture to the dry ingredients, stirring just until the dry ingredients are moistened. Fold in the cranberries. Pour the batter into the prepared pan. Bake for 45 to 50 minutes, or until a toothpick inserted in the center comes out clean. Cool in the pan.

Nutritional information per serving

Calories 152, Protein (g) 2, Carbohydrate (g) 27, Fat (g) 4, Calories from Fat (%) 23, Saturated Fat (g) 0, Dietary Fiber (g) 1, Cholesterol (mg) 13, Sodium (mg) 90
Diabetic Exchanges: *1 starch, 1 other carbohydrate, 0.5 fat*

QUICK TIP

Coat only the bottoms of loaf pans for fruit breads. The ungreased sides allow the batter to cling while rising during baking, helping to form a gently rounded top.

Easy Cranberry Yam Bread

Cream cheese gives this incredible, yet easy, bread a rich flavor packed with the natural sweetness of yams and a burst of cranberries. It will top your quick bread list. Toss in some walnuts for added flavor and crunch.

1 (8-ounce) package reduced-fat cream cheese, softened

1 cup sugar

1 (15-ounce) can sweet potatoes (yams), drained and mashed

2 eggs

1½ cups biscuit baking mix

1 teaspoon ground cinnamon

½ teaspoon ground nutmeg

1 cup dried cranberries, or 1 cup chopped fresh cranberries

MAKES 16 SLICES

Preheat the oven to 350°F. Coat a 9 x 5 x 3-inch loaf pan with nonstick cooking spray.

In a large mixing bowl, cream together the cream cheese and sugar until light and fluffy. Beat in the sweet potatoes and eggs. Stir in the biscuit mix, cinnamon, nutmeg, and cranberries until just blended. Transfer to the prepared pan. Bake for 45 minutes to 1 hour, or until a toothpick inserted in the center comes out clean. Cool in the pan for 15 minutes before serving.

Nutritional information per serving
Calories 189, Protein (g) 4, Carbohydrate (g) 31,
Fat (g) 6, Calories from Fat (%) 26, Saturated Fat (g) 3,
Dietary Fiber (g) 1, Cholesterol (mg) 37, Sodium (mg) 231
Diabetic Exchanges: *1.5 starch, 0.5 fruit, 1 fat*

QUICK TIP

Mini loaves of quick bread make wonderful homemade gifts. Make ahead, wrap in plastic wrap, place in zipper-lock bags, and freeze until ready to give.

Banana Cranberry Bread

Use those overripe bananas with tart cranberries for this wonderful-tasting bread. Take advantage of cranberry season to make this perfect holiday recipe.

2 bananas, peeled
¼ cup sugar
½ cup light brown sugar
¼ cup canola oil
2 eggs
1 teaspoon vanilla extract
1 cup all-purpose flour
¼ teaspoon baking soda
½ teaspoon baking powder
¼ cup buttermilk
1 cup dried cranberries, or 1 cup chopped fresh cranberries
1 teaspoon grated orange rind

MAKES 16 SLICES

Preheat the oven to 350°F. Coat a 9 x 5 x 3-inch loaf pan with nonstick cooking spray.

In a large bowl, beat the bananas until puréed. Add the sugar, brown sugar, canola oil, eggs, and vanilla, and continue beating until creamy.

In a separate, small bowl combine the flour, baking soda, and baking powder. Stir the flour mixture alternately with the buttermilk into the banana mixture, beginning and ending with the flour, mixing only until combined. Stir in the dried cranberries and orange rind. Pour the batter into the prepared pan. Bake for 40 to 45 minutes, or until a toothpick inserted in the center comes out clean. Cool in the pan.

Nutritional information per serving
Calories 144, Protein (g) 2, Carbohydrate (g) 25, Fat (g) 4, Calories from Fat (%) 26, Saturated Fat (g) 1, Dietary Fiber (g) 1, Cholesterol (mg) 27, Sodium (mg) 50
Diabetic Exchanges: *1 starch, 0.5 fruit, 0.5 fat*

QUICK TIP

Don't fret—a large, lengthwise crack in the center is characteristic of quick breads.

❄ Zucchini Bread

This bread resembles carrot bread and is packed with flavor and texture. Many times I substitute golden raisins for dark raisins.

¾ cup whole wheat flour

¾ cup all-purpose flour

½ teaspoon baking soda

½ teaspoon baking powder

1 teaspoon ground cinnamon

2 egg whites

⅓ cup sugar

⅓ cup light brown sugar

⅓ cup canola oil

1 teaspoon vanilla extract

1 cup shredded zucchini, unpeeled

½ cup crushed pineapple, in its own juice

⅓ cup raisins

⅓ cup pecans, toasted, optional

MAKES 16 SLICES

Preheat the oven to 350°F. Coat a 9 x 5 x 3-inch loaf pan with nonstick cooking spray.

In a large bowl, mix the whole wheat flour, flour, baking soda, baking powder, and cinnamon. Add the egg whites, sugars, oil, and vanilla. Mix thoroughly. Fold in the zucchini, pineapple, raisins, and pecans. Pour the batter into the prepared loaf pan. Bake for 40 to 45 minutes, or until a toothpick inserted in the center comes out clean. Cool in the pan.

Nutritional information per serving
Calories 133, Protein (g) 2, Carbohydrate (g) 21, Fat (g) 5, Calories from Fat (%) 31, Saturated Fat (g) 0, Dietary Fiber (g) 1, Cholesterol (mg) 0, Sodium (mg) 66
Diabetic Exchanges: *1 starch, 0.5 fruit, 1 fat*

FOOD FACT

Zucchini has a thin, edible skin and soft seeds—therefore, there's no need to peel.

Mango Bread

Magnificent mangoes make up this hard-to-beat quick bread. If you've never experienced mangoes, here's an ideal recipe to try.

¼ cup margarine

¾ cup sugar

1 egg, lightly beaten

1 cup puréed mango
  (about 2 medium)

1 teaspoon vanilla extract

2 tablespoons lime juice

1½ cups all-purpose flour

1½ teaspoons baking
  powder

½ teaspoon baking soda

½ teaspoon ground
  cinnamon

½ cup chopped walnuts,
  toasted

MAKES 16 SLICES

Preheat the oven to 350°F. Coat a 9 x 5 x 3-inch loaf pan with nonstick cooking spray.

In a large mixing bowl, cream the margarine and sugar, beating well. Add the egg, mango, vanilla, and lime juice. In a separate large bowl, combine the flour, baking powder, baking soda, and cinnamon. Add the mango mixture to the flour mixture, stirring just until the dry ingredients are moistened. Stir in the walnuts. Pour the batter into the prepared loaf pan. Bake for 40 minutes, or until a toothpick inserted in the center comes out clean. Cool in the pan for 10 minutes before serving.

Nutritional information per serving
Calories 152, Protein (g) 2, Carbohydrate (g) 24,
Fat (g) 6, Calories from Fat (%) 33, Saturated Fat (g) 1,
Dietary Fiber (g) 1, Cholesterol (mg) 13, Sodium (mg) 123
Diabetic Exchanges: *1 starch, 0.5 fruit, 1 fat*

QUICK TIP

When buying mangoes, look for a yellowish outer skin tinged with red, which is a sign of ripeness. If you can't find ripe mangoes, papayas will work just as well.

Apricot Bread

Munching on this sweet citrus bread with tart apricots is as good as eating cake. My tasters immediately demanded the recipe.

1 cup diced dried apricots

1 egg

1 cup sugar

2 tablespoons margarine, melted

2 cups all-purpose flour

1 tablespoon baking powder

¼ teaspoon baking soda

¾ cup orange juice

MAKES 16 SLICES

Preheat the oven to 350°F. Coat a 9 x 5 x 3-inch loaf pan with nonstick cooking spray.

Pour boiling water over the apricots to cover, and let stand 5 minutes. Drain apricots, discard water, and set aside.

Meanwhile, in a mixing bowl, beat the egg and sugar. Add the melted margarine.

In a separate large bowl, combine the flour, baking powder, and baking soda. Add the flour mixture alternately with the orange juice to the sugar mixture. Stir in the drained apricots. Pour the batter into the prepared pan. Bake for 50 minutes to 1 hour, or until a toothpick inserted in the center comes out clean. Cool in the pan.

Nutritional information per serving
Calories 152, Protein (g) 2, Carbohydrate (g) 32,
Fat (g) 2, Calories from Fat (%) 11, Saturated Fat (g) 0,
Dietary Fiber (g) 1, Cholesterol (mg) 13, Sodium (mg) 133
***Diabetic Exchanges:** 1.5 starch, 0.5 fruit*

QUICK TIP

Use kitchen scissors to cut dried fruit easily.

Butterscotch Banana Bread

When you're in the mood for banana bread with flair, the butterscotch chips do the trick. For a good, old-fashioned purist's banana bread, leave out the butterscotch chips.

1¾ cups all-purpose flour

2 teaspoons baking powder

½ teaspoon baking soda

½ teaspoon ground cinnamon

½ teaspoon ground nutmeg

¾ cup sugar

1 egg

2 egg whites

1 cup mashed banana (2 large bananas)

¼ cup canola oil

¼ cup skim milk

½ cup butterscotch chips

MAKES 16 SLICES

Preheat the oven to 350°F. Coat a 9 x 5 x 3-inch loaf pan with nonstick cooking spray.

In a large bowl, combine the flour, baking powder, baking soda, cinnamon, and nutmeg; set aside.

In a large mixing bowl, combine the sugar, egg, egg whites, mashed banana, and oil, blending well. Add the flour mixture alternately with the milk to the banana mixture, mixing only until combined. Stir in the butterscotch chips. Pour into the prepared pan. Bake for 50 minutes to 1 hour, or until a toothpick inserted in the center comes out clean. Cool in the pan.

Nutritional information per serving

Calories 167, Protein (g) 3, Carbohydrate (g) 27, Fat (g) 5, Calories from Fat (%) 29, Saturated Fat (g) 2, Dietary Fiber (g) 1, Cholesterol (mg) 13, Sodium (mg) 118
Diabetic Exchanges: *1 starch, 1 other carbohydrate, 1 fat*

FOOD FACT

Quick breads are perfect for the busy cook since there is no rising, punching down, or shaping. Baking powder and baking soda are the leaveners and require gentle mixing. For best results, have the oven preheated, and don't overmix the batter (small lumps are fine) or you will end up with dense, tough bread.

Chocolate Zucchini Bread

The unique combination of chocolate and zucchini produces an exceptionally moist, tasty bread with a carrot cake texture.

1½ cups all-purpose flour

⅓ cup cocoa

1 teaspoon baking soda

1 teaspoon ground cinnamon

¼ teaspoon baking powder

1 cup sugar

2 eggs

⅓ cup canola oil

1 teaspoon vanilla extract

2 cups shredded zucchini

MAKES 16 SLICES

Preheat the oven to 350°F. Coat a 9 x 5 x 3-inch loaf pan with nonstick cooking spray.

In a large bowl, mix the flour, cocoa, baking soda, cinnamon, and baking powder; set aside.

In a separate large bowl, mix the sugar, eggs, oil, and vanilla until well blended. Stir in the zucchini. Add the dry ingredients, and stir until just moistened. Pour into the prepared pan. Bake for 45 to 55 minutes, or until a toothpick inserted in the center comes out clean. Cool in the pan.

Nutritional information per serving

Calories 151, Protein (g) 3, Carbohydrate (g) 23, Fat (g) 5, Calories from Fat (%) 32, Saturated Fat (g) 1, Dietary Fiber (g) 1, Cholesterol (mg) 27, Sodium (mg) 95
Diabetic Exchanges: *1 starch, 0.5 other carbohydrate, 1 fat*

QUICK TIP

Cocoa is a great way to enjoy chocolate without the saturated fat in solid chocolate.

Cinnamon Crescents

Save a trip to the bakery—in just a few minutes you can prepare these easy, melt-in-your-mouth jumbo crescents. My kids like to leave out the pecans, and I like to add raisins—either way, they are outstanding!

¼ cup light brown sugar

¼ cup chopped pecans

1 teaspoon ground cinnamon

2 cups biscuit baking mix

1 tablespoon sugar

½ cup cold water

3 tablespoons margarine, softened

Glaze (recipe follows)

MAKES 8 CRESCENTS

Preheat the oven to 425°F. In a small bowl, combine the brown sugar, pecans, and cinnamon; set aside.

In a separate, large bowl, mix the baking mix, sugar, and water until a soft dough forms; beat vigorously for 30 seconds. Roll the mixture into a ball with hands dusted with baking mix so the dough will not stick. Knead 1 minute. Pat or roll the dough into a 10- to 12-inch circle. Spread with the margarine and sprinkle the brown sugar mixture, and cut into eight wedges. Roll up, beginning at wide edges, to point. Place the crescents on an ungreased baking sheet; shape into a semicircle. Bake for 10 minutes, or until golden brown. Cool slightly on the baking sheet; drizzle with the Glaze (see recipe below).

Glaze

½ cup confectioners' sugar

1 tablespoon margarine, softened

¼ teaspoon vanilla extract

1 tablespoon water

In a small bowl, mix the confectioners' sugar, margarine, vanilla, and water with a fork, adding more water as needed, until blended and smooth.

Nutritional information per serving

Calories 261, Protein (g) 3, Carbohydrate (g) 35, Fat (g) 13, Calories from Fat (%) 44, Saturated Fat (g) 2, Dietary Fiber (g) 1, Cholesterol (mg) 0, Sodium (mg) 447
Diabetic Exchanges: *2 starch, 0.5 other carbohydrate, 2 fat*

Cranberry Pineapple Muffins

Cranberry, pineapple, and pecans, with a touch of cinnamon, make this a popular choice. Dried cranberries will substitute for fresh cranberries.

1 cup all-purpose flour

½ cup whole wheat flour

½ cup quick-cooking oatmeal

¼ cup plus 1 tablespoon sugar, divided

2 teaspoons baking powder

½ teaspoon plus ¼ teaspoon ground cinnamon, divided

¼ cup margarine

1 egg, beaten

1 cup skim milk

1 cup fresh cranberries, coarsely chopped

½ cup unsweetened crushed pineapple, drained

½ cup chopped pecans, optional

MAKES 12 MUFFINS

Preheat the oven to 400°F. Line a muffin pan with paper cups, or coat it with nonstick cooking spray.

In a large bowl, combine the flour, whole wheat flour, oatmeal, ¼ cup sugar, baking powder, ½ teaspoon cinnamon, and margarine with a pastry blender or fork until the mixture resembles coarse crumbs. In a separate small bowl, combine the beaten egg and the milk; add to the dry ingredients, stirring just until moistened. Gently fold in the cranberries, pineapple, and pecans.

Spoon the batter into the prepared pan, filling the cups three-quarters full. Combine 1 tablespoon sugar and ¼ teaspoon cinnamon; sprinkle evenly over the remaining muffin batter. Bake for 20 to 25 minutes, or until golden brown. Remove immediately from the pan, and cool on a wire rack.

Nutritional information per serving

Calories 143, Protein (g) 4, Carbohydrate (g) 22, Fat (g) 5, Calories from Fat (%) 29, Saturated Fat (g) 1, Dietary Fiber (g) 2, Cholesterol (mg) 18, Sodium (mg) 142
Diabetic Exchanges: *1.5 starch, 1 fat*

QUICK TIP

When chopping raisins or dried fruit, coat the knife blade with nonstick cooking spray to prevent sticking.

Chunky Whole Wheat Apple Muffins

Apple, pecans, and raisins enliven this moist, yummy muffin.

1½ cups all-purpose flour, divided

½ cup peeled, chopped baking apples

½ cup whole wheat flour

⅓ cup light brown sugar

1½ teaspoons baking powder

½ teaspoon ground cinnamon

¼ teaspoon salt

½ cup skim milk

3 tablespoons canola oil

2 egg whites, lightly beaten

⅓ cup chopped pecans

⅓ cup golden raisins

MAKES 12 MUFFINS

Preheat the oven to 400°F. Line a muffin pan with papers or coat with a nonstick cooking spray.

In a small bowl, combine ½ cup flour and the apple in a small bowl, tossing to coat; set aside.

In a large bowl, combine the remaining 1 cup flour, whole wheat flour, brown sugar, baking powder, cinnamon, and salt; make a well in the center of the mixture.

In a small bowl, combine the milk, oil, and egg whites; stir well. Add the milk mixture, apple mixture, pecans, and raisins to the flour mixture, stirring just until the dry ingredients are moistened. Spoon the batter into the prepared pan, filling two-thirds full. Bake for 20 minutes, or until golden brown. Cool in pan.

Nutritional information per serving
Calories 173, Protein (g) 4, Carbohydrate (g) 27,
Fat (g) 6, Calories from Fat (%) 31, Saturated Fat (g) 1,
Dietary Fiber (g) 2, Cholesterol (mg) 0, Sodium (mg) 127
***Diabetic Exchanges:** 1.5 starch, 0.5 fruit, 1 fat*

✏️ ❄️ Lemon Raspberry Muffins

Raspberries and lemon pair for a very enticing muffin.

2 cups all-purpose flour
⅔ cup sugar
1 tablespoon baking
　powder
1 cup skim milk
⅓ cup canola oil
1 teaspoon lemon extract
1 egg
2 egg whites
1½ cups fresh or frozen
　raspberries (if frozen,
　no syrup)
1 teaspoon grated
　lemon rind

MAKES 12 TO 16 MUFFINS

Preheat the oven to 425°F. Line a muffin pan with papers, or coat with nonstick cooking spray.

In a large bowl, combine the flour, sugar, and baking powder, mixing well. In a small bowl, combine the milk, oil, lemon extract, egg, and egg whites, blending well. Add to the dry ingredients, stirring just until the ingredients are moistened. Carefully fold in the raspberries and lemon rind. Fill the prepared pan three-quarters full with batter. Bake for 18 to 23 minutes, or until golden brown. Cool 5 minutes; remove from the pan.

Nutritional information per serving
Calories 148, Protein (g) 3, Carbohydrate (g) 23,
Fat (g) 5, Calories from Fat (%) 31, Saturated Fat (g) 0,
Dietary Fiber (g) 1, Cholesterol (mg) 14, Sodium (mg) 111
Diabetic Exchanges: *1.5 starch, 1 fat*

FOOD FACT

Raspberries are an excellent source of Vitamin C and fiber. Wash raspberries just before you're ready to use; washing earlier can ruin these delicate berries.

🥕 ❄️ Tropical Muffins

Tropical paradise in a muffin. If desired, substitute half whole wheat flour.

2 cups all-purpose flour

⅓ cup light brown sugar

2 teaspoons baking powder

½ teaspoon baking soda

1 cup nonfat plain yogurt

2 egg whites

¼ cup canola oil

2 teaspoons coconut extract

1 cup crushed pineapple, well drained

MAKES 12 MUFFINS

Preheat the oven to 400°F. Coat a muffin pan with non-stick cooking spray.

In a large bowl, combine the flour, brown sugar, baking powder, and baking soda. In another bowl, mix together the yogurt, egg whites, oil, and coconut extract. Mix into the flour mixture, stirring just until blended. Fold in the drained pineapple. Spoon the batter into the prepared pan, filling three-quarters full. Bake for 20 to 25 minutes, or until golden. Cool in the pan.

Nutritional information per serving

Calories 167, Protein (g) 4, Carbohydrate (g) 27, Fat (g) 5, Calories from Fat (%) 26, Saturated Fat (g) 0, Dietary Fiber (g) 1, Cholesterol (mg) 0, Sodium (mg) 163 **Diabetic Exchanges:** *1.5 starch, 0.5 fruit, 1 fat*

🥕 ❄️ Surprise Corn Bread

This fulfilling, fabulous corn bread begins with convenience items, so it's a simple indulgence. Corn bread is perfect with chili and barbecued meats.

2 (8-ounce) packages corn muffin mix

2 eggs

⅔ cup skim milk

1 cup picante sauce

1 cup reduced-fat shredded Cheddar cheese

MAKES 12 TO 16 SERVINGS

Preheat the oven to 400°F. Coat a 9 x 9 x 2-inch square pan with nonstick cooking spray.

In a bowl, mix together the corn muffin mix, eggs, and milk, stirring well. Spread half the batter into the prepared pan, and top with the picante sauce and cheese. Carefully spread the remaining batter on top. Bake for 20 minutes, or until golden brown. Cut into squares, and serve warm.

Nutritional information per serving

Calories 146, Protein (g) 4, Carbohydrate (g) 23, Fat (g) 4, Calories from Fat (%) 26, Saturated Fat (g) 2, Dietary Fiber (g) 0, Cholesterol (mg) 30, Sodium (mg) 357 **Diabetic Exchanges:** *1.5 starch, 0.5 fat*

![carrot] ![snowflake] Cheesy Corn Muffins

This deluxe cornmeal muffin goes really well with barbecue. For a quick pickup, make in miniature muffin tins (makes about 4 dozen miniature muffins).

1 cup chopped onion

1 (8½-ounce) can cream-style corn

1 cup shredded reduced-fat sharp Cheddar cheese

⅔ cup fat-free sour cream

2 tablespoons canola oil

2 egg whites

1 tablespoon sugar

1½ cups self-rising cornmeal mix

MAKES 18 MUFFINS

Preheat the oven to 400°F. Coat muffin tins with a non-stick cooking spray.

In a pan coated with nonstick cooking spray, sauté the onion over low heat until tender. In a large bowl, combine the onion with the corn, cheese, sour cream, oil, egg whites, and sugar. Add the cornmeal, and blend well. Fill the muffin tins three-quarters full, and bake for 20 to 25 minutes, or until done. Remove the muffins, and cool on a wire rack.

Nutritional information per serving

Calories 108, Protein (g) 4, Carbohydrate (g) 15, Fat (g) 3, Calories from Fat (%) 27, Saturated Fat (g) 1, Dietary Fiber (g) 1, Cholesterol (mg) 3, Sodium (mg) 292 **Diabetic Exchanges:** *1 starch, 0.5 fat*

![carrot] ![snowflake] Bran Muffins

This batter keeps in the refrigerator for several weeks in a covered plastic or glass container, so you can serve hot muffins in very little time. This quickie is my favorite bran muffin.

4 cups raisin bran cereal

1 cup sugar

2½ cups all-purpose flour

2½ teaspoons baking soda

2 teaspoons ground cinnamon

2 eggs, beaten

⅓ cup canola oil

2 cups buttermilk

MAKES 24 MUFFINS

Preheat the oven to 400°F. Line muffin pans with paper liner, or coat with nonstick cooking spray.

In a large bowl, mix the cereal, sugar, flour, baking soda, and cinnamon together. Add the eggs, oil, and buttermilk, stirring with a spoon until well combined. Fill each muffin cup two-thirds full. Bake for 15 minutes, or until a toothpick inserted in the center of a muffin comes out clean. Cool and remove to wire rack.

Nutritional information per serving

Calories 152, Protein (g) 3, Carbohydrate (g) 27, Fat (g) 4, Calories from Fat (%) 23, Saturated Fat (g) 1, Dietary Fiber (g) 2, Cholesterol (mg) 18, Sodium (mg) 217 **Diabetic Exchanges:** *2 starch, 0.5 fat*

BREADS, MUFFINS, AND BRUNCH

Bread Pudding Florentine

An outstanding brunch recipe that is one of my personal favorites, this can be made the night before and popped into the oven to cook in the morning. It's great for a group.

5 eggs

4 egg whites

3 cups skim milk

¼ cup Dijon mustard

Salt and pepper to taste

1 (16-ounce) loaf day-old French bread, cut into 16 slices, divided

½ pound mushrooms, sliced

1 teaspoon minced garlic

1 onion, chopped

2 (10-ounce) boxes frozen chopped spinach, thawed and squeezed dry

1 tablespoon all-purpose flour

Salt and pepper to taste

1½ cups shredded reduced-fat Swiss cheese, divided

MAKES 10 TO 12 SERVINGS

Coat a 13 x 9 x 2-inch pan with nonstick cooking spray.

In a large mixing bowl, beat the eggs and egg whites with the milk, mustard, salt, and pepper; set aside.

Place half the bread slices in the prepared pan.

In a skillet coated with nonstick cooking spray, sauté the mushrooms, garlic, and onion until tender. Add the spinach and flour, stirring to mix well. Season with salt and pepper to taste. Spread the mixture over the bread layer. Sprinkle with 1 cup of the cheese. Top with the remaining bread. Sprinkle with the remaining ½ cup of the cheese. Pour the egg mixture over the casserole, and refrigerate 2 hours or overnight. Bake at 350°F for 40 to 50 minutes, or until puffed and golden. Serve immediately.

Nutritional information per serving

Calories 230, Protein (g) 15, Carbohydrate (g) 27, Fat (g) 6, Calories from Fat (%) 24, Saturated Fat (g) 3, Dietary Fiber (g) 3, Cholesterol (mg) 97, Sodium (mg) 552
Diabetic Exchanges: *1.5 lean meat, 1.5 starch, 1 vegetable*

Crabmeat Egg Casserole

A crowd-pleasing brunch for those crabmeat fans. Any seafood, or ham, may be used instead of crabmeat.

6 slices whole wheat
   bread or white bread
1½ cups water
1 onion, chopped
½ cup chopped
   green bell pepper
½ cup chopped celery
2 cloves garlic, minced
2 cups shredded reduced-
   fat sharp Cheddar
   cheese
1 (8-ounce) can sliced
   water chestnuts,
   drained
1 pound lump crabmeat,
   picked for shells
1 egg
2 egg whites
½ cup light mayonnaise
Salt and pepper to taste
Several dashes hot
   pepper sauce

MAKES 10 SERVINGS

Preheat the oven to 350°F. Coat a 2- to 3-quart oblong baking dish with nonstick cooking spray.

Place the bread in a large bowl with the water. Let stand 15 minutes.

In a medium skillet coated with nonstick cooking spray, sauté the onion, green pepper, celery, and garlic until tender. Add the shredded cheese to the bread-and-water mixture, stirring together. Carefully stir in the sautéed vegetables, water chestnuts, and crabmeat.

In a medium mixing bowl, beat the egg, egg whites, mayonnaise, salt, pepper, and hot pepper sauce. Combine with the crabmeat mixture, mixing well, and transfer to the prepared dish. Bake for 30 to 40 minutes, or until the filling is set.

Nutritional information per serving
Calories 223, Protein (g) 20, Carbohydrate (g) 13,
Fat (g) 10, Calories from Fat (%) 40, Saturated Fat (g) 4,
Dietary Fiber (g) 2, Cholesterol (mg) 72, Sodium (mg) 521
Diabetic Exchanges: *2.5 lean meat, 0.5 starch, 1 vegetable*

Egg and Green Chile Casserole

A Southwestern egg dish that cuts easily into squares. The sliced tomato topping makes this delicious casserole appealing to the eye.

1 (8-ounce) package reduced-fat Monterey Jack cheese, shredded

1 cup shredded reduced-fat Cheddar cheese

2 (4-ounce) cans chopped green chiles, drained

1 bunch green onions (scallions), chopped

5 eggs

7 egg whites

3 tablespoons nonfat plain yogurt

1 tomato, thinly sliced

MAKES 12 SERVINGS

Coat a 2- to 3-quart oblong glass baking dish with non-stick cooking spray.

Combine both cheeses, green chiles, and green onions; spread on the bottom of the dish. Beat the eggs and egg whites together with the yogurt. Pour over the cheeses, making a space with a fork so the eggs will go through to the bottom. Refrigerate overnight.

Place in a cold oven, and bake for 15 minutes at 350°F. Add sliced tomatoes along the top of the casserole, and continue baking for 15 to 20 minutes longer, or until done. Serve immediately.

Nutritional information per serving

Calories 132, Protein (g) 13, Carbohydrate (g) 3, Fat (g) 7, Calories from Fat (%) 51, Saturated Fat (g) 4, Dietary Fiber (g) 1, Cholesterol (mg) 104, Sodium (mg) 312
Diabetic Exchanges: 2 lean meat

🥕 Tex-Mex Eggs

An open-face omelet with tortillas, Southwestern seasonings, and cheese, this is a great choice for brunch. Serve with salsa for an additional Tex-Mex touch.

5 (6-inch) flour or corn tortillas

1 bunch green onions (scallions), finely chopped

1 red bell pepper, seeded and chopped

2 tablespoons chopped pickled jalapeño pepper

¼ cup finely chopped fresh cilantro

2 eggs

6 egg whites

¼ cup skim milk

1 teaspoon ground cumin

Salt and pepper to taste

⅓ cup shredded reduced-fat sharp Cheddar cheese

MAKES 4 SERVINGS

Preheat the oven to 500°F.

Dip the tortillas into water, drain, and place on a baking sheet coated with nonstick cooking spray. Bake for 4 minutes, turn, and bake for 2 minutes longer, or until crisp; set aside.

In a large skillet coated with nonstick cooking spray, sauté the green onions, red pepper, and jalapeño over medium-high heat until tender. Stir in cilantro and set aside.

In a large bowl, mix the eggs, egg whites, milk, cumin, salt, and pepper. Crumble the crisp tortillas into the egg mixture; let stand for 5 minutes.

Pour the egg mixture into a skillet coated with nonstick cooking spray over medium heat. As the mixture begins to cook, gently lift the edges with a spatula and tilt the pan to allow the uncooked portions to flow underneath. When the eggs are almost set, spoon the vegetable mixture over the top, combining with the eggs. Sprinkle with the cheese, and continue cooking until the eggs are done and the cheese is melted. Serve immediately.

Nutritional information per serving

Calories 223, Protein (g) 16, Carbohydrate (g) 30, Fat (g) 4, Calories from Fat (%) 18, Saturated Fat (g) 2, Dietary Fiber (g) 2, Cholesterol (mg) 112, Sodium (mg) 516
Diabetic Exchanges: *2 very lean meat, 1.5 starch, 1 vegetable*

❄ Steak Creole with Cheese Grits

Ever heard of grillades and grits? This unbelievably flavored dish is served at a true Southern brunch, and it also makes a good light evening meal. See recipe for Quick Cheese Grits, page 80.

3 pounds lean, boneless
    top round steak
¼ teaspoon pepper
¼ cup all-purpose flour
1 onion, thickly sliced
2 green bell peppers,
    seeded and sliced
1 tablespoon minced
    garlic
2 cups canned beef broth
1 (15-ounce) can tomato
    sauce
1 teaspoon light brown
    sugar
1 tablespoon
    Worcestershire sauce
1 teaspoon dried basil
    leaves
1 teaspoon dried thyme
    leaves
1 teaspoon dried
    oregano leaves

MAKES 6 SERVINGS

Trim any fat from the round steak. Season the steak with the pepper, and dredge the steak in the flour, shaking off any excess. In a large skillet coated with nonstick cooking spray, brown the steak over medium-high heat for 5 to 7 minutes on each side. Remove the steak from the skillet and set aside.

Add the onion and bell pepper to the skillet, and cook over moderate heat, stirring occasionally, about 5 minutes. Stir in the garlic, beef broth, tomato sauce, brown sugar, Worcestershire sauce, basil, thyme, and oregano; bring to a boil. Return the steak to the skillet, and cover it with the sauce. Cover and cook over medium-low heat for 1½ to 2 hours, or until the steak is very tender, stirring occasionally. Serve with Quick Cheese Grits (see page 80).

Nutritional information per serving
Calories 381, Protein (g) 57, Carbohydrate (g) 16,
Fat (g) 8, Calories from Fat (%) 21, Saturated Fat (g) 3,
Dietary Fiber (g) 2, Cholesterol (mg) 141, Sodium (mg) 861
Diabetic Exchanges: *6 very lean meat, 0.5 starch, 1.5 vegetable*

Quick Cheese Grits

Cheese grits are hard to beat, especially with this simple recipe.

4 cups water

1 cup skim milk

½ teaspoon salt

1½ cups quick grits

4 ounces reduced-fat pasteurized processed cheese spread

6 ounces reduced-fat sharp Cheddar cheese, shredded

2 tablespoons margarine

1 tablespoon Worcestershire sauce

¼ teaspoon garlic powder

¼ teaspoon cayenne pepper

MAKES 8 TO 10 SERVINGS

In a saucepan, bring the water, milk, and salt to a boil. Add the grits, reduce heat, and cook about 5 minutes, stirring occasionally. Add the cheeses, margarine, Worcestershire sauce, garlic powder, and cayenne pepper. Stir until the margarine and cheeses have melted. Serve immediately.

Nutritional information per serving

Calories 191, Protein (g) 10, Carbohydrate (g) 22, Fat (g) 7, Calories from Fat (%) 33, Saturated Fat (g) 3, Dietary Fiber (g) 0, Cholesterol (mg) 14, Sodium (mg) 462
Diabetic Exchanges: *1 lean meat, 1.5 starch, 0.5 fat*

QUICK TIP

For heartier grits, sauté 2 cups each: onion, green bell pepper, and Canadian bacon, and add to cooked grits along with chopped tomatoes and cheese. It's a great way to start a busy day.

Hot Fruit Casserole

I love serving this dish at a brunch when good fresh fruit is unavailable. Next time you have to bring a luncheon dish, volunteer with this simple, fabulous recipe, which requires little effort with a terrific outcome.

1 (20-ounce) can pineapple chunks in their own juice

2 (16-ounce) packages frozen sliced peaches

1 (16-ounce) can pitted tart red cherries, drained

4 bananas, peeled and sliced

2 tablespoons lemon juice

⅔ cup light brown sugar

1 cup vanilla wafer crumbs

4 tablespoons margarine, cut up

⅓ cup crème de banana liqueur

MAKES 10 TO 12 SERVINGS

Preheat the oven to 350°F.

In a bowl, mix together the pineapple chunks, peaches, and cherries.

Sprinkle the bananas with the lemon juice, add to the other fruit. Transfer half the combined fruit to a 3-quart casserole dish. Sprinkle with half the brown sugar, half the vanilla wafer crumbs, half the margarine, and half the crème de banana. Cover with the remaining fruit liqueur and top with the remaining brown sugar, vanilla wafer crumbs, margarine, and crème de banana liqueur. Bake 35 to 45 minutes, or until the fruit is bubbly. Serve hot.

Nutritional information per serving

Calories 258, Protein (g) 3, Carbohydrate (g) 49, Fat (g) 6, Calories from Fat (%) 20, Saturated Fat (g) 1, Dietary Fiber (g) 3, Cholesterol (mg) 1, Sodium (mg) 86
Diabetic Exchanges: 2 fruit, 1 other carbohydrate, 1 fat

🥕 Basic Pancakes

A favorite family pancake recipe. Make plain pancakes, or for a fun and tasty variation, add 1 cup chopped bananas, blueberries, or even chocolate chips.

1¼ cups all-purpose flour
2 teaspoons baking
    powder
2 tablespoons sugar
Dash salt
1¼ cups skim milk
1 teaspoon vanilla extract
1 tablespoon canola oil

MAKES 10 TO 12 PANCAKES

In a bowl, combine the flour, baking powder, sugar, and salt. Add the milk, vanilla, and oil. Stir only until combined; the batter will be lumpy. Pour the batter into a heated pan, and let cook on one side until bubbles appear on top and the bottom is brown, about 2 to 4 minutes. Flip and cook on other side until browned. Serve with a light syrup.

Nutritional information per serving

Calories 76, Protein (g) 2, Carbohydrate (g) 14, Fat (g) 1, Calories from Fat (%) 16, Saturated Fat (g) 0, Dietary Fiber (g) 0, Cholesterol (mg) 0, Sodium (mg) 95
***Diabetic Exchanges:** 1 starch*

🥕 Baked French Toast

Here's a great recipe to serve a group—especially for kids. Add ½ cup orange juice and/or a little grated orange rind to the egg mixture for a wonderful orange flavor.

1 cup light maple syrup
1 (16-ounce) loaf French
    bread
2 eggs
2 egg whites
2 tablespoons sugar
1½ cups skim milk
1 tablespoon vanilla
    extract
½ teaspoon ground
    cinnamon

MAKES 8 SERVINGS

Coat a 3-quart oblong baking dish with nonstick cooking spray. Pour the maple syrup into the dish. Slice the French bread into 2-inch slices, and place over the syrup.

In another bowl, beat the eggs, egg whites, sugar, skim milk, vanilla, and cinnamon until well blended. Pour the egg mixture over the bread, pressing the bread to soak up the liquid. Cover with plastic wrap and refrigerate overnight, or leave at room temperature for 30 minutes before baking.

Preheat the oven to 350°F. Bake for 40 to 45 minutes, or until golden brown. Serve immediately.

Nutritional information per serving

Calories 261, Protein (g) 9, Carbohydrate (g) 47, Fat (g) 3, Calories from Fat (%) 11, Saturated Fat (g) 1, Dietary Fiber (g) 2, Cholesterol (mg) 54, Sodium (mg) 444
***Diabetic Exchanges:** 0.5 very lean meat, 2 starch, 1 other carbohydrate*

Cereal Mixture

This fabulous mixture is great for a quick morning pickup or for a snack any time of day.

3 tablespoons honey

3 tablespoons margarine

3 tablespoons reduced-
fat peanut butter

3 cups cereal (assorted
crispy wheat, corn,
bran cereal squares)

MAKES 6 (½-CUP) SERVINGS

Preheat the oven to 175°F.

In a microwave oven on high power, combine the honey, margarine, and peanut butter for 30 seconds to one minute, stirring occasionally until smooth. Toss with the cereal, coating well. Spread on a baking sheet, and bake in the oven for 1½ hours.

Nutritional information per serving

Calories 194, Protein (g) 4, Carbohydrate (g) 28, Fat (g) 9, Calories from Fat (%) 38, Saturated Fat (g)1, Dietary Fiber (g) 3, Cholesterol (mg) 0, Sodium (mg) 283
Diabetic Exchanges: *1.5 starch, 1 other carbohydrate, 1.5 fat*

Snack Mix

Sweet-and-salty mixes are always an addictive combination. My family really loves this when they have the munchies.

3 tablespoons sesame oil

3 tablespoons honey

1 tablespoon low sodium
soy sauce

½ teaspoon garlic powder

½ teaspoon onion powder

4 cups honey-nut toasted
rice and corn cereal
squares

6 cups mini-pretzels

1 cup soy nuts

1 cup dry roasted
peanuts

1 cup candy-coated
chocolate pieces

1 cup raisins, optional

MAKES 20 (½-CUP) SERVINGS

Preheat the oven to 250°F.

In a small bowl, whisk together the sesame oil, honey, soy sauce, garlic powder, and onion powder.

In a large bowl, toss together the cereal squares, pretzels, soy nuts, and peanuts. Drizzle the oil mixture over the cereal mixture, tossing gently to coat. Scatter the mixture on a foil-lined jelly roll pan, and bake for 25 minutes, stirring often to prevent too much browning. Turn off the oven and let the cereal stay in the oven for 1 hour to continue crisping. When cool, toss with the chocolate candies and raisins. Store in an airtight container for up to one week.

Nutritional information per serving

Calories 221, Protein (g) 6, Carbohydrate (g) 30, Fat (g) 9, Calories from Fat (%) 36, Saturated Fat (g) 2, Dietary Fiber (g) 2, Cholesterol (mg) 1, Sodium (mg) 309
Diabetic Exchanges: *1 starch, 1 other carbohydrate, 1.5 fat*

Granola

There's no need to buy granola at the grocery store when you can easily prepare this great-tasting crunch mixture. It makes a great snack, or you can sprinkle it on fruit, yogurt, or ice cream.

4 cups old-fashioned
    oatmeal
½ cup wheat bran
2 tablespoons nonfat
    dry milk
1 teaspoon ground
    cinnamon
½ cup sunflower seeds
½ cup pumpkin seeds
⅔ cup honey
2 tablespoons molasses
½ cup dried cranberries
1 cup dried mixed
    fruit bits

MAKES 16 (½-CUP) SERVINGS

Preheat the oven to 300°F. Line a baking sheet with heavy foil to make cleanup a snap.

Mix together the oatmeal, bran, dry milk, cinnamon, sunflower seeds, and pumpkin seeds; spread on the lined pan.

In a small bowl, mix together the honey and molasses. Pour the honey mixture over the cereal, stirring and tossing until well coated. Bake for 30 to 35 minutes, stirring every 15 minutes and cooking until mixture is golden brown. Let cool, and toss with the cranberries and dried mixed fruit. Store in a sealed container or zipper-lock bag.

Nutritional information per serving

Calories 214, Protein (g) 6, Carbohydrate (g) 38,
Fat (g) 6, Calories from Fat (%) 22, Saturated Fat (g) 1,
Dietary Fiber (g) 4, Cholesterol (mg) 0, Sodium (mg) 10
Diabetic Exchanges: *1 starch, 0.5 fruit, 1 other carbohydrate, 1 fat*

Gazpacho with Shrimp 87

White Gazpacho 88

Vichyssoise 89

Cucumber and Avocado Soup 90

Peach Soup 91

Strawberry Soup 91

Soups and Stews

Seafood Gumbo 92

Chicken and Sausage Gumbo 93

Easy Crab Soup 94

Salmon Bisque 94

Broccoli Soup 95

Three Bean Soup 96

Black Bean Soup 97

Chicken, Barley, and Bowtie Soup 98

Chicken Tortilla Soup 99

Corn Soup 100

Spicy Corn and Squash Chowder 101

Shrimp, White Bean, and Pasta Soup 102

Easy Shrimp and Corn Soup 103

Shrimp, Corn, and Sweet Potato Soup 104

Double Potato Bisque 105

Creamy Potato Soup 106

Pumpkin Soup 107

Cream of Spinach and Brie Soup 107

Southwestern Vegetable Soup 108

Beefy Vegetable and Barley Soup 109

Italian Soup 110

Split Pea Soup 111

Onion Soup 112

Wild Rice Soup 113

Artichoke Soup 113

Quick Vegetarian Chili 114

White Chicken Chili 115

Speedy Chili 116

Southwestern Shrimp and Black Bean Chili 117

Southwestern Pork Stew 118

Meatball Stew 119

Quick Beef Stew 120

Gazpacho with Shrimp

This terrific chilled tomato-based soup adds shrimp for a twist. For classic gazpacho, delete the shrimp. Making ahead gives the flavors time to blend.

6 cups tomato juice

2 tablespoons red wine vinegar

1 tablespoon minced garlic

1 cup finely chopped green bell pepper

½ cup finely chopped red bell pepper

1½ cups finely chopped tomato

½ cup chopped onion

1 cup chopped green onion (scallion)

1 teaspoon dried basil leaves

1 teaspoon dried oregano leaves

Dash hot pepper sauce

Salt and pepper to taste

1 pound small cooked, peeled shrimp

MAKES 8 SERVINGS

In a large bowl, mix together the tomato juice, vinegar, and garlic.

In another bowl, combine the green pepper, red pepper, tomato, onion, and green onion. Add half the vegetable mixture to the tomato juice mixture.

Place the remaining half of the vegetable mixture in a food processor, and process until smooth. Add to the tomato juice mixture. Stir in the basil, oregano, hot sauce, salt, pepper, and shrimp.

Cover and refrigerate overnight, or until well chilled. Serve chilled.

Nutritional information per serving
Calories 121, Protein (g) 14, Carbohydrate (g) 13,
Fat (g) 1, Calories from Fat (%) 6, Saturated Fat (g) 0,
Dietary Fiber (g) 3, Cholesterol (mg) 111, Sodium (mg) 779
Diabetic Exchanges: *2 very lean meat, 3 vegetable*

White Gazpacho

Here's the perfect summer soup that includes all the fresh veggies of the season. The longer it's refrigerated, the better it becomes. Serve chilled.

2 cups buttermilk

2 cups fat-free sour cream

3 tablespoons lime juice

½ cup finely chopped green bell pepper

½ cup finely chopped red bell pepper, optional

2 cups peeled, seeded, and finely chopped cucumbers

½ cup chopped green onion (scallion)

2 cups finely chopped tomato

1 cup fat-free canned vegetable (or chicken) broth

Salt and pepper to taste

MAKES 7 SERVINGS

In a large bowl, combine the buttermilk, sour cream, and lime juice. Add the green and red pepper, cucumber, green onion, tomato, chicken broth, salt, and pepper. Refrigerate until well chilled. Serve chilled.

Nutritional information per serving
Calories 133, Protein (g) 8, Carbohydrate (g) 22, Fat (g) 1, Calories from Fat (%) 6, Saturated Fat (g) 0, Dietary Fiber (g) 1, Cholesterol (mg) 2, Sodium (mg) 226
Diabetic Exchanges: *0.5 starch, 0.5 skim milk, 1.5 vegetable*

QUICK TIP

Substitute vegetable broth for chicken broth for a vegetarian treat.

Vichyssoise

Vichyssoise is always a good standby, mild enough for children but sophisticated enough for adults. For a light meal, serve in chilled mugs with a sandwich.

1 tablespoon margarine

1 onion, chopped

3 baking potatoes, peeled and diced

2 (16-ounce) cans fat-free chicken broth

1 (12-ounce) can evaporated skimmed milk

1 cup skim milk

½ cup fat-free sour cream

Salt and pepper to taste

Green onions (scallions), sliced, for garnish

MAKES 8 SERVINGS

In a large pot coated with nonstick cooking spray, melt the margarine; sauté the onion in the margarine until tender, about 3 minutes. Add the potatoes, chicken broth, and evaporated milk. Bring to a boil, lower the heat, and simmer until potato pieces are tender, about 15 minutes.

Transfer the mixture to a food processor or blender, and purée. Whisk in the skim milk and sour cream. Season with the salt and pepper. Refrigerate, covered, and serve chilled with green onions on top.

Nutritional information per serving

Calories 131, Protein (g) 9, Carbohydrate (g) 22, Fat (g) 2, Calories from Fat (%) 10, Saturated Fat (g) 0, Dietary Fiber (g) 2, Cholesterol (mg) 2, Sodium (mg) 411
Diabetic Exchanges: 1 starch, 0.5 skim milk

FOOD FACT

Try substituting half soy milk for the skim milk in this recipe. Including soy protein in your diet may help to reduce the risk of heart disease.

Cucumber and Avocado Soup

A refreshing cold soup with a twist. The delightful combination of cucumber and avocado makes this a recipe you won't want to miss.

3 cups cucumber, peeled and diced

2 cups buttermilk

½ cup chopped avocado, divided

¼ cup chopped red onion, divided

½ teaspoon chopped fresh basil leaves, divided

Salt and pepper to taste

1 teaspoon lime juice

½ cup seeded chopped tomatoes

4 tablespoons nonfat plain yogurt

MAKES 4 SERVINGS

In a blender, combine the cucumber and buttermilk. Add ¼ cup avocado, half the red onion, and half the basil. Blend until very smooth. Season with salt and pepper. Cover and refrigerate until chilled, about 1 hour.

In a small bowl, mix the remaining avocado, onion, and basil, the lime juice, and the tomato. Ladle the cucumber soup into bowls. Dollop each with 1 tablespoon yogurt; top with the tomato mixture. Refrigerate until serving.

Nutritional information per serving
Calories 109, Protein (g) 6, Carbohydrate (g) 13,
Fat (g) 4, Calories from Fat (%) 33, Saturated Fat (g) 1,
Dietary Fiber (g) 2, Cholesterol (mg) 5, Sodium (mg) 146
Diabetic Exchanges: *0.5 skim milk, 1 vegetable, 0.5 fat*

QUICK TIP

To quickly de-seed a cucumber, cut it in half and run the pointed end of a teaspoon down the center, scooping out the seeds. English cucumbers are virtually seedless.

Peach Soup

This is an exceptional cold soup that is so easy to mix together. For a social gathering, serve the soup in a punch bowl and use punch cups.

1½ pounds fresh peaches, peeled, pitted, and sliced, or 1 (28-ounce) can sliced peaches, drained
2 cups nonfat plain yogurt
1 cup fresh orange juice
1 cup pineapple juice
1 tablespoon lemon juice
2 tablespoons sugar
1 tablespoon almond extract

MAKES 10 SERVINGS

Pureé the peaches in a food processor until smooth. Add the yogurt, orange juice, pineapple juice, lemon juice, sugar, and almond extract, blending until smooth. Refrigerate until serving.

Nutritional information per serving
Calories 92, Protein (g) 3, Carbohydrate (g) 18, Fat (g) 0, Calories from Fat (%) 0, Saturated Fat (g) 0, Dietary Fiber (g) 1, Cholesterol (mg) 1, Sodium (mg) 38
Diabetic Exchanges: *1 fruit*

Strawberry Soup

A fruit smoothie in a bowl! A cold soup is nice to serve at a ladies' luncheon on a hot day. This one is high in both fiber and flavor.

1 quart strawberries, hulled
Juice of 1 orange
3 tablespoons confectioners' sugar
1 (12-ounce) can peach nectar
1½ cups nonfat plain yogurt

MAKES 5 SERVINGS

In a food processor, combine the strawberries and orange juice, blending until smooth. Add the sugar. Gradually add the peach nectar, blending well. Add the yogurt, blending until mixed. Refrigerate until serving.

Nutritional information per serving
Calories 141, Protein (g) 5, Carbohydrate (g) 30, Fat (g) 1, Calories from Fat (%) 4, Saturated Fat (g) 0, Dietary Fiber (g) 3, Cholesterol (mg) 1, Sodium (mg) 63
Diabetic Exchanges: *1.5 fruit, 0.5 skim milk*

❄ Seafood Gumbo

The browned flour substitutes for a roux, so you have the nutty flavor without the fat. I always make tons of gumbo and freeze it in containers. Adding fresh fish to the mix for extra flavor makes for a variety of seafood. Prepare rice to serve with the gumbo.

¾ cup all-purpose flour
1 tablespoon minced garlic
2 onions, chopped
2 green bell peppers, seeded and chopped
2 stalks celery, chopped
2 tablespoons chopped parsley
9 cups water
1 (14½-ounce) can diced tomatoes with juices
3 bay leaves
Juice of half a lemon
1 teaspoon dried thyme leaves
¼ teaspoon cayenne pepper
4 whole cloves
Salt and pepper to taste
1 pint claw crabmeat
2 pounds small to medium shrimp, peeled
2 pounds trout, cut into pieces, optional
1 cup chopped green onion (scallion)

MAKES 12 SERVINGS

Preheat the oven to 400°F.

Place the flour on a baking sheet, and bake for 20 to 30 minutes, stirring every 7 minutes, or until the flour is brown (the color of pecan shells). This process also works well in a toaster oven. Set aside.

While the flour is browning, coat a large pot with nonstick cooking spray, and sauté the garlic, onions, green peppers, celery, and parsley until tender. Gradually add the browned flour (the roux), stirring constantly. Gradually add the water, tomatoes, bay leaves, lemon juice, thyme, cayenne pepper, cloves, salt, and pepper. Bring to a boil; lower the heat and cook for 20 minutes.

Add the crabmeat, shrimp, and trout, cooking for another 20 minutes, or until all the seafood is done. Discard the bay leaves and cloves before serving; sprinkle with the green onion and serve over rice.

Nutritional information per serving
Calories 214, Protein (g) 31, Carbohydrate (g) 13,
Fat (g) 4, Calories from Fat (%) 15, Saturated Fat (g) 1,
Dietary Fiber (g) 2, Cholesterol (mg) 149, Sodium (mg) 254
Diabetic Exchanges: *4 very lean meat, 0.5 starch, 1.5 vegetable*

FOOD FACT

A roux is a mixture of flour and fat that is used to flavor and thicken gumbo. The roux turns a deep brown golden color after cooking slowly over low heat.

❄ Chicken and Sausage Gumbo

If you're not in a location with plentiful seafood, chicken and sausage gumbo is the answer. This thicker gumbo is a very popular dinner in my house. The browned flour replaces the traditional roux as a thickening and flavor agent. The gumbo freezes well.

⅔ cup all-purpose flour

2 onions, chopped

1 teaspoon minced garlic

2 green bell peppers, seeded and chopped

2 stalks celery, chopped

10 cups water

1 (14½-ounce) can chopped tomatoes, with their juice

3 to 4 pounds skinless, boneless chicken breasts, cut into pieces

½ teaspoon dried thyme leaves

¼ teaspoon cayenne pepper

1 pound reduced-fat sausage, sliced into ¼-inch pieces

1 bunch green onions (scallions)

1 tablespoon Worcestershire sauce

MAKES 10 TO 12 SERVINGS

Preheat the oven to 400°F. Place the flour on a baking sheet, and bake for 20 to 30 minutes, stirring every 7 minutes, or until the flour is brown (the color of pecan shells). This process works well in a toaster oven. Set aside.

In a large, heavy pot coated with nonstick cooking spray, sauté the onion, garlic, green peppers, and celery until tender. Add the browned flour (the roux), stirring constantly. Gradually add the water, tomatoes, chicken, thyme, and cayenne pepper. Bring to a boil, lower the heat, and simmer for 45 minutes to 1 hour, or until the chicken is tender.

While the gumbo is cooking, brown the sausage in a skillet or in the microwave oven. Add the sausage, green onions, and Worcestershire sauce to the gumbo, cooking 10 more minutes. Skim any fat from the surface of the gumbo. Serve over rice.

Nutritional information per serving

Calories 226, Protein (g) 33, Carbohydrate (g) 16,
Fat (g) 3, Calories from Fat (%) 11, Saturated Fat (g) 1,
Dietary Fiber (g) 2, Cholesterol (mg) 79, Sodium (mg) 464
***Diabetic Exchanges:** 4 very lean meat, 0.5 starch, 1.5 vegetable*

QUICK TIP

When thickening stews and soups with flour, prevent lumps by mixing the flour thoroughly in a cold liquid before adding it to the boiling mixture. To prevent a starchy flavor, heat the thickened liquid to boiling.

Easy Crab Soup

I have prepared this simple, incredible soup at our governor's mansion many times.

1 onion, finely chopped
2 tablespoons margarine
1 (14½-ounce) can
   fat-free chicken broth
½ cup water
1 (12-ounce) can
   evaporated skimmed
   milk
1 pound lump crabmeat
3 green onion stems
   (scallions), finely sliced

MAKES 4 SERVINGS

In a large pot, sauté the onion in the margarine until tender. Add the broth and water. Simmer for 10 minutes over low heat. Add the milk. Stir well, and fold in the crabmeat. Garnish with the green onion slices. Serve immediately.

Nutritional information per serving
Calories 274, Protein (g) 35, Carbohydrate (g) 17,
Fat (g) 7, Calories from Fat (%) 24, Saturated Fat (g) 1,
Dietary Fiber (g) 1, Cholesterol (mg) 90, Sodium (mg) 889
Diabetic Exchanges: *4 very lean meat, 1 skim milk, 1 vegetable*

Salmon Bisque

An easy recipe with a gourmet appeal, this bisque will turn the heads of salmon lovers.

½ pound fresh salmon
   fillet or steak
2 tablespoons margarine
1 bunch green onions
   (scallions), chopped
½ teaspoon minced garlic
⅓ cup all-purpose flour
4 cups skim milk
½ cup tomato purée
2 tablespoons dry sherry
1 teaspoon dried dill
   weed leaves
Salt and white pepper
   to taste

MAKES 6 TO 8 SERVINGS

Poach the salmon over medium-high heat in 1 inch of water until the salmon is done, about 10 to 15 minutes. Cool, flake, and remove any bones or skin; set aside.

   In a large pot, melt the margarine over medium and stir in the green onion and garlic, cooking until tender. Blend in the flour, and gradually add the milk, stirring until thickened. Add the flaked salmon, tomato purée, sherry, dill weed, salt, and pepper. Simmer, covered, for 15 minutes. Serve immediately.

Nutritional information per serving
Calories 134, Protein (g) 11, Carbohydrate (g) 13,
Fat (g) 4, Calories from Fat (%) 28, Saturated Fat (g) 1,
Dietary Fiber (g) 1, Cholesterol (mg) 17, Sodium (mg) 180
Diabetic Exchanges: *1 lean meat, 0.5 starch, 0.5 skim milk*

SOUPS AND STEWS

🥕 ❄️ Broccoli Soup

Broccoli and cheese join together for this wonderful creamy soup that will attract all ages.
Two (10-ounce) packages of frozen chopped broccoli may be used instead of fresh.

4 cups fresh broccoli
   florets
¼ cup water
1 onion, chopped
⅔ cup all-purpose flour
1½ cups skim milk
2 (14½-ounce) cans
   vegetable broth or
   fat-free chicken broth
1 cup shredded reduced-
   fat Monterey Jack
   cheese
Salt and pepper to taste
⅛ teaspoon dried thyme
   leaves

MAKES 6 TO 8 SERVINGS

Cook the broccoli in a microwave dish in the water, covered, for 8 to 10 minutes, or until tender. Drain and set aside.

In a large pot coated with nonstick cooking spray, sauté the onion over medium heat until softened, about 3 to 5 minutes. In a small bowl, mix together the flour and milk. Stir the flour and milk mixture into the onion. Gradually add the vegetable broth and the broccoli. Stir to combine. Cook over medium heat until the mixture comes to a boil, stirring constantly, for about 5 minutes, or until thickened.

Transfer the soup to a food processor or blender, purée the soup, and return to the pot over low heat. Add the cheese, salt, pepper, and thyme, cooking until heated through and the cheese is melted. Serve immediately.

Nutritional information per serving
Calories 121, Protein (g) 9, Carbohydrate (g) 15,
Fat (g) 3, Calories from Fat (%) 24, Saturated Fat (g) 2,
Dietary Fiber (g) 2, Cholesterol (mg) 9, Sodium (mg) 576
Diabetic Exchanges: *0.5 lean meat, 0.5 starch, 1.5 vegetable*

Three Bean Soup

Create your own bean soup with your favorite beans instead of buying packaged soup mixes at the store. You can add ham or sausage for extra flavor when sautéing. This soup is high in fiber.

SOUPS AND STEWS

1 cup dried red kidney beans

1 cup dried Great Northern beans

1 cup dried black beans

1 cup chopped onion

1 green bell pepper, seeded and chopped

1 tablespoon minced garlic

1½ cups diced peeled carrots

8 cups water

2 (10-ounce) cans diced tomatoes and green chilies

1 (15-ounce) can tomato sauce

1½ teaspoons dried oregano leaves

1 teaspoon dried thyme leaves

2 bay leaves

Salt and pepper to taste

MAKES 10 SERVINGS

Rinse the red kidney, Great Northern, and black beans, picking out any bad beans. Place in a large pot with water to cover; soak overnight. Drain and rinse.

In a large pot coated with nonstick cooking spray, sauté the onion, green pepper, garlic, and carrots over medium-high heat for 3 to 5 minutes, or until tender. Add the beans, water, tomatoes and green chilies, tomato sauce, oregano, thyme, and bay leaves; bring to a boil.

Cover, reduce the heat, and continue cooking for 2 hours, or until the beans are tender. Remove and discard the bay leaf. Season with the salt and pepper. Serve.

Nutritional information per serving

Calories 232, Protein (g) 14, Carbohydrate (g) 44, Fat (g) 1, Calories from Fat (%) 3, Saturated Fat (g) 0, Dietary Fiber (g) 13, Cholesterol (mg) 0, Sodium (mg) 480
Diabetic Exchanges: *1 very lean meat, 2.5 starch, 2 vegetable*

FOOD FACT

Beans are high in protein, carbohydrates, and fiber.

❄ Black Bean Soup

Try serving this black bean soup Cuban style: thick soup over rice with chopped onion on top.

1 (1-pound) package
  dried black beans

1½ cups chopped onion

1 teaspoon minced garlic

½ cup chopped green
  bell pepper

½ cup chopped celery

4 ounces lean ham,
  chopped

8 cups water

1 teaspoon
  Worcestershire sauce

1 teaspoon sugar

1 teaspoon ground cumin

4 bay leaves

Salt and pepper to taste

MAKES 6 TO 8 SERVINGS

Rinse and sort the beans; then soak the beans overnight in water. Drain and rinse.

In a large pot coated with nonstick cooking spray, sauté the onion, garlic, green pepper, celery, and ham over medium-low heat until tender, about 5 minutes. Add the beans, water, Worcestershire sauce, sugar, cumin, and bay leaves.

Cook over low heat for 2 hours, or until the beans are tender, adding water if needed. Add the salt and pepper. Discard the bay leaves before serving.

Nutritional information per serving
Calories 244, Protein (g) 17, Carbohydrate (g) 40,
Fat (g) 2, Calories from Fat (%) 8, Saturated Fat (g) 1,
Dietary Fiber (g) 10, Cholesterol (mg) 13, Sodium (mg) 27
Diabetic Exchanges: *1.5 very lean, 2.5 starch, 1 vegetable*

QUICK TIP

Salting the cooking liquid for dried beans tends to slow the cooking and toughen the beans. For best results, salt the beans after they're cooked.

❄ Chicken, Barley, and Bowtie Soup

My kids love chicken soup, and the barley and pasta turn this family favorite into a heartier version.

SOUPS AND STEWS

1½ pounds skinless, boneless chicken breasts, cut into 1-inch pieces
1 cup chopped celery
1 cup chopped onion
2 cups thinly sliced peeled carrots
1 bay leaf
8 cups water
4 cups fat-free canned chicken broth
½ cup pearl barley
Salt and pepper to taste
½ teaspoon dried basil leaves
1 (8-ounce) package bowtie pasta

MAKES 8 TO 10 SERVINGS

Place the chicken, celery, onion, carrots, and bay leaf in a large pot filled with the water and broth. Bring the water and broth to a boil, and add the barley. Reduce the heat, cover, and cook until the chicken and barley are done, about 30 minutes. Season with the salt and pepper, and add the basil.

Meanwhile, cook the pasta according to the package directions, omitting oil and salt. Drain.

Add the pasta to the chicken soup, and remove the bay leaf.

Nutritional information per serving
Calories 219, Protein (g) 21, Carbohydrate (g) 30, Fat (g) 1, Calories from Fat (%) 6, Saturated Fat (g) 0, Dietary Fiber (g) 3, Cholesterol (mg) 39, Sodium (mg) 315
Diabetic Exchanges: *2 very lean meat, 1.5 starch, 1 vegetable*

QUICK TIP

Out of canned chicken broth? Substitute with bouillon cubes. To reduce sodium, use reduced-sodium chicken broth.

❄ Chicken Tortilla Soup

This is a simple Southwestern one-soup meal that will quickly become a family favorite. We make extra tortilla strips to serve with salsa for a terrific snack.

1 cup chopped red onion

½ cup chopped red or green bell pepper

1 teaspoon minced garlic

1 (4-ounce) can chopped green chilies, drained

8 cups fat-free canned chicken broth

2 cups chopped cooked skinless chicken breast

1 cup frozen corn, thawed

¼ cup chopped fresh cilantro, optional

¼ cup lime juice

1 teaspoon ground cumin

1 teaspoon chili powder

4 (6- to 8-inch) flour tortillas, cut into ¼-inch strips

1 cup shredded reduced-fat Monterey Jack cheese

MAKES 4 TO 6 SERVINGS

In a large, heavy pot coated with nonstick cooking spray, sauté the onion, bell pepper, and garlic over medium heat until tender, about 7 minutes. Add the chilies, chicken broth, chicken, corn, cilantro, lime juice, cumin, and chili powder. Simmer, uncovered, for 10 minutes.

While the soup is cooking, preheat the oven to 350°F. Place the tortilla strips on a baking sheet. Bake for 10 to 15 minutes, or until crisp. Spoon the soup into bowls; top with the tortilla strips and cheese.

Nutritional information per serving
Calories 254, Protein (g) 27, Carbohydrate (g) 25,
Fat (g) 5, Calories from Fat (%) 19, Saturated Fat (g) 3,
Dietary Fiber (g) 3, Cholesterol (mg) 50, Sodium (mg) 1,230
Diabetic Exchanges: 3 very lean meat, 1.5 starch, 1 vegetable

QUICK TIP

If you don't have leftover cooked chicken for this recipe, cut chicken breasts into chunks and add to the pot when sautéing the seasonings and cook until done, then add remaining ingredients.

SOUPS AND STEWS

Corn Soup

It's hard to believe this easy and wonderful soup is not full of heavy cream. Serve with sliced green onions as a garnish.

1 onion, chopped
1 green bell pepper, seeded and chopped
½ teaspoon minced garlic
1 (16-ounce) bag frozen sweet corn
1 (8½-ounce) can cream-style corn
1 (10-ounce) can diced tomatoes and green chilies
1 (14½-ounce) can fat-free chicken broth
1 tablespoon Worcestershire sauce
Salt and pepper to taste
2 cups skim milk
⅓ cup all-purpose flour
Sliced green onions (scallions), optional

MAKES 8 SERVINGS

In a pot coated with nonstick cooking spray, sauté the onion, green pepper, and garlic over medium-high heat until tender, about 5 minutes. Add the frozen corn, cream-style corn, diced tomatoes and green chilies, chicken broth, Worcestershire sauce, salt, and pepper.

In a separate bowl, blend together the milk and flour. Gradually stir into the corn mixture. Bring to a boil, lower heat, and cook until the soup thickens, about 15 minutes. Garnish with the green onions.

Nutritional information per serving
Calories 134, Protein (g) 6, Carbohydrate (g) 29, Fat (g) 1, Calories from Fat (%) 5, Saturated Fat (g) 0, Dietary Fiber (g) 3, Cholesterol (mg) 1, Sodium (mg) 424
Diabetic Exchanges: *1.5 starch, 1 vegetable*

QUICK TIP

Instead of frozen corn, use the kernels from leftover corn on the cob in soups.

SOUPS AND STEWS

Spicy Corn and Squash Chowder

When the garden was abundant with squash, I mixed squash with some of my other favorite ingredients, and the outcome was this very tasty chowder. This recipe will appeal to you even if you're not a squash fan.

1 pound yellow squash, thinly sliced

Salt and pepper to taste

1 cup water

1 onion, finely chopped

½ cup chopped green bell pepper

½ teaspoon minced garlic

1 large tomato, chopped

1 (15-ounce) can cream-style corn

1 (4-ounce) can diced green chilies, drained

1 (12-ounce) can evaporated skimmed milk

2 slices reduced-fat American cheese, cut into 1-inch pieces

MAKES 4 SERVINGS

In a medium pot, cook the squash with the salt and pepper in the water, covered, over medium-high heat until the squash is tender, 5 to 7 minutes. Drain and set aside.

In a pot coated with nonstick cooking spray, sauté the onion and green pepper over medium heat until tender, about 5 minutes. Add the garlic and tomato, and sauté for 2 minutes. Stir in the corn, green chilies, squash (breaking up with a fork), and evaporated milk.

Bring to a boil, reduce the heat, and add the cheese; stir until the cheese is melted, and serve.

Nutritional information per serving
Calories 236, Protein (g) 14, Carbohydrate (g) 43,
Fat (g) 2, Calories from Fat (%) 8, Saturated Fat (g) 1,
Dietary Fiber (g) 6, Cholesterol (mg) 11, Sodium (mg) 660
Diabetic Exchanges: *1 starch, 1 skim milk, 3 vegetable*

❄ Shrimp, White Bean, and Pasta Soup

Canadian bacon gives this delicious soup a burst of flavor that enhances the shrimp, beans, and pasta. It freezes well; if too thick when reheating, add more water or chicken broth.

SOUPS AND STEWS

¼ cup chopped Canadian bacon

1 onion, chopped

1 green bell pepper, seeded and chopped

1 teaspoon minced garlic

1½ pounds medium shrimp, peeled

8½ cups water

1 (8-ounce) can tomato sauce

2 (15½-ounce) cans Great Northern beans, drained and rinsed

1½ cups rotini pasta

Salt and pepper to taste

1 bunch green onions (scallions), chopped

MAKES 8 SERVINGS

In a large pot coated with nonstick cooking spray, cook the bacon over medium heat until lightly browned, about 3 minutes. Add the onion, green pepper, and garlic, and sauté until the vegetables are tender, about 5 minutes. Add the shrimp, water, tomato sauce, and beans. Bring to a boil, and add the pasta, cooking until the shrimp and pasta are done. Add the salt, pepper, and green onions; heat for 1 minute, and serve.

Nutritional information per serving

Calories 231, Protein (g) 20, Carbohydrate (g) 4, Fat (g) 1, Calories from Fat (%) 5, Saturated Fat (g) 0, Dietary Fiber (g) 5, Cholesterol (mg) 103, Sodium (mg) 437

Diabetic Exchanges: *2 very lean meat, 2 starch, 1 vegetable*

❄ Easy Shrimp and Corn Soup

This great-tasting soup, so easy to prepare, was noted by Cooking Light magazine as one of the best recipes they tested. They couldn't believe it wasn't full of calories and fat!

1 onion, chopped

1 teaspoon minced garlic

1 green bell pepper, seeded and chopped

1 (8-ounce) package fat-free cream cheese, softened

2 (15-ounce) cans cream-style corn

2 (10-ounce) cans cream of shrimp soup or corn chowder soup or combination

2 cups skim milk

1 (10-ounce) can diced tomatoes and green chilies

1 pound medium shrimp, peeled

Sliced green onions (scallions), for garnish

MAKES 8 SERVINGS

In a large, heavy pot coated with nonstick cooking spray, sauté the onion, garlic, and green pepper until tender, about 5 minutes. Stir in the cream cheese. Add the cream-style corn, soup, milk, tomatoes and green chilies, and shrimp.

Bring to a boil, reduce heat, and cook until the shrimp are done, about 10 minutes. Serve with the green onions. When reheating the soup, if it's too thick, add more milk.

Nutritional information per serving

Calories 230, Protein (g) 18, Carbohydrate (g) 33, Fat (g) 4, Calories from Fat (%) 15, Saturated Fat (g) 2, Dietary Fiber (g) 2, Cholesterol (mg) 81, Sodium (mg) 1,289
Diabetic Exchanges: *1 lean meat, 1.5 starch, 0.5 skim milk, 1 vegetable*

QUICK TIP

Purchase already-peeled shrimp in your seafood market or grocery to avoid the hassle of peeling them yourself.

❄ Shrimp, Corn, and Sweet Potato Soup

These wonderful ingredients blend to make a savory, satisfying soup. Put this recipe at the top of your list.

1 red onion, chopped

½ cup chopped celery

½ teaspoon minced garlic

1 green bell pepper, seeded and chopped

2 cups diced peeled sweet potato (yam)

1 (16-ounce) bag frozen corn

1 (15-ounce) can cream-style corn

1 (10-ounce) can chopped tomatoes and green chilies

1 (6-ounce) can tomato paste

4 cups fat-free canned chicken broth

1½ pounds peeled medium shrimp

Salt and pepper to taste

Sliced green onions (scallions), optional

MAKES 12 SERVINGS

Coat a large pot with nonstick cooking spray, and sauté the onion, celery, garlic, and green pepper until tender. Add the sweet potato, frozen corn, cream-style corn, tomatoes and green chilies, tomato paste, and broth; bring the mixture to a boil. Add the shrimp, bring to a boil, reduce heat and continue cooking until the shrimp are done, about 10 minutes. Season with salt and pepper; garnish with the green onions, if desired, and serve.

Nutritional information per serving

Calories 153, Protein (g) 13, Carbohydrate (g) 26, Fat (g) 1, Calories from Fat (%) 6, Saturated Fat (g) 0, Dietary Fiber (g) 4, Cholesterol (mg) 81, Sodium (mg) 513
Diabetic Exchanges: *1 very lean meat, 1.5 starch, 1 vegetable*

FOOD FACT

Sweet potatoes (yams) are high in fiber and full of vitamins.

Double Potato Bisque

A different twist on bisque. Sweet potato and potato together make a mild, smooth, intensely flavored soup. The sweet potato adds nutrition and color.

1 large sweet potato (yam), peeled and cut into ½-inch cubes (2 cups)

1 large baking potato, peeled and cut into ½-Inch cubes (2 cups)

1 onion, chopped

½ teaspoon minced garlic

1 (14½-ounce) can vegetable broth

1 teaspoon dried thyme leaves

⅛ teaspoon cayenne pepper

1 (12-ounce) can evaporated skimmed milk

Salt and pepper to taste

Green onion stems (scallions), optional

MAKES 4 TO 6 SERVINGS

In a large pot, combine the diced sweet potato, potato, onion, garlic, and vegetable broth; bring to a boil. Reduce the heat and simmer, covered, for 15 minutes, or until the potatoes are tender.

Pour the mixture into a food processor, and blend until smooth; return to the pot. Add the thyme, cayenne, and evaporated milk, and cook over a low heat just until heated through. Season with the salt and pepper. Garnish with the green onion. Serve.

Nutritional information per serving
Calories 115, Protein (g) 7, Carbohydrate (g) 23,
Fat (g) 0, Calories from Fat (%) 0, Saturated Fat (g) 0,
Dietary Fiber (g) 2, Cholesterol (mg) 2, Sodium (mg) 386
Diabetic Exchanges: *1 starch, 0.5 skim milk*

FOOD FACT

The Center for Science in the Public Interest (CSPI) ranked the sweet potato as the most nutritious vegetable.

❄ Creamy Potato Soup

Potato soup is a popular request. You would think this rich soup is a no-no where healthy eating is concerned, but it's completely painless to eat. For the deluxe version, top with shredded reduced-fat Cheddar cheese and a dollop of fat-free sour cream.

1 tablespoon margarine

1 cup chopped onion

½ teaspoon minced garlic

3 tablespoons all-purpose flour

2 (16-ounce) cans fat-free chicken broth

4 cups peeled diced potatoes (about 3 large)

Salt and pepper to taste

1 cup liquid nondairy creamer

Chopped parsley or sliced green onions (scallions), for garnish

MAKES 8 SERVINGS

Melt the margarine in a large pot over medium heat, and sauté the onion and garlic in the margarine until tender, about 5 minutes. Lower the heat and add the flour, stirring until smooth. Gradually add the broth, stirring constantly. Add the potato. Bring to a boil; cover, reduce the heat, and simmer for 20 minutes, stirring occasionally, or until the potato chunks are tender.

Transfer the mixture to a blender or food processor, and blend until smooth, in batches if necessary. Return to the pot. Add salt and pepper, stir in the nondairy creamer, and heat thoroughly. Garnish with the parsley or green onions, and serve.

Nutritional information per serving
Calories 136, Protein (g) 4, Carbohydrate (g) 22,
Fat (g) 4, Calories from Fat (%) 26, Saturated Fat (g) 1,
Dietary Fiber (g) 2, Cholesterol (mg) 0, Sodium (mg) 349
Diabetic Exchanges: *1.5 starch, 0.5 fat*

Pumpkin Soup

This quick soup is especially perfect in the fall.

½ cup finely chopped
  onion
½ teaspoon minced garlic
1 (15-ounce) can
  solid-pack pumpkin
2 (14½-ounce) cans
  fat-free chicken broth
½ cup skim milk
½ teaspoon hot sauce
Salt and pepper to taste
Fat-free sour cream,
  for garnish

MAKES 6 SERVINGS

In a pot coated with nonstick cooking spray, sauté the onion and garlic over medium heat until tender, about 5 minutes. Add the pumpkin, and gradually add the chicken broth and milk. Add the hot sauce, and season with the salt and pepper. Cook until heated through, about 5 minutes. Serve with a dollop of sour cream.

Nutritional information per serving
Calories 45, Protein (g) 4, Carbohydrate (g) 8,
Fat (g) 0, Calories from Fat (%) 0, Saturated Fat (g) 0,
Dietary Fiber (g) 3, Cholesterol (mg) 0, Sodium (mg) 391
Diabetic Exchanges: *0.5 starch*

Cream of Spinach and Brie Soup

Though a tad high in fat, this is a great way to enjoy spinach. You can accompany this rich, velvety soup with lower-fat side dishes or even reduce the amount of Brie.

½ cup chopped onion
⅓ cup all-purpose flour
2 cups skim milk
2 cups fat-free canned
  chicken broth
8 ounces Brie cheese,
  rind removed, cubed
2 cups fresh spinach,
  washed and stemmed
Salt and pepper to taste

MAKES 6 SERVINGS

In a pot coated with nonstick cooking spray, sauté the onion until soft. Stir in the flour for 30 seconds. Gradually stir in the milk and chicken broth. Bring to a boil, stirring constantly until thickened, about 10 minutes. Lower the heat and add the Brie, stirring until melted. Add the spinach, salt, and pepper, stirring until the spinach is wilted. Serve.

Nutritional information per serving
Calories 192, Protein (g) 13, Carbohydrate (g) 11,
Fat (g) 11, Calories from Fat (%) 50, Saturated Fat (g) 7,
Dietary Fiber (g) 1, Cholesterol (mg) 39, Sodium (mg) 495
Diabetic Exchanges: *1.5 high-fat meat, 0.5 starch*

Southwestern Vegetable Soup

You'll really enjoy this veggie soup with a Southwestern flair.

SOUPS AND STEWS

1 cup chopped onion

1 teaspoon minced garlic

2 cups sliced peeled carrots

1 pound red potatoes, peeled and cut into small chunks

2 (14½-ounce) cans vegetable broth

1 (15-ounce) can tomato sauce

1½ cups mild salsa

2 teaspoons dried oregano leaves

2 teaspoons ground cumin

1 (10-ounce) package frozen corn

½ cup sliced green onion (scallion)

½ cup shredded reduced-fat Monterey Jack cheese

MAKES 6 SERVINGS

In a large pot coated with nonstick cooking spray, sauté the onion and garlic over medium heat until tender, 3 to 5 minutes. Add the carrot, potato, vegetable broth, tomato sauce, salsa, oregano, cumin, and corn. Bring the mixture to a boil, lower the heat, and simmer for 20 minutes, or until the carrot and potato chunks are tender. When serving, sprinkle each bowl with the green onion and cheese.

Nutritional information per serving

Calories 221, Protein (g) 9, Carbohydrate (g) 40, Fat (g) 3, Calories from Fat (%) 12, Saturated Fat (g) 1, Dietary Fiber (g) 5, Cholesterol (mg) 5, Sodium (mg) 1,363
Diabetic Exchanges: *1.5 starch, 3 vegetable*

FOOD FACT

Vegetable soup is an easy way to include the recommended servings of vegetables into your daily meals.

❄ Beefy Vegetable and Barley Soup

This wonderfully chunky soup is perfect on a cold night. Instead of mixed veggies, clean out the refrigerator and toss in whatever veggies you like.

2 pounds lean round steak, 2-inches thick

1 onion, chopped

3 stalks celery, chopped

1 bay leaf

2 tablespoons chopped parsley

2 cups water, divided

1 (46-ounce) container low-sodium cocktail vegetable juice

1 (14-ounce) can beef broth

1 red potato, peeled and cut into small cubes

½ cup barley

1 large carrot, peeled and sliced

1 (16-ounce) package frozen mixed vegetables

MAKES 6 TO 8 SERVINGS

Cut the meat into 1-inch cubes. Coat a large, heavy pot with nonstick cooking spray and cook the meat over medium-high heat until browned, stirring often. Add the onion, celery, bay leaf, parsley, and water. Bring to a boil, lower heat, and simmer, covered, for 45 minutes. Add the vegetable juice, broth, potato, and barley. Return to a boil, lower the heat, and cover, cooking for 30 minutes. Add the carrot and mixed vegetables, cover, and continue to cook over low heat for 30 minutes, or until the meat is tender and the barley is done. Remove the bay leaf before serving.

Nutritional information per serving

Calories 278, Protein (g) 31, Carbohydrate (g) 28, Fat (g) 5, Calories from Fat (%) 15, Saturated Fat (g) 2, Dietary Fiber (g) 5, Cholesterol (mg) 71, Sodium (mg) 533
Diabetic Exchanges: *3 lean meat, 1 starch, 3 vegetable*

FOOD FACT

Don't cheat on cooking time with soups and stews. Simmering over low heat helps to extract the maximum flavor from ingredients.

❄ Italian Soup

Rich in flavor and packed full of nutritious and wonderful ingredients, this soup will be high on your list as winter weather arrives.

1 (5-ounce) package Canadian bacon, chopped into pieces

½ teaspoon minced garlic

1 large onion, sliced

⅔ cup chopped peeled carrot

2 zucchini, sliced

1 (28-ounce) can chopped tomatoes with juice

½ cup red wine

Salt and pepper to taste

½ teaspoon dried oregano leaves

4 (10¾-ounce) cans beef consommé

1½ cups water

1 (15-ounce) can red kidney beans, drained and rinsed

2 cups chopped cabbage

1 cup chopped fresh spinach

1 cup shell macaroni

1 teaspoon dried basil leaves

MAKES 10 TO 12 SERVINGS

In a large pot coated with nonstick cooking spray, cook the Canadian bacon over medium heat until brown, about 3 minutes. Stir in the garlic, onion, carrot, zucchini, tomatoes, red wine, salt, pepper, oregano, beef consommé, water, kidney beans, cabbage, and spinach. Bring to a boil, lower the heat, and cook for 10 minutes. Add the macaroni and basil, and continue cooking for 20 minutes, or until the macaroni is done. Serve.

Nutritional information per serving

Calories 144, Protein (g) 12, Carbohydrate (g) 21, Fat (g) 1, Calories from Fat (%) 7, Saturated Fat (g) 0, Dietary Fiber (g) 5, Cholesterol (mg) 6, Sodium (mg) 902
Diabetic Exchanges: *1 very lean meat, 1 starch, 1.5 vegetable*

QUICK TIP

Cabbage is a cruciferous vegetable that has been linked to cancer protection. If you aren't a cabbage fan, including it in soups is a good way to sneak it into your diet.

❄️ Split Pea Soup

Split pea fans—this easy, high-fiber recipe is meant for you.

5 slices center-cut bacon, cut into pieces

1 onion, chopped

½ cup chopped celery

2 cups dried split peas

4 cups water

4 cups fat-free canned chicken broth

1 bay leaf

2 cups sliced carrots

1 potato, peeled and diced

Salt and pepper to taste

½ teaspoon dried thyme leaves

MAKES 6 SERVINGS

In a large pot, sauté the bacon, onion, and celery until tender. Add the peas, water, chicken broth, bay leaf, carrot, potato, salt, pepper, and thyme. Bring the soup to a boil, lower the heat, and cook, covered, for 1½ to 2 hours, or until the peas are very soft. Stir occasionally. If the soup gets too thick, thin with additional broth or water. Remove the bay leaf before serving.

Nutritional information per serving
Calories 355, Protein (g) 21, Carbohydrate (g) 52,
Fat (g) 9, Calories from Fat (%) 21, Saturated Fat (g) 3,
Dietary Fiber (g) 19, Cholesterol (mg) 9, Sodium (mg) 539
Diabetic Exchanges: 2 very lean meat, 3 starch, 1 vegetable, 1 fat

QUICK TIP

Unlike whole peas, split peas don't need soaking before being cooked. Smoked sausage, ham, or bacon are ideal flavor partners for split peas.

Onion Soup

Onion soup is one of my personal favorites, and I prefer this version to some of the high-fat recipes I've tried. The soup is full-flavored without being heavy. I usually melt the cheese on the soup in the microwave.

SOUPS AND STEWS

1 tablespoon margarine

3 large onions (about 2 pounds), halved and thinly sliced

1 teaspoon sugar

3 tablespoons all-purpose flour

2 cups water

2 (14½-ounce) cans beef broth

1 (10½-ounce) can beef consommé

1 teaspoon Worcestershire sauce

2 tablespoons Cognac, optional

8 (½-inch-thick) slices French bread, toasted

1 cup shredded part-skim mozzarella cheese

MAKES 8 SERVINGS

In a large pot coated with nonstick cooking spray, melt the margarine over medium heat. Add the onion, and cook, stirring frequently, for 20 minutes, or until golden. Add the sugar, and stir well. Add the flour, stirring constantly for 1 minute. Gradually add the water, beef broth, and beef consommé. Bring to a boil; cover, reduce the heat, and simmer for 30 minutes. Stir in the Worcestershire sauce and Cognac, if desired.

Preheat the broiler. Place eight ovenproof soup bowls on a baking sheet, and fill with the soup. Top each with a slice of French bread. Sprinkle the cheese evenly over the bread. Broil several minutes, or until the cheese melts.

Nutritional information per serving
Calories 181, Protein (g) 10, Carbohydrate (g) 26,
Fat (g) 4, Calories from Fat (%) 22, Saturated Fat (g) 2,
Dietary Fiber (g) 3, Cholesterol (mg) 8, Sodium (mg) 735
Diabetic Exchanges: *0.5 lean meat, 1 starch, 2 vegetable*

❄ Wild Rice Soup

This hearty, great-tasting soup can be the answer to using leftover chicken or holiday turkey.

½ cup chopped onion

½ cup finely chopped peeled carrot

½ cup all-purpose flour

3 cups fat-free canned chicken broth

1 (6-ounce) package long-grain and wild rice mix

1 cup chopped cooked chicken or turkey

3 tablespoons sherry

MAKES 4 TO 6 SERVINGS

In a large pot coated with nonstick cooking spray, sauté the onion and carrot over medium heat until tender, about 5 minutes. Stir in the flour. Gradually add the broth, and bring the mixture to a boil, stirring constantly.

Meanwhile, prepare the rice according to the package directions, omitting any oil and salt. Add the cooked rice and cooked chicken to the broth mixture, and simmer 5 minutes. Add the sherry. If the soup gets too thick, add more chicken broth or water. Boil 1 minute, and serve.

Nutritional information per serving

Calories 217, Protein (g) 13, Carbohydrate (g) 33, Fat (g) 3, Calories from Fat (%) 13, Saturated Fat (g) 1, Dietary Fiber (g) 1, Cholesterol (mg) 19, Sodium (mg) 754

Diabetic Exchanges: *1 very lean meat, 2 starch*

❄ Artichoke Soup

Throw all the ingredients in the blender, heat, and serve with a smile. Everyone will think you spent hours in the kitchen to prepare this simple yet sensational soup.

3 (14-ounce) cans artichoke hearts, drained

3 (10¾-ounce) cans 98% fat-free cream of mushroom soup

1 cup skim milk

2 cups fat-free canned chicken broth

½ cup dry white wine

Dash cayenne pepper

MAKES 6 TO 8 SERVINGS

Place the artichokes in a food processor, and purée. Add the mushroom soup, milk, broth, white wine, and cayenne pepper. Blend until well combined. Transfer to a pot, and warm over low heat to serve.

Nutritional information per serving

Calories 122, Protein (g) 5, Carbohydrate (g) 17, Fat (g) 3, Calories from Fat (%) 21, Saturated Fat (g) 1, Dietary Fiber (g) 1, Cholesterol (mg) 5, Sodium (mg) 1,201

Diabetic Exchanges: *0.5 starch, 1.5 vegetable, 0.5 fat*

Quick Vegetarian Chili

If you can work a can opener and accept compliments graciously, you can prepare this impressive, hearty chili. Serve with shredded Monterey Jack cheese, if desired.

2 cups salsa

1 (28-ounce) can diced tomatoes, with juice

1 (15-ounce) can pinto beans, drained and rinsed

1 (15-ounce) can red kidney beans, drained and rinsed

1 (19-ounce) can garbanzo beans, drained and rinsed

1 green bell pepper, seeded and chopped

½ teaspoon minced garlic

1 onion, chopped

2 medium zucchini, halved lengthwise and thinly sliced

2 tablespoons chili powder

½ teaspoon ground cumin

1 teaspoon dried oregano leaves

½ teaspoon sugar

MAKES 8 SERVINGS

In a large pot, combine the salsa, tomatoes, pinto beans, kidney beans, garbanzo beans, green pepper, garlic, onion, zucchini, chili powder, cumin, oregano, and sugar. Heat to boiling. Reduce the heat and simmer, covered, for 40 minutes, stirring occasionally.

Nutritional information per serving

Calories 207, Protein (g) 9, Carbohydrate (g) 36, Fat (g) 2, Calories from Fat (%) 7, Saturated Fat (g) 0, Dietary Fiber (g) 11, Cholesterol (mg) 0, Sodium (mg) 924
Diabetic Exchanges: *1 very lean meat, 1.5 starch, 3 vegetable*

FOOD FACT

Beans are a great source of fiber. Fiber reduces the number of calories your body absorbs from other foods you eat. Try to eat 20 to 35 grams of fiber daily.

White Chicken Chili

When you're in the mood for chili, here's an extremely tasty choice with chicken as the star.

1 tablespoon olive oil

2 pounds skinless, boneless chicken breasts, diced

1 onion, chopped

1 teaspoon minced garlic

2 (14½-ounce) cans chopped tomatoes, with juice

2 (14½-ounce) cans fat-free chicken broth

2 (4-ounce) cans chopped green chilies

1 teaspoon dried oregano leaves

½ teaspoon ground cumin

2 (11-ounce) cans cannellini beans, drained

3 tablespoons fresh lime juice

¼ teaspoon pepper

½ cup shredded reduced-fat Monterey Jack cheese

MAKES 8 SERVINGS

Coat a large pot with nonstick cooking spray. Add the olive oil, and cook the diced chicken breasts over medium high heat until done, stirring. Remove the chicken from the pan; set aside.

Add the onion and garlic to the pan, and sauté until tender. Stir in the tomatoes, chicken broth, green chilies, oregano, and cumin, and add the chicken. Bring to a boil, reduce the heat, and simmer for 20 minutes. Add the beans, and cook until heated, about 5 minutes. Add the lime juice and pepper. Spoon into bowls, and serve topped with the cheese.

Nutritional information per serving
Calories 264, Protein (g) 34, Carbohydrate (g) 20,
Fat (g) 5, Calories from Fat (%) 16, Saturated Fat (g) 1,
Dietary Fiber (g) 6, Cholesterol (mg) 70, Sodium (mg) 797
Diabetic Exchanges: *4 very lean meat, 0.5 starch, 2 vegetable*

SOUPS AND STEWS

❄ Speedy Chili

The chipotle salsa gives this excellent, easy-to-make chili a rich, smoky flavor that's hard to beat. If desired, serve with shredded reduced fat cheddar cheese and chopped red onions.

2 pounds ground sirloin
1 teaspoon minced garlic
1 tablespoon chili powder
1 teaspoon ground cumin
1 (16-ounce) jar chipotle chunky salsa
1 (16-ounce) package frozen whole-kernel corn
2 (14½-ounce) cans seasoned beef broth with onion
1 (15-ounce) can red kidney beans, rinsed and drained, optional

MAKES 6 TO 8 SERVINGS

In a large pot, brown the meat and garlic over medium high heat until done. Drain any excess liquid. Add the chili powder, cumin, salsa, corn, beef broth, and beans. Bring the mixture to a boil, reduce the heat, and cook for 15 minutes.

Nutritional information per serving

Calories 212, Protein (g) 26, Carbohydrate (g) 14, Fat (g) 6, Calories from Fat (%) 24, Saturated Fat (g) 2, Dietary Fiber (g) 2, Cholesterol (mg) 60, Sodium (mg) 794
Diabetic Exchanges: 3 lean meat, 1 starch

QUICK TIP

Chipotle peppers are actually dried, smoked jalapeño chilies with a mild, smoky flavor. With chipotle salsa, you can enjoy the flavor without working with the peppers.

Southwestern Shrimp and Black Bean Chili

A wonderful blend of flavors produces this very easy recipe that includes all my favorites: black beans, corn, and shrimp. This chili is not only great tasting but also high in fiber and low in fat.

1 green bell pepper, seeded and chopped

1 red bell pepper, seeded and chopped

1 large onion, chopped

1 cup shredded peeled carrot

1 tablespoon finely chopped pickled jalapeño pepper

½ teaspoon minced garlic

1 tablespoon chili powder

1½ teaspoons dried cumin

1 (14½-ounce) can chopped tomatoes, with juice

1 (16-ounce) can black beans, drained and rinsed

½ cup water

1 pound medium shrimp, peeled

1 (10-ounce) package frozen corn

MAKES 4 TO 6 SERVINGS

In a large pot coated with nonstick cooking spray, sauté the green and red peppers, onion, carrot, jalapeño pepper, and garlic until tender, about 6 to 8 minutes. Stir in the chili powder, cumin, tomatoes, black beans, water, and shrimp; bring to a boil. Reduce the heat, and cook for 5 to 10 minutes, or until the shrimp are pink. Add the corn, and continue cooking 5 minutes longer.

Nutritional information per serving
Calories 205, Protein (g) 17, Carbohydrate (g) 32, Fat (g) 2, Calories from Fat (%) 8, Saturated Fat (g) 0, Dietary Fiber (g) 9, Cholesterol (mg) 90, Sodium (mg) 436
Diabetic Exchanges: 2 very lean meat, 1 starch, 3 vegetable

QUICK TIP

For a time saver, purchase already peeled shrimp at your local seafood market.

❄ Southwestern Pork Stew

Pork, yams, and corn make this an eye-catching, easy one-dish meal that will be repeated often at family dinners.

SOUPS AND STEWS

1¾ pounds pork tenderloin, trimmed of fat and cut into 1-inch cubes

¼ cup all-purpose flour

1 cup chopped red onion

2 cups fat-free canned chicken broth

1 (10-ounce) can chopped tomatoes and green chilies

1¼ pounds sweet potatoes (yams), peeled and cut into 1-inch cubes

1 teaspoon chili powder

½ teaspoon ground cumin

1 (4-ounce) can diced green chilies, drained

1 (16-ounce) package frozen corn

Salt and pepper to taste

MAKES 8 SERVINGS

Toss the pork with the flour to coat. In a large pot coated with nonstick cooking spray, brown the pork over medium heat, about 5 to 7 minutes. Add the onion, and cook until tender. Add the broth, tomatoes and green chilies, sweet potato, chili powder, cumin, green chilies, and corn. Bring the mixture to a boil, lower the heat, and simmer until the potato cubes are tender and the pork is done, approximately 45 minutes. If the stew gets too thick, add more chicken broth. Add the salt and pepper to taste.

Nutritional information per serving
Calories 275, Protein (g) 25, Carbohydrate (g) 37, Fat (g) 4, Calories from Fat (%) 13, Saturated Fat (g) 1, Dietary Fiber (g) 5, Cholesterol (mg) 64, Sodium (mg) 429
Diabetic Exchanges: *3 very lean meat, 2 starch, 1 vegetable*

QUICK TIP

Let soups, stews, and chilis cool; then chill in the refrigerator. The fat will rise to the top, which is perfect for make-ahead meals.

❄ Meatball Stew

If you enjoy meatballs, this stew with a tomato gravy laced with rice and peas proves to be a hearty one-dish meal. Add more broth or water if the stew is too thick for your taste.

- 2 pounds ground sirloin
- 2 egg whites, lightly beaten
- ⅓ cup dry bread crumbs
- 1 onion, finely chopped
- 1 tablespoon minced garlic
- Salt and pepper to taste
- 1 teaspoon dried basil leaves
- 1 teaspoon dried thyme leaves
- 1 green bell pepper, seeded and chopped
- 2 (14½-ounce) cans chopped tomatoes, with juice
- 1 (15-ounce) can tomato sauce
- 2 cups canned beef broth
- ⅔ cup long-grain rice
- 1 (10-ounce) package frozen green peas

MAKES 6 SERVINGS

Preheat the broiler.

In a bowl, combine the meat, egg whites, bread crumbs, onion, garlic, salt, pepper, basil, and thyme. Shape into 30 balls about 1½ inches in diameter. Place the meatballs on a baking sheet coated with nonstick cooking spray. Broil in the oven for 4 to 5 minutes; then turn the meatballs and continue broiling for 4 minutes longer, or until done. Remove from the broiler, and set aside.

In a large pot coated with nonstick cooking spray, sauté the green pepper over medium heat until tender, about 5 minutes. Add the tomatoes, tomato sauce, and beef broth. Bring to a boil, and add the meatballs. Mix in the rice; cover, reduce the heat, and continue cooking for 20 minutes, or until the rice is done. Stir in the peas, cover, and continue cooking for 10 minutes, or until the peas are tender. Serve.

Nutritional information per serving

Calories 391, Protein (g) 40, Carbohydrate (g) 42, Fat (g) 8, Calories from Fat (%) 18, Saturated Fat (g) 3, Dietary Fiber (g) 7, Cholesterol (mg) 80, Sodium (mg) 1,115
Diabetic Exchanges: *4 lean meat, 2 starch, 3 vegetable*

❄ Quick Beef Stew

Everyone needs a basic recipe for this old-time classic.

2 pounds lean boneless
   top round steak,
   trimmed of fat and cut
   into 1-inch cubes
⅓ cup all-purpose flour
2 cups sliced carrots
   (1-inch slices)
1¾ pounds red potatoes,
   peeled and cubed
1 large onion, sliced
½ pound fresh
   mushrooms, quartered
½ teaspoon minced garlic
¼ cup chopped parsley
½ teaspoon dried thyme
   leaves
Salt and pepper to taste
1 (14½-ounce) can
   beef broth
1 cup light beer

MAKES 6 SERVINGS

Combine the meat and flour in a plastic bag; close the bag, and shake.

Coat a large pot with nonstick cooking spray, and cook the meat over high heat until browned, about 8 minutes, stirring often. Add the carrot, potato, onion, mushroom quarters, garlic, parsley, thyme, salt, pepper, beef broth, and beer. Cover, and cook about 1 hour, or until the meat is tender and the vegetables are done.

Nutritional information per serving
Calories 391, Protein (g) 42, Carbohydrate (g) 39,
Fat (g) 6, Calories from Fat (%) 14, Saturated Fat (g) 2,
Dietary Fiber (g) 5, Cholesterol (mg) 94, Sodium (mg) 397
***Diabetic Exchanges:** 4 very lean meat, 2 starch, 2 vegetable*

QUICK TIP

Sirloin tips are lean and tender and can be substituted in the stew.

Caesar Salad 123

Raspberry Spinach Salad 123

Spinach Salad 124

Mixed Greens with Citrus Vinaigrette and Sugared Pecans 125

Mixed Green Salad with Cranberries and Sunflower Seeds 126

Green Salad with Oriental Vinaigrette 127

Orange Almond Mixed Green Salad 127

Salads

Coleslaw Asian-Style 128

Oriental Cabbage Salad 129

Cucumber and Tomato Salad 129

Seven-Layer Salad 130

Black Bean and Corn Salad 131

Corn Salad 131

Macaroni, Tomato, and Corn Salad 132

Sweet-and-Sour Broccoli Salad 133

Marinated Green Beans 133

Black-Eyed Pea and Rice Salad 134

Mediterranean Couscous Salad 135

Loaded Couscous Salad 136

Potato Salad 137

Waldorf Pasta Salad 138

Marinated Crabmeat Salad 139

Pasta Salad with Herb Dijon Vinaigrette 140

Italian Pasta Salad 141

Marinated Pasta and Veggies 142

Southwestern Tortellini Salad 143

Tortellini Shrimp Salad 144

Greek Seafood Pasta Salad 145

Curried Chicken Salad 146

Greek Chicken Salad Bowl 147

Mandarin Chicken Salad 148

Chicken Fiesta Salad 149

Marinated Italian Tuna Salad 150

Deluxe Tuna Salad 151

Tuna and White Bean Salad 152

Salad Niçoise 153

Grilled Tuna Salad with Wasabi-Ginger Vinaigrette 154

Salmon Pasta Salad 155

Wild Rice and Pork Salad 156

Taco Rice Salad 157

Southwestern Rice Salad 158

Paella Salad 159

Pretzel Strawberry Gelatin 160

Cranberry Mold 161

Mango Salad with Citrus Sauce 162

🥕 Caesar Salad

Caesar salad is no longer forbidden with this recipe that is guilt-free yet has the classic flavor.

1 head romaine lettuce,
    torn into pieces
2 tablespoons grated
    Parmesan cheese
1 teaspoon coarsely
    ground black pepper
2 tablespoons lemon juice
1 teaspoon
    Worcestershire sauce
2 tablespoons red wine
    vinegar
½ teaspoon dry mustard
½ teaspoon garlic powder
⅓ cup nonfat plain yogurt
1 cup croutons, optional

MAKES 6 SERVINGS

In a large bowl, combine the lettuce, cheese, and pepper.

In a separate bowl, combine the lemon juice, Worcestershire sauce, vinegar, dry mustard, and garlic powder; blend well. Add the yogurt, and stir well.

Add the dressing to the lettuce mixture, and toss gently to coat. If you'd like, add croutons to the lettuce mixture, and toss gently. Serve immediately.

Nutritional information per serving
Calories 40, Protein (g) 4, Carbohydrate (g) 5,
Fat (g) 1, Calories from Fat (%) 20, Saturated Fat (g) 0,
Dietary Fiber (g) 2, Cholesterol (mg) 2, Sodium (mg) 68
Diabetic Exchanges: *1 vegetable*

🥕 Raspberry Spinach Salad

With its subtly sweet dressing paired with fresh fruit and nuts, this is an outstanding salad selection. Strawberries can be substituted for raspberries. This is very low in saturated fat.

3 tablespoons raspberry
    wine vinegar
3 tablespoons raspberry
    jam
¼ cup canola oil
8 cups fresh spinach,
    washed, stemmed, and
    torn into pieces
¼ cup coarsely chopped
    macadamia nuts
1 cup fresh raspberries
3 kiwis, peeled and sliced

MAKES 8 SERVINGS

Combine the vinegar and jam in a food processor or blender. Add the oil in a thin stream, blending well; set aside.

Carefully toss the fresh spinach, nuts, raspberries, and kiwis with the dressing. Serve immediately.

Nutritional information per serving
Calories 145, Protein (g) 2, Carbohydrate (g) 13,
Fat (g) 10, Calories from Fat (%) 61, Saturated Fat (g) 1,
Dietary Fiber (g) 3, Cholesterol (mg) 0, Sodium (mg) 26
Diabetic Exchanges: *0.5 fruit, 0.5 other carbohydrate, 2 fat*

SALADS

Spinach Salad

Brown sugar and balsamic vinegar join together for a spicy, sweet tart dressing on a salad packed with flavors and textures.

SALADS

1 (12-ounce) bag fresh spinach, washed, stemmed, and torn into pieces

½ cup sliced green onion (scallion)

1 (8-ounce) can sliced water chestnuts, drained

½ cup shredded reduced-fat Monterey Jack cheese

3 tablespoons light brown sugar

⅓ cup fat-free canned chicken broth

3 tablespoons balsamic vinegar

2 dashes hot pepper sauce

1 (11-ounce) can mandarin orange slices, drained

MAKES 6 SERVINGS

Combine the fresh spinach, green onion, water chestnuts, and Monterey Jack cheese. Toss well and set aside.

Combine the brown sugar, chicken broth, vinegar, and hot pepper sauce in a small saucepan. Stir well, and bring to a boil. Remove from the heat, and stir in the mandarin orange slices.

Pour the mandarin mixture over the spinach mixture. Toss gently. Serve immediately.

Nutritional information per serving

Calories 102, Protein (g) 5, Carbohydrate (g) 18, Fat (g) 2, Calories from Fat (%) 17, Saturated Fat (g) 1, Dietary Fiber (g) 3, Cholesterol (mg) 5, Sodium (mg) 150
Diabetic Exchanges: *0.5 lean meat, 1.5 vegetable, 0.5 other carbohydrate*

QUICK TIP

For an easy way to incorporate soy protein into your diet, sprinkle soy nuts on your favorite salad for great taste and extra crunch.

Mixed Greens with Citrus Vinaigrette and Sugared Pecans

The fabulous flavor created by the combination of tangy and crunchy makes this salad extra special.

2 teaspoons olive oil

¼ cup chopped pecans

1 teaspoon sugar

⅛ teaspoon cayenne pepper

9 cups mixed salad greens

½ cup Citrus Vinaigrette (recipe follows)

2 cups fresh orange sections

MAKES 6 SERVINGS

Heat the oil in a nonstick skillet over medium heat; add the pecans. Sprinkle with the sugar and cayenne; sauté 2 minutes, or until the pecans begin to brown. Remove from heat and let cool.

In a large bowl, combine the greens and Citrus Vinaigrette (see recipe below); toss gently. Toss with the oranges and prepared pecans, and serve immediately.

Citrus Vinaigrette

½ cup freshly squeezed orange juice

2 tablespoons lemon juice

2 tablespoons olive oil

1 tablespoon low-sodium soy sauce

1 tablespoon Dijon mustard

1 tablespoon honey

Place the orange juice, lemon juice, olive oil, soy sauce, mustard, and honey in a blender; process until smooth.

Nutritional information per serving
Calories 125, Protein (g) 3, Carbohydrate (g) 14, Fat (g) 8, Calories from Fat (%) 51, Saturated Fat (g) 1, Dietary Fiber (g) 4, Cholesterol (mg) 0, Sodium (mg) 84
Diabetic Exchanges: *1 fruit, 1.5 fat*

SALADS

Mixed Green Salad with Cranberries and Sunflower Seeds

Savory, sweet, and crunchy—this sensational salad is chock-full of simple ingredients.

6 cups mixed greens

½ cup dried cranberries

¼ cup shredded carrot

½ cup sliced green
   onion (scallion)

¼ cup raspberry wine
   vinegar

2 tablespoons red wine
   vinegar

2 tablespoons olive oil

2 tablespoons honey

2 tablespoons sunflower
   seeds

MAKES 8 SERVINGS

Place the greens in a large bowl. Add the cranberries and carrot.

In a small bowl, combine the green onion, raspberry wine vinegar, red wine vinegar, olive oil, and honey, mixing well. Just before serving, pour over the greens mixture, and toss. Sprinkle with the sunflower seeds, and serve.

Nutritional information per serving

*Calories 96, Protein (g) 1, Carbohydrate (g) 13,
Fat (g) 5, Calories from Fat (%) 43, Saturated Fat (g) 1,
Dietary Fiber (g) 2, Cholesterol (mg) 0, Sodium (mg) 14*
Diabetic Exchanges: *0.5 fruit, 0.5 other carbohydrate, 1 fat*

FOOD FACT

Mixed greens are often referred to as "mesclun," a derivative of a Latin word that means "mixture." The key to a good mesclun is a balance of colors, flavors, and textures. Arugula, mustard, and mizuna are examples of spicy greens. Red oak leaf and baby lettuces are mild in flavor.

Green Salad with Oriental Vinaigrette

This is the perfect, low-fat salad to complement any Chinese- or Asian-style dish. The chow mein noodles substitute as the Asian version of the crouton.

2 tablespoons honey
1 teaspoon sugar
1 tablespoon low-sodium
   soy sauce
¼ cup rice wine vinegar
1 teaspoon minced garlic
2 tablespoons olive oil
4 cups mixed greens
¼ cup sliced green
   onion (scallion)
Chow mein noodles,
   optional

MAKES 4 SERVINGS

In the bowl of a food processor, combine the honey, sugar, soy sauce, vinegar, garlic, and oil. Pulse until mixed.

In a separate bowl, combine the mixed greens with the green onion, and toss with the dressing. Top with the crunchy chow mein noodles, and serve.

Nutritional information per serving
Calories 118, Protein (g) 1, Carbohydrate (g) 14,
Fat (g) 7, Calories from Fat (%) 50, Saturated Fat (g) 1,
Dietary Fiber (g) 1, Cholesterol (mg) 0, Sodium (mg) 114
Diabetic Exchanges: *1 other carbohydrate, 1.5 fat*

Orange Almond Mixed Green Salad

Simple enough for the family, yet fancy enough to please guests. This salad is high in flavor and low in saturated fat.

3 tablespoons canola oil
¼ cup red wine vinegar
1 tablespoon lemon juice
2 tablespoons sugar
½ teaspoon salt
½ teaspoon dry mustard
1 (11-ounce) can
   mandarin orange
   segments, drained
¼ cup slivered almonds,
   toasted
1 head red leaf or butter
   lettuce, washed and
   torn into pieces

MAKES 4 SERVINGS

Combine the oil, vinegar, lemon juice, sugar, salt, and dry mustard together in a jar with a lid. Shake, and refrigerate until ready to use.

Toss the mandarin oranges and almonds with the lettuce. Before serving, pour the dressing over the salad, tossing gently.

Nutritional information per serving
Calories 188, Protein (g) 2, Carbohydrate (g) 16,
Fat (g) 14, Calories from Fat (%) 63, Saturated Fat (g) 1,
Dietary Fiber (g) 2, Cholesterol (mg) 0, Sodium (mg) 297
Diabetic Exchanges: *0.5 fruit, 0.5 other carbohydrate, 3 fat*

SALADS

Coleslaw Asian-Style

Slaw is so simple to prepare, and shredded cabbage and shredded carrots can be found at the grocery. The garlic chili sauce gives the slaw some "kick," while the peanuts add crunch.

8 cups shredded cabbage (combination green and red cabbage)

1 cup shredded carrots

1 cup red onion, thinly sliced in rings, halved

1 tablespoon garlic chili sauce

2 tablespoons lime juice

⅓ cup rice wine vinegar

2 tablespoons light brown sugar

3 tablespoons peanut or olive oil

⅓ cup peanuts

MAKES 8 TO 10 SERVINGS

In a large bowl, mix the cabbage, carrots, and red onion.

In a small bowl, whisk together the garlic chili sauce, lime juice, vinegar, brown sugar, and peanut oil.

Toss the dressing with the cabbage mixture. Add the peanuts, mixing well. Refrigerate until serving.

Nutritional information per serving
Calories 102, Protein (g) 2, Carbohydrate (g) 10, Fat (g) 7, Calories from Fat (%) 54, Saturated Fat (g) 1, Dietary Fiber (g) 2, Cholesterol (mg) 0, Sodium (mg) 0
Diabetic Exchanges: 2 vegetable, 1.5 fat

FOOD FACT

Coleslaw is an appealing way to serve cruciferous veggies rich in antioxidants and indoles that help reduce cancer risk.

THE HOLLY CLEGG TRIM & TERRIFIC COOKBOOK

Oriental Cabbage Salad

Picking up a bag of shredded red cabbage makes this a simple salad to prepare, with plenty of flavor and texture.

3 cups shredded red
  cabbage
1 bunch green onions
  (scallions), chopped
¼ cup slivered almonds,
  toasted
1 (3-ounce) package
  Oriental ramen noodle
  soup (with seasoning
  packet)
1 tablespoon canola oil
¼ cup red wine vinegar
1 tablespoon sugar
Salt and pepper to taste

MAKES 4 TO 6 SERVINGS

Combine the cabbage, green onions, and almonds in a large bowl. Coarsely break up the dry soup noodles, and stir into the cabbage mixture.

In a small bowl, mix the oil, seasoning packet, vinegar, sugar, salt, and pepper. Pour over the salad, and toss. Cover with plastic wrap, and refrigerate for 2 hours; serve chilled.

Nutritional information per serving

Calories 136, Protein (g) 3, Carbohydrate (g) 16, Fat (g) 7, Calories from Fat (%) 45, Saturated Fat (g) 1, Dietary Fiber (g) 2, Cholesterol (mg) 0, Sodium (mg) 171
Diabetic Exchanges: *1 starch, 1 fat*

Cucumber and Tomato Salad

A great simple summer salad that is especially good when cucumbers and tomatoes are straight from the garden. The Feta adds a nice Mediterranean touch.

2 cucumbers, peeled and
  thinly sliced
1 cup chopped tomato
½ cup sliced red onion
¼ cup crumbled
  Feta cheese
½ teaspoon minced garlic
⅓ cup white vinegar
½ teaspoon sugar
2 tablespoons olive oil
Salt and pepper to taste

MAKES 6 (½-CUP) SERVINGS

In a bowl, combine the cucumber, tomato, onion, and Feta.

In a small bowl, whisk together the garlic, vinegar, sugar, oil, salt, and pepper. Toss with the cucumber mixture. Refrigerate until serving.

Nutritional information per serving

Calories 81, Protein (g) 2, Carbohydrate (g) 6, Fat (g) 6, Calories from Fat (%) 65, Saturated Fat (g) 2, Dietary Fiber (g) 1, Cholesterol (mg) 6, Sodium (mg) 74
Diabetic Exchanges: *1 vegetable, 1 fat*

Seven-Layer Salad

When you need a salad for a crowd, here's a great make-ahead layered salad with a creamy dressing full of flavors and ingredients. This recipe is my favorite.

½ cup fat-free sour cream

½ cup buttermilk

½ cup crumbled Feta cheese

1 teaspoon sugar

¼ teaspoon dried dill weed leaves

½ teaspoon dried basil leaves

⅛ teaspoon ground white pepper

1 (9-ounce) package spinach tortellini

6 cups torn fresh spinach leaves or romaine lettuce

½ pound fresh mushrooms, sliced

2 Roma (plum) tomatoes, chopped

4 green onions (scallions), chopped

2½ ounces sliced Canadian bacon, pan-cooked and cut into pieces

MAKES 8 TO 10 SERVINGS

To make the dressing, blend the sour cream, buttermilk, feta cheese, sugar, dill weed, basil, and pepper in a food processor until smooth.

Cook the tortellini according to the package directions, omitting any oil and salt. Drain and rinse in cold water.

In a 3-quart oblong dish, layer the spinach leaves, tortellini, mushrooms, tomatoes, and green onions. Pour the dressing over the salad, spreading to cover. Do not toss. Sprinkle with the bacon. Cover and chill at least 2 hours to blend the flavors.

Nutritional information per serving

Calories 112, Protein (g) 7, Carbohydrate (g) 12, Fat (g) 4, Calories from Fat (%) 33, Saturated Fat (g) 2, Dietary Fiber (g) 1, Cholesterol (mg) 44, Sodium (mg) 248
Diabetic Exchanges: *0.5 lean meat, 0.5 starch, 1 vegetable*

QUICK TIP

If you don't have Canadian bacon, substituting lean ham will work fine.

Black Bean and Corn Salad

A blaze of color with simple ingredients creates this outstanding combination that will be popular on anyone's plate. A repeat recipe, for sure!

1 (15-ounce) can black beans, drained and rinsed

1 (11-ounce) can golden sweet corn, drained

1 tomato, chopped

¼ cup fresh chopped cilantro

2 tablespoons chopped red onion

3 tablespoons lemon juice

2 tablespoons olive oil

Salt and pepper to taste

MAKES 6 SERVINGS

In a large bowl, combine the black beans, corn, tomato, cilantro, red onion, lemon juice, olive oil, salt, and pepper. This salad is best refrigerated until it's ready to be served, but it can be served immediately.

Nutritional information per serving

Calories 138, Protein (g) 5, Carbohydrate (g) 18, Fat (g) 6, Calories from Fat (%) 35, Saturated Fat (g) 1, Dietary Fiber (g) 5, Cholesterol (mg) 0, Sodium (mg) 285
Diabetic Exchanges: *0.5 very lean meat, 1 starch, 1 fat*

Corn Salad

A lightly marinated, colorful, flavorful salad.

2 (11-ounce) cans white shoepeg corn, drained

1 (2-ounce) jar diced pimiento, drained

½ cup chopped green bell pepper

½ cup chopped red onion

½ cup chopped celery

¼ cup sugar

2 tablespoons olive oil

¼ cup vinegar (white or red)

Salt and pepper to taste

MAKES 6 SERVINGS

In a large bowl, combine the corn, pimiento, green pepper, onion, celery, sugar, olive oil, vinegar, salt, and pepper. Refrigerate until serving.

Nutritional information per serving

Calories 167, Protein (g) 2, Carbohydrate (g) 28, Fat (g) 5, Calories from Fat (%) 27, Saturated Fat (g) 1, Dietary Fiber (g) 2, Cholesterol (mg) 0, Sodium (mg) 230
Diabetic Exchanges: *1.5 starch, 0.5 other carbohydrate, 1 fat*

SALADS

🥕 Macaroni, Tomato, and Corn Salad

This terrific make-ahead salad includes pasta and fresh summer specialties that appeal to everyone.

1 (8-ounce) package elbow macaroni

1 cup chopped tomato

1 cup thinly sliced green onion (scallion)

1 cup coarsely-chopped, peeled cucumber

1 cup whole-kernel corn (frozen, fresh, or canned)

1 teaspoon dried basil leaves

⅓ cup nonfat plain yogurt

2 tablespoons light mayonnaise

1½ tablespoons lime juice

1 teaspoon minced garlic

Salt and pepper to taste

MAKES 8 TO 10 SERVINGS

Cook the macaroni according to the package directions, drain, and transfer to a large bowl. Add the tomato, green onion, cucumber, and corn.

In a separate bowl, blend the basil, yogurt, mayonnaise, lime juice, and garlic. Toss the dressing with the macaroni mixture, mixing well. Season with the salt and pepper. Cover and refrigerate until ready to serve, or serve immediately.

Nutritional information per serving

Calories 124, Protein (g) 4, Carbohydrate (g) 24, Fat (g) 2, Calories from Fat (%) 11, Saturated Fat (g) 0, Dietary Fiber (g) 2, Cholesterol (mg) 1, Sodium (mg) 36 **Diabetic Exchanges:** *1.5 starch*

FOOD FACT

Store tomatoes at room temperature, stem side up. Never refrigerate them, because refrigeration destroys texture and flavor.

Sweet-and-Sour Broccoli Salad

The subtly sweet dressing mixed with veggies and fruit makes this salad a most requested recipe, delicious with every bite.

4 cups broccoli florets, cut into small pieces
½ cup sliced green onion (scallion)
2 cups red or green grapes or combination
1 head red tip lettuce, torn into pieces
1 tablespoon margarine
¼ cup slivered almonds
½ cup red wine vinegar
¼ cup sugar
2 tablespoons low-sodium soy sauce
1 tablespoon olive oil

MAKES 6 SERVINGS

In a large bowl, combine the broccoli, green onion, grapes, and lettuce; set aside.

In a small skillet coated with nonstick cooking spray, melt the margarine. Add the almonds and sauté until light brown; set aside.

In a small bowl, whisk together the red wine vinegar, sugar, soy sauce, and olive oil. Pour over the broccoli mixture, and toss. Stir in the browned almond slivers. Serve immediately, or refrigerate until ready to serve.

Nutritional information per serving

Calories 163, Protein (g) 3, Carbohydrate (g) 25, Fat (g) 7, Calories from Fat (%) 36, Saturated Fat (g) 1, Dietary Fiber (g) 3, Cholesterol (mg) 0, Sodium (mg) 170
Diabetic Exchanges: *1 fruit, 0.5 other carbohydrate, 1.5 fat*

Marinated Green Beans

Sweet-and-spicy marinated green beans are good at room temperature or chilled. This recipe works well for a party buffet. For a twist, toss in some Feta cheese.

2 pounds fresh green beans, trimmed
¼ cup chopped red onion
2 cups cherry tomato halves
3 tablespoons balsamic vinegar
2 teaspoons Dijon mustard
2 teaspoons sugar
2 tablespoons olive oil
Salt and pepper to taste

MAKES 8 TO 10 SERVINGS

Cook or steam the green beans in a little water in the microwave or on the stove until crisp-tender. Drain. Add the red onion and tomato.

In a small bowl, mix together the vinegar, mustard, sugar, olive oil, salt, and pepper, and toss with the green bean mixture. Serve, or refrigerate until serving.

Nutritional information per serving

Calories 71, Protein (g) 2, Carbohydrate (g) 10, Fat (g) 3, Calories from Fat (%) 36, Saturated Fat (g) 0, Dietary Fiber (g) 4, Cholesterol (mg) 0, Sodium (mg) 29
Diabetic Exchanges: *2 vegetable, 0.5 fat*

Black-Eyed Pea and Rice Salad

Black-eyed peas and rice team up for a salad full of fiber and flavor.

1 (6-ounce) box long-grain and wild rice mix
2 cups cooked white rice
½ cup chopped red onion
¼ cup finely sliced green onion (scallion)
1 red bell pepper, seeded and finely chopped
1 green bell pepper, seeded and finely chopped
¼ cup chopped fresh parsley
½ teaspoon minced garlic
2 (15-ounce) cans black-eyed peas, rinsed and drained
¼ cup olive oil
⅓ cup red wine vinegar
1 tablespoon Dijon mustard
2 jalapeño peppers, seeded and finely chopped
Salt and pepper to taste

MAKES 14 TO 16 SERVINGS

Cook the rice mix according to the directions on the package, omitting margarine; cool. Combine with the white rice, onion, green onion, bell peppers, parsley, garlic, and black-eyed peas.

In a small bowl, combine the olive oil, red wine vinegar, mustard, jalapeño pepper, salt, and pepper. Toss with the rice mixture, and refrigerate until serving.

Nutritional information per serving
Calories 142, Protein (g) 4, Carbohydrate (g) 23,
Fat (g) 4, Calories from Fat (%) 23, Saturated Fat (g) 0,
Dietary Fiber (g) 2, Cholesterol (mg) 0, Sodium (mg) 280
Diabetic Exchanges: *1.5 starch, 0.5 fat*

SALADS

🥕 Mediterranean Couscous Salad

Quick, crisp, and refreshing, this is a must-try salad. If you haven't had couscous, you should know that it is very quick to cook and comes out fluffy, light, and mild in flavor.

2 cups fat-free canned
   chicken broth
½ teaspoon minced garlic
1⅓ cups couscous
½ cup chopped green
   onion (scallion)
⅓ cup chopped parsley
2 cups chopped peeled
   cucumber
3 tablespoons chopped
   fresh mint leaves or 1
   tablespoon dried mint
1 (15-ounce) can
   cannellini beans, rinsed
   and drained
1 cup chopped tomato
½ cup roasted red bell
   peppers or pimentos
   from a jar, cut into
   pieces
⅓ cup sliced kalamata
   olives
¼ cup lemon juice
2 tablespoons olive oil
1½ teaspoons paprika
½ cup crumbled Feta,
   optional
Salt and pepper to taste

MAKES 6 TO 8 SERVINGS

In a saucepan, bring the chicken broth and garlic to a boil. Add the couscous; stir, remove from heat, and cover for 7 minutes. Fluff with a fork, and transfer to a large bowl. Add the green onion, parsley, cucumber, mint, beans, tomato, roasted pepper, and olives to the couscous, mixing well.

In a small bowl, mix together the lemon juice, olive oil, and paprika, and toss with the couscous mixture. Add the Feta, if desired. Season with the salt and pepper to taste. Serve immediately, or refrigerate.

Nutritional information per serving
Calories 244, Protein (g) 8, Carbohydrate (g) 39, Fat (g) 6, Calories from Fat (%) 22, Saturated Fat (g) 1, Dietary Fiber (g) 4, Cholesterol (mg) 0, Sodium (mg) 373
Diabetic Exchanges: *2.5 starch, 1 fat*

FOOD FACT

Couscous is made from semolina and is very quick-cooking. It makes a great alternative to rice or pasta.

Loaded Couscous Salad

Couscous is such a quick side dish to prepare. The fresh veggies combined with the tart cranberries, toasted pine nuts, and goat cheese make this a simple yet sophisticated choice.

½ cup orange juice

1½ cups water

2 cups plain couscous

1 cup dried cranberries

1 cup cubed peeled cucumber

¼ cup chopped parsley

½ cup chopped green onion (scallion)

1 tablespoon Dijon mustard

2 tablespoons distilled vinegar (or whatever is on hand)

2 tablespoons honey

1 clove garlic, minced

½ cup crumbled goat cheese

¼ cup pine nuts, toasted

Salt and pepper to taste

MAKES 16 (½-CUP) SERVINGS

In a saucepan, bring the orange juice and water to a boil. Stir in the couscous, cover; remove from heat and let stand for 5 to 7 minutes. Transfer to a large bowl, and fluff with a fork. Add the cranberries, cucumber, parsley, and green onion, mixing well.

In a small bowl, whisk together the mustard, vinegar, honey, and garlic. Pour the dressing over the couscous, mixing well, and stir in the goat cheese and pine nuts, carefully tossing together. Add the salt and pepper to taste. Serve at room temperature or chilled.

Nutritional information per serving

Calories 166, Protein (g) 5, Carbohydrate (g) 30, Fat (g) 3, Calories from Fat (%) 15, Saturated Fat (g) 1, Dietary Fiber (g) 1, Cholesterol (mg) 4, Sodium (mg) 39
Diabetic Exchanges: *1.5 starch, 0.5 fruit*

QUICK TIP

Pine nuts have a high fat content and can therefore turn rancid quickly. They are best stored airtight in the refrigerator, where they can be kept for up to 3 months.

🥕 Potato Salad

Try this light, marinated potato salad as an alternative to traditional potato salad. It's even easier to make because the potatoes don't need to be peeled.

2 pounds red potatoes
¼ cup chopped parsley
¼ cup chopped green
   onion (scallion)
½ teaspoon minced garlic
¼ teaspoon dry mustard
1 teaspoon sugar
1 teaspoon
   Worcestershire sauce
¼ cup olive oil
¼ cup tarragon vinegar
Salt and pepper to taste

MAKES 6 TO 8 SERVINGS

Place the potatoes with skins on in a pot filled with enough water to cover, and boil until the potatoes are tender when pricked with a fork, about 30 minutes; cut into chunks. Transfer to a bowl, and sprinkle the parsley and green onion over the potatoes.

In a small bowl, combine the garlic, dry mustard, sugar, Worcestershire sauce, olive oil, and vinegar, mixing well. Pour over the potatoes, tossing gently. Season with the salt and pepper.

Let stand at least 4 hours to marinate, stirring every hour. Serve at room temperature.

Nutritional information per serving
Calories 144, Protein (g) 3, Carbohydrate (g) 21,
Fat (g) 7, Calories from Fat (%) 38, Saturated Fat (g) 1,
Dietary Fiber (g) 3, Cholesterol (mg) 0, Sodium (mg) 9
Diabetic Exchanges: *1.5 starch, 1 fat*

QUICK TIP

New potatoes or round red or white potatoes are the best choice for potato salad. This potato salad is great, since you don't even have to peel the potatoes.

Waldorf Pasta Salad

Here's a wonderful way to include apples in a salad, mixed with pasta, pecans, and celery in a tangy, sweet, creamy dressing.

1 (8-ounce) package
 rotini (spiral) pasta
½ cup fat-free sour cream
2 tablespoons light
 mayonnaise
¼ cup lime juice
2 tablespoons sugar
⅓ cup chopped pecans,
 toasted
1 cup chopped celery
1 green apple, cored
 and chopped
2 medium red apples,
 cored and chopped
½ cup chopped green
 onion (scallion)

MAKES 4 TO 6 SERVINGS

Cook the pasta according to the package directions, omitting any oil and salt. Rinse with cold water; drain.

Meanwhile, in a small bowl, stir together the sour cream, mayonnaise, lime juice, and sugar; set aside.

Just before serving, in a large bowl, toss together the pasta, pecans, celery, green and red apples, and green onion. Drizzle with the dressing, and toss gently to coat. Serve immediately or refrigerate.

Nutritional information per serving

Calories 291, Protein (g) 7, Carbohydrate (g) 51, Fat (g) 7, Calories from Fat (%) 21, Saturated Fat (g) 1, Dietary Fiber (g) 5, Cholesterol (mg) 2, Sodium (mg) 78
Diabetic Exchanges: *2 starch, 1 fruit, 0.5 other carbohydrate, 1 fat*

FOOD FACT

Use your favorite variety of red apple in this recipe. America's favorite is Red Delicious. Gala, Pink Lady, Braeburn, and Fuji are other popular choices to include in salads depending on availability.

SALADS

Marinated Crabmeat Salad

This salad has been a family favorite for many years. Make the marinated mixture ahead, and toss with the lettuce before serving. For added nutrition, throw in some carrots or veggies.

¼ cup olive oil

3 tablespoons distilled or wine vinegar

Salt to taste

½ teaspoon pepper

¼ teaspoon dry mustard

⅛ teaspoon dried thyme leaves

¼ teaspoon dried basil leaves

2 tablespoons chopped fresh parsley

1 large red onion, chopped

2 tablespoons lime juice

1 pound lump or white crabmeat, picked for shells

1 head lettuce, washed and torn into bite-size pieces

MAKES 6 TO 8 SERVINGS

In a small bowl, combine the olive oil, vinegar, salt, pepper, mustard, thyme, basil, parsley, onion, and lime juice; mix well. Add the crabmeat, tossing gently. Cover the bowl with plastic wrap, and refrigerate at least 4 hours. Stir occasionally.

Before serving, gently toss the crabmeat and marinade with the lettuce. Serve immediately.

Nutritional information per serving
Calories 144, Protein (g) 14, Carbohydrate (g) 5, Fat (g) 8, Calories from Fat (%) 48, Saturated Fat (g) 1, Dietary Fiber (g) 2, Cholesterol (mg) 43, Sodium (mg) 222
Diabetic Exchanges: *2 very lean meat, 1 vegetable, 1 fat*

FOOD FACT

The greener the lettuce, the more nutrition it contains.

Pasta Salad with Herb Dijon Vinaigrette

This is one of my favorite pasta salads, and sometimes I even toss in other veggies.

2 cups snow peas

1 bunch broccoli, florets only

1 (12-ounce) package tri-colored pasta

1 (6-ounce) package tri-colored stuffed tortellini

½ pound mushroom halves

1 cup cherry tomato halves

1 red bell pepper, seeded and cut into strips

⅓ cup grated Romano cheese

Herb Dijon Vinaigrette (recipe follows)

Herb Dijon Vinaigrette

1 bunch green onions (scallions), sliced

½ cup red wine vinegar

⅓ cup olive oil

2 tablespoons chopped parsley

3 cloves garlic, minced

2 teaspoons dried basil

1 teaspoon dried dill weed

½ teaspoon dried oregano

Salt and pepper to taste

½ teaspoon sugar

1½ teaspoons Dijon mustard

MAKES 10 SERVINGS

Cook the snow peas and broccoli in the microwave until crisp-tender. Drain and set aside.

Cook the pasta and tortellini according to the package directions, omitting any oil and salt. Drain and set aside.

In a large bowl, combine the snow peas, broccoli, pasta, tortellini, mushrooms, tomatoes, red pepper, and cheese. Toss with Herb Dijon Vinaigrette (see recipe below).

FOOD FACT

Dijon mustard is from Dijon, France, and known for its clean, sharp flavor. Always use the type of mustard that is called for in a recipe, or you could end up with a completely different flavor than was intended.

In a small bowl, combine the green onions, red wine vinegar, olive oil, parsley, garlic, basil, dill weed, oregano, salt, pepper, sugar, and mustard, mixing well. Pour over the pasta salad. Refrigerate until serving.

Nutritional information per serving
Calories 286, Protein (g) 10, Carbohydrate (g) 41,
Fat (g) 10, Calories from Fat (%) 30, Saturated Fat (g) 2,
Dietary Fiber (g) 3, Cholesterol (mg) 12, Sodium (mg) 101
Diabetic Exchanges: *2 starch, 2 vegetable, 2 fat*

SALADS

Italian Pasta Salad

Everyone always enjoys the light Dijon vinaigrette in this simple and satisfying salad.

8 ounces ziti pasta

4 ounces tri-colored rotini (spiral) pasta

1 green bell pepper, seeded and chopped

1 red bell pepper, seeded and chopped

½ cup chopped celery

2 teaspoons capers, drained

⅓ cup thinly sliced green onion (scallion)

2 Roma (plum) tomatoes, chopped

½ cup red wine vinegar

¼ cup water

1 tablespoon olive oil

1 teaspoon dried basil leaves

1 teaspoon dried oregano leaves

½ teaspoon minced garlic

1 tablespoon Dijon mustard

¼ cup grated Parmesan cheese

MAKES 8 TO 10 SERVINGS

In a large saucepan, cook both the pastas together according to the package directions, omitting any oil and salt. Rinse, drain, and place in a large bowl. Add the green pepper, red pepper, celery, capers, green onion, and tomatoes.

In a small bowl, combine the vinegar, water, oil, basil, oregano, garlic, mustard, and Parmesan cheese, mixing well. Pour over the pasta mixture, and toss well. Refrigerate until serving.

Nutritional information per serving
Calories 168, Protein (g) 6, Carbohydrate (g) 30,
Fat (g) 3, Calories from Fat (%) 15, Saturated Fat (g) 1,
Dietary Fiber (g) 2, Cholesterol (mg) 2, Sodium (mg) 110
Diabetic Exchanges: *2 starch*

QUICK TIP

For pasta in a cold salad, drain and rinse with cold water.

SALADS

Marinated Pasta and Veggies

The sweet, zesty dressing gives this attractive marinated salad a memorable flavor.

1 (8-ounce) package tubular pasta

1 (15-ounce) can whole-kernel corn, drained

1 (15-ounce) can garbanzo beans, drained and rinsed

2 cups sliced, peeled cucumber

2 tablespoons capers, drained

1 cup chopped tomatoes

½ cup chopped red onion

⅓ cup cider or white vinegar

¼ cup lemon juice

1 tablespoon Dijon mustard

3 tablespoons sugar

2 tablespoons olive oil

MAKES 8 TO 10 SERVINGS

Cook the pasta according to the package directions, omitting any oil and salt; drain.

In a large bowl, mix together the pasta, corn, beans, cucumber, capers, tomatoes, and onion.

In a small bowl, whisk together the vinegar, lemon juice, Dijon mustard, sugar, and oil until well mixed. Pour over the pasta mixture, tossing until well combined.

Refrigerate for several hours, and serve.

Nutritional information per serving
Calories 205, Protein (g) 6, Carbohydrate (g) 37,
Fat (g) 4, Calories from Fat (%) 19, Saturated Fat (g) 0,
Dietary Fiber (g) 3, Cholesterol (mg) 0, Sodium (mg) 248
***Diabetic Exchanges:** 2 starch, 1 vegetable, 0.5 fat*

QUICK TIP

This type of salad works with a variety of beans, so use your favorites. Take advantage of the veggies that are in season by using those them while they're available.

SALADS

Southwestern Tortellini Salad

These ingredients tossed with this incredibly flavored vinaigrette turn an ordinary salad into an outstanding dish.

1 pound cheese-filled
  tri-colored tortellini or
  spiral pasta
1 pint grape tomatoes,
  cut in half
1 (15-ounce) can black
  beans, drained and
  rinsed
1 cup frozen corn,
  defrosted
¼ cup balsamic vinegar
2 tablespoons lime juice
½ cup chopped red onion
½ teaspoon minced garlic
1 teaspoon honey
¼ cup chopped fresh
  cilantro
¼ cup olive oil
Salt and freshly ground
  pepper to taste

MAKES 10 TO 12 SERVINGS

Prepare the tortellini according to the package directions, omitting any oil and salt. Rinse in cold water, and set aside to cool.

In a large bowl, combine the tortellini, tomatoes, black beans, and corn; toss gently.

In a food processor, combine the balsamic vinegar, lime juice, red onion, garlic, honey, and cilantro. Pulse to combine. Add the olive oil gradually through the feed tube with the motor running. Season with the salt and pepper.

Pour the dressing over the salad. Toss, cover, and chill for 30 minutes before serving.

Nutritional information per serving
Calories 202, Protein (g) 8, Carbohydrate (g) 28,
Fat (g) 7, Calories from Fat (%) 30, Saturated Fat (g) 2,
Dietary Fiber (g) 4, Cholesterol (mg) 20, Sodium (mg) 177
Diabetic Exchanges: *1.5 starch, 1 vegetable, 1 fat*

SALADS

Tortellini Shrimp Salad

Shrimp and tortellini tossed with a Dijon vinaigrette team up to make this a popular choice.

SALADS

2 (8-ounce) packages tri-colored tortellini stuffed with Parmesan cheese

1 pound cooked medium shrimp, peeled

⅓ cup grated Romano cheese

4 green onions (scallions), finely sliced

⅓ cup chopped red bell pepper

2 tablespoons dried basil leaves, divided

¼ cup balsamic vinegar

2 tablespoons canola oil

1 teaspoon Dijon mustard

MAKES 8 SERVINGS

Cook the tortellini according to the package directions, omitting any oil and salt. Drain well and cool slightly.

In a large bowl, combine the tortellini, shrimp, cheese, green onions, red pepper, and 1 tablespoon basil.

In a small bowl, combine the vinegar, oil, remaining 1 tablespoon basil, and mustard. Toss with the pasta mixture, and refrigerate until serving.

Nutritional information per serving
Calories 270, Protein (g) 21, Carbohydrate (g) 28,
Fat (g) 8, Calories from Fat (%) 27, Saturated Fat (g) 2,
Dietary Fiber (g) 2, Cholesterol (mg) 145, Sodium (mg) 289
***Diabetic Exchanges:** 2 lean meat, 2 starch*

FOOD FACT

For great cheese flavor, impact, and less fat, use full-flavored cheeses like Romano, Asiago, or Parmesan.

Greek Seafood Pasta Salad

Marinated shrimp and scallops tossed with pasta and Feta create this Greek wonder.
To cook the scallops and shrimp, sauté them in a skillet.

1 pound small shrimp,
  cooked and peeled
1 pound bay scallops,
  cooked
Dill Dressing (recipe
  follows)
1 (12-ounce) package
  tri-colored rotini
  (spiral) pasta
2 cups cherry tomato
  halves
¼ cup thinly sliced black
  olives
3 ounces Feta cheese,
  crumbled

Dill Dressing

½ teaspoon dried dill
  weed leaves
½ teaspoon minced garlic
½ cup chopped red onion
¼ cup fresh lemon juice
3 tablespoons olive oil
Salt and pepper to taste

MAKES 6 TO 8 SERVINGS

Toss the shrimp and scallops with ¼ cup Dill Dressing (see recipe below). Refrigerate the seafood and the remaining dressing until ready to toss together with the other ingredients.

Cook the pasta according to the package directions, omitting any oil and salt. Drain well.

In a large bowl, toss the pasta with the marinated seafood, tomato, olives, Feta, and reserved dressing. Refrigerate until serving.

In a food processor, mix the dill weed, garlic, onion, lemon juice, olive oil, salt, and pepper until well combined.

Nutritional information per serving
Calories 374, Protein (g) 32, Carbohydrate (g) 38,
Fat (g) 10, Calories from Fat (%) 24, Saturated Fat (g) 3,
Dietary Fiber (g) 2, Cholesterol (mg) 144, Sodium (mg) 410
Diabetic Exchanges: *4 lean meat, 2 starch, 1 vegetable*

SALADS

Curried Chicken Salad

The hint of curry (add more if you like) in the light, snappy dressing makes this a marvelous chicken salad for luncheon guests or for just the family at home.

4 cooked skinless, boneless chicken breasts, diced
¾ cup chopped celery
½ cup chopped onion
¼ cup light mayonnaise
¼ cup nonfat plain yogurt
1 teaspoon lemon juice
1 tablespoon low-sodium soy sauce
¼ teaspoon curry powder
¼ cup chopped almonds, toasted
½ cup frozen green peas, thawed

MAKES 4 SERVINGS

In a large bowl, combine the chicken, celery, and onion.

In a small bowl, blend the mayonnaise, yogurt, lemon juice, soy sauce, and curry powder together. Pour the sauce over the chicken mixture, and mix thoroughly. Before serving, fold in the almonds and peas.

Nutritional information per serving
Calories 259, Protein (g) 30, Carbohydrate (g) 10, Fat (g) 11, Calories from Fat (%) 37, Saturated Fat (g) 1, Dietary Fiber (g) 3, Cholesterol (mg) 71, Sodium (mg) 343
Diabetic Exchanges: 4 lean meat, 0.5 starch

QUICK TIP

Curry is a spice with definite flavor that can be found in the spice section of the grocery. Start with a small amount and add to suit your taste.

Greek Chicken Salad Bowl

Throw in some Feta cheese to make a Greek chef salad. The mint gives the salad an adventurous personality.

½ cup lemon juice, divided

1 teaspoon dried mint, divided

¾ teaspoon minced garlic, divided

2 tablespoons red wine vinegar

1½ pounds skinless, boneless chicken breasts, cut into strips

½ cup dry white wine

1 pound fresh spinach, washed, stemmed, and torn into pieces

1½ cups chopped tomatoes

⅓ cup chopped green onion (scallion)

1½ cups chopped peeled cucumber

Salt and pepper to taste

1 tablespoon olive oil

Feta cheese, optional

MAKES 4 TO 6 SERVINGS

In a large bowl, mix together ¼ cup lemon juice, ½ teaspoon mint, ¼ teaspoon garlic, and the vinegar. Add the chicken; toss, cover with plastic wrap, and marinate in the refrigerator for at least 1 hour.

Coat a large skillet with nonstick cooking spray, and cook the chicken over medium-high heat until brown, turning frequently, about 5 minutes. Add the wine, reduce the heat, and simmer for 8 to 10 minutes, or until the chicken is done. Remove the chicken from the pan, and refrigerate until ready to use.

In a large bowl, combine the spinach, tomatoes, green onion, cucumber, and chicken.

In a small bowl, mix together the remaining ¼ cup lemon juice, ½ teaspoon mint, and ½ teaspoon garlic, and the salt, pepper, and oil. Pour the dressing over the salad, add Feta cheese, if desired, and toss to mix well. Serve immediately.

Nutritional information per serving

Calories 198, Protein (g) 29, Carbohydrate (g) 9, Fat (g) 4, Calories from Fat (%) 19, Saturated Fat (g) 1, Dietary Fiber (g) 3, Cholesterol (mg) 66, Sodium (mg) 141
Diabetic Exchanges: *3 very lean meat, 2 vegetable*

Mandarin Chicken Salad

This blaze of color with a burst of flavor and a simple, light lemon dressing is hard to beat. Try grilling the chicken for a nice touch.

1½ pounds skinless, boneless chicken breasts, cut into chunks or strips
1 tablespoon canola oil
3 tablespoons low-sodium soy sauce, divided
½ teaspoon minced garlic
¼ teaspoon ground ginger
1 cup green grapes, cut in half
1 cup chopped celery
½ cup thinly sliced green onion (scallion)
1 (11-ounce) can mandarin orange segments, drained
¼ cup chopped pecans, toasted
1 (6-ounce) container nonfat lemon yogurt
6 cups fresh spinach, washed, stemmed, and torn into pieces
Chinese noodles, for garnish, optional

MAKES 4 TO 6 SERVINGS

In a large bowl, combine the chicken, oil, 2 tablespoons soy sauce, garlic, and ginger, coating the chicken well.

In a skillet coated with nonstick cooking spray, cook the chicken mixture over medium heat for about 5 to 7 minutes, or until the chicken is done. Set aside to cool.

In a large bowl, combine the cooled chicken, grapes, celery, green onion, orange segments, and pecans.

In a separate, small bowl, mix together the yogurt and the remaining 1 tablespoon soy sauce, and pour over the chicken mixture. Cover and refrigerate until the mixture is well chilled, about 2 hours. Serve on the fresh spinach leaves, and sprinkle with Chinese noodles, if desired.

Nutritional information per serving
Calories 262, Protein (g) 30, Carbohydrate (g) 18,
Fat (g) 8, Calories from Fat (%) 26, Saturated Fat (g) 1,
Dietary Fiber (g) 3, Cholesterol (mg) 66, Sodium (mg) 334
Diabetic Exchanges: *3.5 lean meat, 1 fruit, 1 vegetable*

Chicken Fiesta Salad

The well-seasoned chicken with beans, cilantro, tomato, and onion will thrill your Southwestern taste buds. Serve over mixed greens.

1 teaspoon ground cumin

1 teaspoon chili powder

¼ cup all-purpose flour

1½ pounds skinless, boneless chicken breasts, cut into strips

2 cups frozen corn, thawed

1 (15-ounce) can pinto beans, drained and rinsed

1 cup chopped tomato

½ cup chopped red onion

¼ cup chopped fresh cilantro

1 tablespoon olive oil

½ teaspoon minced garlic

½ cup lime juice

¼ cup red wine vinegar

MAKES 6 SERVINGS

In a small bowl, combine the cumin, chili powder, and flour. Coat the chicken with the flour mixture, and in a large skillet coated with nonstick cooking spray, sauté the chicken over medium-high heat, about 5 to 7 minutes or until well done. Set aside.

In a large bowl, combine the corn, pinto beans, tomato, red onion, and cilantro.

In a small bowl, combine the oil, garlic, lime juice, and vinegar. Pour over the corn mixture. Add the chicken strips, tossing to mix. Serve immediately or refrigerate.

Nutritional information per serving

Calories 297, Protein (g) 32, Carbohydrate (g) 33, Fat (g) 5, Calories from Fat (%) 14, Saturated Fat (g) 1, Dietary Fiber (g) 5, Cholesterol (mg) 66, Sodium (mg) 230
Diabetic Exchanges: *3.5 very lean meat, 2 starch, 1 vegetable*

QUICK TIP

For the best flavor, cilantro should only be used when it is fresh. If you are not a cilantro fan, leave it out.

Marinated Italian Tuna Salad

Tuna, mozzarella, and tomatoes highlight this Italian marinade. For an extra touch when tomatoes are in season, use fresh mozzarella.

2 ounces part-skim Mozzarella cheese, cut into small cubes

2 (6-ounce) cans solid white tuna, packed in water, drained

1 cup cherry tomatoes, halved

1 small red onion, cut into thin rings, halved

⅔ cup chopped celery

2 tablespoons olive oil

3 tablespoons red wine vinegar or balsamic vinegar

1½ teaspoons dried basil leaves

¼ teaspoon crushed red pepper flakes

⅛ teaspoon pepper

MAKES 4 TO 6 SERVINGS

In a large bowl, combine the cheese, tuna, tomatoes, onion, and celery.

In a small bowl, mix together the oil, vinegar, basil, red pepper flakes, and pepper. Pour the dressing over the tuna mixture, and toss gently to coat. Cover, and refrigerate for at least 1 hour.

Nutritional information per serving

Calories 159, Protein (g) 17, Carbohydrate (g) 5, Fat (g) 8, Calories from Fat (%) 45, Saturated Fat (g) 2, Dietary Fiber (g) 1, Cholesterol (mg) 30, Sodium (mg) 277
Diabetic Exchanges: *2 very lean meat, 1 vegetable, 1 fat*

QUICK TIP

For a treat, use fresh Mozzarella cheese, available in specialty delis.

Deluxe Tuna Salad

For rave reviews and lots of compliments, dress up tuna salad with these fabulous ingredients.

2 (6-ounce) cans solid white tuna, packed in water, drained

1 (11-ounce) can mandarin orange segments, drained

¼ pound fresh mushrooms, sliced

1 (14-ounce) can artichoke hearts, drained and halved

1 cup sliced water chestnuts, drained

¼ cup light mayonnaise

¼ cup nonfat plain yogurt

1 tablespoon lemon juice

2 teaspoons sugar

1 bunch green onions (scallions), thinly sliced

MAKES 8 SERVINGS

In a large bowl, carefully combine the tuna, oranges, mushrooms, artichoke hearts, and water chestnuts.

In a small bowl, mix the mayonnaise, yogurt, lemon juice, sugar, and green onions, and fold into the tuna mixture. Serve immediately or refrigerate.

Nutritional information per serving

Calories 129, Protein (g) 12, Carbohydrate (g) 11, Fat (g) 4, Calories from Fat (%) 27, Saturated Fat (g) 1, Dietary Fiber (g) 2, Cholesterol (mg) 21, Sodium (mg) 322
Diabetic Exchanges: *1.5 lean meat, 2 vegetable*

FOOD FACT

White tuna is albacore tuna. It has a milder flavor and whiter flesh than the tuna labeled "light."

Tuna and White Bean Salad

This stylishly simple salad is packed with fiber and lots of flavor.

1 (12-ounce) can solid
   white tuna, packed in
   water, drained
1 cup chopped green
   onion (scallion)
1 (15-ounce) can white
   beans, rinsed and
   drained
2 tablespoons chopped
   parsley
½ cup diced celery
⅓ cup lemon juice
1½ tablespoons olive oil
¼ teaspoon dried
   rosemary leaves
¼ teaspoon pepper

MAKES 4 TO 6 SERVINGS

In a large bowl, combine the tuna, green onion, white beans, parsley, and celery, tossing well.

In a small bowl, blend the lemon juice, olive oil, rosemary, and pepper. Pour over the tuna mixture, and stir gently to combine. Refrigerate for 2 hours, or let stand at room temperature for at least 30 minutes before serving.

Nutritional information per serving
Calories 161, Protein (g) 18, Carbohydrate (g) 14,
Fat (g) 5, Calories from Fat (%) 28, Saturated Fat (g) 1,
Dietary Fiber (g) 4, Cholesterol (mg) 24, Sodium (mg) 462
Diabetic Exchanges: *2 lean meat, 1 starch*

QUICK TIP

Try this recipe with grilled fresh tuna for a wonderful treat.

Salad Niçoise

Prepare this French marinated-tuna-and-veggies presentation ahead of time. To wow your taste buds, try using grilled fresh tuna instead of canned.

3 or 4 red potatoes
1 tablespoon chopped
   green onion (scallion)
Salt and pepper to taste
½ pound fresh green
   beans
1 head Boston or
   romaine lettuce, rinsed
Vinaigrette Dressing
   (recipe follows)
2 (9-ounce) cans tuna
   packed in water,
   well drained
Salt and pepper to taste
1 cucumber, peeled and
   thinly sliced
2 ripe tomatoes,
   quartered
2 hard-boiled eggs,
   sliced, optional

Vinaigrette Dressing

½ teaspoon minced garlic
1 tablespoon chopped
   parsley
¼ cup chopped red onion
⅓ cup red wine vinegar
2 tablespoons lemon
   juice
1 teaspoon Dijon
   mustard
3 tablespoons olive oil

MAKES 6 TO 8 SERVINGS

Place the potatoes in a medium saucepan; cover with salted water. Cook, uncovered, until tender when pierced with a fork, about 20 to 25 minutes. Drain, peel, and slice. Combine with the chopped green onion, salt, and pepper; set aside.

Snip the ends off the green beans. In a microwave-safe dish, cook the green beans in a small amount of salted water, covered, in the microwave or on the stovetop until crisp tender. Drain.

Line a large platter with the lettuce. Arrange the green beans over the lettuce. Drizzle with ¼ cup Vinaigrette Dressing (see recipe below). Layer the tuna over the green beans. Sprinkle with salt and pepper. Drizzle with ¼ cup Vinaigrette Dressing. Around the edges of the tuna, arrange the potato slices, cucumber slices, tomato wedges, and egg slices. Pour the remaining Vinaigrette Dressing over all. Cover with plastic wrap, and refrigerate at least 1 hour.

In a small bowl, combine the garlic, parsley, onion, vinegar, lemon juice, mustard, and olive oil, mixing well.

Nutritional information per serving
Calories 193, Protein (g) 18, Carbohydrate (g) 16,
Fat (g) 7, Calories from Fat (%) 32, Saturated Fat (g) 1,
Dietary Fiber (g) 3, Cholesterol (mg) 27, Sodium (mg) 263
Diabetic Exchanges: *2 lean meat, 0.5 starch, 1 vegetable*

SALADS

Grilled Tuna Salad with Wasabi-Ginger Vinaigrette

This vinaigrette has an outstanding taste. Make extra grilled tuna to save for an exciting salad.

3 tablespoons low-sodium soy sauce

¼ cup lime juice

2 teaspoons sugar

1 teaspoon wasabi paste

½ teaspoon ground ginger

2 green onions (scallions), finely chopped

4 grilled tuna steaks, 2 inches thick (about 4 ounces each)

1 medium red onion, thinly sliced

4 cups mixed greens

MAKES 4 SERVINGS

Combine the soy sauce, lime juice, sugar, wasabi, ginger, and green onions in a large bowl, and whisk. Taste for seasoning. Set aside.

Cut the grilled tuna into large chunks, and toss with the vinaigrette. Set aside.

Combine the red onion and greens in a large bowl, and toss well. Place the mixture on four plates. Spoon the tuna on top and serve.

Nutritional information per serving

Calories 165, Protein (g) 27, Carbohydrate (g) 10, Fat (g) 1, Calories from Fat (%) 7, Saturated Fat (g) 0, Dietary Fiber (g) 2, Cholesterol (mg) 53, Sodium (mg) 351
Diabetic Exchanges: *3 very lean meat, 2 vegetable*

QUICK TIP

Substitute your favorite herbs, spices, and flavored oils to create different vinaigrettes.

Salmon Pasta Salad

Fresh salmon is worth the extra effort, but to save time, you can substitute a can of red salmon.

1 pound fresh salmon
   fillet
1 (8-ounce) package
   rotini (spiral) pasta
⅓ cup light mayonnaise
½ cup nonfat plain
   yogurt
½ teaspoon sugar
2 teaspoons dried dill
   weed leaves
½ teaspoon white pepper
1 cup diced celery
1 (14-ounce) can
   artichoke hearts,
   drained and quartered

MAKES 4 TO 6 SERVINGS
Preheat the oven to 325°F.

Place the salmon in a shallow baking dish coated with nonstick cooking spray and bake for 15 minutes, or pan-fry, until the salmon is thoroughly cooked and flakes easily. Set aside to cool.

Cook the pasta according to the package directions, omitting any oil and salt. Drain, rinse, and set aside.

In a small bowl, mix the mayonnaise, yogurt, sugar, dill weed, and pepper. Set aside.

In a large bowl, mix the celery, artichoke hearts, pasta, and dressing. Remove the skin from the salmon, flake into chunks, and add to the pasta mixture, tossing gently. Chill until ready to serve.

Nutritional information per serving
Calories 305, Protein (g) 22, Carbohydrate (g) 35,
Fat (g) 8, Calories from Fat (%) 23, Saturated Fat (g) 1,
Dietary Fiber (g) 2, Cholesterol (mg) 44, Sodium (mg) 311
***Diabetic Exchanges:** 2 lean meat, 2 starch, 1 vegetable*

QUICK TIP

Fresh herbs can be substituted for dried herbs at a ratio of 3:1. In other words, 1 teaspoon of a dried herb equals 1 tablespoon fresh.

SALADS

Wild Rice and Pork Salad

Spruce up this salad with teriyaki or peppered pork tenderloins. If you have pork tenderloin leftovers, this combination makes another hearty yet not heavy meal.

2 (6-ounce) packages long-grain and wild rice

1 (6-ounce) package frozen snow pea pods

1 (8-ounce) can sliced water chestnuts, drained

1 (11-ounce) can mandarin orange segments, drained

2 cups chopped cooked pork tenderloin (about 1¼ pounds)

¼ cup low-sodium soy sauce

¼ cup seasoned rice vinegar

2 tablespoons olive oil

1 teaspoon ground ginger

MAKES 6 TO 8 SERVINGS

Prepare the rice according to the package directions, omitting any oil and salt; set aside.

Prepare the pea pods according to the package directions; set aside.

In a large bowl, combine the cooked rice, pea pods, water chestnut slices, orange segments, and pork, tossing well.

In a small bowl, whisk together the soy sauce, vinegar, oil, and ginger. Pour over the rice salad, and gently toss. Cover and refrigerate for at least 2 hours before serving.

Nutritional information per serving

Calories 343, Protein (g) 25, Carbohydrate (g) 43, Fat (g) 7, Calories from Fat (%) 19, Saturated Fat (g) 2, Dietary Fiber (g) 3, Cholesterol (mg) 56, Sodium (mg) 1,019
Diabetic Exchanges: *3 lean meat, 1.5 starch, 0.5 fruit*

QUICK TIP

Lifting the lid to peek while rice is cooking lets out valuable steam and slows the cooking process.

Taco Rice Salad

This is one of my favorite Southwestern salads. Light but satisfying, it will win you over. Serve with extra salsa and chips. This recipe is also a great way to introduce the younger ones to lettuce, since the meat and rice are the stars of the salad.

1 pound ground sirloin
½ cup finely chopped
   onion
½ teaspoon minced garlic
½ teaspoon ground
   cumin
Salt and pepper to taste
3 cups cooked rice
½ head lettuce, shredded,
   or 4 cups mixed greens
2 tomatoes, chopped
½ cup shredded reduced-
   fat Cheddar cheese
½ cup chopped red onion
¼ cup fat-free sour cream
¼ cup salsa
Low-fat tortilla chips
   (optional)

MAKES 6 SERVINGS

In a large skillet coated with nonstick cooking spray, cook the meat, onion, and garlic over medium heat, stirring to crumble, 5 to 7 minutes or until the meat is done. Drain any excess fat. Add the cumin, salt, pepper, and rice. Remove from the heat, and let cool.

In a large bowl, combine the lettuce, tomatoes, cheese, red onion, and the rice mixture.

In a separate bowl, mix together the sour cream and salsa, and toss lightly with the lettuce-rice mixture. Serve immediately, with extra salsa and chips, if desired.

Nutritional information per serving
Calories 256, Protein (g) 21, Carbohydrate (g) 30,
Fat (g) 6, Calories from Fat (%) 20, Saturated Fat (g) 3,
Dietary Fiber (g) 2, Cholesterol (mg) 45, Sodium (mg) 168
Diabetic Exchanges: 2.5 lean meat, 1.5 starch, 1 vegetable

SALADS

Southwestern Rice Salad

Another make-ahead lifesaver, this full-flavored rice salad is hearty enough to eat on its own and also makes an outstanding side dish for grilled chicken and other meats.

1 (15-ounce) can black beans, rinsed and drained

2 cups cooked rice

1 medium tomato, chopped

1 red bell pepper, seeded and chopped

1 bunch green onions (scallions), sliced

½ cup chopped fresh cilantro leaves

1 small jalapeño pepper, seeded

3 tablespoons olive oil

¼ cup lime juice

½ teaspoon ground cumin

1 cup shredded reduced-fat mild Cheddar cheese

MAKES 10 TO 12 SERVINGS

In a large bowl, combine the beans, rice, tomato, red pepper, green onions, and cilantro.

In a food processor, mince the jalapeño pepper. Add the oil, lime juice, and cumin, and process until well blended. Toss the dressing with the bean mixture. Cover and chill at least 2 hours, or overnight. Just before serving, toss the cheese with the salad.

Nutritional information per serving
Calories 130, Protein (g) 6, Carbohydrate (g) 14, Fat (g) 6, Calories from Fat (%) 38, Saturated Fat (g) 2, Dietary Fiber (g) 3, Cholesterol (mg) 5, Sodium (mg) 173
Diabetic Exchanges: *0.5 lean meat, 1 starch, .05 fat*

QUICK TIP

When buying cilantro, look for bright green leaves that give off a strong fragrance when rubbed.

SALADS

Paella Salad

This festive presentation of colors and textures will quickly convince even the heartiest eaters that a salad can be a satisfying, fulfilling meal, which makes this another favorite of mine.

2 (5-ounce) packages
  saffron yellow rice
¼ cup balsamic vinegar
¼ cup lemon juice
1 tablespoon olive oil
1 teaspoon dried basil
  leaves
⅛ teaspoon pepper
Dash cayenne pepper
1 pound medium cooked
  and peeled shrimp
1 (14-ounce) can
  quartered artichoke
  hearts, drained
¾ cup chopped green
  bell pepper
1 cup frozen green peas,
  thawed
1 cup cherry tomatoes,
  halved
1 (2-ounce) jar diced
  pimiento, drained
½ cup chopped red onion
2 ounces chopped
  prosciutto

MAKES 6 SERVINGS

Prepare the rice according to the package directions, omitting any oil and salt. Set aside.

In a small bowl, mix together the vinegar, lemon juice, oil, basil, pepper, and cayenne; set aside.

In a large bowl, combine the cooked rice with the shrimp, artichoke hearts, green pepper, peas, tomato, pimiento, red onion, and prosciutto, mixing well. Pour the dressing over the rice mixture, tossing to coat. Cover, and refrigerate at least 2 hours before serving.

Nutritional information per serving

Calories 342, Protein (g) 25, Carbohydrate (g) 50,
Fat (g) 5, Calories from Fat (%) 12, Saturated Fat (g) 1,
Dietary Fiber (g) 3, Cholesterol (mg) 156, Sodium (mg) 1,106
Diabetic Exchanges: 2.5 very lean meat, 3 starch, 1 vegetable

FOOD FACT

Paella is a Spanish dish of saffron-flavored rice combined with a variety of meats, shellfish, garlic, onions, peas, artichoke hearts, and tomatoes.

SALADS

Pretzel Strawberry Gelatin

This popular, fabulous recipe may also be served for dessert. No one can ever figure out the ingredients in the pretzel crust—they think there are pecans.

4 tablespoons margarine, melted

2 tablespoons light brown sugar

2 cups crushed pretzels

1 (6-ounce) package strawberry gelatin

2 cups boiling water

3 cups sliced fresh strawberries

4 ounces reduced-fat cream cheese

½ cup sugar

1 envelope dry whipped topping mix

½ cup skim milk

MAKES 16 SERVINGS

Preheat the oven to 350°F.

Combine the margarine, brown sugar, and pretzels, and press into a 13 x 9 x 2-inch baking pan. Bake for 10 minutes; cool.

Meanwhile, dissolve the strawberry gelatin in 2 cups boiling water, stirring until dissolved. Add the strawberry slices. Cool in the refrigerator until the gelatin begins to set.

In a small bowl, beat the cream cheese with the sugar. Prepare the whipped topping according to the package directions, substituting skim milk. Fold into the cream cheese mixture. Spread over the cooled crust.

Pour the semi-firm gelatin mixture over the cream cheese layer. Refrigerate at least 1 hour, or until congealed.

Nutritional information per serving
Calories 179, Protein (g) 3, Carbohydrate (g) 30,
Fat (g) 5, Calories from Fat (%) 26, Saturated Fat (g) 2,
Dietary Fiber (g) 1, Cholesterol (mg) 5, Sodium (mg) 275
Diabetic Exchanges: *0.5 starch, 1.5 other carbohydrate, 1 fat*

SALADS

Cranberry Mold

Throw all these festive ingredients into a food processor—yes, even the peeling on the orange. This is a great cranberry choice for any holiday table.

1 (16-ounce) package
  fresh cranberries
1 whole orange
½ cup chopped pecans
1 cup crushed pineapple,
  in its own juices,
  drained
1 (3-ounce) package
  raspberry gelatin
1 cup boiling water

MAKES 10 SERVINGS

Combine the cranberries, orange, and pecans in a food processor, and mix until chopped finely. Add the crushed pineapple.

Dissolve the gelatin in the boiling water, stirring until dissolved. Combine with the cranberry mixture, mixing well. Pour into a 5-cup mold. Refrigerate until firm.

Nutritional information per serving
Calories 114, Protein (g) 2, Carbohydrate (g) 19,
Fat (g) 4, Calories from Fat (%) 33, Saturated Fat (g) 0,
Dietary Fiber (g) 3, Cholesterol (mg) 0, Sodium (mg) 22
Diabetic Exchanges: *1 fruit, 0.5 other carbohydrate, 1 fat*

QUICK TIP

Purchase cranberries when they're in season and freeze in airtight plastic bags for up to a year.

SALADS

Mango Salad with Citrus Sauce

The lovely, tangy citrus sauce complements the mango salad. Use fresh mangoes when in season. If you ever have extra sauce, refrigerate, or try it over frozen yogurt—it's great.

3 (3-ounce) packages
   lemon gelatin
3 cups boiling water
1 (32-ounce) jar mangoes
   with juice
1 (8-ounce) package
   reduced-fat cream
   cheese
Citrus Sauce
   (recipe follows)

MAKES 12 SERVINGS

In a large bowl, dissolve the gelatin in the boiling water.

Place the mangoes with juice in a food processor. Gradually add the cream cheese, and blend well. Stir in the gelatin mixture. Pour into a 2-quart mold coated with nonstick cooking spray. Refrigerate until set. Serve with Citrus Sauce (see recipe below).

Citrus Sauce

1 egg, slightly beaten
⅔ cup sugar
Juice of 1 lemon
Juice of 1 orange

In a small saucepan, combine the egg, sugar, lemon juice, and orange juice. Bring to a boil, lower the heat, and cook 5 minutes. Remove from the heat, and cool. Store the sauce in the refrigerator; take out 20 minutes before serving, to soften.

Nutritional information per serving
Calories 211, Protein (g) 5, Carbohydrate (g) 40,
Fat (g) 5, Calories from Fat (%) 19, Saturated Fat (g) 3,
Dietary Fiber (g) 0, Cholesterol (mg) 31, Sodium (mg) 166
Diabetic Exchanges: *0.5 fruit, 2 other carbohydrate, 1 fat*

Almond Asparagus 165

Baked Beans 166

White Beans 167

Broccoli with Mustard Vinaigrette 168

Broccoli with Lemon Ginger Sauce 169

Sicilian Broccoli 169

Broccoli Casserole 170

Vegetables

Carrot Soufflé 171

Orange Glazed Carrots 171

Dijon Glazed Carrots 172

Cauliflower Supreme 173

Creamy Corn Casserole 173

Tamale and Corn Casserole 174

Eggplant Parmesan 175

Green Bean and Artichoke Casserole 176

Green Bean Casserole 177

Pineapple Noodle Kugel 178

One-Step Macaroni and Cheese 179

Noodle Pudding 180

Okra and Corn 181

Garlic Smashed Potatoes 181

Horseradish Mashed Potatoes 182

Wasabi Mashed Potatoes 183

Easy Potato Casserole 184

Southwestern Stuffed Potatoes 185

Sweet Potato Oven Fries 186

Roasted Sweet and White Potatoes 187

Sweet Potato Casserole with Praline Topping 188

Praline Stuffed Yams 189

Parmesan Potato Sticks 190

Southwestern Rice 190

Summer Rice 191

Wild Rice and Peppers 191

Rice and Noodles 192

Wild Rice and Barley Pilaf 192

Barley Casserole 193

Dirty Rice 194

Spinach and Black Bean Enchiladas 195

Crêpes Florentine 196

Cheesy Spicy Spinach 197

Spinach Mushroom Casserole 198

Italian Spinach Pie 199

Spinach Oriental 200

Squash Rockefeller 201

Squash Casserole 202

Sautéed Cherry Tomatoes with Basil 203

Corn Bread Dressing 204

Yam Corn Bread Stuffing 205

Wild Rice and Oyster Dressing 206

Basic Eggplant Stuffing 207

Yam Veggie Wraps 208

Almond Asparagus

Low in calories, and the crunch of almonds adds that finishing touch. Remember, almonds contain the type of fat that is good for you.

1½ pounds fresh
    asparagus spears
1 tablespoon margarine
2 tablespoons lemon
    juice
¼ cup slivered almonds,
    toasted
Salt and pepper to taste

MAKES 6 SERVINGS

Trim off the tough ends of the asparagus.

Coat a large skillet with nonstick cooking spray; add the margarine. When the margarine is melted, add the asparagus stems, and sauté at medium heat for 3 to 5 minutes. Add the lemon juice, cover, and simmer until crisp-tender.

Add the almond slivers, and season with the salt and pepper, tossing gently. Serve.

Nutritional information per serving

Calories 83, Protein (g) 4, Carbohydrate (g) 6,
Fat (g) 5, Calories from Fat (%) 51, Saturated Fat (g) 1,
Dietary Fiber (g) 3, Cholesterol (mg) 0, Sodium (mg) 23
Diabetic Exchanges: 1 vegetable, 1 fat

QUICK TIP

When selecting asparagus, pick out stalks that are firm from their closed tips to their green bottoms, avoiding spears with ridges, a sign they are drying out. Peeling asparagus is unnecessary and a lot of work—don't bother.

VEGETABLES

Baked Beans

Using canned beans makes this a great, easy-to-make version of everyone's favorite savory, sweet beans.

2 ounces Canadian
    bacon, chopped into
    ¼-inch pieces
½ pound ground sirloin
1 onion, chopped
½ cup light brown sugar
½ cup tomato sauce
1 tablespoon molasses
1 tablespoon cider
    vinegar
1 tablespoon
    Worcestershire sauce
1 teaspoon onion powder
1 (15-ounce) can butter
    beans, rinsed and
    drained
1 (15-ounce) can red
    kidney beans, rinsed
    and drained
2 (19-ounce) cans small
    white beans, rinsed
    and drained
Salt and pepper to taste

MAKES 12 SERVINGS

Preheat the oven to 350°F.

    In a large skillet, sauté the bacon until slightly brown. Add the sirloin and onion, and cook over medium-high heat until the sirloin is done. Drain any excess fat.

    Combine the meat and bacon with the brown sugar, tomato sauce, molasses, vinegar, Worcestershire sauce, onion powder, butter beans, kidney beans, white beans, salt, and pepper; pour into a 2- or 3-quart baking dish.

    Bake for 40 to 50 minutes, or until bubbly. Serve.

Nutritional information per serving

Calories 187, Protein (g) 14, Carbohydrate (g) 37, Fat (g) 2, Calories from Fat (%) 6, Saturated Fat (g) 0, Dietary Fiber (g) 8, Cholesterol (mg) 12, Sodium (mg) 656
Diabetic Exchanges: *1.5 very lean meat, 2 starch, 1 vegetable*

QUICK TIP

All beans are rich in protein and fiber so select any kind to include in this recipe—use whatever is in your pantry.

✎ ❄ White Beans

Here's a good time to pull out that crockpot to make a nutritious, filling side dish. These beans are great served over rice.

1 pound navy or
   pea beans
½ green bell pepper,
   seeded and chopped
3 stalks celery, chopped
1 onion, chopped
4 cloves garlic, minced
1 tablespoon olive oil
½ cup diced lean ham
3 bay leaves
1 tablespoon garlic
   powder
1 tablespoon
   Worcestershire sauce
2 tablespoons light
   brown sugar, optional
Salt and pepper to taste

MAKES 6 SERVINGS

Soak the beans overnight in water. Rinse and drain.

   In a large pot coated with nonstick cooking spray, sauté the green pepper, celery, onion, and garlic in the olive oil until tender. Add the beans and water to cover. Add the ham, bay leaves, garlic powder, Worcestershire sauce, brown sugar, salt, and pepper. Bring to a boil, lower heat, and simmer, covered, for 2 hours, or until the beans are tender. Remove the bay leaves before serving.

Nutritional information per serving
Calories 313, Protein (g) 20, Carbohydrate (g) 52,
Fat (g) 4, Calories from Fat (%) 11, Saturated Fat (g) 1,
Dietary Fiber (g) 20, Cholesterol (mg) 5, Sodium (mg) 218
Diabetic Exchanges: 2 very lean meat, 3 starch, 1.5 vegetable

VEGETABLES

Broccoli with Mustard Vinaigrette

Dress up broccoli with a light, mustardy dressing.

1 bunch fresh broccoli,
trimmed and cut into
florets

¼ cup finely chopped
green onion (scallion)

2 cloves garlic, minced

½ teaspoon dried
tarragon

½ teaspoon dry mustard

1 tablespoon olive oil

2 tablespoons red wine
vinegar

1 teaspoon Dijon
mustard

⅛ teaspoon salt

¼ teaspoon freshly
ground pepper

MAKES 8 SERVINGS

Place the broccoli in a microwave-safe dish with ¼ cup water. Cover, and cook 8 minutes, or until the broccoli is tender; drain.

Combine the green onion, garlic, tarragon, and dry mustard in a bowl. Whisk the oil into the green onion mixture, stirring to combine. Whisk in the vinegar, Dijon mustard, salt, and pepper.

Pour the vinaigrette over the broccoli, tossing to coat. Serve hot or at room temperature.

Nutritional information per serving
Calories 39, Protein (g) 2, Carbohydrate (g) 4,
Fat (g) 2, Calories from Fat (%) 41, Saturated Fat (g) 0,
Dietary Fiber (g) 2, Cholesterol (mg) 0, Sodium (mg) 69
Diabetic Exchanges: *1 vegetable, 0.5 fat*

FOOD FACT

Broccoli is a good source of beta carotene and vitamin C. It also contains cancer-protective indoles.

VEGETABLES

Broccoli with Lemon Ginger Sauce

When you're bored with broccoli, this light, perky sauce will give it extra personality.

1 bunch broccoli
(about 1½ pounds)

2 tablespoons dry sherry,
optional

½ teaspoon ground
ginger

½ cup fat-free canned
chicken (or vegetable)
broth

2 tablespoons lemon juice

1 teaspoon low-sodium
soy sauce

1 teaspoon cornstarch
mixed with 1½
teaspoons cold water

MAKES 6 SERVINGS

Cut the broccoli into medium-size florets, discarding the stems. Cook the broccoli in ¼ cup water in the microwave, in a microwave-safe covered dish, for 6 to 7 minutes, or until tender, or cook on the stove. Drain and set aside.

In the microwave or in a small pot on the stove, heat together the sherry, ginger, broth, and lemon juice until boiling. Boil for 1 minute, reduce the heat, and add the soy sauce. Gradually add the cornstarch mixture, and cook over medium heat, stirring, until the mixture thickens, about 1 minute. Serve over the hot cooked broccoli.

Nutritional information per serving
Calories 29, Protein (g) 3, Carbohydrate (g) 6, Fat (g) 0, Calories from Fat (%) 0, Saturated Fat (g) 0, Dietary Fiber (g) 3, Cholesterol (mg) 0, Sodium (mg) 96
Diabetic Exchanges: *1 vegetable*

Sicilian Broccoli

Need a quick veggie with some spunk? Your family will adore this broccoli recipe that is prepared in the microwave.

1 (16-ounce) package
broccoli florets

Salt and pepper to taste

⅓ cup chopped onion

¼ cup sliced kalamata
olives

½ cup balsamic vinegar

1 tablespoon olive oil

½ cup shredded part-
skim Mozzarella cheese

MAKES 4 SERVINGS

Lay the broccoli in a 10-inch microwave-safe dish. Add the salt and pepper to taste. Sprinkle with the onion, olives, vinegar, and oil, and microwave for 8 minutes, or until the broccoli is tender. Immediately sprinkle the broccoli with the cheese, and serve when the cheese is melted.

Nutritional information per serving
Calories 154, Protein (g) 7, Carbohydrate (g) 15,
Fat (g) 8, Calories from Fat (%) 46, Saturated Fat (g) 2,
Dietary Fiber (g) 4, Cholesterol (mg) 8, Sodium (mg) 243
Diabetic Exchanges: *3 vegetable, 1.5 fat*

VEGETABLES

Broccoli Casserole

Throw all the ingredients into one dish for a velvety, cheesy broccoli casserole.

2 (10-ounce) packages frozen chopped broccoli, thawed and drained

1 egg

2 egg whites, slightly beaten

3 tablespoons all-purpose flour

1 (12-ounce) carton reduced-fat cottage cheese

6 ounces reduced-fat pasteurized processed cheese spread, cut into pieces

MAKES 6 TO 8 SERVINGS

Preheat the oven to 350°F.

In a large bowl, mix the broccoli, egg, egg whites, flour, cottage cheese, and cheese spread; pour into a 2-quart baking dish coated with nonstick cooking spray.

Bake, uncovered, for 1 hour, or until bubbly. Serve.

Nutritional information per serving

Calories 121, Protein (g) 13, Carbohydrate (g) 9, Fat (g) 4, Calories from Fat (%) 26, Saturated Fat (g) 2, Dietary Fiber (g) 2, Cholesterol (mg) 37, Sodium (mg) 49
Diabetic Exchanges: *1.5 lean meat, 0.5 starch*

QUICK TIP

When buying broccoli, look for heads that are dark to almost purple in color. The purple color means that they are loaded with beta-carotene, a nutrient proven to reduce the risk of heart disease and cancer. Broccoli that is yellow in color has lost its vital nutrients.

VEGETABLES

Carrot Soufflé

I'm so excited to offer everyone this excellent, creamy carrot dish that resembles a pudding. From my 14-year-old to my mother-in-law, this recipe gets high ratings.

2 pounds carrots, peeled and sliced

½ cup sugar

2 egg whites

3 eggs

2 tablespoons all-purpose flour

1½ teaspoons baking powder

3 tablespoons margarine, softened

1 teaspoon vanilla extract

MAKES 6 TO 8 SERVINGS

Preheat the oven to 350°F.

Cook the carrot slices in a small amount of water over medium-high heat or in the microwave until very soft; drain.

In a mixing bowl, beat the carrots and add the sugar, egg whites, and eggs. Mix together the flour and baking powder, and add to the carrot mixture, mixing well. Add the margarine and vanilla, mixing well. Transfer to an oblong 2-quart baking dish coated with nonstick cooking spray, and bake for 35 to 45 minutes or until the center is set. Serve.

Nutritional information per serving

Calories 176, Protein (g) 5, Carbohydrate (g) 26, Fat (g) 6, Calories from Fat (%) 32, Saturated Fat (g) 1, Dietary Fiber (g) 3, Cholesterol (mg) 80, Sodium (mg) 219
Diabetic Exchanges: *2 vegetable, 1 other carbohydrate, 1 fat*

Orange Glazed Carrots

The citrus-sweet flavor complements the carrot and adds color and nutrition to any plate.

1 tablespoon margarine

¼ cup fat-free canned vegetable (or chicken) broth

2 pounds baby carrots or carrots cut into 2-inch pieces

1 cup orange marmalade

Salt and pepper to taste

2 tablespoons chopped parsley

MAKES 8 TO 10 SERVINGS

In a large saucepan, bring the margarine and broth to a boil. Add the carrots, and cook, covered, over medium heat for 10 to 20 minutes, or until crisp-tender. Uncover, and stir in the marmalade. Cook, stirring, over low heat until the liquid has reduced to a glaze, 3 to 5 minutes. Season with the salt and pepper.

Sprinkle with the parsley before serving.

Nutritional information per serving

Calories 125, Protein (g) 1, Carbohydrate (g) 30, Fat (g) 2, Calories from Fat (%) 11, Saturated Fat (g) 0, Dietary Fiber (g) 2, Cholesterol (mg) 0, Sodium (mg) 77
Diabetic Exchanges: *1.5 vegetable, 1.5 other carbohydrate*

Dijon Glazed Carrots

Spicy sweet and a delight to eat—don't miss this recipe.

1 pound carrots, peeled
    and sliced
1 tablespoon margarine
1 tablespoon Dijon
    mustard
2 tablespoons honey
¼ teaspoon white pepper
¼ teaspoon ground
    ginger

MAKES 4 SERVINGS

Steam the carrot slices in water until crisp-tender, about 10 minutes, or cook in the microwave. Drain the cooking liquid.

In a small saucepan, combine the margarine, mustard, honey, pepper, and ginger over low heat, stirring just until combined and the margarine is melted. Pour the sauce over the carrots, toss gently to coat, and serve.

Nutritional information per serving
Calories 111, Protein (g) 1, Carbohydrate (g) 20,
Fat (g) 3, Calories from Fat (%) 24, Saturated Fat (g) 0,
Dietary Fiber (g) 3, Cholesterol (mg) 0, Sodium (mg) 163
***Diabetic Exchanges:** 2 vegetable, 0.5 other carbohydrate, 0.5 fat*

FOOD FACT

Carrots are high in vitamin C, beta-carotene, and potassium.

VEGETABLES

🥕 Cauliflower Supreme

A light cheese sauce coats the cauliflower in this tasty dish.

1 head cauliflower, cut into florets
½ cup plain nonfat yogurt
½ cup shredded reduced-fat sharp Cheddar cheese
½ teaspoon dry mustard
½ teaspoon cayenne pepper
Salt and pepper to taste

MAKES 4 SERVINGS

Preheat the oven to 400°F.

Place the cauliflower in a microwave-safe dish with ⅓ cup water; cook covered in the microwave for 8 minutes, or until crisp-tender. Drain and transfer to a baking dish coated with nonstick cooking spray.

In a small bowl, combine the yogurt, cheese, mustard, cayenne pepper, salt, and pepper, and spread over the cauliflower. Bake, uncovered, for 8 to 10 minutes, or until lightly browned. Serve.

Nutritional information per serving

Calories 97, Protein (g) 9, Carbohydrate (g) 10, Fat (g) 3, Calories from Fat (%) 25, Saturated Fat (g) 2, Dietary Fiber (g) 3, Cholesterol (mg) 8, Sodium (mg) 158
Diabetic Exchanges: *1 lean meat, 2 vegetable*

🥕 ❄️ Creamy Corn Casserole

Everyday pantry ingredients turn this into an extraordinary corn dish.

2 (16-ounce) bags frozen corn
1 (7-ounce) can chopped green chilies, drained
½ cup skim milk
1 (8-ounce) package fat-free cream cheese, cut into pieces
Salt and pepper to taste
½ teaspoon paprika

MAKES 8 TO 10 SERVINGS

Preheat the oven to 350°F.

In a 2-quart baking dish, combine the corn and green chilies.

In a small microwave-safe dish, heat the milk and cream cheese in the microwave until the cream cheese is melted, about 30 seconds. Mix with a fork to blend. Stir into the corn, and season with the salt and pepper. Sprinkle with the paprika. Bake for 30 minutes, or until bubbly. Serve.

Nutritional information per serving

Calories 108, Protein (g) 6, Carbohydrate (g) 22, Fat (g) 1, Calories from Fat (%) 6, Saturated Fat (g) 0, Dietary Fiber (g) 3, Cholesterol (mg) 2, Sodium (mg) 191
Nutritional Exchanges: *1.5 starch*

VEGETABLES

Tamale and Corn Casserole

I love tamales, and here's a great way to enjoy them in a meal. Serve with extra salsa.

2 (15-ounce) cans
chicken, vegetarian, or
reduced-fat meat
tamales
1 (15-ounce) can
cream-style corn
1 (4-ounce) can diced
green chilies
½ cup diced green
onion (scallion)
¼ cup evaporated
skimmed milk
1 (7-ounce) can salsa
verde
1½ teaspoons chili
powder
1 teaspoon ground cumin
1 cup shredded
reduced-fat Monterey
Jack cheese

MAKES 6 TO 8 SERVINGS

Preheat the oven to 375°F.

Cut the tamales into 1-inch pieces. Place in a single layer in a glass, 2-quart casserole dish coated with nonstick cooking spray. Cover with the corn, chilies, and green onion.

In a medium bowl, whisk the evaporated milk, salsa verde, chili powder, and cumin to blend. Pour over the casserole. Sprinkle the cheese over the top. Bake until heated through and bubbling, about 30 to 35 minutes. Serve.

Nutritional information per serving
Calories 207, Protein (g) 11, Carbohydrate (g) 28,
Fat (g) 6, Calories from Fat (%) 27, Saturated Fat (g) 4,
Dietary Fiber (g) 4, Cholesterol (mg) 25, Sodium (mg) 913
Diabetic Exchanges: *1 lean meat, 2 starch*

QUICK TIP

If you live in an area where homemade tamales are available, select your favorite variety for this recipe. Many times, tamales are also located in the freezer section of the grocery store.

VEGETABLES

Eggplant Parmesan

The ultimate version of a favorite of mine, this recipe was featured in Cooking Light *magazine in the "Make It Light" section.*

1 (28-ounce) can
  chopped tomatoes,
  with juice
2 (15-ounce) cans
  tomato sauce
1 (6-ounce) can
  tomato paste
½ cup white wine
1 teaspoon minced garlic
1 tablespoon dried
  basil leaves
1 tablespoon dried
  oregano leaves
2 eggplants, peeled and
  cut into ½-inch slices
3 egg whites
¼ cup water
1½ cups seasoned
  bread crumbs
2½ cups shredded
  reduced-fat Mozzarella
  cheese

MAKES 8 SERVINGS

Preheat the broiler.

In a large saucepan, make the sauce by combining the tomatoes with juice, tomato sauce, tomato paste, white wine, garlic, basil, and oregano. Bring to a boil, lower the heat, and cook 20 minutes.

Meanwhile, soak the eggplant slices in water to cover for 30 minutes. Pat dry.

In a medium bowl, mix the egg whites and water with a fork. Dip the eggplant slices in the egg white mixture, and coat in the bread crumbs. Place the eggplant on a baking sheet coated with nonstick cooking spray, and broil 5 minutes on each side, until lightly browned. Watch closely. Remove and set aside.

Lower the oven temperature to 350°F.

In a 2-quart oblong baking dish, layer half the sauce, half the eggplant, and half the Mozzarella cheese. Repeat the layers. Bake for 20 minutes, or until bubbly and the cheese is melted. Serve.

Nutritional information per serving
Calories 296, Protein (g) 18, Carbohydrate (g) 41,
Fat (g) 6, Calories from Fat (%) 19, Saturated Fat (g) 4,
Dietary Fiber (g) 8, Cholesterol (mg) 21, Sodium (mg) 1520
Diabetic Exchanges: *1.5 lean meat, 1 starch, 5 vegetable*

VEGETABLES

✏ ❄ Green Bean and Artichoke Casserole

Close your eyes and you will think you are eating a stuffed artichoke. Rich and fabulous! Yes, it's a little high in fat, but it's the "good" fat.

2 (16-ounce) packages frozen French-cut green beans, thawed

1 (14-ounce) can artichoke hearts, quartered and drained

2 cups Italian bread crumbs

½ cup olive oil

1 tablespoon minced garlic

⅓ cup grated Parmesan cheese

MAKES 14 TO 16 SERVINGS

Preheat the oven to 350°F.

In a large mixing bowl, combine the green beans, artichoke hearts, bread crumbs, olive oil, garlic, and cheese. Place in a 3-quart oblong casserole coated with nonstick cooking spray, and bake for 30 minutes, or until lightly browned. Serve.

Nutritional information per serving

Calories 149, Protein (g) 4, Carbohydrate (g) 16, Fat (g) 8, Calories from Fat (%) 48, Saturated Fat (g) 1, Dietary Fiber (g) 2, Cholesterol (mg) 2, Sodium (mg) 300
Diabetic Exchanges: *0.5 starch, 1 vegetable, 1.5 fat*

QUICK TIP

Olive oil is a monounsaturated oil which has been shown to be particularly effective against high cholesterol. The majority of the fat in this recipe is from the olive oil, so enjoy!

Green Bean Casserole

When you're looking for a simple, tasty, green bean casserole with kid appeal, it's right here.

1 (16-ounce) package
    frozen French-cut
    green beans
1 onion, chopped
1 tablespoon margarine
2 tablespoons all-purpose
    flour
Salt and pepper to taste
½ cup skim milk
½ cup nonfat plain
    yogurt or fat-free
    sour cream
1 cup shredded reduced-
    fat sharp Cheddar
    cheese

MAKES 8 SERVINGS

Cook the green beans according to the package directions; drain well.

Preheat the boiler.

In a small pot, sauté the onion in the margarine until tender. Blend in the flour, salt, and pepper. Gradually add the milk, stirring and cooking over medium heat until thickened and bubbly. Stir in the yogurt and green beans; heat thoroughly, about two minutes.

Transfer to 1½-quart casserole. Sprinkle with the cheese, and broil in the oven until the cheese melts. Serve.

Nutritional information per serving
Calories 100, Protein (g) 7, Carbohydrate (g) 10,
Fat (g) 4, Calories from Fat (%) 36, Saturated Fat (g) 2,
Dietary Fiber (g) 2, Cholesterol (mg) 8, Sodium (mg) 129
Diabetic Exchanges: *0.5 very lean meat, 2 vegetable, 1 fat*

QUICK TIP

Add edamame (green soybeans, shelled) to your favorite vegetable recipe for added soy protein and great flavor. Edamame can be found in the frozen food section in the grocery store.

Pineapple Noodle Kugel

This noodle pudding with pineapple makes a light side dish with a slightly sweet flavor.

1 (16-ounce) package
   wide noodles

4 tablespoons margarine,
   melted

1 (16-ounce) container
   reduced-fat cottage
   cheese

2 cups nonfat plain
   yogurt

⅔ cup sugar

1 (20-ounce) can crushed
   pineapple, drained

2 teaspoons vanilla
   extract

4 egg whites

MAKES 12 TO 16 SERVINGS

Preheat the oven to 350°F.

Cook the noodles according to the package directions, omitting any oil; drain. Combine with the margarine, cottage cheese, yogurt, sugar, pineapple, and vanilla.

In a medium bowl, beat the egg whites with a mixer on high speed until stiff. Fold into the noodle mixture. Pour into a 13 x 9 x 2-inch baking pan coated with non-stick cooking spray. Bake, uncovered, for 1 to 1¼ hours, 15 minutes, or until mixture is set. Serve.

Nutritional information per serving

*Calories 229, Protein (g) 10, Carbohydrate (g) 37,
Fat (g) 4, Calories from Fat (%) 17, Saturated Fat (g) 1,
Dietary Fiber (g) 1, Cholesterol (mg) 29, Sodium (mg) 194*
Diabetic Exchanges: *1 lean meat, 1.5 starch, 0.5 fruit, 0.5 other carbohydrate*

FOOD FACT

A kugel is a baked pudding usually made with noodles or potatoes and generally served as a side dish.

VEGETABLES

One-Step Macaroni and Cheese

This macaroni and cheese recipe from scratch is easier than the box. Teenagers rate it an A+.

1 (16-ounce) package
  elbow macaroni
1 (8-ounce) package
  reduced-fat Cheddar
  cheese, shredded
1 (12-ounce) can
  evaporated skimmed
  milk
2½ cups skim milk
1 egg, beaten
¼ cup sugar, optional
Salt and pepper to taste

MAKES 10 TO 12 SERVINGS

Preheat the oven to 350°F.

In a 2-quart casserole dish, mix together the macaroni and the cheese.

In a large bowl, mix together the evaporated milk, milk, egg, sugar, salt, and pepper, and pour over the macaroni. Bake, covered, for 1 hour, or until the liquid is almost absorbed. Uncover, and continue baking for 10 minutes. Serve.

Nutritional information per serving
Calories 240, Protein (g) 15, Carbohydrate (g) 34,
Fat (g) 5, Calories from Fat (%) 17, Saturated Fat (g) 3,
Dietary Fiber (g) 1, Cholesterol (mg) 30, Sodium (mg) 188
Diabetic Exchanges: *1 lean meat, 2 starch, 0.5 skim milk*

QUICK TIP

Try using small shells or a small pasta for a variation.

VEGETABLES

Noodle Pudding

A traditional noodle pudding with a rich flavor yet still low in fat.

1 (8-ounce) package
   wide noodles

3 tablespoons margarine,
   melted

½ cup sugar

1 cup reduced-fat
   cottage cheese

4 ounces reduced-fat
   cream cheese

1 cup nonfat plain yogurt

1 egg

2 egg whites

½ teaspoon vanilla
   extract

MAKES 6 TO 8 SERVINGS

Preheat the oven to 350°F.

Boil the noodles according to the package directions, omitting any oil. Rinse, drain, and combine with the margarine, tossing evenly. Place the noodles in a glass 8 x 8 x 2-inch baking dish coated with nonstick cooking spray.

In a food processor or mixer, mix the sugar, cottage cheese, cream cheese, yogurt, egg, egg whites, and vanilla, beating until smooth. Combine with the noodles, mixing well. Bake for 45 minutes to 1 hour, or until the mixture is set. Serve.

Nutritional information per serving

*Calories 282, Protein (g) 12, Carbohydrate (g) 36,
Fat (g) 9, Calories from Fat (%) 30, Saturated Fat (g) 3,
Dietary Fiber (g) 1, Cholesterol (mg) 65, Sodium (mg) 276*
Diabetic Exchanges: *1 very lean meat, 2.5 starch, 1 fat*

Okra and Corn

Okra and tomatoes are popular Southern ingredients. The corn adds a splash of color and flavor to the okra in this simple, few-ingredient recipe.

1 tablespoon margarine
1 onion, chopped
1 (16-ounce) bag frozen cut okra
1 (16-ounce) bag frozen corn
2 (10-ounce) cans diced tomatoes and green chilies

MAKES 6 SERVINGS

In a large pan, heat the margarine over medium heat, and sauté the onion until tender. Add the okra, and cook for 5 minutes, stirring. Add the corn and tomatoes and chilies, cooking and stirring until the okra is tender, about 20 minutes. Serve.

Nutritional information per serving

Calories 130, Protein (g) 5, Carbohydrate (g) 27, Fat (g) 3, Calories from Fat (%) 17, Saturated Fat (g) 0, Dietary Fiber (g) 5, Cholesterol (mg) 0, Sodium (mg) 406
Diabetic Exchanges: *1 starch, 2 vegetable, 0.5 fat*

Garlic Smashed Potatoes

I love this time-efficient, family favorite recipe: you don't even have to peel the potatoes! Many times, I've added shredded Cheddar cheese and cooked bacon for a deluxe version.

3 pounds red potatoes, peeled and quartered
10 garlic cloves, peeled
2 tablespoons margarine
1 cup skim milk
⅓ cup plain nonfat yogurt
½ cup sliced green onion (scallion)
Salt and pepper to taste

MAKES 8 SERVINGS

Preheat the oven to 350°F.

On a baking sheet coated with nonstick cooking spray, spread the potatoes and garlic. Bake for 45 minutes, or until the potatoes are tender.

In a large mixing bowl, mix together the potato mixture, margarine, milk, and yogurt until creamy. Fold in the green onion, and add the salt and pepper to taste. Serve.

Nutritional information per serving

Calories 173, Protein (g) 5, Carbohydrate (g) 32, Fat (g) 3, Calories from Fat (%) 16, Saturated Fat (g) 1, Dietary Fiber (g) 3, Cholesterol (mg) 1, Sodium (mg) 68
Diabetic Exchanges: *2 starch*

VEGETABLES

🥕 Horseradish Mashed Potatoes

If you're a horseradish fan, this variation will be a delightful experience. It's especially good with beef and pork dishes.

3 pounds Yukon Gold
   potatoes
3 tablespoons margarine
½ cup fat-free sour cream
2 tablespoons prepared
   horseradish
1 teaspoon minced garlic
Salt and pepper to taste

MAKES 8 SERVINGS

Place the potatoes in a large pot with water to cover. Bring to a boil, and boil about 30 minutes, or until the potatoes are tender.

Peel the potatoes, and place in a large mixing bowl. Add the margarine, sour cream, horseradish, and garlic, beating until creamy. Season with the salt and pepper and serve.

Nutritional information per serving
Calories 181, Protein (g) 4, Carbohydrate (g) 32,
Fat (g) 4, Calories from Fat (%) 22, Saturated Fat (g) 1,
Dietary Fiber (g) 3, Cholesterol (mg) 0, Sodium (mg) 84
Diabetic Exchanges: *2 starch, 0.5 fat*

QUICK TIP

Beat potatoes until they are light; overbeating will only make them sticky and starchy.

Wasabi Mashed Potatoes

Adding new flavors to familiar ingredients is a great way to introduce new tastes to home cooking. Wasabi and soy sauce add an Asian flair to this incredibly tasty recipe.

2½ pounds baking
  potatoes
2 tablespoons margarine
1 tablespoon low-sodium
  soy sauce
1 teaspoon minced garlic
1 to 2 teaspoons wasabi
½ cup nonfat plain
  yogurt

MAKES 6 TO 8 SERVINGS

Combine the potatoes and enough water to cover in a large saucepan; bring to a boil. Lower the heat, cover, and cook until tender, about 30 to 40 minutes. Drain.

Peel the potatoes, and place them in a mixing bowl with the margarine, blending until smooth. Slowly add the soy sauce, garlic, wasabi, and yogurt, beating until creamy. Serve immediately.

Nutritional information per serving
Calories 139, Protein (g) 4, Carbohydrate (g) 25,
Fat (g) 3, Calories from Fat (%) 19, Saturated Fat (g) 1,
Dietary Fiber (g) 2, Cholesterol (mg) 0, Sodium (mg) 102
Diabetic Exchanges: 1.5 starch

FOOD FACT

Wasabi is a Japanese version of horseradish that comes from the root of an Asian plant. This green condiment has a sharp, pungent, fiery flavor. It is available in the Asian section of grocery stores in both paste and powder form.

Easy Potato Casserole

When you are overwhelmed with preparing dinner, here's a super potato recipe. One night without warning, my husband said, "Company's coming," so I threw this recipe together and everyone asked for a copy. Make this ahead, and refrigerate it until you're ready to cook it.

1 (32-ounce) bag frozen hash brown potatoes

2 cups fat-free sour cream

1 onion, chopped

4 tablespoons margarine, melted

1 (10¾-ounce) can 98% fat-free cream of mushroom soup

6 slices reduced-fat American cheese, cut into pieces

Salt and pepper to taste

Paprika, for garnish

MAKES 8 SERVINGS

Preheat the oven to 350°F.

In a 3-quart casserole dish coated with nonstick cooking spray, combine the potatoes, sour cream, onion, margarine, mushroom soup, cheese, salt, and pepper, mixing well. Sprinkle with the paprika. Bake for $1\frac{1}{4}$ to $1\frac{1}{2}$ hours, or until the casserole is bubbly. Serve.

Nutritional information per serving

Calories 290, Protein (g) 10, Carbohydrate (g) 37, Fat (g) 10, Calories from Fat (%) 33, Saturated Fat (g) 4, Dietary Fiber (g) 2, Cholesterol (mg) 13, Sodium (mg) 663
Diabetic Exchanges: *0.5 lean meat, 2.5 starch, 1 fat*

QUICK TIP

I prefer frozen shredded hash brown potatoes for this recipe, but always use whatever is available at your grocery store.

❄ Southwestern Stuffed Potatoes

Potatoes stuffed with easily available Mexican ingredients make this a cinch. Serve with salsa.

3 medium baking
  potatoes
2 tablespoons margarine
2 tablespoons skim milk
½ cup fat-free or light
  sour cream
1 (4-ounce) can diced
  green chilies, optional
1 (15¼-ounce) can whole-
  kernel corn, drained
4 green onions
  (scallions), chopped
1 cup shredded reduced-
  fat Cheddar cheese
Paprika, for garnish

MAKES 6 SERVINGS

Preheat the oven to 400°F.

Wash the potatoes well, and dry thoroughly. Place the potatoes directly on the oven rack, and bake for approximately 1 hour, or until soft when squeezed.

Reduce the heat to 350°F.

Cut each baked potato in half lengthwise. Scoop out the inside, leaving a thin shell.

In a mixer, mash the potato flesh with the margarine, skim milk, and sour cream, mixing well. Stir in the green chilies, corn, green onions, and cheese, combining well. Spoon the mixture into the shells. Top with the paprika.

Bake for about 15 minutes, or until the cheese is melted and the potatoes are heated. Serve.

Nutritional information per serving
Calories 216, Protein (g) 11, Carbohydrate (g) 29,
Fat (g) 8, Calories from Fat (%) 30, Saturated Fat (g) 3,
Dietary Fiber (g) 4, Cholesterol (mg) 10, Sodium (mg) 381
Diabetic Exchanges: *1 lean meat, 2 starch, 0.5 fat*

VEGETABLES

QUICK TIP

Idaho or Russet: Commonly referred to as baking potatoes, these starchy potatoes make the best baked and mashed potatoes and good fries.
Yukon Gold: Commonly referred to as all purpose potatoes, with their moderate amount of starch, Yukon Golds make good mashed potatoes and decent fries and baked potatoes.
New or Red: Red- or white-skinned potatoes are low in starch and can be waxy. They're best for boiling, great thin-roasted, and okay for other uses.

Sweet Potato Oven Fries

This recipe is requested every time I prepare it for guests on television or at home. It's low in saturated fat and high in fiber. For a sweet variation, sprinkle with 1 teaspoon each cinnamon and nutmeg.

4 medium to large sweet
   potatoes (yams)
¼ cup olive oil
Salt to taste
Parsley, for garnish

MAKES 4 TO 6 SERVINGS

Preheat the oven to 400°F.

Cut the sweet potatoes lengthwise into ½-inch-thick strips, and toss with the olive oil.

Coat a baking sheet with nonstick cooking spray, and arrange the potatoes on the baking sheet. Bake the potatoes for 15 to 20 minutes, or until golden brown on the bottom. Turn the potatoes over, and bake for 15 to 20 more minutes, or until golden brown all over. Sprinkle with the salt, add the parsley for color, and serve.

Nutritional information per serving
Calories 166, Protein (g) 1, Carbohydrate (g) 22,
Fat (g) 9, Calories from Fat (%) 46, Saturated Fat (g) 1,
Dietary Fiber (g) 3, Cholesterol (mg) 0, Sodium (mg) 30
Diabetic Exchanges: *1.5 starch, 1.5 fat*

FOOD FACT

Sweet potatoes should not be refrigerated unless they have been cooked. Store them in a cool, dry location.

VEGETABLES

Roasted Sweet and White Potatoes

I repeat this easy (no peeling needed) recipe whenever I want a zippy side dish that adds to the plate. It's a wonderful way to serve potatoes.

3 tablespoons olive oil

1 pound sweet potatoes (yams) unpeeled, cut into 2-inch chunks

1 pound baking potatoes, unpeeled, cut into 2-inch chunks

4 cloves garlic, unpeeled

¼ cup chopped parsley

1 teaspoon dried thyme leaves

½ teaspoon pepper

Salt to taste

MAKES 8 SERVINGS

Preheat the oven to 450°F.

In a large roasting pan, combine the oil with the potatoes and whole cloves of garlic, tossing to coat. Bake, shaking the pan every 15 minutes, until the potatoes are browned and crisp and the garlic is soft, about 45 minutes to 1 hour. Remove the garlic, press the softened cloves, and slip from the skins, discarding the skins. Toss the potatoes with the garlic, parsley, thyme, pepper, and salt. Serve immediately.

Nutritional information per serving
Calories 143, Protein (g) 3, Carbohydrate (g) 25, Fat (g) 5, Calories from Fat (%) 29, Saturated Fat (g) 1, Dietary Fiber (g) 3, Cholesterol (mg) 0, Sodium (mg) 21
Diabetic Exchanges: *1.5 starch, 1 fat*

FOOD FACT

The sweet potato is not really a potato—not even a distant cousin. Potatoes are tubers; sweet potatoes are roots.

VEGETABLES

Sweet Potato Casserole with Praline Topping

Use freshly baked or canned yams to create this indulgence—too good to save just for holidays.

3 cups cooked mashed
    sweet potatoes (yams)
½ cup sugar
1 egg
1 egg white
1 (5-ounce) can
    evaporated skimmed
    milk
1½ teaspoons vanilla
    extract
Praline Topping
    (recipe follows)

Praline Topping

1 cup light brown sugar
½ cup all-purpose flour
½ teaspoon ground
    cinnamon
6 tablespoons margarine,
    melted
1 teaspoon vanilla extract
½ cup chopped pecans,
    optional

MAKES 8 TO 10 SERVINGS

Preheat the oven to 350°F.

In a mixing bowl, blend together the potatoes, sugar, egg, egg white, evaporated skimmed milk, and vanilla. Place in a 2-quart casserole dish coated with nonstick cooking spray, and cover with Praline Topping (see recipe below). Bake for 45 minutes until topping is browned and casserole is thoroughly heated. Serve.

In a medium bowl, mix together the brown sugar, flour, and cinnamon. Add the margarine, vanilla, and pecans, stirring until crumbly.

Nutritional information per serving

*Calories 333, Protein (g) 5, Carbohydrate (g) 62,
Fat (g) 8, Calories from Fat (%) 20, Saturated Fat (g) 1,
Dietary Fiber (g) 2, Cholesterol (mg) 22, Sodium (mg) 132*
Diabetic Exchanges: *2 starch, 2 other carbohydrate, 1 fat*

QUICK TIP

Sweet potatoes from Louisiana are referred to as yams. Louisiana offers ideal soil and climate conditions to grow sweet potatoes.

Praline Stuffed Yams

Individually stuffed, nutritious, mouth-watering treats with this crumbly topping are hard to beat. This will become a highly requested sweet potato recipe. Make extra and freeze until ready to serve.

3 pounds small to medium sweet potatoes (yams), unpeeled

¼ cup sugar

½ teaspoon ground cinnamon, divided

¼ cup skim milk

2 teaspoons vanilla extract, divided

3 tablespoons margarine, melted

⅓ cup all-purpose flour

¼ cup light brown sugar

¼ cup chopped pecans

MAKES 4 TO 6 SERVINGS

Preheat the oven to 400°F.

Place the potatoes on a baking sheet, and cook for 1 hour, or until tender. Cut a thin slice off the top of each potato. Carefully scoop the pulp into a large bowl, leaving ¼-inch thick shells.

In a mixing bowl, mash the pulp; add the sugar, ¼ teaspoon cinnamon, milk, and 1 teaspoon vanilla, mixing until smooth. Spoon the mixture evenly into the potato shells. Place on a baking sheet.

In a small bowl, mix the margarine, flour, brown sugar, pecans, remaining 1 teaspoon vanilla, and remaining ¼ teaspoon cinnamon together until crumbly. Sprinkle evenly over the potatoes. Reduce the oven to 350°F, and continue baking 15 minutes, or until the topping is brown. Serve.

Nutritional information per serving
Calories 412, Protein (g) 5, Carbohydrate (g) 82,
Fat (g) 9, Calories from Fat (%) 19, Saturated Fat (g) 1,
Dietary Fiber (g) 8, Cholesterol (mg) 0, Sodium (mg) 154
Diabetic Exchanges: *4 starch, 1.5 other carbohydrate, 1 fat*

VEGETABLES

QUICK TIP

Pricking the sweet potato keeps them from bursting during baking. Lining the pan with foil makes an easy clean up.

Parmesan Potato Sticks

Prepare plenty of these crispy, seasoned, oven-baked fries, as they disappear quickly. If your potato sticks are large, you may need more coating.

½ cup Italian bread
    crumbs
2 tablespoons grated
    Parmesan cheese
2 tablespoons chopped
    parsley
Salt and pepper to taste
¼ teaspoon garlic powder
3 medium baking
    potatoes, peeled and
    cut into large sticks
¼ cup skim milk
1 tablespoon margarine,
    melted

MAKES 4 TO 6 SERVINGS

Preheat the oven to 375°F. Line a baking sheet with foil.

In a shallow dish, combine the bread crumbs, cheese, parsley, salt, pepper, and garlic powder. Dip the potatoes in the milk and then in the crumb mixture.

Lay the sticks on the prepared baking sheet. Drizzle with the margarine. Bake for 45 minutes to 1 hour, or until crisp. Serve.

Nutritional information per serving

Calories 117, Protein (g) 5, Carbohydrate (g) 21,
Fat (g) 3, Calories from Fat (%) 20, Saturated Fat (g) 1,
Dietary Fiber (g) 2, Cholesterol (mg) 2, Sodium (mg) 332
Diabetic Exchanges: *1.5 starch*

Southwestern Rice

Mildly flavored with peppers and topped with cheese, this creamy baked rice dish makes you look forward to every bite. It's a great side dish with barbecue.

1 onion, chopped
5 cups cooked rice
2 cups nonfat plain
    yogurt
1 cup reduced-fat
    cottage cheese
2 (4-ounce) cans diced
    green chilies, drained
Salt and pepper to taste
¾ cup shredded reduced-
    fat sharp Cheddar
    cheese

MAKES 10 SERVINGS

Preheat the oven to 350°F.

In a skillet coated with nonstick cooking spray, sauté the onion until tender. Combine with the rice, yogurt, cottage cheese, green chilies, salt, pepper, and cheese. Place in a 2-quart casserole dish coated with nonstick cooking spray. Bake for 20 minutes or until thoroughly heated. Serve.

Nutritional information per serving

Calories 205, Protein (g) 13, Carbohydrate (g) 29,
Fat (g) 4, Calories from Fat (%) 16, Saturated Fat (g) 2,
Dietary Fiber (g) 1, Cholesterol (mg) 11, Sodium (mg) 323
Diabetic Exchanges: *1 very lean meat, 1.5 starch, 0.5 skim milk*

VEGETABLES

Summer Rice

Pick ingredients fresh from the garden for this exciting summer side with a Mediterranean personality.

1 cup chopped onion
1 teaspoon minced garlic
1 cup rice
1 (14½-ounce) can vegetable broth
2 cups chopped tomatoes
1 cup diced cucumber
½ teaspoon dried basil leaves
¼ cup thinly sliced green onion (scallion)
½ cup crumbled Feta cheese

MAKES 6 SERVINGS

In a medium saucepan coated with nonstick cooking spray, sauté the onion and garlic over medium heat for 5 minutes. Add the rice; cook 1 minute, stirring constantly. Add the broth, and bring to a boil. Reduce the heat; cover, and simmer 20 minutes, or until the rice is done. Stir in the tomato, cucumber, and basil, mixing well. Gradually stir in the green onion and Feta cheese. Serve.

Nutritional information per serving
Calories 180, Protein (g) 6, Carbohydrate (g) 32, Fat (g) 3, Calories from Fat (%) 17, Saturated Fat (g) 2, Dietary Fiber (g) 2, Cholesterol (mg) 11, Sodium (mg) 451
Diabetic Exchanges: *1.5 starch, 1.5 vegetable*

Wild Rice and Peppers

Here's the perfect side that keeps the plate attractive while rating very high in flavor. I've made this recipe many times for parties.

1 (6-ounce) box long-grain and wild rice mix
2 tablespoons olive oil
1 bunch green onions (scallions), chopped
1 red bell pepper, seeded, sliced in long, thin slices
1 green bell pepper, seeded, sliced in long, thin slices
½ pound mushrooms, sliced
½ cup cooked white rice

MAKES 6 TO 8 SERVINGS

Cook the wild rice according to the package directions.

In a large skillet, heat the olive oil and sauté the green onions, red and green peppers, and mushrooms until tender, 5 to 7 minutes. Stir in cooked wild rice and white rice, and serve.

Nutritional information per serving
Calories 163, Protein (g) 4, Carbohydrate (g) 23, Fat (g) 7, Calories from Fat (%) 35, Saturated Fat (g) 1, Dietary Fiber (g) 2, Cholesterol (mg) 0, Sodium (mg) 352
Diabetic Exchanges: *1.5 starch, 1 fat*

VEGETABLES

✎ Rice and Noodles

When you can't decide which to serve, enjoy both rice and noodles with a toasty flavor.

1 cup uncooked rice
1 tablespoon margarine
1 cup medium noodles
2¾ cups fat-free canned vegetable (or chicken) broth
Salt and pepper to taste

MAKES 6 SERVINGS

In a heavy saucepan coated with nonstick cooking spray, brown the rice in the margarine, stirring. Add the noodles, broth, salt, and pepper. Bring the mixture to a boil, lower the heat, and simmer, covered, for 20 to 30 minutes, or until the rice and noodles are done. Serve.

Nutritional information per serving
Calories 160, Protein (g) 4, Carbohydrate (g) 30,
Fat (g) 2, Calories from Fat (%) 13, Saturated Fat (g) 0,
Dietary Fiber (g) 1, Cholesterol (mg) 6, Sodium (mg) 309
Diabetic Exchanges: *2 starch*

✎ Wild Rice and Barley Pilaf

Here's a great way to try barley—hearty and simple with a fancy flair.

1 (6-ounce) package long-grain and wild rice mix (with seasoning packet)
½ cup pearl barley
3 cups fat-free canned vegetable (or chicken) broth
1 tablespoon margarine
⅓ cup sliced almonds, toasted

MAKES 6 TO 8 SERVINGS

Preheat the oven to 325°F.

In a large saucepan, combine the rice, the seasoning packet from the rice mix, and the barley, broth, and margarine. Bring to a boil. Reduce the heat, cover, and simmer for 10 minutes. Spoon into a 1½-quart casserole dish coated with nonstick cooking spray. Bake covered for 1 hour, or until the rice and barley are tender and the liquid is absorbed. Fluff the rice mixture with a fork; stir in the almonds. Serve.

Nutritional information per serving
Calories 164, Protein (g) 5, Carbohydrate (g) 28,
Fat (g) 4, Calories from Fat (%) 21, Saturated Fat (g) 0,
Dietary Fiber (g) 3, Cholesterol (mg) 0, Sodium (mg) 567
Diabetic Exchanges: *2 starch, 0.5 fat*

VEGETABLES

Barley Casserole

For a change, serve this rich but wholesome-tasting dish instead of rice. Try using assorted exotic mushrooms for added pizzazz.

1 cup medium barley
1 (1-ounce) envelope
  onion soup mix
4 cups water
1 tablespoon margarine
½ pound fresh
  mushrooms, sliced

FOOD FACT

Barley is a whole grain, high in fiber, which is a good way to include fiber in your diet.

MAKES 6 TO 8 SERVINGS

Preheat the oven to 350°F.

In a 3-quart casserole dish, combine the barley, onion soup mix, and water.

In a small skillet, melt the margarine over medium-low heat and sauté the mushrooms until tender, about 5 minutes. Add to the barley mixture. Cover with a lid or tightly with foil, and bake for 1 to 1¼ hours, or until the barley is done and the liquid is absorbed. Serve.

Nutritional information per serving
Calories 122, Protein (g) 4, Carbohydrate (g) 23,
Fat (g) 2, Calories from Fat (%) 15, Saturated Fat (g) 0,
Dietary Fiber (g) 5, Cholesterol (mg) 0, Sodium (mg) 457
Diabetic Exchanges: *1.5 starch*

VEGETABLES

❄ Dirty Rice

This popular Louisiana dish makes a hearty side or can be a meal itself.

VEGETABLES

1 pound ground sirloin

2 cloves garlic, minced

2 stalks celery, chopped

1 onion, chopped

1 tablespoon chopped
parsley

1 green bell pepper,
seeded and chopped

1 tablespoon
Worcestershire sauce

¼ teaspoon cayenne
pepper

¼ teaspoon pepper

1 cup uncooked rice

1 (14½-ounce) can beef
broth

¾ cup water

MAKES 4 TO 6 SERVINGS

In a large skillet, cook the beef, garlic, celery, onion, parsley, and green pepper over medium-high heat until the meat is done and the vegetables are tender. Add the Worcestershire sauce, cayenne pepper, and pepper, stirring well. Add the rice, broth, and water, mixing well. Bring to a boil; reduce heat, cover, and cook for 25 to 30 minutes, or until the rice is done.

Nutritional information per serving

Calories 227, Protein (g) 19, Carbohydrate (g) 30,
Fat (g) 4, Calories from Fat (%) 14, Saturated Fat (g) 1,
Dietary Fiber (g) 2, Cholesterol (mg) 40, Sodium (mg) 388
Diabetic Exchanges: *2 very lean meat, 1.5 starch, 1 vegetable*

QUICK TIP

This hearty dish can be used as an entrée if desired and served with a salad.

Spinach and Black Bean Enchiladas

This might be one of the best meatless entrées you will ever eat. These simple ingredients give you an enchilada with a"ton of flavor" that will be a standby quick favorite. Try different varieties of tortillas.

1 (10-ounce) package
  frozen chopped
  spinach, thawed
1 (15-ounce) can black
  beans, rinsed and
  drained
1 (1¼-ounce) package
  taco seasoning mix
1 cup water
1 cup fat-free sour cream,
  divided
8 (6- to 8-inch) flour
  tortillas
1 (10-ounce) can
  enchilada sauce
1½ cups shredded
  reduced-fat Cheddar
  cheese
2 tablespoons sliced
  green onion (scallion)

MAKES 8 ENCHILADAS

Preheat the oven to 375°F.

In a skillet, heat the spinach, black beans, taco seasoning mix, and water. Bring to a boil, reduce heat, and cook for 8 to 10 minutes, or until the mixture is thickened. Remove from the heat, and stir in ½ cup sour cream.

On each tortilla, spread 1 tablespoon enchilada sauce, about ⅓ cup spinach mixture, and 1 heaping tablespoon cheese. Roll up each tortilla placing the seam-side down in an oblong baking dish coated with nonstick cooking spray. Spread the remaining enchilada sauce over the filled enchiladas, cover, and bake 15 to 18 minutes. Uncover and sprinkle with the remaining ½ cup cheese. Continue baking for 5 minutes longer, or until the cheese is melted. Serve with the remaining sour cream, and sprinkle with the green onion.

Nutritional information per serving
Calories 266, Protein (g) 14, Carbohydrate (g) 39,
Fat (g) 5, Calories from Fat (%) 18, Saturated Fat (g) 3,
Dietary Fiber (g) 5, Cholesterol (mg) 11, Sodium (mg) 1195
Diabetic Exchanges: *1.5 very lean meat, 2.5 starch*

QUICK TIP

Kale and collards are large, leafy, dark greens, which are a good source of antioxidants that help fight cancer. Cook them by steaming, boiling, or stir-frying them long enough to soften the stems. When the stems are very thick, remove them before cooking.

VEGETABLES

Crêpes Florentine

Buy already made crêpes in the grocery to make this recipe very simple. The cheesy spinach filling baked in crispy crêpes was enthusiastically received at my house.

2 (10-ounce) packages frozen chopped spinach

½ pound fresh mushrooms

½ cup chopped onion

⅓ cup all-purpose flour

1¼ cups skim milk

⅛ teaspoon pepper

⅛ teaspoon ground nutmeg

1 cup shredded reduced-fat Swiss cheese

Salt and pepper to taste

12 commercially prepared crêpes

1 tablespoon margarine, melted

2 tablespoons grated Parmesan cheese

MAKES 12 CRÊPES

Preheat the oven to 350°F.

Cook the spinach as directed on the package, and drain well; set aside.

In a small skillet coated with nonstick cooking spray, sauté the mushrooms and onion until tender, about 5 minutes.

In a 2-quart saucepan, mix the flour and milk, and cook over medium heat, stirring about 5 minutes until smooth and thickened. Add the pepper, nutmeg, Swiss cheese, spinach, mushrooms, and onions. Season to taste. Blend well. Remove from the heat when the cheese is melted.

Place 1 heaping tablespoon of the spinach mixture on a crêpe, with the brown side of the crêpe facing down. Roll the crêpe and place seam down in a 2-quart baking dish coated with nonstick cooking spray. Repeat with the remaining crêpes. Drizzle the crêpes with the melted margarine, and sprinkle with the Parmesan cheese. Bake for 15 to 20 minutes, or until heated.

Nutritional information per serving

Calories 191, Protein (g) 11, Carbohydrate (g) 18, Fat (g) 9, Calories from Fat (%) 41, Saturated Fat (g) 3, Dietary Fiber (g) 2, Cholesterol (mg) 85, Sodium (mg) 177
Diabetic Exchanges: *0.5 lean meat, 1 starch, 1 vegetable, 1.5 fat*

VEGETABLES

Cheesy Spicy Spinach

This special and wonderful cheesy spinach gets requested extremely often.

3 (10-ounce) packages
   frozen chopped
   spinach
½ cup spinach liquid,
   reserved from cooking
   spinach
1 onion, chopped
3 tablespoons all-purpose
   flour
1 cup skim milk
6 ounces mild Mexican
   processed cheese
   spread
1 tablespoon
   Worcestershire sauce
½ teaspoon garlic
   powder

MAKES 10 SERVINGS

Cook the spinach according to the package directions. Drain well, reserving ½ cup spinach liquid; set aside.

In a pan coated with nonstick cooking spray, sauté the onion until tender, about 5 minutes. Add the flour; stir. Gradually add the milk and spinach liquid to make a sauce. Cook over medium heat until the mixture thickens. Add the cheese, Worcestershire sauce, and garlic powder, cooking until the cheese is melted. Add the spinach, mixing well. Serve.

Nutritional information per serving
Calories 107, Protein (g) 8, Carbohydrate (g) 10,
Fat (g) 5, Calories from Fat (%) 38, Saturated Fat (g) 3,
Dietary Fiber (g) 3, Cholesterol (mg) 15, Sodium (mg) 339
Nutritional Exchanges: 0.5 very lean meat, 2 vegetable, 1 fat

QUICK TIP

For a simple and mild Mexican processed cheese spread, substitute a 6-ounce roll of garlic cheese or plain processed cheese spread.

Spinach Mushroom Casserole

Often, I find myself doubling this impressive recipe when guests join us for dinner.

2 (10-ounce) packages frozen chopped spinach

½ pound fresh mushrooms, sliced

3 slices reduced-fat American cheese, diced

1 (5-ounce) can evaporated skimmed milk

¼ teaspoon garlic powder

Salt and pepper, optional

MAKES 6 SERVINGS

Preheat the oven to 350°F.

Cook the spinach according to the package directions; drain well.

Coat a small skillet with nonstick cooking spray, and sauté the mushrooms until tender; set aside.

In a heavy saucepan, melt the cheese in the milk over low heat.

Turn the spinach into a shallow baking dish coated with nonstick cooking spray. Sprinkle with the garlic powder. Add the cheese mixture, and stir until thoroughly mixed. Add the salt and pepper, if desired. Top with the sautéed mushrooms and drippings. Bake, uncovered, for 20 minutes, or until well heated. Serve.

Nutritional information per serving

Calories 89, Protein (g) 8, Carbohydrate (g) 9,
Fat (g) 3, Calories from Fat (%) 29, Saturated Fat (g) 2,
Dietary Fiber (g) 3, Cholesterol (mg) 9, Sodium (mg) 279
Diabetic Exchanges: *0.5 lean meat, 2 vegetable*

QUICK TIP

Introduce yourself to the leafy veggie Swiss chard—it's one of the milder greens! Red-stemmed chard has a faint beet flavor. The best method for preparing Swiss chard is to remove the stems, cut them into pieces, and sauté them with the leaves or simmer them in a skillet with olive oil or garlic. The leaves can be substituted in recipes that call for spinach.

THE HOLLY CLEGG TRIM & TERRIFIC COOKBOOK

Italian Spinach Pie

Here's the perfect solution when you have vegetarians and meat eaters at one table. It makes a special spinach side for any main course and a delicious main dish in its own right.

½ cup chopped onion

2 (10-ounce) packages frozen chopped spinach

1 (14-ounce) can artichoke hearts, quartered, drained

1 cup fat-free or low-fat Ricotta cheese

¼ cup skim milk

2 egg whites, beaten

½ teaspoon garlic powder

1 (8-ounce) can tomato sauce

½ teaspoon dried oregano leaves

½ teaspoon dried basil leaves

1 cup shredded part-skim Mozzarella cheese

MAKES 6 SERVINGS

Preheat the oven to 350°F.

In a skillet coated with nonstick cooking spray, sauté the onion over medium heat until tender, about 5 minutes.

Meanwhile, cook the spinach according to the package directions; drain very well.

In a large bowl, combine the onion, spinach, artichoke hearts, Ricotta cheese, milk, egg whites, and garlic powder, mixing well. Spoon the mixture into a 9-inch pie plate coated with nonstick cooking spray.

Mix the tomato sauce with the oregano and basil, and spread evenly over the spinach. Bake for 15 minutes. Sprinkle with the Mozzarella cheese, and continue baking for 5 to 10 minutes longer, until the cheese is melted. Serve.

Nutritional information per serving

Calories 143, Protein (g) 16, Carbohydrate (g) 13, Fat (g) 3, Calories from Fat (%) 21, Saturated Fat (g) 2, Dietary Fiber (g) 4, Cholesterol (mg) 14, Sodium (mg) 590
Diabetic Exchanges: *1.5 very lean meat, 3 vegetable*

VEGETABLES

QUICK TIP

Some varieties of cheese may be frozen—the lower the moisture content of the cheese, the better it is for freezing. However, once the cheese has been frozen, only use it as a cooking ingredient, not as table cheese. Good freezing cheeses include Cheddar, Mozzarella, Edam, Gouda, Provolone, and Parmesan.

Spinach Oriental

Stir-fry mushrooms and spinach with Oriental seasonings for an instant Asian success.
Prepackaged spinach and sliced mushrooms are time-savers.

½ pound fresh
   mushrooms, sliced
½ cup red onion, thinly
   sliced and separated
   into rings
¼ teaspoon ground
   ginger
1 teaspoon sesame seeds
½ teaspoon minced garlic
¼ cup water
1 teaspoon cornstarch
½ teaspoon sugar
Dash cayenne pepper
1 tablespoon low-sodium
   soy sauce
½ teaspoon dark sesame
   oil, optional
1 (10-ounce) bag fresh
   spinach, washed and
   stemmed

MAKES 4 SERVINGS

Coat a large skillet with nonstick cooking spray; place over medium-high heat until hot. Add the mushrooms, onion, ginger, sesame seeds, and garlic; sauté 5 minutes. Combine the water with the cornstarch, and add to the mushroom mixture along with the sugar, cayenne, soy sauce, and sesame oil; stir well. Add the spinach, and cook about 2 minutes, while stirring constantly, until the spinach begins to wilt.

Nutritional information per serving

Calories 48, Protein (g) 4, Carbohydrate (g) 8,
Fat (g) 1, Calories from Fat (%) 14, Saturated Fat (g) 0,
Dietary Fiber (g) 3, Cholesterol (mg) 0, Sodium (mg) 157
Diabetic Exchanges: *1.5 vegetable*

FOOD FACT

Spinach and other dark, leafy greens are rich in bone-fortifying calcium and folic acid, which may help protect against heart disease.

VEGETABLES

Squash Rockefeller

Make ahead, refrigerate, and bake before serving. Visually attractive and full of flavor, this stand-out recipe is really good.

6 yellow medium squash
2 (10-ounce) packages
   frozen chopped spinach
1 bunch green onions
   (scallions), chopped
½ cup finely chopped
   parsley
3 stalks celery, chopped
2 cloves garlic, minced
¼ cup margarine
½ cup Italian
   bread crumbs
Hot pepper sauce to taste
Salt and pepper to taste

MAKES 12 STUFFED SQUASH

Preheat the oven to 350°F.

Cut the squash in half lengthwise. Steam in ½ inch water, covered, on the stove or in the microwave, until almost tender. Cool slightly, and scoop out the pulp, being careful not to break the shell; discard the pulp.

Cook the spinach according to the package directions; drain well.

In a skillet coated with nonstick cooking spray, sauté the green onions, parsley, celery, and garlic in the margarine until tender. Combine with the spinach, bread crumbs, hot pepper sauce, salt, and pepper, mixing well.

Stuff the squash shells with the mixture. Bake for 20 minutes, or until well-heated. Serve.

Nutritional information per serving
Calories 89, Protein (g) 3, Carbohydrate (g) 11,
Fat (g) 4, Calories from Fat (%) 40, Saturated Fat (g) 1,
Dietary Fiber (g) 4, Cholesterol (mg) 0, Sodium (mg) 162
Diabetic Exchanges: *2 vegetable, 1 fat*

VEGETABLES

Squash Casserole

This recipe has been in my family for years, and we always look forward to having it. Even if you're not a squash fan, this creamy-corn, squash casserole will win you over. For the holidays, make it ahead and freeze uncooked. Defrost to room temperature and bake.

2 pounds fresh squash,
   thinly sliced
2 green bell peppers,
   seeded and chopped
1 large onion, chopped
2 tablespoons canola oil
1 (15-ounce) can
   cream-style corn
1 tablespoon sugar
¼ cup cornmeal
Salt and pepper to taste

MAKES 6 TO 8 SERVINGS

Preheat the oven to 350°F.

Steam the fresh squash until very tender on top of the stove for about 10 minutes in ¼ cup water or in the microwave; drain. Mash or purée the squash in a food processor.

In a large skillet, sauté the green pepper and onion in the oil until tender.

Combine the puréed squash, onion mixture, corn, sugar, and cornmeal. Add the salt and pepper.

Place the mixture in a 2-quart casserole dish coated with nonstick cooking spray. Bake for 30 minutes, or until bubbly and thoroughly heated. Serve.

Nutritional information per serving
*Calories 136, Protein (g) 3, Carbohydrate (g) 25,
Fat (g) 4, Calories from Fat (%) 24, Saturated Fat (g) 0,
Dietary Fiber (g) 4, Cholesterol (mg) 0, Sodium (mg) 173*
Diabetic Exchanges: *1 starch, 1.5 vegetable, 0.5 fat*

VEGETABLES

Sautéed Cherry Tomatoes with Basil

Stir-fry these juicy tomatoes with a few ingredients for a tomato statement.

1 pound cherry or
  grape tomatoes
1 garlic clove, minced
1 tablespoon dried
  basil leaves
2 tablespoons chopped
  parsley
½ teaspoon dried
  thyme leaves
1 teaspoon sugar
Salt and freshly ground
  pepper to taste

MAKES 6 SERVINGS

Wash the tomatoes, and dry them well.

In a small bowl, combine the garlic, basil, parsley, and thyme.

Heat a skillet coated with nonstick cooking spray over medium heat, and add the tomatoes. Sprinkle with the sugar, salt, and pepper, and toss briefly until well heated. Stir in the garlic mixture, and sauté for 1 minute, or until the sugar melts and the mixture is heated thoroughly. Serve immediately.

Nutritional information per serving
Calories 22, Protein (g) 1, Carbohydrate (g) 5,
Fat (g) 0, Calories from Fat (%) 0, Saturated Fat (g) 0,
Dietary Fiber (g) 1, Cholesterol (mg) 0, Sodium (mg) 8
Diabetic Exchanges: *1 vegetable*

FOOD FACT

Tomatoes contain the carotenoid lycopene, which protects against cancer-causing pollutants.

VEGETABLES

Corn Bread Dressing

Use corn bread mixes to ease preparation of this traditional favorite. Prepare year-round to make your baked chicken more popular than ever.

2 (8½-ounce) boxes corn muffin mix

1 egg

⅓ cup skim milk

4 ounces bulk light sausage, optional

2 onions, chopped

1 green bell pepper, seeded and chopped

1 teaspoon minced garlic

1 cup chopped celery

1 (10¾-ounce) can 98% fat-free cream of mushroom soup

1 (16-ounce) can fat-free vegetable (or chicken) broth

1 teaspoon poultry seasoning

Salt and pepper to taste

¼ cup chopped parsley

¼ cup chopped green onion (scallion)

MAKES 8 SERVINGS

Preheat the oven to 350°F.

Prepare the corn muffin mix with the egg and milk, and bake in a 13 x 9 x 2-inch pan according to the package directions. Crumble and set aside.

In a large skillet coated with nonstick cooking spray, sauté the sausage, onion, green pepper, garlic, and celery until tender. Add the cream of mushroom soup, broth, poultry seasoning, salt, pepper, and crumbled corn bread. Stir in the parsley and green onion.

Transfer to a 2-quart casserole, and bake for 30 minutes, or until lightly browned and heated. Serve.

Nutritional information per serving

Calories 292, Protein (g) 6, Carbohydrate (g) 54, Fat (g) 7, Calories from Fat (%) 20, Saturated Fat (g) 2, Dietary Fiber (g) 2, Cholesterol (mg) 28, Sodium (mg) 836
Diabetic Exchanges: *3 starch, 2 vegetable, 1 fat*

VEGETABLES

Yam Corn Bread Stuffing

If you're looking for something new when preparing stuffing, try this savory corn bread–yam combination.

2 cups chopped, peeled, sweet potatoes (yams)

1 cup chopped onion

1 cup sliced celery

2 tablespoons margarine

¼ cup chopped parsley

1 teaspoon ground ginger

5 cups crumbled cooked corn bread

¼ cup chopped pecans, toasted

Vegetable (or chicken) broth, as needed

MAKES 10 SERVINGS

Preheat the oven to 375°F.

In a large skillet, cook the sweet potatoes, onion, and celery in the margarine over medium-high heat for 7 to 10 minutes, or until just tender. Spoon the mixture into a large mixing bowl. Stir in the parsley and ginger. Add the corn bread and pecans, and toss gently to coat. Add enough broth to moisten. Place the stuffing in a 2-quart oblong casserole. Bake, uncovered, for 45 minutes, or until heated through. Serve.

Nutritional information per serving

Calories 211, Protein (g) 5, Carbohydrate (g) 29, Fat (g) 9, Calories from Fat (%) 37, Saturated Fat (g) 2, Dietary Fiber (g) 3, Cholesterol (mg) 19, Sodium (mg) 355
Diabetic Exchanges: *2 starch, 1.5 fat*

VEGETABLES

QUICK TIP

For a time-efficient approach, prepare the cornbread and toast the pecans a day ahead. Sweet potatoes are packed with vitamins and enhance the nutritional value of this recipe.

Wild Rice and Oyster Dressing

Make ahead, refrigerate, and bake before serving. The hint of sherry with wild rice and oysters is the perfect blend for a really wonderful dish.

2 (6-ounce) packages long-grain and wild rice mix

2 (10-ounce) jars oysters

1 teaspoon minced garlic

½ pound fresh mushrooms, sliced

½ cup chopped onion

3 tablespoons all-purpose flour

1 (5-ounce) can evaporated skimmed milk

2 tablespoons dry sherry

¼ cup chopped green onion (scallion)

¼ cup chopped parsley

MAKES 6 TO 8 SERVINGS

Preheat the oven to 350°F.

Prepare the wild rice according to the package directions; set aside.

Drain the oysters, reserving ½ cup oyster liquid; set the liquid aside.

In a large skillet coated with nonstick cooking spray, sauté the garlic, mushrooms, and onion until tender. Add the oysters, and cook for several minutes. Add the flour, and gradually stir in the milk and the reserved ½ cup oyster liquid, mixing well. Cook over medium heat until the mixture thickens, stirring constantly. Add the sherry, cooked wild rice, green onion, and parsley. Transfer the mixture to a 2-quart baking dish. Bake, uncovered, for 30 minutes, or until heated through. Serve.

Nutritional information per serving
Calories 270, Protein (g) 12, Carbohydrate (g) 43,
Fat (g) 5, Calories from Fat (%) 17, Saturated Fat (g) 1,
Dietary Fiber (g) 2, Cholesterol (mg) 40, Sodium (mg) 771
Diabetic Exchanges: *1 lean meat, 3 starch*

VEGETABLES

Basic Eggplant Stuffing

Use as a dressing or even an eggplant casserole. Add cooked shrimp for a seafood version.

16 cups cubed, peeled eggplant (about 3 large)

2 cups chopped onion

1 tablespoon minced garlic

1 cup chopped celery

1 green bell pepper, seeded and chopped

1 bunch green onions (scallions), chopped

1 (8-ounce) bag herb stuffing mix

⅓ cup grated Parmesan cheese

¾ cup fat-free canned vegetable (or chicken) broth

MAKES 10 TO 12 SERVINGS

Preheat the oven to 350°F.

In a large pot, boil the eggplant, in water to cover, for about 20 to 25 minutes, or until tender. Drain and set aside.

In a large skillet coated with nonstick cooking spray, sauté the onion, garlic, celery, and green pepper until tender, about 8 minutes. Add the green onions, herb stuffing mix, Parmesan cheese, and eggplant, mixing well. Gradually stir in the broth until moistened. If needed, adjust the amount of broth.

Pour the mixture into a 3-quart casserole dish coated with nonstick cooking spray. Bake for 20 to 30 minutes, or until heated through. Serve.

Nutritional information per serving
Calories 130, Protein (g) 6, Carbohydrate (g) 25,
Fat (g) 2, Calories from Fat (%) 11, Saturated Fat (g) 1,
Dietary Fiber (g) 5, Cholesterol (mg) 2, Sodium (mg) 454
Diabetic Exchanges: *1 starch, 2 vegetable*

VEGETABLES

Yam Veggie Wraps

This quick and wonderful flavor combo makes a wrap to remember. Shred sweet potatoes with a grater or in a food processor. This is a high-fiber recipe.

1 sweet potato (yam), peeled and shredded (about 1 cup)

½ cup chopped red onion

1 cup canned black beans, rinsed and drained

2 green onions (scallions), sliced

¼ cup chopped roasted peanuts

2 tablespoons light Italian or Caesar dressing

1 teaspoon honey

6 (6- to 8-inch) flour tortillas, warmed to soften

MAKES 6 WRAPS

In a skillet coated with nonstick cooking spray, sauté the shredded yam over medium-high heat for about 5 minutes, or until crisp-tender. Transfer to a bowl.

In the same skillet coated with nonstick cooking spray, sauté the red onion until tender. Add the sautéed onion, black beans, green onions, and peanuts to the shredded yams, mixing well.

In a small bowl, mix together the dressing and honey, and toss with the yam mixture to coat.

Fill the tortillas, and wrap. Serve.

Nutritional information per serving
Calories 226, Protein (g) 8, Carbohydrate (g) 39, Fat (g) 4, Calories from Fat (%) 16, Saturated Fat (g) 0, Dietary Fiber (g) 6, Cholesterol (mg) 0, Sodium (mg) 554
Diabetic Exchanges: *0.5 very lean, 2.5 starch*

FOOD FACT

Sweet potatoes contain virtually no fat or sodium, and one medium potato is only about 150 calories. Sweet potatoes are high in vitamins A and C, beta carotene, iron, potassium, and fiber.

Oven-Fried Parmesan Chicken 211

Simple Baked Crusty Chicken 212

Dijon Rosemary Chicken 212

Honey Pecan Chicken 213

Company Chicken 214

Chicken Breasts Diane 215

Easy Marinated Chicken 216

Poultry

Skillet Pizza Chicken 217

Italian Chicken 218

Chicken Divan 219

Chicken Cherry Jubilee 220

Chicken Breasts Florentine 221

Chicken Breasts with Artichokes and Mushrooms 222

Lemon Feta Chicken 223

Paprika Chicken 223

Indoor Barbecued Chicken 224

Peanut Chicken 225

Ginger Chicken and Black Beans 226

Chinese Chicken and Broccoli Stir-Fry 227

Chicken Full-of-Flavor 228

Cranberry Chicken with Wild Rice 229

Chicken and Dumplings 230

One-Dish Chicken Casserole 231

Chicken Roll-Ups 232

Salsa Chicken 233

Tequila Chicken 234

Chicken Fajita Pizza 235

Southwestern Chicken with Bean Sauce 236

Mexican Chicken Casserole 237

Chicken and Black Bean Enchiladas 238

Cornish Hens with Wild Rice Stuffing 239

Turkey Steaks with Prosciutto 240

Honey-Glazed Turkey Breast 241

Turkey Jambalaya 242

Oven-Fried Parmesan Chicken

A family favorite—with this recipe, you won't miss fried chicken.

¾ cup nonfat plain yogurt

¼ cup lemon juice

1½ tablespoons Dijon mustard

1 teaspoon garlic, minced

½ teaspoon dried oregano leaves

8 skinless, boneless chicken breasts

2 cups Italian bread crumbs

¼ cup grated Parmesan cheese

2 tablespoons margarine, melted

QUICK TIP

Try this recipe with chicken tenders or strips to make pick-ups. Serve with the Jezebel Sauce on page 42 for a zesty dipping sauce.

MAKES 8 SERVINGS

Preheat the oven to 350°F.

Combine the yogurt, lemon juice, mustard, garlic, and oregano. Pour over the chicken, coating it. Marinate, covered, 2 hours or overnight in the refrigerator.

Drain the chicken. Mix together the bread crumbs and cheese, and coat the chicken. Place on a baking sheet coated with nonstick cooking spray, and chill for 1 hour (time permitting).

Drizzle the chicken with the margarine. Bake for 45 minutes to 1 hour, or until tender and golden brown. Serve immediately.

Nutritional information per serving

Calories 293, Protein (g) 33, Carbohydrate (g) 23, Fat (g) 7, Calories from Fat (%) 21, Saturated Fat (g) 1, Dietary Fiber (g) 1, Cholesterol (mg) 69, Sodium (mg) 680
Diabetic Exchanges: *3 lean meat, 1.5 starch*

POULTRY

Simple Baked Crusty Chicken

A no-fuss favorite in my house, this is a real kid-pleaser. The gravy is great on rice.

2 pounds skinless,
   boneless chicken breasts
⅔ cup biscuit baking mix
2 tablespoons olive oil
1 teaspoon minced garlic
1 tablespoon all-purpose
   flour
1 (16-ounce) can fat-free
   chicken broth

MAKES 8 SERVINGS

Preheat the oven to 375°F.

Coat the chicken in the baking mix. Place in a 3-quart oblong casserole dish coated with nonstick cooking spray. Bake for 40 minutes to one hour.

Meanwhile, in a saucepan, mix together the olive oil and garlic, and add the flour. Whisk in the chicken broth, cooking over medium-high heat until thickened. Pour over the chicken, baking covered, for an additional 20 minutes, or until chicken is done. Serve.

Nutritional information per serving

Calories 203, Protein (g) 28, Carbohydrate (g) 7, Fat (g) 6, Calories from Fat (%) 29, Saturated Fat (g) 1, Dietary Fiber (g) 0, Cholesterol (mg) 66, Sodium (mg) 355
Diabetic Exchanges: 3 lean meat, 0.5 starch

Dijon Rosemary Chicken

This quick-to-fix chicken pops right in the oven for those busy evenings. Absolutely incredibly tasty and kid appealing. I watched a group of teenagers devour this dish in record time one night.

1½ to 2 pounds skinless,
   boneless chicken
   breasts
2 tablespoons Dijon
   mustard
¼ teaspoon garlic powder
1 teaspoon dried
   rosemary leaves
Pepper to taste
¼ cup grated Parmesan
   cheese

MAKES 6 SERVINGS

Preheat the oven to 350°F.

Line a baking sheet with foil. Lay the chicken on the foil.

In a small bowl, mix together the mustard and garlic powder, and spread on top of each chicken breast. Sprinkle with the rosemary and pepper. Top with the cheese. Bake for 45 to 50 minutes, or until the chicken is done. Serve.

Nutritional information per serving

Calories 150, Protein (g) 28, Carbohydrate (g) 0, Fat (g) 3, Calories from Fat (%) 18, Saturated Fat (g) 1, Dietary Fiber (g) 0, Cholesterol (mg) 69, Sodium (mg) 271
Diabetic Exchanges: 3 very lean meat

POULTRY

Honey Pecan Chicken

You'll enjoy the fabulous flavor of this chicken! For a glowing presentation, slice the chicken and arrange on a plate to show off the dark-crusted poultry with the moist inside.

1 cup Wheat Chex cereal crumbs

⅓ cup finely chopped pecans

2 tablespoons honey

2 tablespoons low-sodium soy sauce

6 skinless, boneless chicken breasts

Salt and pepper to taste

MAKES 6 SERVINGS

Preheat the oven to 425°F.

Cover a baking sheet with foil, and spray with nonstick cooking spray.

On a plate or on waxed paper, combine the cereal crumbs and pecans.

In a bowl, mix together the honey and soy sauce.

Season the chicken with salt and pepper. Dip both sides of the chicken breast into the honey mixture; then roll in the pecan mixture to coat. Arrange the chicken on the pan. Bake for 12 to 15 minutes on each side, or until the chicken is done. Serve.

Nutritional information per serving
Calories 262, Protein (g) 29, Carbohydrate (g) 23,
Fat (g) 7, Calories from Fat (%) 22, Saturated Fat (g) 1,
Dietary Fiber (g) 3, Cholesterol (mg) 66, Sodium (mg) 376
Diabetic Exchanges: *3 lean meat, 1 starch, 0.5 other carbohydrate*

POULTRY

QUICK TIP

If you're in a pinch and don't have Wheat Chex, use bread crumbs or another wheat cereal.

❄ Company Chicken

Household ingredients dress up chicken for a special evening.

8 skinless, boneless
   chicken breasts or
   thighs
Salt and pepper to taste
2 tablespoons olive oil
1 bunch green onions
   (scallions), chopped
½ teaspoon minced garlic
½ pound fresh
   mushrooms, sliced
½ cup white wine
1 (28-ounce) can diced
   tomatoes in juice
½ cup fat-free canned
   chicken broth

MAKES 8 SERVINGS

Season the chicken breasts with the salt and pepper. In a large skillet coated with nonstick cooking spray, heat the olive oil and brown the chicken pieces. Remove from the pan and set aside.

Add the green onions, garlic, and mushrooms to the pan, and sauté until tender. Add the white wine, tomatoes, and broth. Bring to a boil, adjust the seasonings, and reduce to a simmer. Add the chicken, cover, and continue to cook for about 30 to 40 minutes, or until the chicken is tender. Serve.

Nutritional information per serving
Calories 197, Protein (g) 28, Carbohydrate (g) 7,
Fat (g) 5, Calories from Fat (%) 23, Saturated Fat (g) 1,
Dietary Fiber (g) 2, Cholesterol (mg) 66, Sodium (mg) 242
Diabetic Exchanges: *3 lean meat, 1.5 vegetable*

FOOD FACT

White meat is the leanest part of the chicken, but if you prefer dark meat, make sure you use skinless thighs.

Chicken Breasts Diane

This light and flavorful recipe is a quick dinner solution. Try serving it with the wild rice, which complements the chicken.

6 skinless, boneless
   chicken breasts
Salt and pepper to taste
1 tablespoon olive oil
1 bunch green onions
   (scallions), chopped
Juice of 1 lemon
2 tablespoons chopped
   parsley
1 tablespoon Dijon
   mustard
⅓ cup fat-free canned
   chicken broth

MAKES 6 SERVINGS

Place the chicken breasts between sheets of waxed paper, and pound slightly with a mallet to flatten, if desired. Sprinkle with salt and pepper.

In a large skillet, heat the olive oil. Cook the chicken on each side until done, about 15 minutes total. Remove from the skillet, and set aside.

Add the green onions, lemon juice, parsley, and mustard to the skillet. Cook, stirring constantly, for 1 minute. Whisk in the broth, and stir until smooth. Return the chicken to the pan, and serve with the sauce.

Nutritional information per serving
Calories 155, Protein (g) 27, Carbohydrate (g) 2,
Fat (g) 4, Calories from Fat (%) 23, Saturated Fat (g) 1,
Dietary Fiber (g) 0, Cholesterol (mg) 66, Sodium (mg) 171
Diabetic Exchanges: *3 very lean meat*

POULTRY

FOOD FACT

Flat leaf or Italian parsley has a stronger flavor than the curly leaf parsley that is commonly used as a garnish.

❄ Easy Marinated Chicken

With its intense flavors, this marinade is super to use with other meats.

2 tablespoons olive oil
⅓ cup sherry
1 tablespoon lemon juice
⅓ cup finely chopped
onion
½ teaspoon minced garlic
1 teaspoon dried
rosemary leaves
Pepper to taste
6 skinless, boneless
chicken breasts

MAKES 6 SERVINGS

In a small bowl, whisk together the olive oil, sherry, lemon juice, onion, garlic, rosemary, and pepper.

Place the chicken in a shallow glass dish, and pour the marinade over it. Cover, and refrigerate 2 hours to overnight.

Broil or grill the chicken until done, 5 to 7 minutes on each side, basting with the marinade. Serve.

Nutritional information per serving

Calories 145, Protein (g) 26, Carbohydrate (g) 0,
Fat (g) 4, Calories from Fat (%) 24, Saturated Fat (g) 1,
Dietary Fiber (g) 0, Cholesterol (mg) 66, Sodium (mg) 74
Diabetic Exchanges: *3 very lean meat*

QUICK TIP

Mix the marinade in zipper-lock bags to marinate the chicken. Just throw away the used bag for easy clean up.

Skillet Pizza Chicken

When there's no time to cook, prepare this family-pleasing dish pizza style. For best results, try to find thin chicken breasts, or pound them with a mallet.

1 egg white

¼ cup buttermilk

¼ cup grated Parmesan cheese

½ teaspoon dried oregano leaves

½ teaspoon dried basil leaves

½ cup all-purpose flour

½ cup bread crumbs

2 pounds skinless, boneless chicken breasts, pounded thin

2 cups tomato pasta sauce

1 cup shredded part-skim Mozzarella cheese

QUICK TIP

Select your favorite blend of pasta sauce—from roasted garlic to Parmesan cheese—to boost the taste of this dish.

MAKES 6 SERVINGS

In a shallow bowl, combine the egg white and buttermilk, beating lightly.

On a plate, combine the Parmesan cheese, oregano, basil, flour, and bread crumbs. Dip each piece of chicken in the egg and then in the flour mixture, making sure to completely coat each piece. Set the chicken aside.

Heat a large nonstick skillet coated with nonstick cooking spray over medium heat. Add the chicken, and cook until lightly browned. Turn the chicken, and cook several more minutes, or until almost done. Lower the heat, and cover the chicken with the pasta sauce. Top with the Mozzarella, cover the pan, and cook several more minutes, or until the cheese is melted. Serve.

Nutritional information per serving
Calories 361, Protein (g) 46, Carbohydrate (g) 24,
Fat (g) 8, Calories from Fat (%) 20, Saturated Fat (g) 4,
Dietary Fiber (g) 2, Cholesterol (mg) 102, Sodium (mg) 736
Diabetic Exchanges: *5.5 very lean meat, 1.5 starch*

POULTRY

Italian Chicken

Chicken, rice, and seasonings all in one dish—it seems too easy for such a good Italian experience.

POULTRY

1½ cups water

1 cup uncooked rice

1 (10-ounce) can diced tomatoes and green chilies, drained

½ cup chopped onion

½ cup shredded part-skim Mozzarella cheese

2 teaspoons dried basil leaves, divided

2 teaspoons dried oregano leaves, divided

1 teaspoon minced garlic

1½ pounds skinless, boneless chicken breasts, cut into strips

¼ cup grated Parmesan cheese

MAKES 4 SERVINGS

Preheat the oven to 375°F.

In a 2- to 3-quart oblong baking dish coated with nonstick cooking spray, combine the water, rice, tomatoes and chilies, onion, Mozzarella, 1 teaspoon of the basil, 1 teaspoon of the oregano, and the garlic, stirring well. Top the rice mixture with the chicken strips, and sprinkle with the remaining 1 teaspoon basil, 1 teaspoon oregano, and the Parmesan. Bake, covered, for 45 minutes. Uncover and continue baking 15 minutes longer, or until the chicken is tender and the rice is cooked. Serve.

Nutritional information per serving

Calories 444, Protein (g) 50, Carbohydrate (g) 43, Fat (g) 7, Calories from Fat (%) 14, Saturated Fat (g) 3, Dietary Fiber (g) 2, Cholesterol (mg) 112, Sodium (mg) 580
Diabetic Exchanges: *6 very lean meat, 2.5 starch, 1 vegetable*

Chicken Divan

A standby that is a guaranteed hit in any home. Use this recipe to make another meal out of leftover chicken. Frozen chopped broccoli can be substituted for fresh.

2 bunches fresh broccoli

3 cups chopped, cooked chicken breasts (about 1 pound skinless, boneless chicken breasts)

1 cup skim milk

1 (10¾-ounce) can 98% fat-free cream of chicken soup

1 teaspoon lemon juice

⅛ teaspoon pepper

3 tablespoons all-purpose flour

3 tablespoons water

½ cup finely crushed whole wheat bread crumbs or plain bread crumbs

1 tablespoon margarine, melted

1 cup shredded reduced-fat sharp Cheddar cheese

MAKES 6 SERVINGS

Preheat the oven to 350°F.

Cut off the stems of the broccoli, leaving florets. Place in a 2-quart casserole with ⅓ cup water. Cover and cook on high in a microwave for 8 minutes, or until tender; drain.

Arrange the broccoli in an oblong dish. Spoon the chicken on top of the broccoli.

In a heavy saucepan, combine the milk, soup, lemon juice, and pepper, stirring well.

In a small bowl, combine the flour and water. Add to the soup mixture. Bring to a boil over medium heat, stirring constantly with a wire whisk, about 5 minutes. The mixture will get thick and bubbly. Pour evenly over the chicken.

In a small bowl, combine the bread crumbs and margarine. Sprinkle over the soup mixture. Top with the shredded cheese. Bake for 20 minutes, or until thoroughly heated. Serve.

Nutritional information per serving

Calories 296, Protein (g) 33, Carbohydrate (g) 18, Fat (g) 10, Calories from Fat (%) 30, Saturated Fat (g) 4, Dietary Fiber (g) 2, Cholesterol (mg) 74, Sodium (mg) 678
Diabetic Exchanges: *4 lean meat, 1 starch*

❄ Chicken Cherry Jubilee

Sweet and spicy: a timeless, delicious combination.

3 pounds skinless, boneless chicken breasts and thighs
Salt and pepper to taste
2 onions, thinly sliced
1 cup water
1 (12-ounce) bottle chili sauce
½ cup light brown sugar
1 cup sherry
1 (16-ounce) can pitted dark cherries, drained

MAKES 10 TO 12 SERVINGS

Preheat the broiler.

Season the chicken with the salt and pepper. Place in a 3-quart oblong pan, and cover with the sliced onion. Broil until the chicken is brown, 5 to 7 minutes.

Meanwhile, in a medium saucepan, combine the water, chili sauce, brown sugar, sherry, and cherries over low heat, until melted together.

When the chicken is brown, remove and discard the onion and transfer the chicken to a baking dish. Lower the oven temperature to 325°F. Pour the sauce over the chicken. Bake, covered, for 1½ hours, or until chicken is very tender. Serve.

Nutritional information per serving
Calories 236, Protein (g) 25, Carbohydrate (g) 25,
Fat (g) 3, Calories from Fat (%) 11, Saturated Fat (g) 1,
Dietary Fiber (g) 1, Cholesterol (mg) 80, Sodium (mg) 849
Diabetic Exchanges: *3 very lean meat, 0.5 fruit, 1 other carbohydrate*

QUICK TIP

Try this dish during the holiday season for a rich-tasting festive entrée. Serve with wild rice.

POULTRY

Chicken Breasts Florentine

Impressive for company and a favorite in my home. Prepare early in the day, refrigerate, and bake it when you're ready.

8 skinless, boneless
   chicken breasts

All-purpose flour
   (about ⅓ cup)

2 tablespoons olive oil

Salt and pepper to taste

1 (10-ounce) package
   frozen chopped spinach

8 thin square slices
   part-skim Mozzarella
   cheese (about 6 ounces)

½ cup fat-free canned
   chicken broth

¼ cup white wine

¼ cup lemon juice

QUICK TIP

Spinach is a source
of beta-carotene,
vitamin C, and folate.

MAKES 8 SERVINGS

Preheat the oven to 325°F.

Dust the chicken breasts with the flour. In a large skillet coated with nonstick cooking spray, heat the olive oil and sauté the breasts about 5 minutes on each side, until lightly browned, and season to taste. Remove to a 3-quart oblong dish coated with nonstick cooking spray.

Cook the spinach according to the package directions; squeeze and drain well. Top each chicken breast with the cooked spinach and a slice of mozzarella cheese.

Add the chicken broth to the same pan used to sauté the breasts. Add the wine and lemon juice, scraping the pan to remove the drippings, and stirring until heated. Pour the sauce over the chicken. If preparing the chicken ahead of time, refrigerate it at this point. Bake for 20 minutes, or until the chicken is done. The cheese should be melted and the chicken heated thoroughly. Serve.

Nutritional information per serving

Calories 241, Protein (g) 33, Carbohydrate (g) 7,
Fat (g) 8, Calories from Fat (%) 32, Saturated Fat (g) 3,
Dietary Fiber (g) 1, Cholesterol (mg) 78, Sodium (mg) 238
Diabetic Exchanges: *4 lean meat, 0.5 starch*

POULTRY

❄ Chicken Breasts with Artichokes and Mushrooms

My mother's standby recipe when we're all coming to town. She always makes it ahead of time, freezes it, and pulls it out to bake for an eagerly awaiting group.

2 pounds skinless,
   boneless chicken breasts
Onion powder to taste
Paprika to taste
Salt and pepper to taste
1 (14-ounce) can
   artichoke hearts,
   drained and quartered
½ pound fresh
   mushrooms, sliced
1 bunch green onions
   (scallions), chopped
½ teaspoon minced garlic
2 tablespoons margarine
2 tablespoons all-purpose
   flour
⅔ cup fat-free canned
   chicken broth
3 tablespoons sherry

MAKES 8 SERVINGS

Preheat the oven to 350°F.

Season the chicken heavily with the onion powder, paprika, salt, and pepper. Place the chicken in the bottom of a 3-quart casserole dish coated with nonstick cooking spray. Place the artichoke hearts around the chicken.

In a medium skillet coated with nonstick cooking spray, sauté the mushrooms, green onions, and garlic until tender. Place the mushroom mixture on top of the chicken.

In the same skillet, melt the margarine, and add the flour, stirring. Gradually add the chicken broth and sherry, cooking until smooth and the sauce comes to a boil. Pour the sauce over all in the casserole.

Bake, covered, for 1 hour. Remove the cover, and continue baking for 15 minutes to brown the chicken. Serve.

Nutritional information per serving
Calories 184, Protein (g) 28, Carbohydrate (g) 6,
Fat (g) 4, Calories from Fat (%) 22, Saturated Fat (g) 1,
Dietary Fiber (g) 1, Cholesterol (mg) 66, Sodium (mg) 250
Diabetic Exchanges*: 3 very lean meat, 1 vegetable*

QUICK TIP

To omit sherry, wine, or any other alcoholic beverage from a recipe, substitute another liquid such as chicken broth or water.

Lemon Feta Chicken

For a last-minute dinner, remember this recipe featuring Feta and lemon.

8 skinless, boneless
chicken breasts

¼ cup lemon juice,
divided

1 tablespoon dried
oregano leaves, divided

¼ teaspoon pepper

3 ounces crumbled
Feta cheese

3 tablespoons chopped
green onion (scallion)

MAKES 8 SERVINGS

Preheat the oven to 350°F.

Place the chicken in a 13 x 9 x 2-inch baking dish, and drizzle with half the lemon juice. Sprinkle with half the oregano and all of the pepper. Top with the cheese and green onion. Drizzle with the remaining lemon juice and oregano. Bake, covered, for 45 minutes to 1 hour, or until done. Serve.

Nutritional information per serving

Calories 158, Protein (g) 28, Carbohydrate (g) 2, Fat (g) 4, Calories from Fat (%) 22, Saturated Fat (g) 2, Dietary Fiber (g) 0, Cholesterol (mg) 75, Sodium (mg) 193
Diabetic Exchanges: *4 very lean meat*

Paprika Chicken

Fast to prepare, and will disappear even faster from the plate. The paprika gives this dish nice color, and the sherry adds to the sauce.

8 skinless, boneless
chicken breasts

Salt and pepper to taste

4 tablespoons lemon
juice, divided

1 tablespoon paprika

1 teaspoon minced garlic

1 tablespoon low-sodium
soy sauce

¾ cup dry sherry

1 bunch green onions
(scallions), sliced

MAKES 8 SERVINGS

Pound the chicken breasts to a ½-inch thickness. Season with the salt, pepper, 3 tablespoons of lemon juice, and paprika.

Coat a large skillet with nonstick cooking spray, and place over medium heat. Cook the chicken breasts on each side until browned, 5 to 7 minutes. Add the garlic, the remaining 1 tablespoon lemon juice, the soy sauce, and the sherry to the pan. Cook for 5 minutes. Sprinkle the green onions into the pan, and cook 3 to 5 minutes more, or until the chicken is done. Serve.

Nutritional information per serving

Calories 146, Protein (g) 27, Carbohydrate (g) 3, Fat (g) 2, Calories from Fat (%) 10, Saturated Fat (g) 0, Dietary Fiber (g) 1, Cholesterol (mg) 66, Sodium (mg) 126
Diabetic Exchanges: *3 very lean meat*

POULTRY

❄ Indoor Barbecued Chicken

When you have that craving for barbecue but don't feel like grilling or it's too chilly outside, try this indoor method.

⅔ cup ketchup

2 tablespoons lemon juice

2 tablespoons Worcestershire sauce

2 tablespoons honey

1 teaspoon minced garlic

8 skinless, boneless chicken breast halves

QUICK TIP

Use this homemade barbecue sauce when grilling outside. It works especially well with ribs or meat.

MAKES 8 SERVINGS

Preheat the broiler.

In a small saucepan, combine the ketchup, lemon juice, Worcestershire sauce, honey, and garlic. Bring to a boil, stirring frequently, then reduce the heat and simmer 2 minutes. Remove from the heat.

Place the chicken on a foil-lined pan, and coat both sides with the sauce. Broil 10 to 15 minutes; then turn and baste, and continue cooking 10 to 15 minutes longer, or until the chicken is done. Serve.

Nutritional information per serving

Calories 166, Protein (g) 27, Carbohydrate (g) 11,
Fat (g) 1, Calories from Fat (%) 8, Saturated Fat (g) 0,
Dietary Fiber (g) 0, Cholesterol (mg) 66, Sodium (mg) 358
Diabetic Exchanges: *3 very lean meat, 0.5 other carbohydrate*

POULTRY

Peanut Chicken

Fast, full of flavor, and a favorite. Crunchy peanuts add the finishing touch.

1 tablespoon peanut oil

2 pounds skinless, boneless chicken breasts, cut into strips

½ cup thinly sliced green onion (scallion)

½ teaspoon minced garlic

1 tablespoon cornstarch

¼ teaspoon ground ginger

Dash cayenne pepper

1¼ cups fat-free canned chicken broth

2 tablespoons honey

¼ cup low-sodium soy sauce

½ pound sliced mushrooms, optional

⅓ cup roasted peanuts

MAKES 8 SERVINGS

Heat the oil in a wok or large skillet. Add the chicken, and brown over medium-high heat, about 7 to 10 minutes. Add the green onion, garlic, cornstarch, ginger, cayenne, chicken broth, honey, soy sauce, and mushrooms. Cook, stirring constantly, until thickened. Cover and cook over low heat, 15 to 20 minutes. Sprinkle with the peanuts, and serve.

Nutritional information per serving

Calories 204, Protein (g) 29, Carbohydrate (g) 8, Fat (g) 6, Calories from Fat (%) 27, Saturated Fat (g) 1, Dietary Fiber (g) 1, Cholesterol (mg) 66, Sodium (mg) 368
Diabetic Exchanges: *4 lean meat, 0.5 other carbohydrate*

QUICK TIP

Purchase roasted peanuts in a jar or use whatever peanuts you have in your pantry.

POULTRY

Ginger Chicken and Black Beans

Intrigue your taste buds with peaches, ginger, and black beans, which mesh together for this sweet and savory dish.

2½ pounds skinless, boneless chicken breasts

Salt and pepper to taste

½ teaspoon garlic powder

1 teaspoon paprika

1 (15-ounce) can light sliced peaches, drained and cut into chunks

1 teaspoon ground ginger

2 tablespoons lime juice

1 teaspoon minced garlic

½ cup chopped green onion (scallion)

2 (15-ounce) cans black beans, undrained

MAKES 6 SERVINGS

Preheat the oven to 350°F.

Place the chicken in a 2-quart oblong baking dish. Season with the salt and pepper, garlic powder, and paprika. In a bowl, combine the peaches, ginger, lime juice, garlic, green onions, and black beans. Spoon this mixture over the chicken, cover, and bake for 50 to 60 minutes, or until the chicken is tender. Serve.

Nutritional information per serving

Calories 361, Protein (g) 52, Carbohydrate (g) 27, Fat (g) 4, Calories from Fat (%) 9, Saturated Fat (g) 1, Dietary Fiber (g) 9, Cholesterol (mg) 110, Sodium (mg) 563
Diabetic Exchanges: *6 very lean meat, 1.5 starch, 0.5 fruit*

QUICK TIP

In this recipe, the beans are not rinsed. However, if you are watching your sodium, rinse the beans and it will be fine in your diet.

Chinese Chicken and Broccoli Stir-Fry

Two family favorites, chicken and broccoli, are stir-fried for a tasty Chinese-style meal. My kids thought the flavor was better than at our favorite Chinese restaurant. Serve over rice.

2 pounds skinless, boneless chicken breasts, cut into strips
1 tablespoon cornstarch
½ teaspoon ground ginger
1 teaspoon crushed red pepper flakes
Salt and pepper to taste
3 tablespoons olive oil
1 bunch broccoli, florets only
1 tablespoon minced garlic
3 tablespoons low-sodium soy sauce
¼ cup sherry
1 teaspoon sugar
1 bunch green onions (scallions), cut into 2-inch slices
1 red bell pepper, seeded and cut into strips

MAKES 4 TO 6 SERVINGS

In a large bowl, toss the chicken strips with the cornstarch, ginger, red pepper flakes, salt, and pepper.

In a large skillet, heat the olive oil. Add the chicken, broccoli, garlic, soy sauce, sherry, and sugar, stirring and cooking over high heat, about 7 minutes. Add the green onions and red pepper, and continue cooking and stirring for another 10 minutes, or until the chicken is done. Serve.

Nutritional information per serving
Calories 266, Protein (g) 37, Carbohydrate (g) 7, Fat (g) 9, Calories from Fat (%) 30, Saturated Fat (g) 1, Dietary Fiber (g) 2, Cholesterol (mg) 88, Sodium (mg) 308
Diabetic Exchanges: 4.5 lean meat, 1.5 vegetable

QUICK TIP

Sometimes I substitute with a green pepper if red peppers are too expensive or difficult to find.

POULTRY

❄ Chicken Full-of-Flavor

This time-saving, one-pan, full-of-flavor recipe is ideal for busy nights.

¼ cup all-purpose flour

Salt and pepper to taste

8 skinless, boneless chicken breasts

1 tablespoon olive oil

1 bunch green onions (scallions), sliced

½ pound fresh mushrooms, sliced

1 cup fat-free canned chicken broth

½ cup dry white wine

1 tablespoon lemon juice

1 tablespoon chopped parsley

MAKES 8 SERVINGS

In a small bowl, combine the flour, salt, and pepper. Dredge the chicken breasts in the flour mixture.

In a skillet coated with nonstick cooking spray, heat the olive oil; cook the chicken until golden brown, 7 to 10 minutes, and no longer pink inside. Remove to a platter.

Coat the skillet again with nonstick cooking spray, and add the green onions and mushroom slices, cooking and stirring until tender. Pour in the chicken broth, wine, and lemon juice; bring to a boil, stirring. Cook for 5 minutes, or until slightly thickened. Reduce the heat to low, and stir in the parsley. Return the chicken to the pan; cook over low heat for 10 to 12 minutes until the chicken is tender. Serve.

Nutritional information per serving
Calories 172, Protein (g) 28, Carbohydrate (g) 5,
Fat (g) 3, Calories from Fat (%) 17, Saturated Fat (g) 1,
Dietary Fiber (g) 1, Cholesterol (mg) 66, Sodium (mg) 155
Diabetic Exchanges*: 3 very lean meat, 0.5 starch*

POULTRY

Cranberry Chicken with Wild Rice

Get in the holiday mood with this cranberry-orange chicken dish that's both satisfying and pretty on the plate.

1 (16-ounce) can whole-berry cranberry sauce

2 tablespoons orange liqueur or orange juice

2 tablespoons lemon juice

½ teaspoon dry mustard

1½ pounds skinless, boneless chicken breasts

1 (6-ounce) package long grain and wild rice mix

2 tablespoons grated orange rind

¼ cup sliced green onion (scallion)

MAKES 4 TO 6 SERVINGS

Preheat the oven to 350°F.

In a medium saucepan over medium heat or in a microwave-safe pan, combine the cranberry sauce, orange liqueur, lemon juice, and mustard, cooking until hot.

Place the chicken in a baking dish, and pour the cranberry sauce over the chicken. Bake, uncovered, for 45 minutes, or until the chicken is done.

Meanwhile, cook the wild rice according to the package directions, omitting any oil and salt. When the rice is done, stir in the orange rind and green onion.

To serve, place the rice on a plate, and top with the chicken and cranberry sauce.

Nutritional information per serving
Calories 357, Protein (g) 29, Carbohydrate (g) 53,
Fat (g) 2, Calories from Fat (%) 4, Saturated Fat (g) 0,
Dietary Fiber (g) 2, Cholesterol (mg) 66, Sodium (mg) 511
Diabetic Exchanges: *3 very lean meat, 1.5 starch, 2 other carbohydrate*

QUICK TIP

Include the toasted pecans and dried cranberries in the rice for a dish full of texture and a flavor that's equally impressive. For a regular, nightly dinner, I usually leave the pecans and cranberries out.

POULTRY

❄ Chicken and Dumplings

This Southern comfort dish is great in the winter months and popular in my home. If you prefer a thicker soup, mix a little soup and flour together; then return the mixture to the pot. If you like lots of dumplings, double the recipe and add them all to the soup.

2 pounds skinless, boneless chicken breasts, cut into small serving pieces

3 quarts water

Salt and pepper to taste

2 (10¾-ounce) cans 98% fat-free cream of mushroom soup

6 chicken bouillon cubes

½ cup all-purpose flour

1 celery stalk, cut into pieces

1 onion, quartered

4 carrots, peeled and sliced

2 cups self-rising flour

2 tablespoons canola oil

¾ cup skim milk

MAKES 6 TO 8 SERVINGS

Place the chicken in a large pot with the water, salt, pepper, mushroom soup, bouillon cubes, all-purpose flour mixed with a little water to make a smooth paste, celery, onion, and carrot slices. Bring to a boil. Reduce the heat to medium, and cook 30 minutes, or until the chicken is tender.

Meanwhile, make the dumplings. In a small bowl, combine with a fork the self-rising flour, oil, and milk. Turn onto a floured surface, and roll the dough ⅛-inch thick. Cut into thin strips.

Remove the celery and onion, bring the broth to a boil, and drop in the dumplings. Cook on medium heat, covered, for 10 minutes or until the dumplings are done. Serve in big bowls.

Nutritional information per serving
Calories 368, Protein (g) 32, Carbohydrate (g) 40,
Fat (g) 7, Calories from Fat (%) 18, Saturated Fat (g) 1,
Dietary Fiber (g) 2, Cholesterol (mg) 70, Sodium (mg) 1,869
Diabetic Exchanges: *3 lean meat, 2.5 starch, 1 vegetable*

QUICK TIP

If you're watching your sodium intake, use a smaller amount of the bouillon cubes, or cut them out of the recipe entirely.

❄ One-Dish Chicken Casserole

Leftover chicken combined with pantry ingredients makes this recipe an ideal choice when you're short of time.

1 (10¾-ounce) can 98% fat-free cream of chicken soup

1 cup water

½ cup skim milk

1 pound cooked, skinless, boneless chicken breasts, diced

1 (6-ounce) package quick-cooking long-grain and wild rice mix

1 (10-ounce) package frozen peas, thawed

½ cup shredded reduced-fat Cheddar cheese

½ teaspoon dry mustard

1 teaspoon dry rosemary leaves

Salt and pepper to taste

¼ cup dry bread crumbs

2 tablespoons margarine, melted

MAKES 4 TO 6 SERVINGS

Preheat the oven to 400°F.

In a 2-quart baking dish coated with nonstick cooking spray, mix together the soup, water, and milk. Add the chicken, rice mix and seasoning packet, peas, cheese, mustard, rosemary, salt, and pepper. Mix well.

In a small bowl, combine the bread crumbs with the melted margarine, and sprinkle over the chicken. Bake for 25 minutes, or until bubbly. Serve.

Nutritional information per serving

Calories 383, Protein (g) 34, Carbohydrate (g) 37, Fat (g) 10, Calories from Fat (%) 24, Saturated Fat (g) 3, Dietary Fiber (g) 3, Cholesterol (mg) 74, Sodium (mg) 1,056
Diabetic Exchanges: *3.5 lean meat, 2.5 starch*

FOOD FACT

Brown rice has a high-fiber bran coating; it goes rancid quickly and really should be stored for only 6 months in the pantry. It will last longer kept in the refrigerator.

POULTRY

Chicken Roll-Ups

A different twist to preparing chicken with a fancy flair—use broccoli or canned asparagus if you wish.

4 skinless, boneless chicken breasts

1 tablespoon Dijon mustard

⅓ pound fresh asparagus, trimmed

2 tablespoons all-purpose flour

½ teaspoon dried thyme leaves, divided

¼ teaspoon garlic powder

¼ teaspoon paprika

⅛ teaspoon white pepper

1 tomato, sliced

1 red onion, thinly sliced

½ cup fat-free canned chicken broth

½ cup dry white wine

MAKES 4 SERVINGS

Preheat the oven to 350°F.

Pound the chicken breasts to ½ inch thick. Spread each with the mustard. Place 2 asparagus spears on each chicken breast, and roll up, securing with a toothpick.

Combine the flour with ¼ teaspoon thyme, the garlic powder, paprika, and pepper. Roll the chicken breasts in the flour mixture.

Place the tomato and onion slices in an 1½-quart oblong baking dish coated with nonstick cooking spray. Arrange the chicken rolls on top.

In a small bowl, combine the chicken broth, wine, and remaining ¼ teaspoon thyme. Pour over the chicken. Cover loosely with foil. Bake for 30 minutes, basting occasionally. Uncover and bake 10 to 15 minutes longer, or until the chicken is done. Serve.

Nutritional information per serving
Calories 185, Protein (g) 29, Carbohydrate (g) 10,
Fat (g) 2, Calories from Fat (%) 8, Saturated Fat (g) 0,
Dietary Fiber (g) 2, Cholesterol (mg) 66, Sodium (mg) 246
Diabetic Exchanges: *3 very lean meat, 2 vegetable*

POULTRY

Salsa Chicken

I love to prepare this easy, flavorful dish. Cover the chicken with all the ingredients, and pop into the oven. Yellow rice goes well with this recipe.

2 pounds skinless, boneless chicken breasts

2 cups salsa

1 (15-ounce) can whole-kernel corn, drained

1½ cups shredded reduced-fat Monterey Jack cheese

½ cup sliced green onion (scallion), optional

MAKES 8 SERVINGS

Preheat the oven to 350°F.

Place the chicken in a 2-quart casserole coated with nonstick cooking spray. Cover with the salsa and corn. Cover, and bake for 1 hour.

Uncover, sprinkle with the cheese, and continue cooking for 5 minutes, or until done. Sprinkle with the green onion, if desired. Serve.

Nutritional information per serving
Calories 240, Protein (g) 33, Carbohydrate (g) 10, Fat (g) 6, Calories from Fat (%) 23, Saturated Fat (g) 3, Dietary Fiber (g) 1, Cholesterol (mg) 77, Sodium (mg) 578
Diabetic Exchanges: *4 lean meat, 0.5 starch*

QUICK TIP

To make grating cheese easier, place soft cheese such as Monterey Jack in the freezer for 10 to 15 minutes before grating.

Tequila Chicken

The homemade tomato salsa baked with the tequila infused chicken makes this quick dish a simple sensation. If you don't want to flame this dish, just bring the mixture to a boil for several minutes. Be careful when flaming any dish—make sure the area is clear.

1¾ pounds skinless, boneless chicken breasts
2 teaspoons ground cumin
2 tablespoons triple sec
2 tablespoons tequila
2 tomatoes, chopped
2 tablespoons chopped fresh cilantro
1 tablespoon lime juice
1 teaspoon chopped jalapeño pepper
⅓ cup chopped onion
⅔ cup shredded reduced-fat Monterey Jack cheese

MAKES 6 SERVINGS

Preheat the oven to 350°F.

Coat the chicken breasts on both sides with the cumin. In a large skillet coated with nonstick cooking spray, sauté the breasts over medium heat until brown on both sides, 5 minutes in all.

In a small bowl, combine the triple sec and tequila. Remove the pan from the heat, add the liqueur, and ignite very carefully with a match—a high flame will arise.

In a medium bowl, mix together the tomatoes, cilantro, lime juice, jalapeño, and onion; add to the chicken mixture when the flame goes out.

Transfer the chicken and salsa mixture to a baking dish, and bake for 15 minutes. Sprinkle with the shredded cheese, and continue baking until the cheese is melted, about 5 more minutes. Serve immediately.

Nutritional information per serving
Calories 226, Protein (g) 35, Carbohydrate (g) 6,
Fat (g) 4, Calories from Fat (%) 17, Saturated Fat (g) 2,
Dietary Fiber (g) 1, Cholesterol (mg) 84, Sodium (mg) 170
Diabetic Exchanges: *4.5 very lean meat, 1 vegetable*

POULTRY

Chicken Fajita Pizza

This quick dish is simple enough to please the kids while still satisfying the adults.

1 pound skinless, boneless chicken breasts, cut into strips
1 teaspoon chili powder
Salt and pepper to taste
½ teaspoon garlic powder
1 medium onion, thinly sliced
1 green bell pepper, seeded and thinly sliced into strips
1 (10-ounce) can prepared pizza crust or Boboli crust
½ cup prepared picante sauce
1 cup shredded reduced-fat Monterey Jack cheese

MAKES 8 SERVINGS

Preheat the oven to 425°F.

In a large skillet coated with nonstick cooking spray, sauté the chicken over medium heat until done, 7 to 10 minutes. Stir in the chili powder, salt, pepper, and garlic powder. Add the onion and green pepper, cooking until the vegetables are tender, another 3 minutes.

Coat a pizza pan with nonstick cooking spray; unroll the dough, and place in the pan. Starting at the center, press out the dough with your hands. Bake for 6 to 8 minutes, or until light golden brown.

Remove from the oven, and spoon the chicken mixture over the partially baked crust. Spoon the picante sauce over the chicken, and sprinkle with the cheese. Return to the oven, and bake for 10 to 12 minutes, or until the crust is crisp.

Nutritional information per serving
Calories 214, Protein (g) 21, Carbohydrate (g) 21, Fat (g) 5, Calories from Fat (%) 20, Saturated Fat (g) 2, Dietary Fiber (g) 2, Cholesterol (mg) 41, Sodium (mg) 471
Diabetic Exchanges: 2.5 lean meat, 1 starch, 1 vegetable

QUICK TIP

If you don't have a pizza cutter, try using kitchen scissors to cut your pizza instead.

POULTRY

❄ Southwestern Chicken with Bean Sauce

The beans dissolve to create a wonderful flavored sauce for the chicken. Top with cheese and chopped green onions, and serve with yellow rice.

POULTRY

2 pounds skinless, boneless chicken breasts

1 (16-ounce) can fat-free refried beans

½ cup chopped red onion

1 (16-ounce) jar salsa

1 cup shredded reduced-fat sharp Cheddar cheese, optional

¼ cup chopped green onion (scallion), optional

MAKES 6 TO 8 SERVINGS

Preheat the oven to 350°F.

Place the chicken breasts in a 2-quart oblong baking dish coated with nonstick cooking spray. Spread the beans to cover the top of the chicken. Sprinkle with the onions. Pour the salsa evenly over the top. Cover with foil, and bake 80 minutes, or until the chicken is done. Sprinkle with the cheese and green onion, if desired, and serve.

Nutritional information per serving

Calories 193, Protein (g) 29, Carbohydrate (g) 11, Fat (g) 1, Calories from Fat (%) 7, Saturated Fat (g) 0, Dietary Fiber (g) 3, Cholesterol (mg) 66, Sodium (mg) 558
Diabetic Exchanges: *3.5 very lean meat, 1 starch*

QUICK TIP

Try different flavored salsas for a twist to this recipe. Make sure you purchase fat-free refried beans!

❄ Mexican Chicken Casserole

This recipe is so good that it once won the heart of a man and inspired a proposal.
I just think it's a great-tasting casserole—I have my man.

1½ cups fat-free canned chicken broth

1 cup skim milk

½ cup all-purpose flour

½ cup nonfat plain yogurt

1 (10-ounce) can diced tomatoes and green chilies, drained

1 (4-ounce) can diced green chilies, drained

1 tablespoon chili powder

1 teaspoon dried oregano leaves

Salt and pepper to taste

1 onion, chopped

1 red or green bell pepper, seeded and chopped

½ teaspoon minced garlic

10 (6- to 8-inch) flour tortillas, cut into quarters

1 pound cooked skinless, boneless, chicken breasts cut into chunks

1 cup shredded reduced-fat sharp Cheddar cheese

MAKES 6 TO 8 SERVINGS

Preheat the oven to 350°F.

In a large saucepan, bring the chicken broth to a simmer. In a small bowl, whisk the milk into the flour to make a smooth paste. Add to the chicken broth, bring to a boil, reduce heat, and cook until thickened and smooth, stirring constantly. Remove from the heat, and stir in the yogurt, tomatoes and green chilies, diced green chilies, chili powder, and oregano. Season with the salt and pepper; set aside.

In a medium skillet coated with nonstick cooking spray, sauté the onion, bell pepper, and garlic until tender.

Line the bottom of a shallow 3-quart baking dish with half the tortillas. Sprinkle half the chicken and half the onion mixture over the tortillas. Spoon half the sauce evenly on the top. Repeat the layers, ending with the cheese. Bake for 25 to 30 minutes, or until bubbly. Serve.

Nutritional information per serving
Calories 278, Protein (g) 22, Carbohydrate (g) 37,
Fat (g) 4, Calories from Fat (%) 14, Saturated Fat (g) 2,
Dietary Fiber (g) 3, Cholesterol (mg) 38, Sodium (mg) 791
Diabetic Exchanges: *2.5 very lean meat, 2 starch, 1 vegetable*

QUICK TIP

Try flavored tortillas for added variety.

POULTRY

❄ Chicken and Black Bean Enchiladas

Super recipe! Try flavored salsas to kick up the flavor, and leave the beans out of the kids' servings if necessary.

1¼ pounds skinless, boneless chicken breasts

3 slices center-cut bacon

½ teaspoon minced garlic

1½ cups salsa, divided

1 (15-ounce) can black beans, undrained

1 red or green bell pepper, seeded and chopped, optional

1 teaspoon ground cumin

Salt and pepper to taste

1 bunch green onions (scallions), chopped

12 (6- to 8-inch) flour tortillas

6 ounces reduced-fat Monterey Jack cheese, shredded

MAKES 6 SERVINGS

Preheat the oven to 350°F.

Cut the chicken into chunks; set aside.

In a skillet, cook the bacon until crisp. Remove the bacon to a paper towel to soak any excess grease; discard any grease in the skillet.

In the same skillet, coated with nonstick cooking spray, sauté the chicken and garlic until the chicken is almost done, 5 to 7 minutes. Stir in ½ cup salsa, the beans, bell pepper, cumin, salt, and pepper. Simmer until thickened, about 5 minutes, stirring occasionally, or until the chicken is done. Stir in the green onions and reserved bacon.

Divide the chicken-bean mixture among 12 tortillas, placing the mixture down the center of each tortilla. Top with 1 tablespoon shredded cheese. Roll up and place seam-side down in a 13 x 9 x 2-inch baking dish coated with nonstick cooking spray. Spoon the remaining 1 cup salsa evenly over the enchiladas. Top with the remaining cheese. Bake for 15 minutes, or until thoroughly heated and the cheese is melted.

Nutritional information per serving

Calories 455, Protein (g) 40, Carbohydrate (g) 50, Fat (g) 8, Calories from Fat (%) 17, Saturated Fat (g) 4, Dietary Fiber (g) 6, Cholesterol (mg) 73, Sodium (mg) 1326
Diabetic Exchanges: *4 lean meat, 3 starch, 1 vegetable*

Cornish Hens with Wild Rice Stuffing

These glazed hens with fruits and a superb stuffing are a special-occasion dish. The stuffing may be used with any main dish. Make sure you remove the skin before eating.

8 Cornish game hens (about 1½ pounds each)

1 tablespoon paprika

1 tablespoon garlic powder

Salt and pepper to taste

2 onions, chopped

2 green bell peppers, seeded and chopped

4 celery stalks, chopped

1 tablespoon minced garlic

1 bunch green onions (scallions), chopped

3 (6-ounce) packages long-grain and wild rice mix

1 cup peach preserves

3 tablespoons honey

2 tablespoons light brown sugar

½ cup golden raisins

4 baking apples, cored and sliced

MAKES 16 SERVINGS

Preheat the oven to 350°F.

Clean and rinse the Cornish game hens. Lay the hens in a large casserole dish, and pat dry. Season with the paprika, garlic powder, salt, and pepper; set aside.

In a large pot coated with nonstick cooking spray, sauté the onion, green pepper, celery, garlic, and green onions until tender, about 7 minutes. Add all of the long grain and wild-rice mix and water according to the package directions, omitting any oil and salt. Cook until the rice is done and the liquid is absorbed, about 35 to 40 minutes. Stuff each of the Cornish game hens with equal amounts of the wild rice mixture.

In another saucepan, heat the peach preserves, honey, and brown sugar over medium-low heat until the mixture is bubbly, about 4 minutes. Pour over the stuffed hens. Sprinkle with the raisins and sliced apples. Bake for 1½ to 2 hours, or until the hens are done. You might have to cover them with foil during the last 30 minutes if the hens get too brown. To serve, cut each hen in half, and serve with the dressing.

Nutritional information per serving
Calories 404, Protein (g) 34, Carbohydrate (g) 58,
Fat (g) 5, Calories from Fat (%) 11, Saturated Fat (g) 1,
Dietary Fiber (g) 3, Cholesterol (mg) 132, Sodium (mg) 574
Diabetic Exchanges: *4 medium-fat meat, 1.5 starch, 1 fruit,*
1.5 other carbohydrate

POULTRY

Turkey Steaks with Prosciutto

A turkey dish is a nice change of fare, and this absolutely delicious recipe will leave quite an impression.

4 turkey breast cutlets or
   steaks (about 1 pound)
Salt and pepper to taste
¼ cup all-purpose flour
2 tablespoons olive oil
½ cup fat-free canned
   chicken broth
½ teaspoon minced garlic
4 thin slices prosciutto
   (about 2 ounces)
¼ cup Marsala wine
2 tablespoons chopped
   parsley

QUICK TIP

A boneless, skinless chicken breast can be substituted for a turkey breast cutlet.

MAKES 4 SERVINGS

Place the turkey steaks between sheets of waxed paper, and pound them to about ¼ inch thick. Sprinkle with salt and pepper. Coat lightly in the flour, and shake off the excess.

Heat the oil, and cook the turkey steaks until golden brown, 5 to 7 minutes; turn, and cook until done on other side. Add the chicken broth and garlic to the pan, and heat. Top each steak with prosciutto. Pour in the Marsala wine, and cook for a few minutes, reducing the sauce. Sprinkle with the parsley; serve.

Nutritional information per serving
Calories 263, Protein (g) 32, Carbohydrate (g) 8,
Fat (g) 10, Calories from Fat (%) 35, Saturated Fat (g) 2,
Dietary Fiber (g) 0, Cholesterol (mg) 89, Sodium (mg) 383
Diabetic Exchanges: *4 lean meat, 0.5 starch*

Honey-Glazed Turkey Breast

A sweet, spicy glaze infuses the turkey with flavor for a great everyday meal. My family enjoys the leftovers for sandwiches the next day.

1 (5-pound) turkey breast
Salt and pepper to taste
⅓ cup honey
3 tablespoons Dijon
   mustard
1½ teaspoons dried
   rosemary leaves

MAKES 10 TO 12 SERVINGS
Preheat the oven to 325°F.

Remove the skin from the turkey breast and discard; place the breast in a roaster pan. Season with the salt and pepper.

In a small bowl, mix together the honey, Dijon mustard, and rosemary. Pour half the glaze over the turkey breast, and bake, uncovered, for about 2 hours, or until the meat thermometer registers 170° to 175°F in the thickest part of the breast. You may want to add a little water to the bottom of pan, if needed. During the final 15 minutes of baking, brush the remaining glaze over the turkey breast. Serve.

Nutritional information per serving
Calories 188, Protein (g) 33, Carbohydrate (g) 8,
Fat (g) 1, Calories from Fat (%) 7, Saturated Fat (g) 0,
Dietary Fiber (g) 0, Cholesterol (mg) 95, Sodium (mg) 152
Diabetic Exchanges: *4.5 very lean meat, 0.5 carbohydrate*

QUICK TIP

If you prefer to cook the breast with the skin on, remove the skin before eating.

❄ Turkey Jambalaya

Turn leftover turkey into another meal with this superb combination of ingredients, or buy a roasted chicken to use instead of turkey.

1 pound reduced-fat sausage

1 large onion, chopped

1 pound fresh mushrooms, sliced

2 (6-ounce) packages long-grain and wild rice mix

4 cups cooked, diced turkey breasts or thighs

1 (2¼-ounce) can sliced black olives, drained

1 (14-ounce) can artichoke hearts, drained and quartered

½ cup chopped green onion (scallion)

MAKES 8 TO 10 SERVINGS

Cut the sausage into slices, and brown about 5 minutes in a large pot coated with nonstick cooking spray. Add the onion and mushrooms, cooking until tender. Drain off any excess grease.

Add the wild rice, seasoning packet, and water to the sausage mixture, and cook according to the package directions. Add the turkey, olives, and artichoke hearts, tossing gently. Top with the chopped green onion, and serve.

Nutritional information per serving

Calories 294, Protein (g) 28, Carbohydrate (g) 38, Fat (g) 3, Calories from Fat (%) 9, Saturated Fat (g) 1, Dietary Fiber (g) 2, Cholesterol (mg) 64, Sodium (mg) 1,055
Diabetic Exchanges: 3 very lean meat, 2 starch, 1.5 vegetable

QUICK TIP

The word Jambalaya refers to a Spanish Cajun seasoned rice dish with a mixture of several combinations of meat, poultry, sausage, and vegetables. This is an easy, yet sophisticated, version.

Barbecued Brisket 245

Italian-Style Pot Roast 246

Tenderloin Mexicana 247

Grilled Flank Steak 247

Stuffed Flank Steak 248

Sirloin Steak Strips 249

Smothered Round Steak 250

Meat

Beef Stir-Fry 251

Traditional Meat-and-Macaroni Casserole 252

Southwestern Grilled Beef Fajitas 253

Beef and Chicken Shish Kabobs 254

Crispy Southwestern Lasagna 255

Mexican Lasagna 256

Tamale Pie 257

Italian Meat Loaf 258

Italian Eggplant, Meat, and Rice 259

Stuffed Peppers 260

Meatballs for a Crowd 261

Mock Cabbage Rolls 262

Stuffed Cabbage 263

Moussaka 264

Old-Fashioned Pork Chop Casserole 266

Barbecued Pork Roast 267

Pork Florentine Wellington with Green Peppercorn Sauce 268

Pork Tenderloin Diane with Wild Rice 269

Glazed Pork Tenderloin 270

Grilled Pork Tenderloin Oriental 271

Pork Medallions with Brandy Sauce 272

Pork Tenderloin with Mustard Sauce 273

Sweet-and-Sour Pork 274

Italian Pork, Squash, and Tomatoes 275

Veal Saltimbocca 276

Veal Marengo 277

Veal Elegante 278

Veal with Tomatoes 279

Honey Mustard Lamb Chops 280

Lamb Loin Chops with Mint Sauce 281

Asian Meat Marinade 282

❄ Barbecued Brisket

Who needs to mess with a grill when you have this wonderful recipe that cooks itself? Put it in the oven, forget about it, and return to a tender, tasty brisket. My entire family adores this dish. If you have any, leftovers make great sandwiches.

1 (5-pound) trimmed
   beef brisket
Salt and pepper to taste
1 tablespoon garlic
   powder
½ cup light brown sugar
½ cup Worcestershire
   sauce
2 cups chipotle salsa

MAKES 12 TO 14 SERVINGS

Trim any excess fat from the brisket. Season the brisket with the salt, pepper, and garlic powder. In a small bowl, mix together the brown sugar, Worcestershire sauce, and salsa, and spread over the brisket. Cover, and refrigerate overnight.

Preheat the oven to 300°F.

Place the brisket and marinade in the oven in a heavy pot. Bake, covered, for 5 to 6 hours, or until the brisket is tender. Serve.

Nutritional information per serving
Calories 289, Protein (g) 35, Carbohydrate (g) 11,
Fat (g) 10, Calories from Fat (%) 33, Saturated Fat (g) 3,
Dietary Fiber (g) 0, Cholesterol (mg) 96, Sodium (mg) 378
Diabetic Exchanges: *5 lean meat, 0.5 other carbohydrate*

QUICK TIP

Brisket becomes very tender as long as it is cooked for a long time with plenty of moisture. To serve, slice the meat against the grain, even though it's tempting to tear strips of cooked brisket.

MEAT

❄ Italian-Style Pot Roast

Everyone always enjoys a pot roast, and this hearty and flavorful Italian version has a wonderful gravy. This recipe also works well in a slow cooker. Serve rice or potatoes with the gravy.

1 (4- to 5-pound) round roast

2 cups canned beef broth

½ cup Burgundy wine

3 tablespoons tomato paste

1 (28-ounce) can chopped tomatoes, with juice

1 teaspoon minced garlic

1 tablespoon dried basil leaves

1 tablespoon dried oregano leaves

2 bay leaves

1 pound carrots, peeled and cut into 1-inch pieces

3 onions, quartered

1 pound fresh mushrooms, halved

3 tablespoons all-purpose flour

MAKES 8 TO 10 SERVINGS

Preheat the oven to 350°F.

Place the roast in a large pot or Dutch oven. Pour in the beef broth and wine. Add the tomato paste, and stir. Add the tomatoes with juice. Blend in the garlic, basil, oregano, and bay leaves. Cover, and cook in the oven for 1½ hours. Turn the meat over, and add the carrots, onions, and mushrooms. Cover, and continue cooking for 1 to 1½ hours, or until the meat is tender. Transfer the meat to a carving board.

Remove a small amount of the sauce, and mix with the flour to form a paste. Place the Dutch oven over medium-high heat, and bring the remaining sauce to a boil. Whisk in the paste to thicken the sauce.

Slice the meat against the grain. Remove the bay leaves from the sauce, and discard. Serve the sliced meat with the vegetables and the sauce.

Nutritional information per serving
Calories 332, Protein (g) 41, Carbohydrate (g) 18, Fat (g) 10, Calories from Fat (%) 27, Saturated Fat (g) 3, Dietary Fiber (g) 5, Cholesterol (mg) 111, Sodium (mg) 384
Diabetic Exchanges: 5 lean meat, 3 vegetable

FOOD FACT

Round roasts include top round, bottom round, rump, and eye of round, which are leaner than other cuts of meat.

❄ Tenderloin Mexicana

Splurge with a reasonable portion of this terrific tenderloin. Include nutritional sides on the plate. This tastes even better when it's grilled.

4 (5-ounce) beef
  tenderloin steaks
¼ cup lime juice
2 tablespoons chili
  powder
1 tablespoon minced
  garlic
½ teaspoon ground
  cumin
¼ teaspoon crushed red
  pepper flakes
Salt and pepper

MAKES 4 SERVINGS

Place the steaks in a wide, shallow dish.

In a small bowl, combine the lime juice, chili powder, garlic, cumin, and red pepper flakes. Pour over the steaks, and rub to coat. Marinate if time permits.

Heat a large, heavy nonstick skillet over medium-high heat. Add the steaks, and cook 4 minutes on each side for medium-rare. Season with salt and pepper to taste. Serve.

Nutritional information per serving

Calories 237, Protein (g) 30, Carbohydrate (g) 3, Fat (g) 11, Calories from Fat (%) 43, Saturated Fat (g) 4, Dietary Fiber (g) 1, Cholesterol (mg) 88, Sodium (mg) 105
Diabetic Exchanges: *4 lean meat*

Grilled Flank Steak

My family requests this simple savory sensation often. A friend says this is her standard summer party recipe. Broil inside if desired.

2 pounds flank steak
2 tablespoons dry
  red wine
1 tablespoon red wine
  vinegar
1 tablespoon prepared
  horseradish
1 tablespoon ketchup
½ teaspoon pepper
1 teaspoon dried thyme
  leaves
1 teaspoon minced garlic

MAKES 6 SERVINGS

Trim any visible fat from the meat.

Combine the wine, vinegar, horseradish, ketchup, pepper, thyme, and garlic, and pour over meat. Cover, and marinate in the refrigerator for 8 hours or overnight, turning occasionally.

Grill, covered, over a hot fire about 7 minutes on each side. Serve rare, and cut diagonally across the grain into thin slices.

Nutritional information per serving

Calories 241, Protein (g) 32, Carbohydrate (g) 0, Fat (g) 12, Calories from Fat (%) 46, Saturated Fat (g) 5, Dietary Fiber (g) 0, Cholesterol (mg) 78, Sodium (mg) 135
Diabetic Exchanges: *4.5 meat*

MEAT

❄ Stuffed Flank Steak

Roasted peppers are available in the grocery stores in jars for a time saver. The stuffing infuses the meat with intense flavors—quite a presentation, with a taste to match. If you like, the butcher can butterfly your meat.

1 green bell pepper,
   roasted (recipe follows)
1 red bell pepper,
   roasted
   (recipe follows)
1 (10-ounce) bag fresh
   spinach
1 teaspoon minced garlic
½ cup Italian bread
   crumbs
½ cup grated Parmesan
   cheese
3 pounds lean flank
   steak, butterflied
Salt and pepper to taste

MAKES 6 TO 8 SERVINGS

Preheat the oven to 350°F.

Combine the roasted peppers (see recipe below), spinach, garlic, bread crumbs, and Parmesan cheese in a food processor, and process until chopped into small pieces and well mixed. Place the mixture on the flank steak. Starting with the long side, roll the steak up jelly roll style. Season with the salt and pepper. Secure with a toothpick. Place in a baking pan, and bake for 45 minutes. Slice into pinwheels, and serve.

Roasting Peppers

Preheat the oven to 400°F. Place the peppers on a pan, and bake for 30 minutes, or until browned. Place in a paper bag for 20 minutes. Then take out of the bag, remove the skins easily, and use the rest of the peppers in the recipe.

Nutritional information per serving
Calories 343, Protein (g) 40, Carbohydrate (g) 9,
Fat (g) 16, Calories from Fat (%) 42, Saturated Fat (g) 7,
Dietary Fiber (g) 2, Cholesterol (mg) 93, Sodium (mg) 361
***Diabetic Exchanges:** 5 lean meat, 0.5 starch*

MEAT

❄ Sirloin Steak Strips

You'll find yourself preparing this recipe for its excellent, quick, rich sauce. This meat dish gets rave reviews from kids.

2 pounds sirloin steak, trimmed of fat

Salt and pepper to taste

1 teaspoon minced garlic

½ cup dry red wine

½ cup canned beef broth

2 tablespoons Dijon mustard

3 tablespoons minced parsley

QUICK TIP

For leaner cuts of meat, use a meat whose name ends in "loin," such as *sirloin* and *tenderloin.*.

MAKES 6 TO 8 SERVINGS

Cut the steak into strips about ¾ inch thick. Heat a large skillet coated with nonstick cooking spray over medium-high heat, and sauté the steak on both sides until done, about 5 to 7 minutes. Season with the salt and pepper.

Remove the meat, and add the garlic and wine to the pan. Boil until reduced by half, stirring well. Add the beef broth and mustard, stirring until blended. Boil until slightly thickened, and add the parsley. Return the meat to the pan, heat with the sauce, and serve.

Nutritional information per serving
Calories 159, Protein (g) 24, Carbohydrate (g) 0,
Fat (g) 5, Calories from Fat (%) 30, Saturated Fat (g) 2,
Dietary Fiber (g) 0, Cholesterol (mg) 69, Sodium (mg) 219
Diabetic Exchanges: *3 lean meat*

MEAT

✳ Smothered Round Steak

My family likes this dish's terrific gravy with rice. Toss in some baby carrots if desired. Get the dish going, turn the burner to low heat, and have time to do other things.

2 pounds round steak, trimmed of fat

Salt and pepper to taste

¼ cup all-purpose flour

1 medium onion, chopped

1 teaspoon minced garlic

1 (10-ounce) can diced tomatoes and green chilies

2 cups beef broth

MAKES 4 TO 6 SERVINGS

Season the meat with the salt and pepper, and dust both sides with the flour.

In a large skillet coated with nonstick cooking spray, brown the steak over medium-high heat on both sides, about 6 minutes in all. Add the onion, garlic, tomato and green chilies, and broth, and bring to a boil. Reduce the heat, cover, and simmer for 1½ hours, or until the meat is tender. Serve.

Nutritional information per serving
Calories 245, Protein (g) 38, Carbohydrate (g) 8,
Fat (g) 6, Calories from Fat (%) 22, Saturated Fat (g) 2,
Dietary Fiber (g) 1, Cholesterol (mg) 94, Sodium (mg) 592
Diabetic Exchanges: *4.5 lean meat, 1.5 vegetable*

QUICK TIP

Even though round steak is a less tender cut of meat, this recipe cooks the meat for a long time, and the meat is extremely soft.

MEAT

❄ Beef Stir-Fry

Early in the morning, marinate and refrigerate the meat. For your quick evening meal,
toss the ingredients together and serve over rice. You can also use the marinade for a whole
flank steak, and grill or broil in the oven.

⅓ cup low-sodium soy
   sauce
¼ cup honey
1 teaspoon ground ginger
2 teaspoons minced garlic
2 pounds flank steak,
   trimmed of fat and
   cut into strips
1 onion, coarsely chopped
4 cups broccoli florets
1 green or red bell
   pepper, seeded
   and cut into strips
½ cup quartered
   fresh mushrooms
1 large tomato, chopped
1 (8-ounce) can water
   chestnuts, drained

MAKES 6 TO 8 SERVINGS

Combine the soy sauce, honey, ginger, and garlic in a baking dish; coat both sides of the meat with the mixture, and marinate in the refrigerator, covered, for at least 1 hour.

    In a wok or large shallow skillet coated with nonstick cooking spray, stir-fry the steak, onion, broccoli, and pepper over a medium-high heat for 5 to 7 minutes. Add the mushrooms, tomato, and water chestnuts, and cook for 3 more minutes, or until the vegetables are tender and the meat is done. The meat is best served rare.

Nutritional information per serving
Calories 258, Protein (g) 26, Carbohydrate (g) 18,
Fat (g) 9, Calories from Fat (%) 32, Saturated Fat (g) 4,
Dietary Fiber (g) 3, Cholesterol (mg) 59, Sodium (mg) 348
Diabetic Exchanges: *3 lean meat, 0.5 starch, 1.5 vegetable*

FOOD FACT

The best cuts of beef for stir-frying are flank and sirloin, which are more tender and full-flavored. To make slicing beef into strips easier, freeze for 15 to 30 minutes.

MEAT

❄ Traditional Meat-and-Macaroni Casserole

These basic ingredients come together to create a fun, family-appealing meal.

1 onion, chopped

1 green bell pepper, seeded and chopped

½ pound fresh mushrooms, sliced

1 pound ground sirloin

1 cup shell macaroni

1 (15-ounce) can tomato sauce

3 tablespoons tomato paste

1 (15¼-ounce) can whole-kernel corn, drained

1 tablespoon chili powder

Salt and pepper to taste

1 cup shredded reduced-fat Cheddar cheese

MAKES 8 SERVINGS

Preheat the oven to 350°F.

In a large pot coated with nonstick cooking spray, sauté the onion, green pepper, mushrooms, and meat until the vegetables are tender and the meat is done.

Cook the macaroni according to the package directions, omitting any oil and salt. Drain; add to the meat mixture. Add the tomato sauce, tomato paste, corn, and chili powder. Season with the salt and pepper.

Transfer to a 2-quart casserole, and top with the shredded cheese. Bake for 20 minutes, or until well heated. Serve.

Nutritional information per serving

Calories 227, Protein (g) 20, Carbohydrate (g) 26, Fat (g) 6, Calories from Fat (%) 22, Saturated Fat (g) 3, Dietary Fiber (g) 3, Cholesterol (mg) 38, Sodium (mg) 527
Diabetic Exchanges: 2 lean meat, 1 starch, 2 vegetable

MEAT

❄ Southwestern Grilled Beef Fajitas

This marinade is packed with flavor and makes the best fajitas. Serve with tortillas, cheese, tomatoes, and salsa or the condiments of your choice.

1 (10-ounce) can
  light beer
¼ cup chopped cilantro
½ teaspoon minced garlic
¼ cup lime juice
2 tablespoons red wine
  vinegar
1 tablespoon
  Worcestershire sauce
1 tablespoon grated
  lime peel
1 teaspoon ground cumin
1 tablespoon chili powder
Salt and pepper
2 pounds flank steak

MAKES 6 TO 8 SERVINGS

In a zipper-lock bag, combine the beer, cilantro, garlic, lime juice, vinegar, Worcestershire sauce, lime peel, cumin, chili powder, salt, and pepper. Add the meat, seal the bag, and refrigerate overnight. Drain well, and grill or broil the meat until done—flank steak should be served rare. Slice and serve.

Nutritional information per serving

*Calories 185, Protein (g) 24, Carbohydrate (g) 1,
Fat (g) 9, Calories from Fat (%) 45, Saturated Fat (g) 4,
Dietary Fiber (g) 0, Cholesterol (mg) 59, Sodium (mg) 103*
Diabetic Exchanges: *3 lean meat*

QUICK TIP

After cooking flank steak, always slice the meat against the "grain"— diagonal to the natural cut of meat—or it will be tough. Flank steak is sometimes labeled "skirt steak."

MEAT

Beef and Chicken Shish Kabobs

This recipe has one of the best marinades. I prepared this quick recipe on the Today *show for a grilled, one-dish meal.*

MEAT

2 pounds skinless, boneless chicken breasts, cut into 1½-inch cubes

2 pounds sirloin tip, cut into 1½-inch cubes

1 pint cherry tomatoes

1 pound fresh mushrooms

2 green bell peppers, seeded and cut into chunks

1 onion, cut into chunks

Orange and Wine Marinade (recipe follows)

Orange and Wine Marinade

1 cup dry red wine

¼ cup low-sodium soy sauce

1 cup orange juice

1 tablespoon dried thyme leaves

1 tablespoon dried rosemary leaves

2 tablespoons Worcestershire sauce

1 teaspoon pepper

1 tablespoon minced garlic

MAKES 8 TO 10 SKEWERS

Place the chicken, meat, tomatoes, mushrooms, peppers, and onion in a large bowl, and pour the Orange and Wine Marinade (see recipe below) over them. Refrigerate overnight.

Assemble the chicken, meat, and vegetables on metal skewers, without crowding the pieces together, and grill on a hot grill 5 to 10 minutes or until done, turning frequently. Baste with the remaining marinade while grilling. Serve.

QUICK TIP

When making kabobs, don't crowd the ingredients on the skewers—leave a little space between each piece.

In a medium bowl, mix together the wine, soy sauce, orange juice, thyme, rosemary, Worcestershire sauce, pepper, and garlic.

Nutritional information per serving
Calories 252, Protein (g) 43, Carbohydrate (g) 8,
Fat (g) 5, Calories from Fat (%) 18, Saturated Fat (g) 2,
Dietary Fiber (g) 2, Cholesterol (mg) 107, Sodium (mg) 311
Diabetic Exchanges: *6 very lean meat, 1.5 vegetable*

❄ Crispy Southwestern Lasagna

This popular and exciting twist to lasagna is simple to prepare, with no noodles to cook. I prefer blending the cottage cheese in a food processor until it's smooth. Ricotta cheese may be substituted for the cottage cheese.

1 pound ground sirloin

1 (14½-ounce) can diced tomatoes, with juice

1 (4-ounce) can diced green chilies, drained

2 teaspoons chili powder

1½ teaspoons ground cumin

1 teaspoon minced garlic

Salt and pepper to taste

2 egg whites

2 cups reduced-fat or fat-free cottage cheese

14 (6-inch) corn or flour tortillas, cut into quarters

1 (15¼-ounce) can whole-kernel corn, drained

8 ounces reduced-fat Monterey Jack cheese, shredded

MAKES 8 TO 10 SERVINGS

Preheat the oven to 350°F.

In a large skillet coated with nonstick cooking spray, cook the meat over medium heat until done, and drain any excess liquid. Add the tomatoes and juice, green chilies, chili powder, cumin, garlic, salt, and pepper; set aside.

In a small bowl, blend the egg whites and cottage cheese well; set aside.

Coat a 13 x 9 x 2-inch baking dish with nonstick cooking spray. Cover the bottom of the baking dish with six quartered tortillas. Layer of all the corn, half the meat mixture, half the cheese, four quartered tortillas, then all of the cottage cheese mixture, the remaining half of the meat mixture, and the remaining four quartered tortillas, and top with the remaining cheese. Bake, uncovered, for 30 minutes. Serve.

Nutritional information per serving

Calories 239, Protein (g) 25, Carbohydrate (g) 20, Fat (g) 7, Calories from Fat (%) 26, Saturated Fat (g) 3, Dietary Fiber (g) 3, Cholesterol (mg) 40, Sodium (mg) 537
Diabetic Exchanges: *3 lean meat, 1 starch, 1 vegetable*

QUICK TIP

Purchase ground meat in bulk for savings. Mold into patties, wrap well, and freeze to pull out later for hamburgers on the spot.

MEAT

❄ Mexican Lasagna

Use different-flavored salsas to add extra kick to this very tasty lasagna family pleaser.

1 pound ground sirloin
½ cup chopped celery
½ cup chopped onion
½ teaspoon minced garlic
¼ cup chopped green
    bell pepper
1 (16-ounce) jar salsa
1 (14-ounce) can
    enchilada sauce,
    divided
Salt and pepper to taste
4 slices reduced-fat
    American cheese
1 cup fat-free cottage
    cheese
1 egg white, beaten
6 (6- to 8-inch) flour
    tortillas, cut into thirds

MAKES 8 SERVINGS

Preheat the oven to 350°F.

In a large skillet coated with nonstick cooking spray, cook the meat, celery, onion, garlic, and green pepper over medium heat until the meat is done, about 8 to 10 minutes. Drain any excess liquid. Add the salsa, two-thirds of the enchilada sauce, and the salt and pepper. Bring to a boil; reduce the heat, and simmer 10 minutes.

Meanwhile, combine the American and cottage cheeses and the egg white in a food processor, mixing until blended and the American cheese is in pieces; set aside.

In a skillet coated with nonstick cooking spray, heat the remaining enchilada sauce a little at a time, and fry the flour tortillas until soft. Remove, continuing to add sauce and fry tortillas until all have been cooked.

Spoon one-third of the meat mixture into a 2-quart oblong baking dish coated with nonstick cooking spray. Spoon half the cheese mixture over the meat. Top with half the tortillas. Repeat the layers, ending with the meat. Bake for 25 minutes. Let stand for 5 minutes before cutting.

Nutritional information per serving

Calories 230, Protein (g) 20, Carbohydrate (g) 22, Fat (g) 5, Calories from Fat (%) 22, Saturated Fat (g) 3, Dietary Fiber (g) 2, Cholesterol (mg) 40, Sodium (mg) 998
Diabetic Exchanges: *2.5 lean meat, 1.5 starch*

MEAT

❄ Tamale Pie

In the mood for tamales? This easy-to-make layered tortilla-and-meat dish is great for a crowd of all ages.

2 pounds ground sirloin
1 onion, chopped
1 teaspoon minced garlic
1 (8-ounce) can tomato sauce
1 (16-ounce) jar thick and chunky salsa
1 teaspoon ground cumin
1 teaspoon chili powder
1 (15-ounce) can cream-style corn
6 (6- to 8-inch) flour tortillas, cut into 1-inch strips
¾ cup shredded reduced-fat Cheddar cheese

MAKES 10 TO 12 SERVINGS

Preheat the oven to 350°F.

In a large skillet coated with nonstick cooking spray, cook the meat, onion, and garlic over medium heat, until the meat is done, about 7 minutes. Drain any excess grease. Add the tomato sauce, salsa, cumin, chili powder, and corn, mixing well.

Coat a 13 x 9 x 2-inch baking pan with nonstick cooking spray, and layer one-third of the meat mixture. Cover the mixture with one-third of the tortilla strips, and repeat the layers, starting with a fourth of the remaining meat mixture and topping with a third of the tortilla strips. Continue layering, ending with the meat mixture. Cover and bake for 35 to 40 minutes, or until thoroughly heated. Sprinkle with the cheese, and continue cooking for another 5 minutes, or until the cheese is melted. Cool for 5 minutes, and serve.

Nutritional information per serving
Calories 200, Protein (g) 19, Carbohydrate (g) 20,
Fat (g) 5, Calories from Fat (%) 22, Saturated Fat (g) 2,
Dietary Fiber (g) 1, Cholesterol (mg) 44, Sodium (mg) 605
Diabetic Exchanges: *2 lean meat, 1 starch, 1 vegetable*

MEAT

❄ Italian Meat Loaf

Sometimes I add spinach to this very moist meat loaf packed with flavor. It will turn anyone into a meat loaf fan.

2 pounds ground sirloin
1 egg white
1 cup tomato juice
Salt and pepper to taste
½ teaspoon minced garlic
1 teaspoon dried
   oregano leaves
1 teaspoon dried basil
   leaves
1 onion, chopped
4 ounces sliced part-skim
   Mozzarella cheese
4 ounces sliced lean ham

MAKES 6 SERVINGS

Preheat the oven to 350°F.

In a large bowl, combine the meat, egg white, tomato juice, salt, pepper, garlic, oregano, and basil.

In a small skillet coated with nonstick cooking spray, sauté the onion until tender. Add the cooked onion to the meat mixture, mixing well. Put half the meat mixture into a 9 x 5 x 3-inch loaf pan, top with the Mozzarella cheese and ham, and cover with the remaining meat mixture. Bake for 1 hour, or until meat is done. Serve.

Nutritional information per serving
Calories 266, Protein (g) 39, Carbohydrate (g) 5,
Fat (g) 11, Calories from Fat (%) 35, Saturated Fat (g) 5,
Dietary Fiber (g) 1, Cholesterol (mg) 98, Sodium (mg) 532
Diabetic Exchanges: *5 lean meat, 1 vegetable*

QUICK TIP

Add ½ cup salsa or picante sauce to one pound ground beef for a moist and flavorful hamburger.

❄ Italian Eggplant, Meat, and Rice

Eggplant and zucchini are disguised in this rice dressing–style dish topped with tomato sauce and cheese. It's a wonderful, crowd-pleasing Italian casserole.

2 medium eggplants, peeled and cubed

1 zucchini, thinly sliced

1 tablespoon minced garlic

4 ounces light bulk sausage

½ pound ground sirloin

Salt and pepper to taste

1 tablespoon plus 1 teaspoon dried basil leaves, divided

1 tablespoon plus 1 teaspoon dried oregano leaves, divided

3 cups cooked rice

1 (15-ounce) can tomato sauce

1½ cups shredded part-skim Mozzarella cheese

MAKES 6 TO 8 SERVINGS

Preheat the oven to 350°F.

In a large pot coated with nonstick cooking spray, sauté the eggplants, zucchini, garlic, sausage, and meat over medium heat until the meat is done and the vegetables are very tender, about 10 minutes. Drain any excess liquid. Add the salt and pepper, 1 tablespoon basil, 1 tablespoon oregano, and the cooked rice, tossing well.

Spread the mixture in a 2-quart casserole dish coated with nonstick cooking spray. In a small bowl, combine the tomato sauce with the remaining 1 teaspoon basil and 1 teaspoon oregano, and spread over the eggplant-rice mixture. Sprinkle with the Mozzarella, and bake, uncovered, for 20 to 30 minutes, or until the mixture is hot and the cheese is melted. Serve.

Nutritional information per serving
Calories 246, Protein (g) 17, Carbohydrate (g) 30,
Fat (g) 7, Calories from Fat (%) 24, Saturated Fat (g) 3,
Dietary Fiber (g) 4, Cholesterol (mg) 39, Sodium (mg) 502
Diabetic Exchanges: *2 lean meat, 1 starch, 3 vegetable*

MEAT

QUICK TIP

For added fiber, substitute brown or wild rice in dishes that call for rice.

❄ Stuffed Peppers

The stuffing is so delicious that you could put this hearty mixture in a casserole dish, bake it, and make a meal of it. If you feel color-creative, use red, yellow, or orange bell peppers.

6 medium green bell
   peppers, seeded
1 pound ground sirloin
1 cup chopped fresh
   mushrooms
¾ cup chopped onion
1 cup tomato sauce
1 tablespoon minced
   garlic
1 teaspoon dried basil
   leaves
1 teaspoon dried
   oregano leaves
1 tablespoon
   Worcestershire sauce
Salt and pepper to taste
2 cups cooked rice
½ cup (2 ounces)
   shredded part-skim
   Mozzarella cheese

MAKES 6 SERVINGS

Preheat the oven to 350°F.

Cut the tops off the green peppers, and remove the cores. Trim the stems from the tops, and discard. Chop the remaining tops; set aside.

Arrange the pepper shells in a steamer over boiling water, cover, and steam for 5 to 10 minutes, or until tender. Drain the shells, and set aside.

In a large skillet coated with nonstick cooking spray, combine the meat, mushrooms, onion, and reserved chopped green pepper. Cook over medium heat until the meat is brown, about 7 minutes; drain off any excess grease. Add the tomato sauce, garlic, basil, oregano, Worcestershire sauce, salt, and pepper. Bring to a boil; reduce the heat and simmer 5 minutes. Mix in the rice.

Spoon the mixture into the pepper shells; then place the peppers upright in an 8-inch square baking dish. Sprinkle with the Mozzarella. Bake for 15 minutes, or until the cheese is melted and the peppers are thoroughly heated. Serve.

Nutritional information per serving

Calories 242, Protein (g) 21, Carbohydrate (g) 29,
Fat (g) 5, Calories from Fat (%) 19, Saturated Fat (g) 2,
Dietary Fiber (g) 3, Cholesterol (mg) 45, Sodium (mg) 346
***Diabetic Exchanges:** 2 lean meat, 1 starch, 3 vegetable*

MEAT

❄ Meatballs for a Crowd

This recipe makes a huge pot of these meatballs, so I usually serve them and freeze the remainder.

4 pounds ground sirloin
1 tablespoon onion
   powder
1 tablespoon dried
   oregano leaves
1 tablespoon dried basil
½ teaspoon pepper
1 tablespoon minced garlic
2 tablespoons
   Worcestershire sauce
2 tablespoons
   low-sodium soy sauce
1 cup Italian bread crumbs
3 egg whites
Tomato Sauce
   (recipe follows)

Tomato Sauce

1 cup finely chopped
   onion
2 (28-ounce) cans
   chopped tomatoes,
   with juice
2 (6-ounce) cans tomato
   paste
2 cups water
1 tablespoon minced garlic
1 tablespoon dried
   oregano leaves
1 tablespoon dried basil
¼ teaspoon pepper

MAKES 14 TO 16 SERVINGS

Preheat the broiler.

In a large bowl, mix together the meat, onion powder, oregano, basil, pepper, garlic, Worcestershire sauce, soy sauce, bread crumbs, and egg whites until well combined. Shape the mixture into meatballs, using about ¼ cup of the mixture for each.

Place the meatballs on a baking sheet coated with nonstick cooking spray. Broil about 6 to 8 minutes on each side. Transfer the meatballs to the pot of Tomato Sauce (see recipe below), and continue cooking for 30 minutes. Serve with pasta.

QUICK TIP

To keep your hands from getting sticky when shaping meatballs or other sticky foods, moisten them with cool water.

While the meatballs are broiling, place the onion in a large pot coated with nonstick cooking spray. Over medium-high heat, sauté the onion until tender, about 5 minutes. Add the tomatoes, tomato paste, water, garlic, oregano, basil, and pepper. Bring to a boil, lower the heat, and simmer for 30 minutes. Add the meatballs to the sauce.

Nutritional information per serving
Calories 213, Protein (g) 26, Carbohydrate (g) 17,
Fat (g) 5, Calories from Fat (%) 22, Saturated Fat (g) 2,
Dietary Fiber (g) 4, Cholesterol (mg) 60, Sodium (mg) 395
Diabetic Exchanges: *3 lean meat, 0.5 starch, 2 vegetable*

MEAT

❄ Mock Cabbage Rolls

This recipe is a quick and easy alternative to individually stuffing all those cabbage leaves. Shredded cabbage is available in bags at the grocery store.

1½ pounds ground sirloin
1 onion, chopped
1 teaspoon minced garlic
¼ teaspoon pepper
3 cups cooked rice
1 (¾-pound) head
  cabbage, coarsely
  shredded
1 (26-ounce) jar pasta
  sauce
¼ cup light brown sugar
1 cup shredded part-skim
  Mozzarella cheese,
  optional

QUICK TIP

When cooking rice, remember that rice triples in volume when it's cooked, so make sure you use a big enough pot.

MAKES 6 TO 8 SERVINGS
Preheat the oven to 350°F.

In a large skillet, cook the meat, onion, and garlic over medium heat until the meat is done, about 7 minutes. Drain any excess liquid. Add the pepper and cooked rice, mixing well. Spoon the meat mixture into a 4-quart casserole dish coated with nonstick cooking spray. Top with the shredded cabbage.

In a medium bowl, mix together the pasta sauce and brown sugar. Pour the sauce over the cabbage. Bake, covered, for 1¼ hours, or until the cabbage is tender. Sprinkle with the Mozzarella, and continue baking for 5 minutes, or until the cheese is melted. Serve.

Nutritional information per serving
Calories 307, Protein (g) 24, Carbohydrate (g) 37,
Fat (g) 7, Calories from Fat (%) 22, Saturated Fat (g) 3,
Dietary Fiber (g) 3, Cholesterol (mg) 53, Sodium (mg) 541
Diabetic Exchanges: *3 lean meat, 1 starch, 1 vegetable, 1 other carbohydrate*

MEAT

❄ Stuffed Cabbage

This recipe is from my grandmother. Storing the cabbage overnight in the freezer simplifies the typical preparation of boiling cabbage leaves to soften, so I usually double the recipe and freeze some.

3 pounds green cabbage
(about 2 large heads)

2 pounds ground sirloin

1 onion, chopped

2 egg whites

1 cup uncooked rice

Salt and pepper to taste

1 (15-ounce) can tomato
sauce

¾ cup water

½ cup light brown sugar

½ cup crushed ginger
snap cookie crumbs

¼ cup lemon juice

QUICK TIP

When you're buying cabbage, look for tight, firm, heavy heads with no broken or bruised leaves.

MAKES 12 (2-ROLL) SERVINGS

Preheat the oven to 350°F.

Place the cabbage in the freezer overnight. Defrost, and cut out the core. Carefully tear the leaves away from the head (they will pull off easily now); set aside.

In a large bowl, combine the meat, onion, egg whites, rice, salt, and pepper. Place about ¼ cup meat mixture in the hollow of each cabbage leaf. Fold the sides of the leaf over the stuffing; roll up from the thick end of the leaf. Repeat with all leaves large enough to roll up, until the stuffing is used up. Place the stuffed leaves in a deep, oblong 3- to 4-quart casserole dish. A roaster also works well.

To make the sauce, in another bowl combine the tomato sauce, water, brown sugar, cookie crumbs, and lemon juice. Pour over the stuffed cabbage. Cover, and bake for 2 to 2½ hours. When the cabbage rolls are done, the rice and meat will be cooked and the cabbage will be tender.

Nutritional information per serving
Calories 248, Protein (g) 19, Carbohydrate (g) 35,
Fat (g) 4, Calories from Fat (%) 15, Saturated Fat (g) 1,
Dietary Fiber (g) 3, Cholesterol (mg) 40, Sodium (mg) 306
Diabetic Exchanges: *2 lean meat, 1 starch, 1 vegetable, 1 other carbohydrate*

MEAT

❄ Moussaka

My Greek neighbor showed me how to make moussaka, a Greek lasagna with a unique taste that serves a crowd. This hearty meal is worth the time spent preparing it.

2 large eggplants, peeled
  and cut into ½-inch
  slices
2 baking potatoes,
  peeled and cut into
  ½-inch slices
½ teaspoon sugar
Meat Sauce
  (recipe follows)
White Sauce
  (recipe follows)
1 cup shredded reduced-
  fat Cheddar cheese

Meat Sauce
1 onion, chopped
1 teaspoon minced garlic
1 pound ground sirloin
½ cup dry white wine
½ cup chopped parsley
1 (14½-ounce) can diced
  tomatoes
1 (10¾-ounce) can
  tomato pureé
Dash allspice
¼ teaspoon ground
  cinnamon
Salt and pepper to taste

MAKES 12 SERVINGS
Preheat the broiler.

Place the eggplant and the potato on a baking sheet, spray the vegetables with nonstick cooking spray, and broil about 4 inches from the heat until the vegetables are golden in color, about 5 minutes on each side.

Preheat the oven to 350°F; coat a 13 x 9 x 2-inch baking pan with nonstick cooking spray.

Lay half the potato slices in the bottom of the prepared baking pan. Layer half the eggplant on top, and sprinkle with the sugar. Layer with all of the Meat Sauce (see recipe below). Top with the remaining potato and eggplant. Pour the White Sauce (see recipe at right) over the top to cover. Bake for 35 to 40 minutes, or until the vegetables are tender. Sprinkle with the cheese, and continue baking for 5 to 10 minutes, or until the cheese is melted. Cool for 5 minutes, and serve.

In a large skillet coated with nonstick cooking spray, sauté the onion, garlic, and meat over medium heat until the meat is done and the vegetables are tender, about 5 minutes. Drain any excess grease. Add the white wine, parsley, tomato, tomato pureé, allspice, cinnamon, salt, and pepper. Bring to a boil, stirring constantly. Reduce the heat, and simmer, uncovered, for 20 minutes.

MEAT

White Sauce (for Moussaka)

¼ cup all-purpose flour
2 cups skim milk
⅛ teaspoon allspice
Salt and pepper to taste

In a medium saucepan, stir together the flour and milk. Bring to a boil over medium-high heat, stirring until thickened, about 5 minutes. Remove from the heat, and add the allspice, salt, and pepper.

Nutritional information per serving
Calories 158, Protein (g) 14, Carbohydrate (g) 19,
Fat (g) 4, Calories from Fat (%) 20, Saturated Fat (g) 2,
Dietary Fiber (g) 4, Cholesterol (mg) 26, Sodium (mg) 252
Diabetic Exchanges: *1.5 lean meat, 0.5 starch, 2 vegetable*

FOOD FACT

The traditional Greek moussaka is a baked, layered casserole usually made with lamb.

MEAT

❄ Old-Fashioned Pork Chop Casserole

In this simple dish, you get gravy, meat, and rice in a no-fail combination that makes a nice family dinner.

⅔ cup uncooked rice

1 (6-ounce) package long-grain and wild rice mix

3 cups hot water

8 bone-in loin pork chops, trimmed of fat (½ inch thick)

Salt and pepper to taste

1 (10¾-ounce) can 98% fat-free cream of celery soup

⅔ cup skim milk

⅓ cup chopped green onion (scallion)

MAKES 6 TO 8 SERVINGS

Preheat the oven to 350°F.

In a medium bowl, combine the rice, the wild rice with its seasoning packet, and the hot water. Place the rice mixture in a 13 x 9 x 2-inch baking dish coated with nonstick cooking spray; lay the pork chops on top, and season with salt and pepper. Cover, and bake for 1 hour.

In a small bowl, mix together the cream of celery soup, milk, and green onion. Uncover the casserole, and pour the soup mixture over the pork chops. Return the casserole, uncovered, to the oven, and bake for 15 minutes longer, or until thoroughly heated. Serve.

Nutritional information per serving
Calories 292, Protein (g) 26, Carbohydrate (g) 33,
Fat (g) 5, Calories from Fat (%) 17, Saturated Fat (g) 2,
Dietary Fiber (g) 1, Cholesterol (mg) 66, Sodium (mg) 640
***Diabetic Exchanges:** 3 lean meat, 2 starch*

FOOD FACT

Loin pork chops are from the ultra-lean tenderloin. Loin or center-loin are equally good, whether boneless or bone-in.

MEAT

❄ Barbecued Pork Roast

A pork roast is a nice change, and this tasty barbecued meat is a no-trouble approach for barbecue cravings. The leftovers make great sandwiches.

1 (3-pound) boneless, rolled loin pork roast

3 large cloves garlic, sliced thinly

1 teaspoon pepper

1 teaspoon dried thyme leaves

1 onion, sliced

½ cup fat-free canned chicken broth

½ cup cider vinegar

1 (6-ounce) can tomato paste

¼ cup lemon juice

2 tablespoons Worcestershire sauce

2 tablespoons light brown sugar

1 tablespoon Dijon mustard

½ teaspoon paprika

MAKES 6 TO 8 SERVINGS

Preheat the oven to 350°F.

Trim any excess fat from the pork roast. Cut deep slits in the roast, and insert the garlic slices. Combine the pepper and thyme; rub over the surface of the roast.

In a saucepan coated with nonstick cooking spray, sauté the onion over medium heat. Add the chicken broth, vinegar, tomato paste, lemon juice, Worcestershire sauce, brown sugar, Dijon mustard, and paprika, stirring until the mixture comes to a boil. Remove from heat.

Place the roast in a pot coated with nonstick cooking spray, and cover with the barbecue sauce. Bake for 1½ to 2 hours, or until very tender. Slice, and serve with the sauce.

Nutritional information per serving

Calories 314, Protein (g) 39, Carbohydrate (g) 13, Fat (g) 11, Calories from Fat (%) 33, Saturated Fat (g) 4, Dietary Fiber (g) 2, Cholesterol (mg) 94, Sodium (mg) 198
Diabetic Exchanges: *6 lean meat, 2 vegetable*

MEAT

❄ Pork Florentine Wellington with Green Peppercorn Sauce

Easy elegance with a terrific taste. It literally took me only minutes to wrap these tenderloins for such an impressive pork preparation. Wonderful stuffing with a very tasty Peppercorn Sauce.

2 (10-ounce) packages frozen chopped spinach
½ pound fresh mushrooms, sliced
1 onion, chopped
½ teaspoon minced garlic
2 (1-pound) pork tenderloins, trimmed of fat
Salt and pepper to taste
1 package phyllo dough
Green Peppercorn Sauce (recipe follows)

MAKES 6 TO 8 SERVINGS

Preheat the oven to 375°F.

Cook the spinach according to the package directions; drain, squeeze dry, and set aside.

In a large skillet coated with nonstick cooking spray, sauté the mushrooms, onion, and garlic until tender. Add the spinach. Transfer the mixture to a food processor, and pulse until puréed.

Season each tenderloin with the salt and pepper. Mold the spinach mixture around the sides and top of each tenderloin.

On waxed paper, lay each sheet of phyllo dough, coated with nonstick cooking spray, until 10 sheets of phyllo dough are stacked. Place a spinach-covered tenderloin on one end of the phyllo dough, and roll up, tucking the ends on each side under. Repeat the procedure with another 10 sheets of phyllo dough and the other tenderloin. Spray each wrapped tenderloin with nonstick cooking spray, and transfer to a baking sheet. Bake for 45 minutes, or until a meat thermometer reads 160°F. Slice, and serve with Green Peppercorn Sauce (see recipe at right).

FOOD FACT

Phyllo is tissue-thin pastry dough found frozen in most grocery stores. Phyllo sheets become dry and brittle quickly, so don't remove the sheets from their wrapping until you're ready to use them.

MEAT

Green Peppercorn Sauce

1 cup beef broth

2 teaspoons Dijon mustard

¼ cup dried green peppercorns

1 cup evaporated skimmed milk

MAKES 1½ CUPS SAUCE

In a small saucepan, combine the beef broth, mustard, and peppercorns. Bring to a boil over medium heat. Lower the heat, and cook until the sauce is reduced by half and thickens. Add the milk, and heat until the sauce thickens. *Do not boil.*

Nutritional information per serving

Calories 385, Protein (g) 34, Carbohydrate (g) 43,
Fat (g) 8, Calories from Fat (%) 19, Saturated Fat (g) 2,
Dietary Fiber (g) 6, Cholesterol (mg) 75, Sodium (mg) 582
Diabetic Exchanges: *3 lean meat, 2 starch, 0.5 skim milk, 1.5 vegetable*

❄ Pork Tenderloin Diane with Wild Rice

Brown the tenderloins while the rice is cooking, for a fast-to-fix, one-dish meal with pizzazz.

1 (6-ounce) package long-grain and wild rice mix

2 pounds pork tenderloin, trimmed of fat, cut crosswise into 16 slices, each about 1 inch thick

Salt and pepper to taste

2 tablespoons margarine

¼ cup lemon juice

2 tablespoons Worcestershire sauce

1 tablespoon Dijon mustard

1 tablespoon chopped parsley

MAKES 6 TO 8 SERVINGS

Cook the wild rice according to the package directions, omitting any oil and salt.

Meanwhile, sprinkle the pork slices with the salt and pepper. Heat the margarine in a heavy skillet. Cook the slices 3 to 4 minutes on each side, until browned and cooked through, working in batches if necessary. Remove to a serving platter, and cover to keep warm.

Add the lemon juice, Worcestershire sauce, and mustard to the skillet. Cook over medium heat, stirring with the pork juices, until heated thoroughly, about 3 minutes. Return the pork to the sauce. Serve the pork and sauce over the rice, sprinkled with the parsley.

Nutritional information per serving

Calories 248, Protein (g) 26, Carbohydrate (g) 18,
Fat (g) 7, Calories from Fat (%) 27, Saturated Fat (g) 2,
Dietary Fiber (g) 0, Cholesterol (mg) 67, Sodium (mg) 483
Diabetic Exchanges: *3 lean meat, 1 starch*

❄ Glazed Pork Tenderloin

Pork tenderloin is a lean cut of meat that can be kept in the freezer to pull out for a quick dinner. This glaze enhances the meat with a subtly sweet, spicy flavor. Time permitting, let the meat marinate in the sauce.

2 tablespoons Dijon
   mustard
½ teaspoon minced garlic
½ teaspoon dried
   rosemary leaves
½ teaspoon dried thyme
   leaves
¼ teaspoon pepper
2 tablespoons honey
2 (1-pound) pork
   tenderloins, trimmed
   of fat

MAKES 6 TO 8 SERVINGS

Preheat the oven to 325°F.

   In a small bowl, mix together the mustard, garlic, rosemary, thyme, pepper, and honey. Coat the tenderloins with the mixture, and baste during cooking.

   Place the tenderloins on a baking sheet coated with nonstick cooking spray or on a rack in a shallow roasting pan. Bake for 40 to 45 minutes, or until a meat thermometer inserted into the thickest portion registers 160°F. Slice the tenderloins, and serve.

Nutritional information per serving
Calories 160, Protein (g) 24, Carbohydrate (g) 5,
Fat (g) 4, Calories from Fat (%) 24, Saturated Fat (g) 1,
Dietary Fiber (g) 0, Cholesterol (mg) 67, Sodium (mg) 138
Diabetic Exchanges: *3 lean meat, 1 other carbohydrate*

QUICK TIP

Tenderloins come two to a package. If one will be enough for you to serve, halve the recipe and freeze the other tenderloin.

THE HOLLY CLEGG TRIM & TERRIFIC COOKBOOK

MEAT

❄ Grilled Pork Tenderloin Oriental

This fabulous marinade (also great with flank steak) infuses the meat with tons of flavor.

¼ cup orange juice

¼ cup low-sodium
   soy sauce

3 tablespoons honey

1 tablespoon chopped
   garlic

1 bay leaf

½ teaspoon pepper

½ teaspoon dry mustard

½ teaspoon ground
   ginger

½ teaspoon onion
   powder

2 (1-pound) pork
   tenderloins, trimmed
   of fat

SERVES 6 TO 8

In a shallow dish, combine the orange juice, soy sauce, honey, garlic, bay leaf, pepper, mustard, ginger, and onion powder. Add the pork tenderloins. Marinate in the refrigerator at least 4 hours (time permitting) or overnight.

Grill the pork over medium-hot coals for 20 to 25 minutes, or bake at 350°F, basting with the marinade mixture, for 50 minutes, or until a meat thermometer registers 160°F. Discard unused marinade. Serve.

Nutritional information per serving
Calories 144, Protein (g) 24, Carbohydrate (g) 1,
Fat (g) 4, Calories from Fat (%) 27, Saturated Fat (g) 1,
Dietary Fiber (g) 0, Cholesterol (mg) 67, Sodium (mg) 243
Diabetic Exchanges: *3 lean meat*

QUICK TIP

The best way to test pork's doneness is with a meat thermometer. Cutting it to check on doneness lets too many good juices run out.

MEAT

❄ Pork Medallions with Brandy Sauce

This succulent, moist tenderloin is served with a rich, intensely flavored sauce.

1 (2 to 2½-pound)
   boneless pork
   tenderloin, trimmed
   of fat
Black pepper as needed
Brandy Sauce
⅔ cup canned fat-free
   chicken broth
2 tablespoons chopped
   green onions (scallions)
½ cup evaporated
   skimmed milk
2 tablespoons brandy
2 tablespoons margarine
1 tablespoon lemon juice
Salt to taste
⅛ teaspoon white
   pepper

MAKES 6 TO 8 SERVINGS

Preheat the oven to 325°F.

Rub the tenderloin with the black pepper. Place on a rack in a shallow baking pan coated with nonstick cooking spray. Roast until a meat thermometer registers 160°F (about 30 minutes per pound).

Meanwhile, for the Brandy Sauce, in a saucepan, combine the chicken broth and green onions. Bring to a boil; reduce the heat, cover, and simmer 2 minutes. Add the evaporated milk and brandy. Simmer, uncovered, over medium heat until the sauce is reduced to ⅔ cup, about 5 minutes. Add the margarine to the sauce, 1 tablespoon at a time, stirring constantly with a wire whisk. Stir in the lemon juice, salt, and white pepper. To serve, cut the meat and top with the sauce.

Nutritional information per serving
Calories 188, Protein (g) 25, Carbohydrate (g) 2,
Fat (g) 7, Calories from Fat (%) 35, Saturated Fat (g) 2,
Dietary Fiber (g) 0, Cholesterol (mg) 68, Sodium (mg) 151
Diabetic Exchanges: *3 lean meat*

MEAT

❄ Pork Tenderloin with Mustard Sauce

Many times I've served this on a buffet line with rolls. The mustard sauce superbly complements the tenderloin, adding a touch of sophistication.

¼ cup low-sodium
　soy sauce
¼ cup bourbon
2 tablespoons light
　brown sugar
2 pounds pork tenderloin,
　trimmed of fat
Mustard Sauce
　(recipe follows)

MAKES 6 TO 8 SERVINGS

In an 11 x 7 x 1½-inch baking dish, combine the soy sauce, bourbon, and brown sugar. Add the tenderloins. Cover and refrigerate at least 2 hours, turning occasionally.

Preheat the oven to 325°F.

Remove the meat from the marinade, discarding the marinade; place the tenderloins on a rack in a shallow roasting pan. Bake for 45 minutes, or until a meat thermometer inserted into the thickest portion registers 160°F. Serve with the Mustard Sauce (see recipe below).

Mustard Sauce

⅔ cup fat-free sour cream
⅔ cup light mayonnaise
2 tablespoons dry
　mustard
½ cup thinly sliced green
　onion (scallion)

MAKES ABOUT 1½ CUPS

In a small bowl, combine the sour cream, mayonnaise, dry mustard, and green onion. Cover, and chill in the refrigerator until ready to serve.

Nutritional information per serving
Calories 249, Protein (g) 27, Carbohydrate (g) 7,
Fat (g) 11, Calories from Fat (%) 43, Saturated Fat (g) 2,
Dietary Fiber (g) 0, Cholesterol (mg) 74, Sodium (mg) 420
Diabetic Exchanges: *3.5 lean meat, 0.5 other carbohydrate*

QUICK TIP

The leanest cuts of pork have "loin" names. Pork rib chops and boneless rib roasts are also good choices.

MEAT

Sweet-and-Sour Pork

Thumbs up for this version of sweet-and-sour pork. Diners clean their plates and say, "Forget going to Chinese restaurants, when I can enjoy this dish at home."

1½ pounds lean boneless pork tenderloin, trimmed of fat, sliced into thin slices

1 (8-ounce) can tomato sauce

¼ cup rice wine vinegar

2 tablespoons light brown sugar

1 tablespoon low-sodium soy sauce

¼ teaspoon minced garlic

⅛ teaspoon cayenne pepper

1 (20-ounce) can pineapple chunks with juice

1 green bell pepper, seeded and cut into 1-inch pieces

½ cup chopped green onion (scallion)

1 (11-ounce) can mandarin orange segments, drained

2 tablespoons cornstarch

3 cups cooked rice

MAKES 6 SERVINGS

Coat a skillet with nonstick cooking spray, and cook the pork over medium-high heat for 3 to 5 minutes, or until browned, stirring frequently. Add the tomato sauce, vinegar, brown sugar, soy sauce, garlic, and cayenne pepper, and bring to a boil. Cover, reduce the heat, and simmer for 10 minutes, or until the pork is tender.

Drain the pineapple, reserving the juice. To the pork mixture, add the pineapple, green pepper, green onion, and mandarin oranges; cover and simmer 5 minutes longer, or until the vegetables are crisp-tender.

Combine the cornstarch with the reserved pineapple juice, and stir into the pork mixture. Cook, stirring constantly, until thickened and boiling. To serve, spoon the pork mixture over the rice.

Nutritional information per serving
Calories 366, Protein (g) 27, Carbohydrate (g) 52,
Fat (g) 4, Calories from Fat (%) 11, Saturated Fat (g) 1,
Dietary Fiber (g) 2, Cholesterol (mg) 67, Sodium (mg) 339
Diabetic Exchanges: *3 lean meat, 1.5 starch, 1.5 fruit, 1 vegetable*

MEAT

❄ Italian Pork, Squash, and Tomatoes

This summer specialty showcases seasonal squash in a one-dish skillet with an array of wonderful herbs and seasonings.

2 pounds pork tenderloin, trimmed of fat, cut into 1½-inch cubes

2 cups sliced yellow squash (about 3 squash)

1 large zucchini, sliced

1 green bell pepper, seeded and coarsely chopped

1 onion, coarsely chopped

1 teaspoon minced garlic

4 large Roma (plum) tomatoes, quartered

1 teaspoon dried basil leaves

1 teaspoon dried oregano leaves

1 (28-ounce) can chopped tomatoes, with juice

MAKES 6 TO 8 SERVINGS

Heat a large skillet coated with nonstick cooking spray over high heat, and add the pork, squash, zucchini, green pepper, onion, garlic, Roma tomatoes, basil, and oregano. Cook, stirring, until the meat begins to brown and the vegetables are crisp-tender, about 10 minutes. Add the chopped tomatoes, and continue cooking, covered, over medium heat until the meat is done and the vegetables are tender, about 20 minutes. Serve.

Nutritional information per serving

Calories 199, Protein (g) 26, Carbohydrate (g) 13, Fat (g) 4, Calories from Fat (%) 19, Saturated Fat (g) 1, Dietary Fiber (g) 5, Cholesterol (mg) 67, Sodium (mg) 177
Diabetic Exchanges: *3 lean meat, 3 vegetable*

QUICK TIP

Store summer squash like crookneck yellow squash, pattypan, and zucchini in plastic bags in the refrigerator for no more than 5 days.

MEAT

❄ Veal Saltimbocca

This impressive dish is made company-capable by preparing it early and transferring it to a 2-quart casserole dish to reheat. My family enjoys this combination of veal and prosciutto in a light cheese sauce.

10 small lean veal
   scallopine (thin slices)
¼ cup all-purpose flour
10 tablespoons shredded
   part-skim Mozzarella
   cheese
10 slices prosciutto
   (about 2 ounces)
1½ cups fat-free canned
   chicken broth
½ cup white wine
Chopped parsley,
   for garnish

MAKES 4 TO 6 SERVINGS

Dust the veal with the flour. In a nonstick skillet coated with nonstick cooking spray, brown on both sides. Remove the veal from the pan, and top with the cheese. Place the prosciutto over the cheese (it will adhere to the cheese).

Add the chicken broth and wine to the pan, scraping to get all pieces off the pan. Reduce the liquid by half by boiling for about 5 minutes. Carefully place the prepared veal in the pan, cooking over low heat for 10 minutes, or until heated. Garnish with the chopped parsley, and serve.

Nutritional information per serving

Calories 195, Protein (g) 26, Carbohydrate (g) 5,
Fat (g) 6, Calories from Fat (%) 28, Saturated Fat (g) 3,
Dietary Fiber (g) 0, Cholesterol (mg) 94, Sodium (mg) 461
Diabetic Exchanges: 3.5 lean meat, 0.5 starch

FOOD FACT

Prosciutto is the Italian word for ham. This special Italian-style ham has been seasoned, salt cured, and air dried. When you purchase prosciutto, it is ready to eat.

MEAT

❄ Veal Marengo

This intensely herb-flavored sauce cooked with the veal teams up with fresh tomatoes and mushrooms. Quick and tasty, it's perfect to serve with pasta.

½ cup white wine, divided

2 pounds lean veal scallopine

1 onion, chopped

½ pound fresh mushrooms, sliced

½ teaspoon minced garlic

1 teaspoon dried basil leaves

1 teaspoon dried oregano leaves

1 bay leaf

1 cup chopped Roma (plum) tomato

1 bunch green onions (scallions), chopped

2 tablespoons chopped parsley

MAKES 8 SERVINGS

In a large skillet coated with nonstick cooking spray, bring ¼ cup white wine to a simmer. Add the veal, and brown on both sides. Add the onion, mushrooms, garlic, basil, oregano, bay leaf, tomato, and the remaining ¼ cup white wine. Cook, stirring, until the mushrooms and onions are tender and the veal is cooked through, about 7 minutes. Add the green onions and parsley, and continue cooking for 5 more minutes. Remove and discard the bay leaf before serving.

Nutritional information per serving
Calories 157, Protein (g) 24, Carbohydrate (g) 5,
Fat (g) 3, Calories from Fat (%) 20, Saturated Fat (g) 1,
Dietary Fiber (g) 1, Cholesterol (mg) 94, Sodium (mg) 104
Diabetic Exchanges: *3 very lean meat, 1 vegetable*

FOOD FACT

Marengo refers to a veal or chicken dish in which the meat is braised with tomatoes, onions, garlic, and wine. It is said to have been created by Napoleon's chef after the 1800 Battle of Marengo.

MEAT

❄ Veal Elegante

This veal with wonderful, savory-flavored sauce goes well with capellini.

1½ pounds thinly sliced
  veal scallopine

½ cup all-purpose flour

Salt and pepper to taste

2 tablespoons olive oil

1 cup sliced fresh
  mushrooms

1 green bell pepper,
  seeded and sliced

½ cup sliced green onion
  (scallion)

1 teaspoon minced garlic

1⅓ cups fat-free canned
  chicken broth

2 tablespoons lemon juice

MAKES 6 SERVINGS

Trim any fat from the veal. Combine the flour with the salt and pepper, and dredge the veal in the flour. In a large skillet coated with nonstick cooking spray, heat the olive oil over medium-high heat. Sauté the veal cutlets about 1½ minutes on each side, or just until done. Remove from the skillet, and set aside.

To the same skillet, add the mushrooms, green pepper, green onion, and garlic, cooking over low heat for about 5 minutes, or until almost tender. Add the chicken broth and lemon juice, scraping up the browned bits from the bottom of the pan. Bring to a boil, lower the heat, and return the veal to the sauce. Cook for 3 to 5 minutes, or until the veal is heated through. Serve immediately.

Nutritional information per serving
Calories 222, Protein (g) 25, Carbohydrate (g) 11,
Fat (g) 8, Calories from Fat (%) 33, Saturated Fat (g) 2,
Dietary Fiber (g) 1, Cholesterol (mg) 94, Sodium (mg) 238
Diabetic Exchanges: *3 lean meat, 0.5 starch*

QUICK TIP

When a recipe calls for mushrooms, try substituting shiitake or portabello mushrooms for a more intense mushroom flavor.

MEAT

❄ Veal with Tomatoes

Veal and pasta together is a natural, and with its spices, olives, and prosciutto, this dish has a distinct, flavorful personality.

1 large onion, thinly sliced

1 pound veal scallopine, cut into 1-inch strips

2 tablespoons all-purpose flour

½ cup dry white wine

1 teaspoon minced garlic

Salt and pepper to taste

1 teaspoon dried oregano leaves

1 teaspoon dried thyme leaves

5 medium Roma (plum) tomatoes, cut into wedges

1 (2¼-ounce) can sliced ripe black olives, drained

2 ounces prosciutto, cut into 1-inch slices

2 tablespoons chopped parsley

MAKES 6 SERVINGS

In a large skillet coated with nonstick cooking spray, sauté the onion over medium heat until tender, about 5 minutes. Sprinkle the veal with the flour, and add to the skillet, stirring constantly, cooking the veal until lightly browned.

Stir in the wine, garlic, salt, pepper, oregano, and thyme. Bring to a boil; cover, reduce the heat, and simmer 8 to 10 minutes, or until the veal is almost tender. Add the tomatoes and olives; cover and simmer 5 minutes, or until thoroughly heated. Add the prosciutto; cover, and let stand 2 minutes. Sprinkle with the parsley, and serve.

Nutritional information per serving
Calories 162, Protein (g) 19, Carbohydrate (g) 9, Fat (g) 5, Calories from Fat (%) 27, Saturated Fat (g) 1, Dietary Fiber (g) 2, Cholesterol (mg) 71, Sodium (mg) 334
Diabetic Exchanges: *2.5 lean meat, 1.5 vegetable*

QUICK TIP

Overcooking any cut of veal will toughen and ruin its delicate texture.

MEAT

Honey Mustard Lamb Chops

When you're in the mood for lamb, rosemary and honey mustard pair together to make this simple preparation a very special dish.

3 tablespoons honey

2 tablespoons Dijon
mustard

8 (4-ounce) lean lamb
loin chops (2 pounds)

1 teaspoon minced garlic

1 tablespoon dried
rosemary leaves

⅛ teaspoon pepper

MAKES 4 SERVINGS

In a small bowl, combine the honey and mustard; set aside.

Trim any excess fat from the chops. Rub both sides of the chops with the garlic, and press the rosemary and pepper onto both sides.

Place on a broiler pan covered with foil. Broil the chops close to heat for about 5 minutes. Turn the chops, and spread with the honey mixture; broil for several minutes more, or until done. Serve.

Nutritional information per serving
Calories 235, Protein (g) 26, Carbohydrate (g) 14, Fat (g) 7, Calories from Fat (%) 30, Saturated Fat (g) 3, Dietary Fiber (g) 0, Cholesterol (mg) 81, Sodium (mg) 264
Diabetic Exchanges: *4 lean meat, 1 other carbohydrate*

QUICK TIP

Lamb ribs and loin should be cooked rare to medium rare, since overcooking lamb makes it dry and tough. These cuts are the most tender and least fatty.

MEAT

Lamb Loin Chops with Mint Sauce

Marinate this savory sensation ahead to cook when needed. The light mint sauce perfectly complements the lamb.

1 tablespoon dried mint
1 teaspoon ground cumin
1 teaspoon garlic powder
½ teaspoon ground
   cinnamon
Salt and pepper to taste
1½ pounds lamb loin
   chops
Mint Sauce
   (recipe follows)

Mint Sauce

1 tablespoon olive oil
¼ teaspoon minced garlic
1 tablespoon lemon juice
1 teaspoon dried mint
¼ cup fat-free canned
   chicken broth

MAKES 4 SERVINGS

In a large zipper-lock bag, combine the mint, cumin, garlic powder, cinnamon, salt, and pepper. Add the lamb chops, and shake the bag. Refrigerate until ready to cook.

Heat a large nonstick skillet coated with nonstick cooking spray over medium-high heat. Place the lamb chops in the skillet, and cook until crusty and browned, about 5 minutes on each side. Serve with the Mint Sauce (see recipe below).

In a microwave-safe dish or in a small pot on the stove, heat the oil, garlic, lemon juice, mint, and chicken broth until bubbly hot.

Nutritional information per serving
Calories 170, Protein (g) 20, Carbohydrate (g) 2,
Fat (g) 9, Calories from Fat (%) 49, Saturated Fat (g) 2,
Dietary Fiber (g) 0, Cholesterol (mg) 61, Sodium (mg) 104
Diabetic Exchanges: 3 lean meat

MEAT

❄ Asian Meat Marinade

This recipe makes enough marinade that you could increase the amount of meat if necessary. Marinade-infused flavor colors every bite of this marvelous dish. Try with different cuts of beef or pork.

1 cup mirin
1 teaspoon ground
   ginger
1 serrano chile pepper,
   minced
1 teaspoon minced garlic
2 green onions
   (scallions), sliced
1 cup light beer
1 cup low-sodium
   soy sauce
½ cup chopped cilantro,
   optional
6 (4-ounce) beef
   tenderloin fillets

MAKES 6 SERVINGS

In a shallow dish, mix together the mirin, ginger, serrano chile, garlic, green onions, beer, soy sauce, and cilantro; add the fillets. Marinate the fillets for at least 2 hours, time permitting. Grill, or pan-sear on a hot skillet about 5 to 10 minutes on each side, depending on how well-cooked you like the meat. Serve immediately.

Nutritional information per serving
Calories 177, Protein (g) 24, Carbohydrate (g) 0, Fat (g) 8, Calories from Fat (%) 44, Saturated Fat (g) 3, Dietary Fiber (g) 0, Cholesterol (mg) 70, Sodium (mg) 1,093
Diabetic Exchanges: *3 lean meat*

QUICK TIP

If mirin is not available, substitute 2 tablespoons vermouth mixed with 1 teaspoon sugar. If you don't have vermouth, use another light sweet wine.

Pecan Trout with Dijon Sauce 285

Spicy Baked Fish 286

Fish Florentine 287

Mediterranean Catch 288

Pizza Baked Fish 289

Baked Fish with Shrimp Stuffing 290

Trout Eggplant Parmesan 291

Seafood

Fish Fry 292

Superb Salmon Steaks 293

Salmon Framboise 294

Glazed Salmon 294

Salmon Patties with Horseradish Caper Sauce 295

Tuna Steaks with Horseradish Sauce 296

Crabmeat au Gratin 297

Crabmeat Enchiladas 298

Crab Cakes 299

Shrimp Fried Rice 300

Italian Shrimp (Barbecue Shrimp) 301

Broiled Marinated Shrimp 302

Shrimp with Caper Clam Sauce 303

Shrimp Clemanceau 304

Shrimp with Mango Salsa 305

Shrimp Tacos with Tropical Salsa 306

Grilled Shrimp 307

Shrimp Sauté 307

Scampi Italian Style 308

Shrimp-and-Spinach Skillet Surprise 309

Shrimp-and-Spinach White Pizza 310

Cheesy Shrimp Rice Casserole 311

Speedy Shrimp Jambalaya 312

Crawfish Elegante 313

Crawfish Étouffée 314

Crawfish and Rice Casserole 315

Scallop Stir-Fry with Crispy Noodle Pancakes 316

Broiled Scallops 317

Seafood Casserole 318

Seafood and Wild Rice Casserole 319

Baked Italian Oysters 320

Pecan Trout with Dijon Sauce

The fish can also be pan-sautéed in a skillet, if you prefer. The simple sauce and toasted pecans are prepared in a snap, and this dish is elegant enough for company.

6 (4-ounce) trout fillets
Salt and pepper to taste
½ cup Italian bread crumbs
¼ cup nonfat plain yogurt
1 tablespoon Dijon mustard
1 tablespoon lemon juice
3 tablespoons chopped pecans, toasted
½ cup sliced green onion (scallion), optional

MAKES 6 SERVINGS

Preheat the broiler.

Season the fillets with the salt and pepper. In a rectangular baking dish coated with nonstick cooking spray, arrange the fillets in a single layer. Top evenly with the bread crumbs. Cook under the broiler about 5 to 7 minutes, or until the fish flakes easily when tested with a fork.

Meanwhile, combine the yogurt, mustard, and lemon juice in a small bowl. Transfer to a serving dish. Spoon 1 tablespoon sauce over the hot fish, and sprinkle the pecans evenly over each fillet. Sprinkle with the green onion, if desired. Serve immediately.

Nutritional information per serving
Calories 206, Protein (g) 26, Carbohydrate (g) 8,
Fat (g) 7, Calories from Fat (%) 32, Saturated Fat (g) 1,
Dietary Fiber (g) 1, Cholesterol (mg) 67, Sodium (mg) 246
Diabetic Exchanges: *3 lean meat, 0.5 starch*

QUICK TIP

To test fish for doneness, prod it with a fork at its thickest point. Properly cooked fish is opaque, has milky white juices and just begins to flake easily. Don't overcook or it will be dry.

SEAFOOD

Spicy Baked Fish

A quick, tasty, and popular choice for preparing trout, catfish, orange roughy, or any mild-flavored fish.

1 pound fish fillets

2 tablespoons light mayonnaise

1 teaspoon lemon juice

½ teaspoon prepared mustard

½ teaspoon sugar

¼ teaspoon Worcestershire sauce

½ teaspoon garlic powder

⅛ teaspoon cayenne pepper

Paprika, as needed

MAKES 4 SERVINGS

Preheat the oven to 500°F. Rinse the fish fillets, and pat dry.

In a small dish, combine the mayonnaise, lemon juice, mustard, sugar, Worcestershire sauce, garlic powder, and cayenne pepper.

Lay the fish in an oblong baking dish coated with nonstick cooking spray. Spread the mayonnaise mixture over the fillets. Let sit to marinate for 30 minutes. Sprinkle with the paprika. Bake for 10 to 15 minutes, or until the fish flakes easily with a fork. Serve immediately.

Nutritional information per serving

Calories 108, Protein (g) 17, Carbohydrate (g) 2, Fat (g) 3, Calories from Fat (%) 29, Saturated Fat (g) 0, Dietary Fiber (g) 0, Cholesterol (mg) 25, Sodium (mg) 142
Diabetic Exchanges: *3 very lean meat*

QUICK TIP

Don't overcook fish—cook it just until it begins to flake.

SEAFOOD

Fish Florentine

Any fresh fish such as flounder, trout, or orange roughy would work well with this recipe. Creamy spinach and dill-seasoned fish pair together for simple gourmet dining.

2 (10-ounce) packages frozen chopped spinach

¼ cup all-purpose flour

1 cup skim milk

½ cup fat-free canned chicken broth

½ cup fat-free sour cream

2 pounds fish fillets

1 teaspoon dried dill weed leaves

Salt and pepper to taste

2 tablespoons lemon juice

MAKES 6 SERVINGS

Preheat the oven to 350°F.

Cook the spinach according to the package directions. Drain very well; set aside.

Place the flour in a small saucepan, and gradually whisk in the milk and chicken broth. Cook over medium heat until thickened, stirring about 5 minutes. Remove from the heat, and fold in the sour cream. Stir 1 cup of the sauce into the spinach, mixing well.

Spread the creamed spinach on the bottom of a 2-quart casserole dish coated with nonstick cooking spray. Arrange the fish fillets over the spinach. Sprinkle the fish with the dill weed, salt, and pepper; drizzle with the lemon juice. Pour the remaining sauce over the fish.

Bake, covered with foil, for 30 minutes, or until the fish is done and flakes easily when tested with a fork. Serve immediately.

Nutritional information per serving
Calories 220, Protein (g) 35, Carbohydrate (g) 14,
Fat (g) 2, Calories from Fat (%) 9, Saturated Fat (g) 1,
Dietary Fiber (g) 3, Cholesterol (mg) 73, Sodium (mg) 282
Diabetic Exchanges: *4 very lean meat, 0.5 starch, 1 vegetable*

SEAFOOD

Mediterranean Catch

Feta, tomatoes, peppers, and oregano give this delectable fish dish a Greek flair.

1 large onion, sliced

1 large green bell pepper, seeded and cut into thin strips

1 cup sliced Roma (plum) tomatoes

1 tablespoon minced garlic

2 pounds firm-textured fish fillets (such as redfish, snapper, grouper)

Salt and pepper to taste

1 teaspoon dried oregano leaves

½ cup crumbled Feta cheese

1 tablespoon chopped parsley, optional

MAKES 6 SERVINGS

Preheat the oven to 375°F.

In a large skillet coated with nonstick cooking spray, sauté the onion and green pepper over medium heat until tender, about 5 minutes. Add the tomato slices and garlic, stirring for several more minutes.

Arrange the fish in a single layer in a 3-quart oblong baking dish coated with nonstick cooking spray. Season with salt and pepper, and sprinkle with the oregano. Spoon the vegetable mixture over the seasoned fish. Sprinkle with the Feta.

Bake for 20 to 25 minutes, or until the fish flakes easily with a fork. Sprinkle with the parsley, and serve immediately.

Nutritional information per serving

Calories 204, Protein (g) 31, Carbohydrate (g) 7, Fat (g) 5, Calories from Fat (%) 24, Saturated Fat (g) 2, Dietary Fiber (g) 2, Cholesterol (mg) 75, Sodium (mg) 257
Diabetic Exchanges: *4 lean meat, 1.5 vegetable*

SEAFOOD

❄ Pizza Baked Fish

Now you can have all the appealing flavors of pizza in a fish dish.

½ pound sliced fresh
  mushrooms, divided
⅔ cup chopped onion
½ teaspoon minced garlic
¾ cup water
½ cup tomato paste
1 teaspoon dried basil
  leaves
1 teaspoon dried
  oregano leaves
¼ teaspoon sugar
⅛ teaspoon crushed red
  pepper flakes
Salt and pepper
2 pounds red snapper
  fillets or fish of choice
1 green bell pepper,
  seeded and sliced
  into rings
1 cup shredded part-skim
  Mozzarella cheese

MAKES 6 SERVINGS

Preheat the oven to 400°F.

In a skillet coated with nonstick cooking spray, combine half the mushrooms, the onion, and the garlic, and sauté over medium heat until tender, about 5 minutes. Add the water, tomato paste, basil, oregano, sugar, red pepper flakes, salt, and pepper. Bring to a boil, reduce the heat, and simmer, uncovered, for 5 minutes, stirring occasionally. Remove from the heat.

Place the fish in a 2-quart oblong baking dish coated with nonstick cooking spray. Season with the salt and pepper, and pour the sauce over the fish. Top with the remaining mushrooms and the green pepper rings.

Bake the fish for 15 minutes. Sprinkle with the Mozzarella, and continue baking for 5 minutes, or until the fish flakes with a fork and the cheese is melted. Serve immediately.

Nutritional information per serving

*Calories 243, Protein (g) 38, Carbohydrate (g) 10,
Fat (g) 5, Calories from Fat (%) 20, Saturated Fat (g) 2,
Dietary Fiber (g) 3, Cholesterol (mg) 67, Sodium (mg) 204*
Diabetic Exchanges: *5 very lean meat, 2 vegetable*

SEAFOOD

Baked Fish with Shrimp Stuffing

Fish sandwiched with a shrimp stuffing baked in a tomato sauce is the ultimate! Make ahead and refrigerate until time to bake. Use the fish of your choice.

1 tablespoon minced garlic

¾ cup sliced green onion (scallion), divided

1 pound small peeled shrimp

1½ cups Italian bread crumbs

Salt and pepper to taste

2 pounds fish fillets (such as trout)

1 (15-ounce) can tomato sauce

½ cup dry white wine or clam juice

1 teaspoon sugar

1 tablespoon minced parsley

MAKES 6 SERVINGS

Preheat the oven to 350°F. Coat a 2-quart oblong baking dish with nonstick cooking spray.

In a large skillet coated with nonstick cooking spray, sauté the garlic, ½ cup green onion, and the shrimp, stirring, until done. Add the bread crumbs, and season to taste; set aside.

Arrange half the fish fillets along the bottom of the prepared baking dish. Season with the salt and pepper. Top the fish with all the shrimp mixture. Arrange the remaining fish fillets on top, and season with the salt and pepper.

In a small bowl, combine the tomato sauce, wine, sugar, and parsley. Pour over the fish. Bake, uncovered, for 30 to 40 minutes, or until the fish flakes easily with a fork. Sprinkle with the remaining ¼ cup green onion, and serve immediately.

Nutritional information per serving

Calories 391, Protein (g) 48, Carbohydrate (g) 27,
Fat (g) 7, Calories from Fat (%) 17, Saturated Fat (g) 1,
Dietary Fiber (g) 2, Cholesterol (mg) 197, Sodium (mg) 1,000
Diabetic Exchanges: *6 very lean meat, 1.5 starch, 1 vegetable*

SEAFOOD

Trout Eggplant Parmesan

This recipe gets a thumbs-up and is well worth the extra steps for the eggplant, topped with fried fish, red sauce, and cheese. (Prepare early in the day, and bake just before serving.)

1 eggplant, peeled
1 cup chopped tomatoes
1 (15-ounce) can tomato sauce
1 onion, chopped
1 green bell pepper, seeded and chopped
1 teaspoon dried oregano leaves
1 teaspoon dried basil leaves
1 tablespoon minced garlic
Salt and pepper to taste
⅛ teaspoon cayenne pepper
⅓ cup grated Parmesan cheese
½ cup Italian bread crumbs
½ cup all-purpose flour
1 tablespoon chopped parsley
½ cup skim milk
1½ pounds trout fillets
1½ cups shredded part-skim Mozzarella cheese

MAKES 6 SERVINGS

Preheat the broiler. Coat a 2-quart oblong casserole dish with nonstick cooking spray.

Cut the eggplant into ½-inch slices. Place the eggplant in a broiler pan, and broil for 5 minutes on each side. Remove the eggplant, and place in the bottom of the prepared casserole dish.

Preheat the oven to 350°F.

In a large saucepan, stir together the chopped tomatoes, tomato sauce, onion, green pepper, oregano, basil, garlic, salt, pepper, and cayenne pepper. Bring the mixture to a boil, reduce the heat, and cook for about 7 minutes; set aside.

In a small shallow bowl, combine the Parmesan cheese, bread crumbs, flour, and parsley. In another small shallow bowl, place the milk. Dip the fillets first in the milk and then in the Parmesan cheese mixture, pressing to coat.

In a large skillet coated with nonstick cooking spray, sauté the fish until crisp and cooked through, several minutes on each side. Remove the fillets from the skillet, and place them on top of the eggplant in the casserole dish. Spread the tomato mixture over the cooked fillets. Sprinkle with the Mozzarella cheese. Bake for 10 minutes, or until the cheese is melted. Serve immediately.

Nutritional information per serving
Calories 382, Protein (g) 38, Carbohydrate (g) 32, Fat (g) 11, Calories from Fat (%) 26, Saturated Fat (g) 5, Dietary Fiber (g) 4, Cholesterol (mg) 88, Sodium (mg) 826
Diabetic Exchanges: *4 lean meat, 1 starch, 3 vegetable*

Fish Fry

In the South, we love those fish frys with fresh fish. Here's my version without the guilt.
If you can't find the seasoned fish fry, substitute cornmeal with seasonings.

½ cup skim milk

1 teaspoon garlic powder

Dash cayenne pepper

1 teaspoon Dijon mustard

Salt and pepper to taste

2 pounds fish fillets
   (such as trout)

1 cup commercially
   prepared seasoned
   fish fry

1 teaspoon baking
   powder

2 tablespoons canola oil

¼ cup lemon juice

2 tablespoons chopped
   parsley

MAKES 6 SERVINGS

In a large bowl, combine the milk, garlic powder, cayenne pepper, mustard, salt, and pepper. Add the fish fillets, and refrigerate for at least 30 minutes and up to several hours.

On a plate, combine the fish fry and baking powder. Remove each fillet, and roll in the fish fry mix to cover; set aside.

In a large frying pan coated with nonstick cooking spray, heat the oil over medium-high heat, and sauté the fish on each side for several minutes, or until flaky. Sprinkle with the lemon juice and parsley, heat for a minute longer, and serve immediately.

Nutritional information per serving

Calories 313, Protein (g) 33, Carbohydrate (g) 19,
Fat (g) 10, Calories from Fat (%) 31, Saturated Fat (g) 1,
Dietary Fiber (g) 1, Cholesterol (mg) 90, Sodium (mg) 853
Diabetic Exchanges: 4 lean meat, 1.5 starch

QUICK TIP

The best way to thaw frozen fish is in milk. The milk draws out the frozen taste and gives the fish a fresh flavor.

Superb Salmon Steaks

Fast and easy, this dish never fails to wow the eaters. Double the recipe as needed.

1 tablespoon Dijon
mustard

1 tablespoon honey

1 pound 1-inch-thick
salmon steaks

½ teaspoon dried
tarragon leaves

1 Roma (plum) tomato,
sliced

1 tablespoon drained
capers

¼ cup white wine

MAKES 2 TO 3 SERVINGS

Preheat the oven to 400°F.

In a small bowl, combine the mustard and honey. Place the salmon steaks in a baking dish, and coat with the mustard mixture. Sprinkle with the tarragon, sliced tomato, and capers. Pour the wine in the dish. Bake for 18 to 25 minutes, or until done as desired. Serve immediately.

Nutritional information per serving

Calories 215, Protein (g) 31, Carbohydrate (g) 7,
Fat (g) 5, Calories from Fat (%) 23, Saturated Fat (g) 1,
Dietary Fiber (g) 0, Cholesterol (mg) 79, Sodium (mg) 309
Diabetic Exchanges: 4 very lean meat, 0.5 other carbohydrate

FOOD FACT

Salmon is a fatty fish providing a good supply of health protective omega-3 fatty acids. It's also a good source of high-quality protein.

SEAFOOD

Salmon Framboise

Fine dining with simple elegance that will thrill your taste buds.

1 cup dry white wine
¼ cup raspberry
  preserves
1 tablespoon green
  peppercorns
4 (6-ounce) salmon fillets

MAKES 4 SERVINGS

In a small bowl, mix the wine, preserves, and green peppercorns. Pour over the salmon fillets, and refrigerate for 4 hours.

Preheat the oven to 375°F. Bake the fillets for 20 minutes, or until done as desired. Serve immediately.

Nutritional information per serving

Calories 277, Protein (g) 34, Carbohydrate (g) 15,
Fat (g) 6, Calories from Fat (%) 20, Saturated Fat (g) 1,
Dietary Fiber (g) 1, Cholesterol (mg) 88, Sodium (mg) 128
Diabetic Exchanges: *5 very lean meat, 1 other carbohydrate*

Glazed Salmon

Easy elegance! Diners say this is the best salmon they have ever had. The glaze on the crispy, crusted salmon takes only minutes to prepare—and to disappear from the plate.

¼ cup honey
2 tablespoons low-
  sodium soy sauce
2 tablespoons lime juice
1 tablespoon Dijon
  mustard
4 (6-ounce) salmon fillets

MAKES 4 SERVINGS

In a small bowl, whisk together the honey, soy sauce, lime juice, and mustard. Marinate the salmon in the sauce in the refrigerator for several hours, or until ready to cook.

In a nonstick skillet coated with nonstick cooking spray, cook the salmon on each side, 3 to 5 minutes, until golden brown, crispy, and just cooked through. Transfer the salmon to a platter. Add the remaining honey glaze to the skillet, and simmer, stirring, until the mixture comes to a boil. Return the salmon to the pan, heat thoroughly, and serve immediately.

Nutritional information per serving

Calories 273, Protein (g) 35, Carbohydrate (g) 19,
Fat (g) 6, Calories from Fat (%) 20, Saturated Fat (g) 1,
Dietary Fiber (g) 0, Cholesterol (mg) 88, Sodium (mg) 400
Diabetic Exchanges: *5 very lean meat, 1 other carbohydrate*

Salmon Patties with Horseradish Caper Sauce

Try using fresh salmon to whip up these wonderful croquettes for a light evening meal or lunch or as an appetizer. The sauce adds fat to the recipe, so just watch your portions. It's so good.

1¼ pounds salmon fillets, skinned

⅓ cup finely chopped onion

3 tablespoons light mayonnaise

½ teaspoon dried dill weed leaves

½ cup Italian bread crumbs

Salt and pepper to taste

Horseradish Caper Sauce (recipe follows)

MAKES 6 PATTIES

Trim the salmon, and cut into 2-inch cubes; place in a food processor, or chop finely by hand. Add the onion, mayonnaise, dill weed, and bread crumbs, mixing well. Season to taste with the salt and pepper.

Coat a skillet with nonstick cooking spray, and heat. Shape the salmon mixture into 6 patties; brown the patties over high heat for 1 minute. Lower the heat, and continue cooking for a few minutes; turn over, and continue cooking about 3 more minutes, or until the salmon is done. Do not overcook. Serve with Horseradish Caper Sauce (see recipe below).

Horseradish Caper Sauce

¼ cup light mayonnaise

2 tablespoons prepared horseradish

1 tablespoon lemon juice

1 tablespoon finely chopped onion

1 teaspoon capers, drained

In a small bowl, stir together the mayonnaise, horseradish, lemon juice, onion, and capers. Refrigerate until serving.

Nutritional information per serving

Calories 212, Protein (g) 21, Carbohydrate (g) 10, Fat (g) 10, Calories from Fat (%) 41, Saturated Fat (g) 1, Dietary Fiber (g) 1, Cholesterol (mg) 55, Sodium (mg) 377
Diabetic Exchanges: *3 lean meat, 0.5 starch*

SEAFOOD

Tuna Steaks with Horseradish Sauce

Impressive, intensely herb-flavored tuna seared in the pan with this distinctive sauce is a winning selection. Serve the Horseradish Sauce with other recipes, too.

1½ to 2 pounds tuna steaks, 1- to 2-inches thick

3 tablespoons finely chopped blanched almonds

¼ cup all-purpose flour

1 teaspoon minced garlic

1 tablespoon dried basil leaves

1 tablespoon dried thyme leaves

1 tablespoon dried rosemary leaves

1 teaspoon coarsely ground pepper

2 tablespoons water

2 tablespoons white wine, optional

Horseradish Sauce (recipe follows)

Horseradish Sauce

⅔ cup light mayonnaise

1½ tablespoons prepared horseradish

1½ tablespoons grainy or other spicy mustard

MAKES 4 SERVINGS

Rinse and trim the tuna steaks.

In a food processor or with a fork, combine the almonds, flour, garlic, basil, thyme, rosemary, pepper, and water to make a paste. Spread the paste on both sides of the tuna steaks, and refrigerate until ready to use.

Heat a skillet coated with nonstick cooking spray over medium heat until hot, and cook the tuna steaks 3 to 5 minutes on each side, depending on thickness, until done. Tuna is usually served rare. If desired, wine can be added to the pan while cooking. Serve with Horseradish Sauce (see recipe below).

FOOD FACT

Tuna is high in omega-3 fatty acids, which have been linked with possible protection against heart disease.

MAKES 1 CUP SAUCE

In a small bowl, combine the mayonnaise, horseradish, and mustard, mixing well.

Nutritional information per serving
Calories 386, Protein (g) 40, Carbohydrate (g) 14,
Fat (g) 18, Calories from Fat (%) 43, Saturated Fat (g) 3,
Dietary Fiber (g) 2, Cholesterol (mg) 94, Sodium (mg) 497
***Diabetic Exchanges:** 5 very lean meat, 1 starch, 2.5 fat*

SEAFOOD

❄ Crabmeat au Gratin

You won't even be able to tell this is a healthier version of one of the Louisiana greats.

1 cup thinly sliced green
onion (scallion)

2 tablespoons finely
chopped fresh parsley

3 tablespoons margarine

3 tablespoons all-purpose
flour

Salt and pepper to taste

1½ cups skim milk

1 tablespoon sherry,
optional

1½ to 2 pounds lump
crabmeat

1 cup shredded reduced-
fat sharp Cheddar
cheese

MAKES 6 TO 8 SERVINGS

Preheat the oven to 375°F.

In a saucepan, sauté the green onion and parsley in the margarine until tender. Stir in the flour. Add the salt and pepper. Gradually add the milk, stirring over low heat until the mixture thickens and is bubbly. Remove the pan from the heat; add the sherry. Gently fold in the crabmeat.

Place the mixture in a casserole dish or individual ramekins. Sprinkle with the cheese. Bake for 10 to 15 minutes, or until the cheese is melted. Serve.

Nutritional information per serving
*Calories 204, Protein (g) 25, Carbohydrate (g) 6,
Fat (g) 8, Calories from Fat (%) 36, Saturated Fat (g) 3,
Dietary Fiber (g) 1, Cholesterol (mg) 73, Sodium (mg) 488*
Diabetic Exchanges: *3.5 lean meat, 0.5 starch*

QUICK TIP

The price of fresh crabmeat is determined by the quality, and goes from lump, backfin lump, white, and claw. In Au Gratin you should use lump or white crabmeat.

SEAFOOD

❄ Crabmeat Enchiladas

These simple enchiladas are enhanced with a tasty white sauce, resulting in a mildly flavored, creamy Southwestern dish.

1 pound lump white
    crabmeat, picked for
    shells
½ cup chopped onion
¾ cup shredded reduced-
    fat Monterey Jack
    cheese
1 (4-ounce) can chopped
    green chilies
16 to 18 (6- to 8-inch)
    tortillas (flour, flavored,
    or whole wheat)
White Sauce
    (recipe follows)
¼ cup shredded reduced-
    fat Cheddar cheese
Sliced green onion,
    optional

White Sauce

2 tablespoons chopped
    onion
2 cloves garlic, minced
1 tablespoon margarine
¼ cup all-purpose flour
1 (14½-ounce) can
    fat-free chicken broth
1 (4-ounce) can chopped
    green chilies, drained
1 cup nonfat plain yogurt
    or sour cream

MAKES 8 SERVINGS

Preheat the oven to 350°F.

In a mixing bowl, combine the crabmeat, onion, Monterey Jack cheese, and green chilies.

Warm the tortillas a few seconds in the microwave to make them easier to roll. Place 1 heaping tablespoon of the filling on the edge of each tortilla, rolling up with the filling in the center.

Place the filled tortillas in a 2-quart baking dish. Pour the White Sauce over the filled tortillas. Sprinkle with the Cheddar cheese and green onion. Bake for 30 minutes, or until thoroughly heated, and serve.

QUICK TIP

When you're watching your fat intake, the sharper the cheese the better, because you can use less of it for the same amount of flavor.

In a medium saucepan, sauté the onion and garlic in the margarine until tender. Add the flour, and gradually add the chicken broth and green chilies. Bring to a boil, stirring, until the mixture thickens; reduce heat. Stir in the yogurt until smooth. Pour over the filled enchiladas.

Nutritional information per serving

Calories 316, Protein (g) 22, Carbohydrate (g) 45, Fat (g) 5, Calories from Fat (%) 13, Saturated Fat (g) 2, Dietary Fiber (g) 3, Cholesterol (mg) 42, Sodium (mg) 1,065
Diabetic Exchanges: *2 very lean meat, 3 starch*

SEAFOOD

Crab Cakes

Go gourmet with ease by preparing this mouthwatering recipe—an absolutely terrific crab cake. Make early in the day, refrigerate, and cook before serving.

1 pint lump white crabmeat, picked for shells

⅓ cup finely diced green bell pepper

½ cup thinly sliced green onion (scallion)

1 (11-ounce) can Mexi-corn, drained

⅓ cup light mayonnaise

¾ cup Italian bread crumbs

1 egg, beaten

½ teaspoon hot pepper sauce

½ cup cornmeal

MAKES 12 CRAB CAKES

In a large bowl, combine the crabmeat, green pepper, green onion, corn, mayonnaise, bread crumbs, egg, and hot pepper sauce. Mix well.

Place the cornmeal in a shallow dish. Shape the crabmeat mixture into 12 equal cakes. Dredge each cake in the cornmeal to coat both sides well.

In a large skillet coated with nonstick cooking spray, set over medium-low heat, carefully add the crab cakes; cook until golden brown and cooked through, about 4 minutes on each side. Serve warm.

Nutritional information per serving
Calories 116, Protein (g) 7, Carbohydrate (g) 14, Fat (g) 3, Calories from Fat (%) 26, Saturated Fat (g) 1, Dietary Fiber (g) 1, Cholesterol (mg) 35, Sodium (mg) 347
Diabetic Exchanges: *0.5 lean meat, 1 starch*

QUICK TIP

Always use your fingers to pick over crabmeat, fresh or canned, to make sure there are no tiny pieces of shells.

SEAFOOD

❄ Shrimp Fried Rice

This really is a family favorite—it tastes like you ordered it from a Chinese restaurant. For a vegetable fried rice, just delete the shrimp; you can even add cooked chicken to please your taste buds. A good choice!

2 eggs, lightly beaten
1 tablespoon peanut oil
1 pound peeled small shrimp
1 cup chopped onion
½ pound fresh mushrooms, sliced
3 tablespoons low-sodium soy sauce, plus additional for serving
1 tablespoon minced garlic
4 cups cooked rice
1 cup sliced green onion (scallion)
1 (5-ounce) can sliced water chestnuts, drained
1 cup frozen green peas
1 tablespoon sesame oil

MAKES 6 SERVINGS

In a large skillet coated with nonstick cooking spray, cook the eggs without stirring (as with an omelet) until the eggs are almost dry; set aside.

In a large skillet, heat the peanut oil over high heat. Add the shrimp, onion, and mushroom slices, sautéing until the mushroom slices are tender, 5 to 7 minutes. Stir in 3 tablespoons soy sauce, the garlic, and rice; cook about 3 minutes, stirring frequently. Add the green onion, water chestnuts, peas, and sesame oil. Cut the egg into thin strips, add to the skillet, and stir. Stir-fry 1 minute more to heat the water chestnuts and peas. Serve with additional soy sauce, if desired.

Nutritional information per serving
Calories 320, Protein (g) 20, Carbohydrate (g) 42,
Fat (g) 7, Calories from Fat (%) 21, Saturated Fat (g) 2,
Dietary Fiber (g) 4, Cholesterol (mg) 178, Sodium (mg) 376
Diabetic Exchanges: *2 lean meat, 2 starch, 2 vegetables*

SEAFOOD

Italian Shrimp (Barbecue Shrimp)

Italian or Barbecue Shrimp is probably one of the best recipes in this book. I've made it all over the country to the same overwhelming response. Make sure to have a loaf of hot French bread to dip in the unbelievable sauce.

¼ cup olive oil

½ cup fat-free Italian dressing

6 cloves garlic, minced

1 teaspoon hot pepper sauce

¼ cup Worcestershire sauce

8 bay leaves

2 teaspoons paprika

1 teaspoon dried oregano leaves

1 teaspoon dried rosemary leaves

1 teaspoon dried thyme leaves

1 teaspoon pepper

1 teaspoon salt, optional

2 pounds unpeeled headless large shrimp

2 ounces dry white wine

MAKES 4 TO 6 SERVINGS

In a large, heavy skillet, combine the oil, Italian dressing, garlic, hot pepper sauce, Worcestershire sauce, bay leaves, paprika, oregano, rosemary, thyme, pepper, and salt. Cook over medium heat until the sauce begins to boil. Add the shrimp. Cook approximately 10 minutes. Add the wine, and cook another 5 to 7 minutes, or until the shrimp are done. Serve the shrimp with the sauce.

Nutritional information per serving

Calories 206, Protein (g) 20, Carbohydrate (g) 6, Fat (g) 10, Calories from Fat (%) 46, Saturated Fat (g) 2, Dietary Fiber (g) 1, Cholesterol (mg) 180, Sodium (mg) 610
***Diabetic Exchanges**: 3 lean meat, 0.5 other carbohydrate*

FOOD FACT

Shrimp are high in omega-3 fatty acids.

SEAFOOD

Broiled Marinated Shrimp

This simply prepared dish has an abundance of flavor. You can marinate early in the day and prepare later. It's perfect for grilling as well.

2 pounds unpeeled
   large shrimp
Salt and pepper to taste
2 tablespoons olive oil
1 lemon, thinly sliced
¼ cup lemon juice
¼ cup Worcestershire
   sauce
1 teaspoon minced garlic
2 bay leaves
1 teaspoon dried
   oregano leaves

MAKES 4 TO 6 SERVINGS

Spread the shrimp in a 13 x 9 x 2-inch baking pan coated with nonstick cooking spray or lined with foil. Sprinkle with the salt and pepper.

In a small bowl, combine the olive oil, sliced lemon, lemon juice, Worcestershire sauce, garlic, bay leaves, and oregano. Mix well, and pour evenly over the shrimp. Refrigerate, and marinate 30 minutes to 1 hour.

When ready to cook, preheat the broiler. Place the pan under the broiler for 10 to 15 minutes, until the shrimp are done, turning the shrimp once. Serve immediately.

Nutritional information per serving
Calories 143, Protein (g) 19, Carbohydrate (g) 3,
Fat (g) 6, Calories from Fat (%) 36, Saturated Fat (g) 1,
Dietary Fiber (g) 0, Cholesterol (mg) 179, Sodium (mg) 317
Diabetic Exchanges: *3 lean meat*

FOOD FACT

Shrimp contains above average concentrations of selenium, an enzyme believed to function as an antioxidant.

Shrimp with Caper Clam Sauce

Clam juice, found with the canned seafood in the grocery store, adds a nice touch to the sauce in this quick, tasty recipe.

2 pounds peeled
   large shrimp
¼ cup all-purpose flour
2 tablespoons olive oil
1 to 1½ cups clam juice
   or fat-free canned
   chicken broth
1 tablespoon Dijon
   mustard
1 teaspoon
   Worcestershire sauce
½ teaspoon minced
   garlic
¼ cup green onion
   (scallion)
1 tablespoon capers,
   drained
1 tablespoon minced
   parsley
¼ cup white wine,
   optional

MAKES 8 SERVINGS

Toss the shrimp with the flour. In a large skillet, heat the olive oil, and cook the shrimp until done, 5 to 7 minutes. Remove the shrimp from the pan.

In the same skillet, combine 1 cup clam juice and the mustard, Worcestershire sauce, garlic, and green onion, scraping the pan to remove the bits, cooking 2 minutes. Add the capers, parsley, and white wine, and continue cooking 1 minute. Add the shrimp to the pan, tossing gently with the sauce. Add more clam juice or water if the sauce is too thick. Serve.

Nutritional information per serving
Calories 130, Protein (g) 18, Carbohydrate (g) 4,
Fat (g) 4, Calories from Fat (%) 31, Saturated Fat (g) 1,
Dietary Fiber (g) 0, Cholesterol (mg) 161, Sodium (mg) 470
Diabetic Exchanges: *2.5 lean meat, 0.5 starch*

FOOD FACT

Capers are little buds from a plant native to the Mediterranean that are picked, sun dried, and then pickled in a vinegar brine. They are high in sodium, so use in moderation or even rinse before using.

SEAFOOD

Shrimp Clemanceau

A heavenly sauce tops off this mixture of crispy potatoes, shrimp, and peas, for a one-dish meal.

2 large baking potatoes, cubed (about 5 cups)
2 tablespoons margarine
¼ cup minced garlic
2 bunches green onions (scallions), chopped
½ pound fresh mushrooms, sliced
2½ pounds peeled medium shrimp
2 tablespoons finely chopped parsley
¼ cup white wine
1 tablespoon lemon juice
1 tablespoon Worcestershire sauce
1 (10-ounce) package frozen green peas
Salt and pepper to taste

MAKES 8 SERVINGS

Preheat the oven to 400°F.

Place the cubed potatoes on a baking sheet coated with nonstick cooking spray. Bake, stirring occasionally, for 30 to 40 minutes, or until browned and crisp-tender.

In a large skillet, melt the margarine, and sauté the garlic, green onions, and mushrooms until tender, stirring frequently. Add the shrimp, parsley, wine, lemon juice, and Worcestershire sauce, and cook, stirring, until the shrimp are done, 5 to 7 minutes.

Cook the peas according to the package directions; drain.

In a 2-quart oblong casserole, combine the cooked potatoes, peas, and the shrimp mixture removed from the skillet with a slotted spoon. Reduce the liquid in the skillet by half, and pour over the shrimp-potato mixture. Season to taste. Toss gently, and serve.

Nutritional information per serving
Calories 254, Protein (g) 27, Carbohydrate (g) 27,
Fat (g) 4, Calories from Fat (%) 15, Saturated Fat (g) 1,
Dietary Fiber (g) 4, Cholesterol (mg) 202, Sodium (mg) 337
Diabetic Exchanges: *3 very lean meat, 1.5 starch, 1 vegetable*

SEAFOOD

Shrimp with Mango Salsa

The hot jalapeños and cilantro with the sweet mango make exotic, exciting flavors. Serve this wonderful combination over rice or as a salsa.

2 tablespoons sliced pickled jalapeño pepper (from a jar)

⅓ cup chopped red onion

½ cup chopped red bell pepper

½ cup fresh cilantro leaves

2 ripe medium-size mangoes

4 tablespoons lime juice, divided

1 tablespoon olive oil

1 pound peeled medium shrimp

1 teaspoon minced garlic

¼ cup tequila

Salt and pepper to taste

MAKES 4 SERVINGS

Place the jalapeño, onion, red pepper, and cilantro in a food processor, and pulse until chopped. Peel the mangoes and chop, adding the jalapeño mixture. Add 2 tablespoons lime juice, and transfer to a bowl.

Heat the oil in a large skillet over medium heat, and stir-fry the shrimp and garlic until the shrimp is almost done, about 5 minutes. Add the remaining 2 tablespoons lime juice and the tequila, and cook for about 5 minutes, or until the shrimp are done. Add the salt and pepper. Stir the shrimp into the salsa mixture, and serve.

Nutritional information per serving

Calories 230, Protein (g) 18, Carbohydrate (g) 22, Fat (g) 5, Calories from Fat (%) 18, Saturated Fat (g) 1, Dietary Fiber (g) 3, Cholesterol (mg) 161, Sodium (mg) 226
Diabetic Exchanges: *2.5 lean meat, 1.5 fruit*

QUICK TIP

Refrigerate ripe mangoes in a plastic bag for up to 5 days. Be careful of the mango juice as it will stain your clothing.

SEAFOOD

Shrimp Tacos with Tropical Salsa

Abundance of color and flavor—the shrimp and veggies served with the salsa make a refreshing, light meal.

1 yellow or red bell pepper, seeded and sliced

1 red onion, sliced

½ teaspoon minced garlic

1½ pounds peeled medium shrimp

½ teaspoon ground cumin

½ teaspoon chili powder

1 cup chopped tomatoes

1 (11-ounce) can Mexi-corn, drained (optional)

8 (6- to 8-inch) flour tortillas

1 cup shredded reduced-fat Monterey Jack cheese

Tropical Salsa (recipe follows)

MAKES 8 SHRIMP TACOS

In a large skillet coated with nonstick cooking spray, sauté the bell pepper, onion, and garlic over medium-high heat for 2 minutes. Add the shrimp, cumin, chili powder, and tomatoes, cooking until the shrimp are done, 5 to 7 minutes. Stir in Mexi-corn.

On each tortilla, divide evenly the shrimp mixture and the cheese, and fold over in half. If desired, heat in the microwave or heat the tortillas before filling. Serve with Tropical Salsa (see recipe below).

QUICK TIP

To heat tortillas, wrap them loosely in plastic wrap and heat them in a microwave on high for about 1 minute. If you prefer, wrap in foil and warm in a 250°F oven for 10 minutes.

Tropical Salsa

1 (8-ounce) can pineapple chunks in own juice, drained

1 (11-ounce) can mandarin orange segments, drained

1 tablespoon lemon juice

2 green onions (scallions), chopped

1 tablespoon diced green chilies

1 tablespoon chopped fresh cilantro

Coarsely chop the pineapple and oranges.

In a medium bowl, combine the pineapple, oranges, lemon juice, green onions, green chilies, and cilantro. Refrigerate until ready to use.

Nutritional information per serving
Calories 238, Protein (g) 20, Carbohydrate (g) 31, Fat (g) 3, Calories from Fat (%) 13, Saturated Fat (g) 2, Dietary Fiber (g) 2, Cholesterol (mg) 129, Sodium (mg) 506
Diabetic Exchanges: *2.5 very lean meat, 1 starch, 0.5 fruit, 1 vegetable*

SEAFOOD

Grilled Shrimp

The shrimp burst with flavor from this simple citrus marinade. Have fun—use the shrimp in shish kabobs.

⅓ cup lime juice
1 tablespoon honey
2 tablespoons low-sodium
   soy sauce
2 tablespoons
   Worcestershire sauce
1 cup orange juice
1 tablespoon minced
   garlic
2 pounds peeled large
   shrimp

MAKES 6 SERVINGS

In a small glass or stainless steel bowl, mix the lime juice, honey, soy sauce, Worcestershire sauce, orange juice, and garlic. Add the shrimp, and marinate 15 minutes. Grill the shrimp on hot coals, or broil in the oven for several minutes on each side, or until done. Serve.

Nutritional information per serving

Calories 116, Protein (g) 23, Carbohydrate (g) 1,
Fat (g) 1, Calories from Fat (%) 10, Saturated Fat (g) 0,
Dietary Fiber (g) 0, Cholesterol (mg) 215, Sodium (mg) 433
Diabetic Exchanges: 3.5 very lean meat

Shrimp Sauté

A few ingredients sautéed with shrimp created this family favorite. Great over rice, fettuccine, or patty shells.

2 tablespoons margarine
1 bunch green onions
   (scallions), chopped
2 cloves garlic, minced
1 tablespoon
   Worcestershire sauce
1 teaspoon dried basil
   leaves
2 pounds peeled medium
   shrimp
2 cups nonfat plain
   yogurt

MAKES 6 SERVINGS

In a large skillet, melt the margarine, and sauté the green onions and garlic until tender. Add the Worcestershire sauce and basil. Add the shrimp, and cook until the shrimp are done (turn pink), 5 to 7 minutes. Gradually stir in the yogurt, and heat thoroughly. *Do not boil.* Serve.

Nutritional information per serving

Calories 197, Protein (g) 28, Carbohydrate (g) 8,
Fat (g) 5, Calories from Fat (%) 24, Saturated Fat (g) 1,
Dietary Fiber (g) 0, Cholesterol (mg) 217, Sodium (mg) 384
Diabetic Exchanges: 3.5 very lean meat, 0.5 skim milk

SEAFOOD

Scampi Italian Style

When you arrive home from work exhausted and starving, sauté the shrimp and seasonings in a skillet, and serve with pasta for an irresistible dinner.

2 tablespoons olive oil
1 pound peeled large
  shrimp
1 teaspoon minced garlic
2 green onions
  (scallions), chopped
3 tablespoons dry sherry
1 tomato, diced
1 teaspoon
  Worcestershire sauce
½ teaspoon hot pepper
  sauce
¼ teaspoon white pepper
⅛ teaspoon dried
  oregano leaves
⅛ teaspoon dried thyme
  leaves
2 tablespoons chopped
  parsley

MAKES 4 SERVINGS

Heat the olive oil in a large skillet, and sauté the shrimp until they begin to turn pink. Add the garlic and green onions, sautéing for 1 minute longer. Add the sherry, tomato, Worcestershire sauce, hot pepper sauce, pepper, oregano, thyme, and parsley. Cook about 5 minutes, or until the shrimp are fully cooked and the sauce has thickened slightly. Serve.

Nutritional information per serving
Calories 161, Protein (g) 18, Carbohydrate (g) 3,
Fat (g) 8, Calories from Fat (%) 44, Saturated Fat (g) 1,
Dietary Fiber (g) 1, Cholesterol (mg) 161, Sodium (mg) 209
Diabetic Exchanges: 2.5 very lean meat, 1 fat

QUICK TIP

Substitute fresh herbs for the dried in this recipe, or use whatever fresh you have and mix it with dried.

Shrimp-and-Spinach Skillet Surprise

Mandarin oranges and pine nuts give this dish a burst of flavor. This incredible recipe takes minutes to prepare and is great served over wild rice.

2 tablespoons olive oil

1 red bell pepper, seeded and chopped

1 cup sliced red onion

1 teaspoon minced garlic

2 pounds peeled medium shrimp

3 sprigs fresh basil leaves, chopped, or ½ teaspoon dried basil leaves

½ cup cherry or grape tomatoes, halved

2 cups fresh spinach, washed and stemmed

2 tablespoons pine nuts

1 (11-ounce) can mandarin orange segments, drained

MAKES 6 TO 8 SERVINGS

In a large skillet, heat the olive oil, and sauté the red pepper, onion, and garlic for 5 to 7 minutes. Add the shrimp, cooking over medium-high heat until the shrimp are done, 5 to 7 minutes. Add the basil, tomatoes, and spinach, cooking until the spinach begins to wilt. Add the pine nuts and oranges, cooking until well heated. Serve.

Nutritional information per serving

Calories 156, Protein (g) 18, Carbohydrate (g) 8, Fat (g) 5, Calories from Fat (%) 31, Saturated Fat (g) 1, Dietary Fiber (g) 1, Cholesterol (mg) 161, Sodium (mg) 196
Diabetic Exchanges: 2.5 lean meat, 0.5 fruit

FOOD FACT

Bell peppers have more vitamin C than oranges and most melons.

SEAFOOD

Shrimp-and-Spinach White Pizza

Shrimp in a white sauce topped with spinach adds intrigue to the traditional pizza.

1 (12-inch) Italian Boboli
crust

1¼ cups evaporated
skimmed milk

2 tablespoons cornstarch

½ teaspoon minced garlic

Salt and pepper to taste

1 pound peeled small
shrimp

½ pound sliced
fresh mushrooms

3 cups fresh spinach,
washed and stemmed

½ teaspoon dried
oregano leaves

½ teaspoon dried basil
leaves

1 cup shredded part-skim
Mozzarella cheese

MAKES 8 SERVINGS

Preheat the oven to 425°F. Place the crust into a round 12-inch pizza pan coated with nonstick cooking spray.

Meanwhile, in a small pot, whisk together the milk and cornstarch until blended. Cook over medium-high heat, stirring until thickened. Stir in the garlic, and season with the salt and pepper. Spread the white sauce over the crust, and set aside.

In a skillet coated with nonstick cooking spray, cook the shrimp until pink, about 5 minutes; drain. Add the mushroom slices, and continue cooking for several minutes. Add the spinach, stirring until wilted; drain, and spoon the shrimp mixture over the white sauce. Sprinkle with the oregano and basil. Top with the Mozzarella cheese. Bake for 8 to 10 minutes, or until the crust is golden brown and the cheese is melted. Slice and serve.

Nutritional information per serving
Calories 275, Protein (g) 23, Carbohydrate (g) 33,
Fat (g) 6, Calories from Fat (%) 19, Saturated Fat (g) 3,
Dietary Fiber (g) 1, Cholesterol (mg) 93, Sodium (mg) 503
Diabetic Exchanges: *2 very lean meat, 1.5 starch, 0.5 skim milk*

QUICK TIP

For a different twist, use Brie instead of Mozzarella in this recipe. Brie and spinach work nicely together.

SEAFOOD

❄ Cheesy Shrimp Rice Casserole

Shrimp and rice team up with cheese and salsa for a quick family favorite. Use leftover rice or rice of your choice.

1 onion, chopped

1 teaspoon minced garlic

1½ pounds peeled
   medium shrimp

1 (8-ounce) can
   mushroom stems and
   pieces

⅓ cup chunky salsa

1½ cups shredded
   reduced-fat Cheddar
   cheese

1 tablespoon
   Worcestershire sauce

½ cup evaporated
   skimmed milk

1 bunch green onions
   (scallions), sliced

3 cups cooked rice

MAKES 6 SERVINGS

In a large skillet coated with nonstick cooking spray, sauté the onion, garlic, shrimp, and mushrooms over medium-high heat for 5 to 7 minutes. Add the salsa, cheese, Worcestershire sauce, milk, and green onions. Stir in the rice, and cook until the cheese is melted and well combined, about 10 minutes. Serve.

Nutritional information per serving

Calories 313, Protein (g) 31, Carbohydrate (g) 30, Fat (g) 6, Calories from Fat (%) 19, Saturated Fat (g) 4, Dietary Fiber (g) 2, Cholesterol (mg) 177, Sodium (mg) 623
Diabetic Exchanges: *3.5 very lean meat, 1.5 starch, 1 vegetable*

FOOD FACT

One cup of rice has 30% of the recommended daily allowance of iron and is also an excellent source of fiber.

SEAFOOD

Speedy Shrimp Jambalaya

Talk about easy, talk about good—here's the recipe. Serve over rice, pasta, patty shells, corn bread, or biscuits.

1 (16-ounce) jar roasted-pepper-and-garlic chunky salsa or other flavored salsa

8 ounces reduced-fat smoked sausage, diced

½ pound peeled small shrimp

1 teaspoon dried thyme leaves

1 bunch green onions (scallions), sliced, divided

¼ teaspoon cayenne pepper

¾ cup fat-free sour cream

MAKES 4 TO 6 SERVINGS

In a large skillet, mix the salsa, sausage, shrimp, thyme, and ⅓ cup green onions. Heat to a boil. Reduce the heat to low, and cook 10 minutes.

Meanwhile, in a small bowl, mix the cayenne pepper and sour cream. Serve the jambalaya with a dollop of sour cream mixture, and sprinkle with the remaining green onions.

Nutritional information per serving
Calories 140, Protein (g) 13, Carbohydrate (g) 14,
Fat (g) 1, Calories from Fat (%) 10, Saturated Fat (g) 0,
Dietary Fiber (g) 1, Cholesterol (mg) 67, Sodium (mg) 766
***Diabetic Exchanges:** 1.5 very lean meat, 1 starch*

QUICK TIP

One-half cup salsa is equal to one serving of vegetables. Add salsa to your favorite recipe to sneak in those veggies.

SEAFOOD

❄ Crawfish Elegante

This healthier version of a classic favorite will satisfy even gourmets. Crabmeat may be substituted for crawfish. For dinner, serve over rice, patty shells, or pasta, and for an amazing appetizer, serve with melba rounds.

3 tablespoons margarine

1 bunch green onions (scallions), chopped

½ cup chopped parsley

3 tablespoons all-purpose flour

1 (12-ounce) can evaporated skimmed milk

3 tablespoons sherry

1 pound crawfish tails, rinsed and drained

Salt and pepper to taste

Dash cayenne pepper

MAKES 6 TO 8 SERVINGS

In a small skillet, melt the margarine, and sauté the green onions and parsley. Blend in the flour. Gradually add the milk, stirring constantly until the sauce thickens and bubbles. Add the sherry and crawfish tails, stirring gently. Season with the salt, pepper, and cayenne pepper; serve.

Nutritional information per serving

Calories 141, Protein (g) 14, Carbohydrate (g) 9, Fat (g) 5, Calories from Fat (%) 33, Saturated Fat (g) 1, Dietary Fiber (g) 0, Cholesterol (mg) 77, Sodium (mg) 163
Diabetic Exchanges: *1.5 lean meat, 0.5 skim milk*

QUICK TIP

When crawfish is purchased in airtight plastic bags, it has already been cooked and only needs to be reheated.

SEAFOOD

Crawfish Étouffée

Étouffée is a very popular Louisiana recipe, and this quick and "better for you" recipe is the best one of them all. Purchase crawfish tails in sealed bags in the freezer section of the grocery store.

1½ cups finely chopped
onions
⅓ cup finely chopped
green bell pepper
½ teaspoon minced garlic
2 tablespoons margarine
2 tablespoons
all-purpose flour
1 pound peeled
crawfish tails, rinsed
and drained
1 cup water
Dash cayenne pepper
Dash Worcestershire
sauce
Salt and pepper to taste
Juice of 1 lemon
1 bunch green onions
(scallions), tops only,
finely sliced

MAKES 4 SERVINGS

In a large skillet coated with nonstick cooking spray, sauté the onions, green pepper, and garlic in the margarine until tender. Stir in the flour, and cook 1 minute. Add the crawfish tails and water. Cover, and simmer over low heat for 10 minutes. Add the cayenne pepper, Worcestershire sauce, salt, pepper, and lemon juice. Add the green onions, and cook for 5 minutes longer. If the mixture is too thick, add more water. Serve over cooked rice.

Nutritional information per serving
Calories 195, Protein (g) 21, Carbohydrate (g) 12,
Fat (g) 7, Calories from Fat (%) 33, Saturated Fat (g) 1,
Dietary Fiber (g) 2, Cholesterol (mg) 151, Sodium (mg) 179
Diabetic Exchanges: 2.5 lean meat, 2 vegetable

FOOD FACT

The word *étouffée* is a French word that means "to smother." This popular Cajun-style dish is a thick spicy stew of crawfish and veggies served over rice.

❄ Crawfish and Rice Casserole

Cooked shrimp may be substituted in this crowd-pleasing dish. Use wild rice if desired.

2 tablespoons olive oil

2 large onions, chopped

2 large green bell
peppers, seeded
and chopped

2 pounds crawfish tails,
rinsed and drained

1 (8-ounce) package
fat-free cream cheese,
cubed

1 (10¾-ounce) can 98%
fat-free cream of
mushroom soup

4 ounces light
pasteurized processed
cheese spread, cubed

6 cups cooked rice

2 bunches green onions
(scallions), chopped

1 teaspoon minced garlic

¼ teaspoon cayenne
pepper

Dash white pepper

MAKES 12 TO 14 SERVINGS

Preheat the oven to 350°F. Coat a 2- or 3-quart casserole dish with nonstick cooking spray.

In a large skillet, heat the oil over medium heat, and sauté the onion and pepper until tender, about 5 minutes. Add the crawfish tails and cream cheese, cooking until the cream cheese is creamy. Add the cream of mushroom soup and cheese spread, cooked rice, green onions, garlic, cayenne, and white pepper.

Transfer the mixture to the prepared dish coated with nonstick cooking spray. Bake, uncovered, for 30 minutes, or until well heated. Serve.

Nutritional information per serving

*Calories 225, Protein (g) 18, Carbohydrate (g) 28,
Fat (g) 4, Calories from Fat (%) 18, Saturated Fat (g) 1,
Dietary Fiber (g) 2, Cholesterol (mg) 92, Sodium (mg) 414*
Diabetic Exchanges: *2 very lean meat, 1.5 starch, 1 vegetable*

SEAFOOD

Scallop Stir-Fry with Crispy Noodle Pancakes

This scallop specialty is equally good served over rice—if you feel adventurous, try the noodle pancakes, as they are a tasty complement to the dish.

1 cup fat-free canned chicken broth

¼ cup oyster sauce

1 tablespoon cornstarch

½ teaspoon sesame oil

2 tablespoons canola oil, divided

½ pound fresh mushrooms, sliced

1 (6-ounce) package frozen snow peas, thawed

4 green onions (scallions), sliced

1 pound sea scallops, halved crosswise

½ teaspoon ground ginger

Crispy Noodle Pancakes (recipe follows)

MAKES 4 TO 6 SERVINGS

In a small bowl, combine the chicken broth, oyster sauce, cornstarch, and sesame oil. Heat 1 tablespoon canola oil in a wok or large, heavy skillet over high heat. Stir-fry the mushrooms; add the snow peas, and stir-fry until crisp- tender, about 3 minutes. Transfer to a bowl.

In the same skillet, heat the remaining 1 tablespoon canola oil over high heat; add the green onions and scallops, stir-frying several minutes, or until the scallops turn opaque. Stir the broth mixture and ginger into the skillet, stirring until the sauce thickens. Return the vegetables to the skillet, stirring until thoroughly heated. Spoon over Noodle Pancakes (see recipe at right), and serve.

FOOD FACT

To best cook scallops, dry with paper towels to remove excess moisture before sautéing them. Cook in a single layer in the skillet, making sure they don't touch one another; otherwise, they will steam instead of brown.

Crispy Noodle Pancakes

8 ounces plain Chinese
    noodles
½ cup chopped green
    onion (scallion)
1 teaspoon plus 1
    tablespoon canola
    oil, divided
1 tablespoon sesame oil

Cook the noodles according to the package directions, stirring occasionally. Drain. Rinse with cold water, and drain well.

In a medium bowl, toss with the green onion and 1 teaspoon canola oil.

Heat 1 tablespoon canola oil and the sesame oil in a heavy 9-inch skillet over medium heat. Drop the mixture onto the skillet, and flatten slightly. Cook without stirring, until light brown, about 6 minutes. Turn, and cook the second side until light brown, about 6 minutes. Drain on paper towels.

Nutritional information per serving
Calories 365, Protein (g) 27, Carbohydrate (g) 40,
Fat (g) 12, Calories from Fat (%) 29, Saturated Fat (g) 1,
Dietary Fiber (g) 7, Cholesterol (mg) 37, Sodium (mg) 817
Diabetic Exchanges: 3 very lean meat, 2.5 starch, 1 vegetable, 1 fat

Broiled Scallops

Honey mustard with a touch of curry glazes the scallops for tons of flavor.

¼ cup Dijon mustard
¼ cup honey
½ teaspoon ground curry
1 teaspoon lemon juice
2 pounds sea scallops

FOOD FACT

Scallops are low in fat.

MAKES 8 SERVINGS

In a large bowl, combine the mustard, honey, curry, and lemon juice, mixing well. Add the scallops, and marinate 15 minutes. Transfer to a baking pan, and broil in the oven about 4 inches from the heat until golden brown on the outside and opaque in the middle, 4 to 5 minutes. (Do not turn.) Serve.

Nutritional information per serving
Calories 140, Protein (g) 19, Carbohydrate (g) 12,
Fat (g) 1, Calories from Fat (%) 6, Saturated Fat (g) 0,
Dietary Fiber (g) 0, Cholesterol (mg) 37, Sodium (mg) 363
Diabetic Exchanges: 3 very lean meat, 1 other carbohydrate

Seafood Casserole

This mouthwatering dish also may be served as an appetizer or in a chafing dish with patty shells or melba toasts.

½ cup chopped onion

2 cloves garlic, minced

1 pound peeled shrimp

¼ cup all-purpose flour

¾ cup fat-free canned chicken broth

1 (5-ounce) can evaporated skimmed milk

1 teaspoon dried dill weed leaves

1 (14-ounce) can quartered artichoke hearts, drained

1 pound lump crabmeat, picked for shells

1 cup shredded reduced-fat sharp Cheddar cheese

MAKES 6 SERVINGS

In a skillet coated with nonstick cooking spray, sauté the onion, garlic, and shrimp until pink, about 5 minutes. Stir in the flour and gradually add the chicken broth, stirring until smooth and it comes to a boil. As the sauce thickens, add the milk, stirring until mixed. Add the dill weed. Gently fold in the artichoke hearts, crabmeat, and cheese, heating until the cheese is melted and thoroughly heated. Serve in individual dishes or a in casserole dish.

Nutritional information per serving
Calories 254, Protein (g) 38, Carbohydrate (g) 12,
Fat (g) 5, Calories from Fat (%) 18, Saturated Fat (g) 3,
Dietary Fiber (g) 1, Cholesterol (mg) 176, Sodium (mg) 756
Diabetic Exchanges: 5 very lean meat, 0.5 starch, 1 vegetable

QUICK TIP

In sauces, always gradually add cheese toward the end of cooking, stirring just until cheese is melted and blended throughout.

SEAFOOD

Seafood and Wild Rice Casserole

Easy and excellent for your family or friends. I have cooked this recipe numerous times over the years.

1 (6-ounce) package long-grain and wild rice mix

1 pound peeled cooked shrimp

1 pound white or lump crabmeat picked for shells

1 (10-ounce) package frozen green peas

1 cup chopped celery

1 green bell pepper, seeded and chopped

1 onion, chopped

½ cup light mayonnaise

1 teaspoon Worcestershire sauce

Salt and pepper to taste

MAKES 6 TO 8 SERVINGS

Preheat the oven to 350°F.

Cook the rice mix according to the package directions, omitting any oil. Add the shrimp, crabmeat, peas, celery, green pepper, onion, mayonnaise, Worcestershire sauce, salt, and pepper, tossing carefully. Pour into a 2-quart casserole coated with nonstick cooking spray. Bake for 20 to 30 minutes, or until heated through; serve.

Nutritional information per serving

Calories 287, Protein (g) 29, Carbohydrate (g) 27, Fat (g) 7, Calories from Fat (%) 21, Saturated Fat (g) 1, Dietary Fiber (g) 3, Cholesterol (mg) 159, Sodium (mg) 837
Diabetic Exchanges: *4 very lean meat, 1.5 starch, 1 vegetable*

SEAFOOD

❄ Baked Italian Oysters

Here's a lighter version of a New Orleans restaurant favorite of ours. This one has all the taste but not the fat.

⅓ cup olive oil

1 tablespoon minced garlic

1 bunch green onions (scallions), sliced

½ cup chopped parsley

2 cups bread crumbs

2 cups Italian bread crumbs

⅓ cup grated Parmesan cheese

2 tablespoons lemon juice

2 teaspoons dried oregano leaves

¼ teaspoon cayenne pepper

1 teaspoon dried tarragon leaves

Salt and pepper to taste

2 pints oysters, with liquid

MAKES 10 SERVINGS

Preheat the oven to 450°F.

In a large skillet, heat the olive oil, and sauté the garlic, green onions, and parsley for several minutes. Add the bread crumbs, Italian bread crumbs, Parmesan cheese, lemon juice, oregano, cayenne pepper, tarragon, salt, and pepper. Stir in the oysters and enough oyster liquid to make the mixture moist.

Transfer the mixture to a shallow 2-quart casserole dish. Bake for 20 to 30 minutes, or until the oysters are cooked and the mixture browned. Serve.

Nutritional information per serving
Calories 327, Protein (g) 15, Carbohydrate (g) 37,
Fat (g) 13, Calories from Fat (%) 36, Saturated Fat (g) 3,
Dietary Fiber (g) 2, Cholesterol (mg) 55, Sodium (mg) 805
Diabetic Exchanges: *1 very lean meat, 2.5 starch, 2 fat*

SEAFOOD

Perfect Pasta 323

Vermicelli with Fresh Tomatoes 324

Penne with Spinach, Sun-Dried Tomatoes, and Goat Cheese 325

Spicy Southwestern Pasta 326

Thai Pasta Dish 327

Vodka Pasta 328

Sensational Meatless Spaghetti Sauce 329

Pasta

Rigatoni with Roasted Tomato Sauce 330

Excellent Eggplant Pasta 331

Eggplant, Spinach, and Pasta 332

Mediterranean Capellini 333

Tortellini and Eggplant Casserole 334

Eggplant Manicotti with Cheesy Spinach Filling 335

Double Squash Pasta Toss 336

Chicken and Linguine 337

Chicken Primavera 338

Greek Lemon Chicken over Pasta 339

Chicken Mediterranean Pasta 340

Chicken and Spinach Cannelloni 341

Chicken Vermicelli 342

Shrimp and Angel Hair 343

Shrimp Fettuccine 344

Shrimp with Feta and Pasta 345

Shrimp with Oranges and Pasta 346

Shrimp Ziti Primavera 347

Basil Shrimp with Fettuccine 348

Shrimp, Salsa, and Pasta Casserole 349

Angel Hair with Crabmeat 350

Smoked Salmon, Snap Peas, and Pasta 351

Crawfish Fettuccine 352

Scallop, Pepper, and Pasta Toss 353

Old-Fashioned Lasagna 354

Quick Chicken Lasagna 355

Vegetable Lasagna 356

Seafood Lasagna 357

Mediterranean Lasagna 358

Jumbo Stuffed Shells 359

Meaty Spinach Manicotti with Tomato Sauce 360

Magnificent Meat Sauce with Spaghetti 361

Chinese Pork Vermicelli 362

Perfect Pasta

I find myself making this recipe time and time again when I need a pasta side dish.

12 ounces capellini
   (angel hair) pasta
3 tablespoons olive oil
½ teaspoon minced garlic
1 tablespoon finely
   chopped parsley

MAKES 6 TO 8 SERVINGS

Cook the pasta according to the package directions, omitting any oil and salt. Drain and set aside.

In a small skillet, heat the olive oil and sauté the garlic and parsley for a few minutes. Toss with the pasta, and serve.

Nutritional information per serving
Calories 204, Protein (g) 6, Carbohydrate (g) 32,
Fat (g) 6, Calories from Fat (%) 26, Saturated Fat (g) 1,
Dietary Fiber (g) 1, Cholesterol (mg) 0, Sodium (mg) 3
Diabetic Exchanges: *2 starch, 1 fat*

PASTA

Vermicelli with Fresh Tomatoes

Here's an incredible and satisfying recipe for when tomatoes are in season.

2 pounds tomatoes,
    chopped
1 onion, chopped
½ teaspoon minced garlic
1 tablespoon dried basil
    leaves
⅓ cup olive oil
Salt and pepper to taste
1 (16-ounce) package
    vermicelli pasta
1 cup shredded reduced-
    fat Cheddar cheese,
    optional

MAKES 8 SERVINGS

In a large bowl, mix the tomatoes, onion, garlic, basil, olive oil, salt, and pepper together. Let stand at room temperature for 1 hour.

Cook the vermicelli according to the package directions, omitting any oil and salt. Drain, and toss with the sauce. Sprinkle with the cheese, and serve.

Nutritional information per serving
Calories 324, Protein (g) 9, Carbohydrate (g) 50,
Fat (g) 10, Calories from Fat (%) 28, Saturated Fat (g) 1,
Dietary Fiber (g) 3, Cholesterol (mg) 0, Sodium (mg) 15
Diabetic Exchanges: 3 starch, 1.5 vegetable, 1.5 fat

QUICK TIP

Always cook pasta uncovered at a fast, continuous boil so that the pasta can move freely and will cook more evenly. The rapid boil also helps to prevent sticking.

PASTA

Penne with Spinach, Sun-Dried Tomatoes, and Goat Cheese

This easy recipe has the fabulous characteristics of a trendy restaurant dish.

½ cup sun-dried tomatoes (not oil-packed)

⅔ cup boiling water

12 ounces penne or other tubular pasta

2 tablespoons olive oil

1 tablespoon minced garlic

6 cups stemmed fresh spinach, washed

1 tablespoon dried basil leaves

2 tablespoons balsamic vinegar

Salt and pepper to taste

½ cup crumbled goat cheese

QUICK TIP

Any short pasta, such as ziti, rigatoni, or mostaccioli, is a substitute for penne.

MAKES 4 TO 6 SERVINGS

In a small bowl, combine the sun-dried tomatoes and boiling water; set aside to soften, about 10 minutes. Coarsely chop the sun-dried tomatoes, and reserve the soaking liquid.

Meanwhile, prepare the pasta according to the package directions, omitting any oil and salt. Drain, and set aside.

In a large skillet coated with nonstick cooking spray, heat the oil and add the garlic, sun-dried tomatoes with soaking liquid, spinach, basil, vinegar, salt, and pepper, cooking until the spinach is just wilted, about 5 minutes. Stir in the goat cheese and pasta, heating until the cheese begins to melt. Serve immediately.

Nutritional information per serving
Calories 322, Protein (g) 12, Carbohydrate (g) 48, Fat (g) 9, Calories from Fat (%) 25, Saturated Fat (g) 3, Dietary Fiber (g) 3, Cholesterol (mg) 10, Sodium (mg) 63
Diabetic Exchanges: *3 starch, 1 vegetable, 1.5 fat*

PASTA

Spicy Southwestern Pasta

This sensational Southwestern meatless pasta will be devoured in minutes. Use a food processor to purée the tomatoes until they are mushy.

1 (28-ounce) can whole
   tomatoes, puréed,
   with their juice
1 onion, chopped
1½ teaspoons chili
   powder
½ teaspoon ground
   cumin
1 teaspoon dried
   oregano leaves
½ teaspoon minced garlic
½ teaspoon sugar
¼ teaspoon ground
   cinnamon
¼ teaspoon crushed red
   pepper flakes
Salt and pepper to taste
1 (16-ounce) package
   rotini pasta
1 (16-ounce) can black
   beans, drained and
   rinsed
1 (10-ounce) package
   frozen corn kernels
1 (4-ounce) can chopped
   green chilies, drained
1 cup shredded reduced-
   fat Cheddar cheese,
   optional

MAKES 6 TO 8 SERVINGS

In a large pot coated with nonstick cooking spray, add the tomato purée with juice, onion, chili powder, cumin, oregano, garlic, sugar, cinnamon, red pepper flakes, salt, and pepper. Bring to a boil, reduce the heat, and simmer, covered, to blend the flavors, about 15 minutes.

Meanwhile, cook the pasta according to the package directions, omitting any oil and salt. Drain well.

Stir the black beans, corn, and green chilies into the sauce. Cook until the corn is crisp-tender, about 5 minutes. Remove from the heat. To serve, toss the black bean mixture with the pasta. If desired, serve with the shredded cheese.

Nutritional information per serving
Calories 323, Protein (g) 13, Carbohydrate (g) 65,
Fat (g) 2, Calories from Fat (%) 5, Saturated Fat (g) 0,
Dietary Fiber (g) 8, Cholesterol (mg) 0, Sodium (mg) 349
Diabetic Exchanges: 4 starch, 1 vegetable

FOOD FACT

Rinse canned beans before cooking with them to reduce the sodium content.

🥕 Thai Pasta Dish

Here's a quick trip to Bangkok, in a mainstreamed version you can enjoy in your own home. The Thai stir-fry sauce gives this dish a surprising, sweet, and fiery flavor. My family loves it.

1 (8-ounce) package
vermicelli pasta

1 cup fresh bean sprouts

½ cup sliced green onion
(scallion)

½ cup whole baby corn,
drained

2 tablespoons chopped
peanuts

1 (4-ounce) can
mushrooms, drained

3 egg whites

½ teaspoon garlic
powder

1 cup bottled pad thai or
sweet-and-sour stir-fry
sauce

MAKES 4 TO 6 SERVINGS

Cook the pasta according to the package directions, omitting any oil and salt. Drain; set aside.

In a small bowl, toss together the bean sprouts, green onion, corn; set aside.

In a large skillet coated with nonstick cooking spray, sauté the mushrooms over medium heat until hot, about 1 minute. In a small bowl, beat the egg whites slightly with the garlic powder. Pour over the mushrooms, cooking and stirring for 1 minute. Stir in the bottled sauce, pasta, and vegetable mixture. Continue cooking, tossing gently, until the pasta is heated through and the egg whites are cooked, about 5 to 8 minutes. Toss in the peanuts, and serve immediately.

Nutritional information per serving
Calories 236, Protein (g) 10, Carbohydrate (g) 45,
Fat (g) 2, Calories from Fat (%) 8, Saturated Fat (g) 0,
Dietary Fiber (g) 4, Cholesterol (mg) 0, Sodium (mg) 453
Diabetic Exchanges: *2 starch, 1 other carbohydrate*

QUICK TIP

If you can't find fresh bean sprouts, substitute 1 (14-ounce) can of bean sprouts, drained. If you can't find or don't like baby corn, substitute 1 (14-ounce) can of white corn, drained. The dish is very tasty either way.

PASTA

Vodka Pasta

Don't let the vodka scare you; it cooks into a very light creamy tomato sauce that your family will adore.

2 tablespoons olive oil

¾ cup finely chopped onion

1 (28-ounce) can diced tomatoes, drained

½ cup vodka

1 (12-ounce) can evaporated skimmed milk

¼ teaspoon crushed red pepper flakes

Salt and pepper to taste

1 (16-ounce) package penne or other tubular pasta

¼ cup grated Parmesan cheese

¼ cup sliced green onion (scallion) stems, optional

MAKES 6 TO 8 SERVINGS

In a large skillet over medium heat, heat the olive oil and sauté the onion until tender, about 5 minutes. Add the tomatoes. Stir in the vodka, and cook over medium-high heat until it comes to a boil, about 5 minutes. Reduce heat, add the milk, stirring constantly, and add the crushed red pepper, salt, and pepper. Continue cooking for 3 to 5 minutes, or until thoroughly heated.

Meanwhile, prepare the pasta according to the package directions, omitting any oil and salt. Drain well. Add to the tomatoes, mixing well. Toss with the Parmesan cheese, sprinkle with the sliced green onion stems, and serve.

Nutritional information per serving
Calories 349, Protein (g) 13, Carbohydrate (g) 54, Fat (g) 5, Calories from Fat (%) 14, Saturated Fat (g) 1, Dietary Fiber (g) 3, Cholesterol (mg) 4, Sodium (mg) 244
Diabetic Exchanges: *3 starch, 0.5 skim milk, 1 vegetable*

QUICK TIP

When cooking pasta, don't salt water until after it has come to a boil. Salted water has a higher boiling point and takes longer to boil.

PASTA

Sensational Meatless Spaghetti Sauce

You can put this classic red sauce on the stove late in the afternoon and let it cook while you get other things done. It reheats and freezes well, so make a big batch.

1 onion, chopped

1 teaspoon minced garlic

¼ cup chopped parsley

1 green bell pepper, seeded and chopped

1 pound fresh mushrooms, chopped

2 (6-ounce) cans tomato paste

1 (28-ounce) can whole Italian tomatoes, chopped, with their juice

1 (15-ounce) can tomato sauce

1 cup water

1 tablespoon Worcestershire sauce

1 tablespoon sugar

½ cup dry red wine

1 tablespoon dried basil leaves

2 bay leaves

1 (16-ounce) package spaghetti

Grated Parmesan cheese, optional

MAKES 6 TO 8 SERVINGS

In a large, heavy pot coated with nonstick cooking spray, sauté the onion and garlic over medium heat until tender, about 5 minutes. Add the parsley, green pepper, mushrooms, tomato paste, tomatoes with their juice, tomato sauce, water, Worcestershire sauce, sugar, wine, basil, and bay leaves. Simmer over low heat for at least 1 hour.

Cook the spaghetti according to the package directions, omitting any oil and salt. Drain, and serve with the sauce, discarding the bay leaves. Sprinkle with the Parmesan cheese, if desired. Serve immediately.

Nutritional information per serving

Calories 333, Protein (g) 12, Carbohydrate (g) 67, Fat (g) 1, Calories from Fat (%) 3, Saturated Fat (g) 0, Dietary Fiber (g) 7, Cholesterol (mg) 0, Sodium (mg) 485
Diabetic Exchanges: *3 starch, 4 vegetable*

FOOD FACT

Tomato products offer lycopene, a substance thought to fight cancer.

PASTA

Rigatoni with Roasted Tomato Sauce

The roasted tomatoes give this sauce a rich, smoky flavor. They are easy to do—my sister, who hates to do anything extra, has prepared this recipe successfully.

1 (16-ounce) package rigatoni or other tubular pasta
8 to 10 Roma (plum) tomatoes
1 tablespoon minced garlic
½ cup sliced fresh mushrooms
¼ cup green peas
Salt and pepper to taste
1 tablespoon dried basil leaves
¼ cup grated Parmesan cheese

MAKES 6 SERVINGS

Cook the rigatoni according to the package directions, omitting any oil and salt. Drain, and set aside.

Meanwhile, preheat the broiler or grill, and broil or grill the tomatoes until black on the outside, turning occasionally, about 15 minutes. *Do not peel!* Place in a food processor, and purée; set aside.

In a large skillet coated with nonstick cooking spray, sauté the garlic over medium heat until light brown, stirring, about 1 minute. Add the mushrooms; continue cooking until the mushrooms are tender, about 4 minutes. Add the tomato purée and peas, and cook 3 minutes or until well heated. Add the salt and pepper, basil, and Parmesan cheese, mixing well. Toss with the rigatoni, and serve.

Nutritional information per serving
Calories 327, Protein (g) 13, Carbohydrate (g) 63,
Fat (g) 3, Calories from Fat (%) 8, Saturated Fat (g) 1,
Dietary Fiber (g) 3, Cholesterol (mg) 3, Sodium (mg) 91
Diabetic Exchanges: *4 starch*

Excellent Eggplant Pasta

A one-pan, high-fiber dinner that eggplant lovers will praise.

1 (12-ounce) package
vermicelli pasta

1½ tablespoons olive oil

1 small (1-pound)
eggplant, peeled and
sliced ¼-inch thick

1 teaspoon minced garlic

1 green bell pepper,
seeded and cut into
thin strips

½ pound fresh
mushrooms, sliced

1 tablespoon dried
basil leaves

½ teaspoon crushed red
pepper flakes

1 large tomato, chopped

2 tablespoons grated
Parmesan cheese

MAKES 4 TO 6 SERVINGS

Cook the vermicelli according to the package directions, omitting any oil and salt. Drain, set aside, and keep warm.

While the pasta is cooking, heat the olive oil in a large skillet. Add the eggplant and garlic, cover, and cook about 5 minutes, or until the eggplant is just tender, stirring occasionally. Stir in the pepper strips, mushrooms, basil, and red pepper flakes; cook until tender, about 6 minutes. Stir in the chopped tomatoes, and cook until the mixture is heated through, 5 to 7 minutes. Toss with the cooked pasta and Parmesan cheese. Serve immediately.

Nutritional information per serving
Calories 293, Protein (g) 11, Carbohydrate (g) 52, Fat (g) 5, Calories from Fat (%) 16, Saturated Fat (g) 1, Dietary Fiber (g) 5, Cholesterol (mg) 2, Sodium (mg) 50
Diabetic Exchanges: *3 starch, 2 vegetable, 0.5 fat*

FOOD FACT

Eggplant is a very low calorie vegetable that is high in fiber and anthycyanosides, antioxidants that help fight cancer and heart disease.

PASTA

Eggplant, Spinach, and Pasta

Eggplant, tomatoes, and basil together make a true Sicilian dish. This light red sauce highlights these wonderful veggies, which are standouts. A good dish during tomato season. For a different version, I made this dish without the eggplant, and it was wonderful.

2 tablespoons olive oil

1 cup chopped onion

1 teaspoon minced garlic

5 cups cubed, peeled eggplant (about 1 pound)

4 cups fresh stemmed spinach, chopped

2 cups chopped tomatoes

2 tablespoons chopped fresh basil leaves

Salt and pepper to taste

1 (8-ounce) can tomato sauce

1 (16-ounce) package tubular pasta

⅓ cup grated fresh Parmesan cheese

MAKES 6 TO 8 SERVINGS

In a large skillet, heat the olive oil over medium-high heat, and sauté the onion and garlic until tender, about 5 minutes. Add the eggplant; sauté about 5 minutes, or until lightly browned. Add the spinach, tomatoes, basil, salt, pepper, and tomato sauce; reduce the heat, and simmer 15 minutes.

Meanwhile, cook the pasta according to the package directions, omitting any oil and salt. Add the pasta to the eggplant mixture, and toss. Sprinkle with the Parmesan cheese, and serve.

Nutritional information per serving

Calories 303, Protein (g) 11, Carbohydrate (g) 52, Fat (g) 6, Calories from Fat (%) 17, Saturated Fat (g) 1, Dietary Fiber (g) 4, Cholesterol (mg) 3, Sodium (mg) 258
Diabetic Exchanges: *3 starch, 2 vegetable, 0.5 fat*

QUICK TIP

When you're buying eggplant, look for smooth, taut skin with a fresh-looking green cap at the stem. Store eggplant in your refrigerator, and use it as soon as possible because the inside will become soft and bitter within a few days.

PASTA

Mediterranean Capellini

A deluxe red sauce enhanced with capers and seasonings makes this a light dinner or pasta side dish. Feta cheese may be substituted for the Parmesan.

1 (12-ounce) package
capellini (angel hair)
pasta

2 tablespoons olive oil

1 tablespoon minced
garlic

1 red onion, chopped

1 red bell pepper, seeded
and finely chopped

1 (14½-ounce) can
chopped tomatoes
with their juice

1 (10-ounce) can diced
tomatoes and green
chilies

1 teaspoon drained
capers

2 teaspoons dried basil
leaves

1 teaspoon dried
oregano leaves

½ teaspoon crushed red
pepper flakes

¼ cup grated Parmesan
cheese

MAKES 4 TO 6 SERVINGS

Cook the capellini according to the package directions, omitting any oil and salt. Drain, set aside.

While the pasta is cooking, heat the oil in a large pan and sauté the garlic, onion, and red pepper over medium heat until tender, about 5 minutes. Add the tomatoes with their juice, tomatoes and green chilies, capers, basil, oregano, and red pepper flakes. Simmer for 20 minutes. Toss with the pasta and Parmesan cheese. Serve immediately.

Nutritional information per serving

*Calories 309, Protein (g) 11, Carbohydrate (g) 52,
Fat (g) 7, Calories from Fat (%) 20, Saturated Fat (g) 2,
Dietary Fiber (g) 4, Cholesterol (mg) 3, Sodium (mg) 389*
Diabetic Exchanges: *3 starch, 1.5 vegetable, 1 fat*

PASTA

Tortellini and Eggplant Casserole

A great and easy combination that creates a delicious vegetarian meal resembling a variation on eggplant Parmesan.

1 (9-ounce) package cheese tortellini

1 medium eggplant, peeled and cut into 1-inch cubes

1 medium green bell pepper, seeded and chopped

1 cup chopped onion

1 teaspoon minced garlic

1 (15-ounce) can tomato sauce

1 teaspoon balsamic or red wine vinegar

1 teaspoon dried basil leaves

Salt and pepper to taste

½ cup shredded part-skim Mozzarella cheese

MAKES 4 SERVINGS

Preheat the oven to 350°F. Cook the tortellini according to the package directions, omitting any oil and salt. Drain, and set aside.

In a large nonstick skillet, sauté the eggplant, green pepper, onion, and garlic. Cook, stirring often, 10 to 12 minutes, or until the vegetables are tender. Add the tomato sauce, vinegar, basil, salt, and pepper. Bring to a boil, reduce heat, and simmer for 5 minutes.

Spoon half the eggplant mixture into a baking dish coated with nonstick cooking spray. Top with half the tortellini. Repeat the layers with the remaining eggplant and tortellini. Sprinkle the Mozzarella cheese over the top. Cook for 10 to 15 minutes, or until the cheese melts and the casserole is heated through. Serve immediately.

Nutritional information per serving

Calories 300, Protein (g) 15, Carbohydrate (g) 48, Fat (g) 6, Calories from Fat (%) 17, Saturated Fat (g) 3, Dietary Fiber (g) 7, Cholesterol (mg) 42, Sodium (mg) 769
Diabetic Exchanges: *0.5 lean meat, 2 starch, 4 vegetable, 0.5 fat*

QUICK TIP

Store eggplants in a cool, dry place and use within one to two days of purchase. For longer storage (up to 5 days) place the eggplant in a plastic bag and store it in a refrigerator or vegetable drawer.

PASTA

Eggplant Manicotti with Cheesy Spinach Filling

This meatless, high-fiber manicotti creatively uses eggplant instead of pasta—a fabulous way to enjoy veggies disguised in this tasty roll with a rich, wonderful tomato sauce.

1 (15-ounce) container reduced-fat Ricotta cheese

¼ cup grated Asiago or Parmesan cheese

1¼ cups chopped fresh baby spinach

¼ teaspoon nutmeg

1 egg white

Salt and pepper to taste

2 medium eggplants, peeled, cut lengthwise into 8⅓-inch slices

3 tablespoons olive oil

Tomato Sauce (recipe follows)

1 cup shredded part-skim Mozzarella cheese

Tomato Sauce

1 onion, chopped

⅔ cup chopped carrot

1 teaspoon chopped garlic

½ cup dry red wine

1 (28-ounce) can crushed tomatoes with purée

1 cup fat-free canned chicken broth

1 teaspoon dried basil

Salt and pepper to taste

MAKES 8 SERVINGS

Preheat the oven to 350°F.

In a medium bowl, mix together the Ricotta and Asiago cheeses, spinach, nutmeg, egg white, salt, and pepper.

Arrange the eggplants on foil-lined pans or baking pans coated with nonstick cooking spray. Drizzle with the olive oil. Sprinkle with salt and pepper. Bake until the eggplant slices are tender, about 12 to 15 minutes; cool.

Place one eggplant slice on the work surface. Place about 2 tablespoons of the Ricotta mixture near the narrower end of the eggplant slice. Roll up, enclosing the filling. Repeat with the remaining eggplant slices and filling. Spread half the Tomato Sauce (see recipe below) over the bottom of a 13 x 9 x 2-inch glass baking dish coated with nonstick cooking spray. Arrange the eggplant in a single layer atop the Tomato Sauce. Spoon the remaining sauce over the eggplant rolls. Sprinkle with the Mozzarella cheese. Bake until heated through, about 15 to 20 minutes. Serve immediately.

In a large, heavy saucepan coated with nonstick cooking spray, sauté the onion, carrot, and garlic over medium-high heat until tender, 5 to 7 minutes. Add the wine, crushed tomatoes, broth, and basil, and bring to a boil. Reduce the heat; cover, and simmer for 15 to 20 minutes to blend the flavors. Season with the salt and pepper.

Nutritional information per serving

Calories 236, Protein (g) 13, Carbohydrate (g) 20, Fat (g) 11, Calories from Fat (%) 40, Saturated Fat (g) 4, Dietary Fiber (g) 5, Cholesterol (mg) 24, Sodium (mg) 462
Diabetic Exchanges: *1 very lean meat, 4 vegetable, 1.5 fat*

PASTA

Double Squash Pasta Toss

Great for a light evening dinner or lunch, this is one of my favorite simple summer recipes to take advantage of farmers' markets or homegrown squash and tomatoes.

2 tablespoons olive oil

1 tablespoon minced garlic

2 cups thinly sliced zucchini

2 cups thinly sliced yellow squash

2 cups coarsely chopped red onion

1 teaspoon dried basil leaves

1 teaspoon dried oregano leaves

2 cups coarsely chopped tomatoes

3 tablespoons balsamic vinegar

Salt and pepper to taste

1 (16-ounce) package ziti or other tubular pasta

¼ cup grated Parmesan cheese

MAKES 6 TO 8 SERVINGS

In a large skillet, heat the olive oil over medium-high heat, and cook the garlic, zucchini, yellow squash, and onion until very tender, about 5 to 8 minutes. Add the basil, oregano, tomatoes, vinegar, salt, and pepper; lower the heat and cook 2 minutes longer, or until well heated.

Meanwhile, prepare the pasta according to the package directions, omitting any oil and salt. Drain, and add to the squash mixture. Add the Parmesan cheese, toss, and serve.

Nutritional information per serving
Calories 298, Protein (g) 10, Carbohydrate (g) 52, Fat (g) 6, Calories from Fat (%) 17, Saturated Fat (g) 1, Dietary Fiber (g) 4, Cholesterol (mg) 3, Sodium (mg) 70
Diabetic Exchanges: *3.5 starch, 3 vegetable, 1 fat*

FOOD FACT

Crookneck (yellow) squash and zucchini are referred to as summer squash. Summer squash have thin, edible skins and soft seeds. In general, the smaller the squash, the more tender it will be.

PASTA

Chicken and Linguine

The roasted chicken and onion add an abundance of flavor to this simple preparation.

3 tablespoons olive oil

1 medium onion, thinly sliced in rings

2 cloves garlic, minced

1 teaspoon dried basil leaves

¼ teaspoon crushed red pepper flakes

1½ pounds skinless, boneless chicken breasts, cut into pieces

8 ounces linguine pasta

¼ cup grated Parmesan cheese

Salt and pepper, optional

MAKES 4 SERVINGS

Preheat the oven to 400°F.

In a 2-quart oblong pan, stir together the olive oil, onion rings, garlic, basil, and red pepper. Roll the chicken pieces in the oil mixture, and leave in the pan. Bake the chicken, uncovered, about 45 minutes.

Approximately 10 minutes before the chicken is done, cook the linguine according to the package directions, omitting any oil and salt. Drain.

When the chicken is done, add the pasta, cheese, salt, and pepper to the dish, mixing well. Serve immediately.

Nutritional information per serving

Calories 534, Protein (g) 50, Carbohydrate (g) 47, Fat (g) 15, Calories from Fat (%) 26, Saturated Fat (g) 3, Dietary Fiber (g) 2, Cholesterol (mg) 104, Sodium (mg) 233
Diabetic Exchanges: *4.5 very lean meat, 3 starch, 2 fat*

QUICK TIP

In the mood for a really quick and great tasting chicken dish? Serve the chicken as an entrée and make your choice of sides.

PASTA

Chicken Primavera

This is one of my standby favorites when I want a satisfying dish packed with flavor that looks as good as it is to eat.

1 (12-ounce) package
    linguine
1½ pounds skinless,
    boneless chicken
    breasts, cut into chunks
    or strips
¼ cup olive oil
1 teaspoon minced garlic
½ pound fresh
    mushrooms, sliced
1 onion, chopped
1 red bell pepper, seeded
    and chopped
½ teaspoon dried
    oregano leaves
½ teaspoon dried basil
    leaves
½ teaspoon thyme leaves
Salt and pepper to taste
1 cup frozen peas
¼ cup grated Parmesan
    cheese

MAKES 6 TO 8 SERVINGS

Cook the linguine according to the package directions, omitting any oil and salt; drain.

In a large skillet, cook the chicken pieces in the olive oil and garlic over medium high heat until lightly brown and done, about 7 minutes. Watch carefully, tossing to keep from sticking. Add the mushrooms, onion, red pepper, oregano, basil, thyme, salt, and pepper, sautéing until tender. Add the peas, tossing until heated. Add the pasta to the vegetable mixture, combining well. Add the Parmesan cheese, and serve.

Nutritional information per serving
Calories 359, Protein (g) 29, Carbohydrate (g) 38,
Fat (g) 10, Calories from Fat (%) 24, Saturated Fat (g) 2,
Dietary Fiber (g) 3, Cholesterol (mg) 52, Sodium (mg) 139
Diabetic Exchanges: *3 very lean meat, 2 starch, 1.5 vegetable, 1 fat*

Greek Lemon Chicken over Pasta

With its touch of Greek style, this wonderfully marinated, lemony chicken in a light sauce with Feta and pasta is a delightful eating experience.

½ cup white wine

3 tablespoons olive oil, divided

¼ cup plus 1 tablespoon lemon juice

Salt and pepper to taste

4 cloves garlic, minced

8 skinless, boneless chicken breasts

½ cup milk

2 tablespoons all-purpose flour

1 tablespoon prepared mustard

1 teaspoon dried dill weed leaves

¼ cup finely chopped parsley

1 cup nonfat plain yogurt

1 (16-ounce) capellini (angel hair) pasta

½ cup crumbled Feta cheese

½ cup shredded Muenster or reduced-fat Swiss cheese

MAKES 8 SERVINGS

In a small bowl, combine the wine, 1 tablespoon olive oil, ¼ cup lemon juice, the salt, pepper, and garlic. Mix well.

Pound the chicken breasts slightly, and place in a shallow casserole. Pour the marinade over the chicken to cover, and refrigerate up to 12 hours. Discard the marinade.

Coat a skillet with nonstick cooking spray, and heat the remaining 2 tablespoons oil. Sauté the chicken until tender, 7 to 10 minutes. Slice and set aside.

In a small saucepan, stir the milk into the flour, and add the mustard. Cook over medium heat, stirring constantly until thickened. Remove from the heat, and add the remaining 1 tablespoon lemon juice, the dill weed, and the parsley. Stir in the yogurt, mixing well.

Cook the pasta according to the package directions, omitting any oil and salt. Gently toss the pasta with the sauce and the Feta cheese. Place in a 13 x 9 x 2-inch baking dish, and top with the sliced chicken breasts and Muenster cheese. Broil until the cheese is golden. Serve immediately.

Nutritional information per serving

Calories 478, Protein (g) 39, Carbohydrate (g) 49, Fat (g) 12, Calories from Fat (%) 22, Saturated Fat (g) 4, Dietary Fiber (g) 2, Cholesterol (mg) 82, Sodium (mg) 428
Diabetic Exchanges: *4 lean meat, 3.5 starch*

Chicken Mediterranean Pasta

Use leftover chicken, or leave it out to create a vegetarian dish. My mother-in-law came over and enjoyed this dish for dinner, then again the next day as a cold pasta salad.

1 cup chopped onion

1 tablespoon minced garlic

1 tablespoon dried basil leaves

1 teaspoon dried thyme leaves

1 (10-ounce) can diced green chilies and tomatoes

1 (8-ounce) can tomato sauce

4 skinless, boneless chicken breasts, cut into strips

Salt and pepper to taste

2 tablespoons capers, drained

1 (2¼-ounce) can chopped black olives, drained

1 (16-ounce) package linguine pasta

¼ cup grated Parmesan cheese

½ cup finely minced parsley

MAKES 6 SERVINGS

In a large skillet coated with nonstick cooking spray, sauté the onion and garlic over medium heat until tender, about 5 minutes. Add the basil, thyme, chilies and tomatoes, tomato sauce, and chicken. Season with the salt and pepper. Simmer slowly for 15 to 20 minutes, stirring occasionally until the chicken is cooked through. Add the capers and olives.

Meanwhile, cook the pasta according to the package directions, omitting any oil and salt. Drain, and toss with the Parmesan cheese. Pour the sauce over the pasta; toss, sprinkle with the parsley, and serve immediately.

Nutritional information per serving

Calories 428, Protein (g) 31, Carbohydrate (g) 65,
Fat (g) 4, Calories from Fat (%) 9, Saturated Fat (g) 1,
Dietary Fiber (g) 4, Cholesterol (mg) 47, Sodium (mg) 717
Diabetic Exchanges: 2.5 very lean meat, 4 starch, 1 vegetable

❄ Chicken and Spinach Cannelloni

With a simple white sauce, spinach, and shells, turn leftover chicken into a scrumptious meal.

3 cups skim milk, divided

1 onion, quartered

3 bay leaves

2 whole cloves

2 tablespoons cornstarch

¼ cup grated Parmesan
cheese

¼ teaspoon white pepper

1 cup finely chopped
fresh mushrooms

½ cup finely chopped
onion

½ teaspoon minced garlic

1 (10-ounce) bag fresh
spinach, coarsely
chopped

1 pound cooked skinless,
boneless chicken
breasts, cut into small
chunks

⅛ teaspoon white pepper

1 (8-ounce) package
cannelloni shells

MAKES 8 SERVINGS

Preheat the oven to 350°F.

In a large saucepan, combine 2 cups milk and the quartered onion, bay leaves, and cloves; heat until hot. In a small bowl, combine remaining 1 cup milk and the cornstarch; stir well. Gradually add the cornstarch mixture to the hot milk mixture, stirring constantly and cooking until thickened and bubbly, 5 to 7 minutes. Remove the onion, bay leaves, and cloves. Add the Parmesan cheese and ¼ teaspoon white pepper to the milk mixture; set the sauce aside.

In a skillet coated with nonstick cooking spray, sauté the mushrooms, chopped onion, and garlic until tender, 5 to 7 minutes. Add the spinach, cooking and stirring occasionally until the spinach wilts and the liquid has evaporated, 3 to 5 minutes. Remove from the heat, and add the chicken and ⅛ teaspoon white pepper; mix well and set aside.

Meanwhile, cook the shells according to the package directions, omitting any oil and salt. Spoon ½ cup sauce over the bottom of a 13 x 9 x 2-inch baking dish. Fill the shells with the chicken mixture, and arrange in the dish. Pour the remaining sauce over the shells. Cover, and bake for 30 minutes, or until bubbly and heated. Serve.

Nutritional information per serving
Calories 237, Protein (g) 23, Carbohydrate (g) 30,
Fat (g) 2, Calories from Fat (%) 9, Saturated Fat (g) 1,
Dietary Fiber (g) 2, Cholesterol (mg) 37, Sodium (mg) 173
Diabetic Exchanges: *2 very lean meat, 1.5 starch, 0.5 skim milk*

PASTA

❄ Chicken Vermicelli

This great and very tasty recipe is perfect to take to a friend or freeze for another time, since it makes enough to fill two casseroles. For a quick and equally good version, use cooked chicken and canned broth. If you plan to freeze the chicken vermicelli, don't bake it beforehand.

6 pounds skinless chicken breasts

Salt and pepper to taste

2 celery stalks, cut in half

2 onions, 1 halved and 1 chopped

1 (16-ounce) package vermicelli pasta

1 tablespoon margarine

1 green bell pepper, seeded and chopped

2 cups chopped celery

½ teaspoon minced garlic

1 (8-ounce) can mushrooms, drained

1 cup all-purpose flour

4 cups reserved chicken broth

1 (10-ounce) can diced tomatoes and green chilies

¼ teaspoon cayenne pepper

1 tablespoon Worcestershire sauce

½ cup grated Parmesan cheese

¼ cup chopped parsley

1 cup chopped green onion (scallion)

MAKES 14 TO 16 SERVINGS

Preheat the oven to 300°F.

Place the chicken in a large pot, and add water to cover. Add the salt and pepper, celery stalks, and halved onion; bring to a boil. Reduce heat and cook for 30 minutes, or until the chicken is done. Reserve the broth, discarding the celery and onion. Cool slightly; then debone the chicken and cut into bite-size pieces.

Meanwhile, cook the vermicelli according to the package directions, omitting any oil and salt. Drain and set aside.

In a large pot, melt the margarine over medium heat, and sauté the chopped onion, green pepper, celery, and garlic until tender. Add the mushrooms. Gradually stir in the flour, mixing for 30 seconds. Gradually add the chicken broth, stirring. Add the tomatoes and green chilies, cayenne pepper, and Worcestershire sauce. Add the chicken and vermicelli, mixing well.

Divide the mixture into two 2-quart shallow casseroles coated with nonstick cooking spray. Top each casserole with half the Parmesan cheese, parsley, and green onion, and bake for 20 to 30 minutes, or until thoroughly heated. Serve immediately.

Nutritional information per serving
Calories 329, Protein (g) 30, Carbohydrate (g) 30,
Fat (g) 9, Calories from Fat (%) 24, Saturated Fat (g) 3,
Dietary Fiber (g) 2, Cholesterol (mg) 74, Sodium (mg) 291
Diabetic Exchanges: *3 lean meat, 2 starch*

PASTA

Shrimp and Angel Hair

I prepared this snappy and spicy recipe on The Phil Donahue Show *years ago, and it stole the show.*

5 ounces Canadian bacon, diced

1 green bell pepper, seeded and chopped

1 onion, chopped

3 stalks celery, chopped

5 cloves garlic, minced

2 teaspoons dried basil leaves

2 teaspoons dried oregano leaves

1 bay leaf

¼ cup all-purpose flour

1 (10-ounce) can chopped tomatoes and green chilies

2 pounds peeled medium shrimp

1 (16-ounce) package capellini (angel hair) pasta

1 large bunch green onions (scallions), thinly sliced

MAKES 8 TO 10 SERVINGS

In a large skillet coated with nonstick cooking spray, cook the Canadian bacon over medium heat until it begins to brown, about 3 minutes. Add the green pepper, onion, celery, garlic, basil, oregano, and bay leaf, sautéing until tender, 5 to 7 minutes. Gradually add the flour and the tomatoes and green chilies, stirring. Add the shrimp, cooking 7 to 10 minutes or until pink and done, still stirring.

Meanwhile, cook the angel hair according to the package directions, omitting any oil; drain. Toss with the shrimp mixture, and add the green onions. Serve immediately.

Nutritional information per serving

Calories 279, Protein (g) 22, Carbohydrate (g) 42,
Fat (g) 2, Calories from Fat (%) 8, Saturated Fat (g) 1,
Dietary Fiber (g) 3, Cholesterol (mg) 115, Sodium (mg) 453
Diabetic Exchanges: *2 very lean meat, 2.5 starch, 1 vegetable*

QUICK TIP

Drain but don't rinse pasta unless using for a cold salad. Always reserve a small amount of the pasta cooking liquid. Toss pasta with the sauce, and if the sauce is too thick, add some of the reserved cooking liquid a little at a time.

PASTA

Shrimp Fettuccine

A stylishly simple, family-favorite, one-dish evening meal.

1 pound peeled
  large shrimp
¼ cup white wine
1 bunch green onions
  (scallions), sliced
2 cloves garlic, minced
½ pound fresh
  mushrooms, sliced
1 (6-ounce) package
  frozen snow peas
2 tablespoons olive oil
1 (8-ounce) package
  fettuccine pasta
¼ cup chopped parsley
½ cup grated Romano
  cheese

MAKES 6 TO 8 SERVINGS

Marinate the shrimp in the white wine for 30 minutes, if time permits.

In a large skillet, stir-fry the green onions, garlic, mushrooms, and snow peas in the olive oil over medium-high heat for about 5 minutes. When the vegetables are crisp-tender, add the shrimp and wine, and sauté until the shrimp are pink.

Prepare the fettuccine according to the package directions, omitting any oil. Drain. Add the fettuccine to the shrimp mixture along with the parsley and Romano cheese, tossing gently. Serve immediately.

Nutritional information per serving
Calories 220, Protein (g) 15, Carbohydrate (g) 25,
Fat (g) 6, Calories from Fat (%) 25, Saturated Fat (g) 2,
Dietary Fiber (g) 2, Cholesterol (mg) 74, Sodium (mg) 160
Diabetic Exchanges: *1.5 very lean meat, 1.5 starch, 0.5 fat*

QUICK TIP

When the water reaches a rapid, rolling boil, add 1 tablespoon of salt for every 1 pound of pasta if salt is desired.

PASTA

Shrimp and Feta with Pasta

Easy make-ahead recipe, since most of the work is done ahead of time with the ingredients marinating. During tomato season this is a super stand-by recipe.

2 pounds peeled, cooked shrimp

½ cup crumbled Feta cheese

1 bunch green onions (scallions), sliced

2 teaspoons dried oregano

2½ cups chopped tomatoes

2 tablespoons sliced black olives

Salt and pepper to taste

1 (16-ounce) package fettuccine pasta

MAKES 6 TO 8 SERVINGS

In a large bowl, combine the shrimp, Feta, green onions, oregano, tomatoes, olives, salt, and pepper. Let stand at room temperature for at least 1 hour.

Cook the pasta according to the package directions omitting any oil; drain. Add the pasta to the shrimp mixture, tossing. Serve immediately.

Nutritional information per serving

Calories 366, Protein (g) 33, Carbohydrate (g) 47, Fat (g) 5, Calories from Fat (%) 11, Saturated Fat (g) 2, Dietary Fiber (g) 3, Cholesterol (mg) 230, Sodium (mg) 388
Diabetic Exchanges: *3.5 very lean meat, 3 starch*

QUICK TIP

Try different varieties of Feta to intensify the flavor of this dish.

PASTA

Shrimp with Oranges and Pasta

A burst of citrus flavor, shrimp, pasta, and Brie cheese make this an easy gourmet delight.

1 (16-ounce) package ziti or other tubular pasta

1 red onion, sliced

1 teaspoon chopped jalapeño chile pepper

2 pounds peeled, medium shrimp

1 teaspoon minced garlic

½ cup orange juice

2 oranges, seeded and separated into segments

1 teaspoon dried basil leaves

6 ounces Brie cheese, rind removed, sliced

MAKES 6 TO 8 SERVINGS

Cook the pasta according to the package directions, omitting any oil and salt. Drain; set aside.

In a large skillet coated with nonstick cooking spray, sauté the onion, jalapeño, shrimp, and garlic over medium-high heat until the shrimp are done, 5 to 8 minutes. Add the orange juice, orange segments, and basil, stirring well, and cook just until heated through. Toss the pasta with the shrimp sauce, and add the Brie, stirring gently until the cheese is melted.

Nutritional information per serving

Calories 382, Protein (g) 27, Carbohydrate (g) 50, Fat (g) 8, Calories from Fat (%) 18, Saturated Fat (g) 4, Dietary Fiber (g) 3, Cholesterol (mg) 156, Sodium (mg) 294
Diabetic Exchanges: *3 lean meat, 3 starch, 0.5 fruit*

QUICK TIP

When boiling pasta, use 4 to 6 cups of water per pound of pasta.

PASTA

Shrimp Ziti Primavera

For a vegetarian meal, leave out the shrimp, and don't worry about losing any of the flavor—this intense sauce is a winner on its own. Be creative with your choice of veggies.

1 (16-ounce) package ziti or other tubular pasta

2 pounds peeled, medium shrimp

2 tablespoons minced garlic

1 bunch green onions (scallions), sliced

1 pound fresh asparagus spears, cut into 2-inch pieces

½ pound fresh mushrooms, sliced

2 cups chopped tomatoes

Salt and pepper to taste

⅛ teaspoon crushed red pepper flakes

½ cup dry white wine

1 tablespoon dried basil leaves

1 tablespoon dried oregano leaves

1 tablespoon dried thyme leaves

¼ cup grated Parmesan cheese

1 tablespoon chopped parsley

MAKES 8 SERVINGS

Cook the pasta according to the package directions, omitting any oil and salt. Drain; set aside.

Heat a large skillet coated with nonstick cooking spray, and cook the shrimp, garlic, and green onions, stirring constantly, until the shrimp just turn pink. Add the asparagus, mushrooms, tomatoes, salt, pepper, red pepper flakes, wine, basil, oregano, and thyme to the skillet, and continue cooking until the shrimp are done and the vegetables are tender, 5 to 7 minutes. Add the pasta, Parmesan, and parsley, tossing well. Serve immediately.

Nutritional information per serving

Calories 346, Protein (g) 26, Carbohydrate (g) 51, Fat (g) 3, Calories from Fat (%) 8, Saturated Fat (g) 1, Dietary Fiber (g) 4, Cholesterol (mg) 137, Sodium (mg) 225
Diabetic Exchanges: *2 very lean meat, 3 starch, 1.5 vegetable*

PASTA

Basil Shrimp with Fettuccine

I usually don't insist on fresh herbs, but fresh basil is the star ingredient for this recipe.

2 tablespoons olive oil

1 pound peeled, medium shrimp

4 cups chopped tomatoes

⅓ cup chopped fresh basil leaves

¼ cup sliced black olives

1 teaspoon minced garlic

1 bunch green onions (scallions), sliced

Salt and pepper to taste

¼ teaspoon cayenne pepper

1 (8-ounce) package fettuccine pasta

Grated Romano cheese, optional

MAKES 4 SERVINGS

In a large skillet, heat the oil over medium-high heat, and cook the shrimp, tomatoes, basil, olives, garlic, and green onions. Season with the salt, pepper, and cayenne pepper. Cook, stirring frequently, until the shrimp are pink, about 7 minutes.

Meanwhile, cook the fettuccine according to the package directions, omitting any oil and salt. Drain, and place in a serving dish. Pour the shrimp and sauce over the pasta, and toss together. Sprinkle with the cheese. Serve immediately.

Nutritional information per serving

Calories 397, Protein (g) 24, Carbohydrate (g) 54, Fat (g) 10, Calories from Fat (%) 22, Saturated Fat (g) 1, Dietary Fiber (g) 4, Cholesterol (mg) 135, Sodium (mg) 252
Diabetic Exchanges: *2 very lean meat, 3 starch, 2 vegetable, 1 fat*

QUICK TIP

Drain but do not rinse pasta when it is used in a hot dish. Toss the pasta immediately with the sauce, and if the sauce is too thick, try adding some reserved cooking liquid a little at a time until the desired consistency is reached.

Shrimp, Salsa, and Pasta Casserole

The combination of a custardy layer, salsa, shrimp, and cheese makes this the perfect light evening meal.

1 (8-ounce) package capellini (angel hair) pasta

1 egg white

1 egg

1 (5-ounce) can evaporated skimmed milk

1 cup nonfat plain yogurt

⅓ cup chopped green onions (scallions)

1 teaspoon dried basil leaves

1 teaspoon dried oregano leaves

1 teaspoon minced garlic

1 (16-ounce) jar mild chunky salsa

1 pound peeled, medium shrimp

1½ cups shredded reduced-fat Cheddar cheese

MAKES 6 SERVINGS

Preheat the oven to 350°F.

Cook the pasta according to the package directions, omitting any oil and salt. Drain and set aside.

In a medium bowl, blend together the egg white, egg, evaporated milk, yogurt, green onions, basil, oregano, and garlic; set aside. Spread half the pasta over the bottom of a 13 x 9 x 2-inch baking dish coated with nonstick cooking spray. Cover with the salsa. Layer the shrimp over the salsa. Spread the remaining pasta over the shrimp. Pour the egg mixture evenly over the pasta.

Bake, uncovered, 30 minutes, or until the shrimp are pink and the liquid is absorbed. Sprinkle with the cheese and continue baking for 5 to 10 minutes, or until the cheese is melted. Remove from the oven, and let stand 10 minutes before serving.

Nutritional information per serving

Calories 334, Protein (g) 24, Carbohydrate (g) 40, Fat (g) 6, Calories from Fat (%) 18, Saturated Fat (g) 3, Dietary Fiber (g) 1, Cholesterol (mg) 99, Sodium (mg) 640
Diabetic Exchanges: *2 very lean meat, 2 starch, 0.5 skim milk*

PASTA

Angel Hair with Crabmeat

There is no compromise on flavor when crabmeat and Italian seasonings create a light, lovely sauce.

1 (8-ounce) package capellini (angel hair) pasta
2 tablespoons olive oil
½ cup chopped onion
1 teaspoon minced garlic
½ pound fresh mushrooms, sliced
2 tablespoons chopped parsley
1 teaspoon dried basil leaves
1 teaspoon dried oregano leaves
1 teaspoon lemon juice
1 pound lump white crabmeat
Salt and pepper to taste

MAKES 4 TO 6 SERVINGS

Cook the pasta according to the package directions, omitting any oil. Drain and set aside.

Meanwhile, coat a large skillet with nonstick cooking spray, and heat the oil. Sauté the onion, garlic, and mushrooms over medium-high heat until tender, 5 to 7 minutes. Add the parsley, basil, oregano, and lemon juice, cooking a few more minutes. Gently, stir in the crabmeat. Add the pasta, carefully tossing to mix well. Season to taste, and serve.

Nutritional information per serving
Calories 282, Protein (g) 23, Carbohydrate (g) 33, Fat (g) 6, Calories from Fat (%) 20, Saturated Fat (g) 1, Dietary Fiber (g) 2, Cholesterol (mg) 57, Sodium (mg) 291
Diabetic Exchanges: *2.5 very lean meat, 2 starch, 1 vegetable*

QUICK TIP

Different pastas can be substituted in recipes. For best results, mix and match thin, delicate noodles with light thin sauces and thick heavier noodles with heavier sauces.

PASTA

Smoked Salmon, Snap Peas, and Pasta

Add the salmon before serving—it loses its translucency and delicate texture when heated.

1 (16-ounce) package
    fusilli (corkscrew) pasta
1 cup chopped onion
½ pound fresh sugar
    snap peas
2 tablespoons olive oil
1 (12-ounce) can
    evaporated skimmed
    milk
2 tablespoons capers,
    drained
1 tablespoon chopped
    fresh dill weed
Salt and pepper to taste
4 ounces smoked salmon

MAKES 8 SERVINGS

Cook the fusilli in boiling water according to the package directions, omitting any oil and salt; drain well.

In a large skillet coated with nonstick cooking spray, sauté the onion and snap peas in the olive oil over medium-high heat until tender, 3 to 5 minutes. Add the evaporated skimmed milk, capers, dill weed, salt, and pepper, cooking until well heated, about 5 minutes. Remove from the heat, dice the smoked salmon, and toss with the pasta. Serve immediately.

Nutritional information per serving
Calories 315, Protein (g) 14, Carbohydrate (g) 52,
Fat (g) 5, Calories from Fat (%) 15, Saturated Fat (g) 1,
Dietary Fiber (g) 3, Cholesterol (mg) 5, Sodium (mg) 407
Diabetic Exchanges: *0.5 very lean meat, 3 starch, 0.5 skim milk*

FOOD FACT

Smoked salmon is a rich source of protein, vitamin A, and omega-3 oils.

PASTA

❄ Crawfish Fettuccine

If you're a crawfish fan, this dish will soon be high on your list. It is great for crowds, and it freezes well. Cooked shrimp can be used instead of crawfish.

1 (16-ounce) package
   fettuccine pasta
2 pounds crawfish tails
¼ cup margarine
1 large onion, chopped
2 green bell peppers,
   seeded and chopped
1 red bell pepper, seeded
   and chopped
1 teaspoon minced garlic
¼ cup all-purpose flour
1½ cups skim milk
½ pound light
   pasteurized cheese
   spread
2 tablespoons chopped
   parsley
1 tablespoon
   Worcestershire sauce
¼ teaspoon cayenne
   pepper

MAKES 8 TO 10 SERVINGS

Cook the fettuccine according to the package directions, omitting any oil and salt. Drain; set aside.

Rinse the crawfish tails; drain well, and set aside.

In a large pot, melt the margarine and sauté the onion, green pepper, red pepper, and garlic over medium heat until tender, 5 to 7 minutes. Add the flour, stirring until mixed. Gradually add the milk, stirring until smooth. Add the cheese, stirring until melted. Add the crawfish, parsley, Worcestershire sauce, and cayenne pepper. Toss with the pasta, heat thoroughly, and serve.

Nutritional information per serving
Calories 378, Protein (g) 28, Carbohydrate (g) 45,
Fat (g) 9, Calories from Fat (%) 22, Saturated Fat (g) 3,
Dietary Fiber (g) 2, Cholesterol (mg) 131, Sodium (mg) 539
Diabetic Exchanges: *3 lean meat, 3 starch*

FOOD FACT

Crawfish is a shell fish that can be purchased already peeled and ready to use in airtight bags either fresh or frozen.

PASTA

Scallop, Pepper, and Pasta Toss

With an abundance of color and flavor, this fabulous dish is a great way to serve scallops. Use either bay or sea scallops, and add more if desired.

1 (8-ounce) package fettuccine pasta

1 tablespoon olive oil

1 cup chopped red onion

1 red bell pepper, seeded and cut in strips

1 green bell pepper, seeded and cut in strips

8 ounces bay scallops

1 teaspoon minced garlic

1 cup frozen corn kernels

2 tablespoons lemon juice

1 teaspoon dried basil leaves

½ cup sliced green onion (scallion)

Pepper to taste

MAKES 4 TO 6 SERVINGS

Cook the fettuccine according to the package directions, omitting any oil and salt. Drain, set aside.

Coat a large skillet with nonstick cooking spray, and heat the olive oil. Sauté the onion, red pepper, and green pepper over medium-high heat for 5 to 7 minutes until tender; set aside.

Over medium-high heat, stir-fry the scallops, garlic, and corn until the scallops are opaque. Stir in the lemon juice, basil, green onion, and pepper. Toss the scallop and pepper mixture with the pasta, and serve.

Nutritional information per serving

Calories 244, Protein (g) 13, Carbohydrate (g) 41, Fat (g) 3, Calories from Fat (%) 13, Saturated Fat (g) 0, Dietary Fiber (g) 3, Cholesterol (mg) 12, Sodium (mg) 68
Diabetic Exchanges: *1 very lean meat, 2.5 starch, 1 vegetable*

QUICK TIP

Scallops are available in two sizes. Sea scallops are about 2 inches in diameter and bay scallops are about ½ inch in diameter. Both work well in this recipe.

PASTA

❄ Old-Fashioned Lasagna

Here is a lighter version of our traditional family-favorite lasagna, but with no compromise on taste. It freezes well.

½ pound lasagna noodles
1 teaspoon minced garlic
1 onion, chopped
1½ pounds ground sirloin
Salt and pepper to taste
2 teaspoons dried basil leaves
1 tablespoon chopped parsley
1 teaspoon dried oregano leaves
½ cup finely chopped carrots
2 (6-ounce) cans tomato paste
1½ cups hot water
1 large egg white
1 (15-ounce) container reduced fat ricotta cheese
1 cup shredded part-skim Mozzarella cheese

MAKES 8 SERVINGS

Preheat the oven to 350°F.

Cook the noodles according to the package directions, omitting any oil and salt. Drain and set aside.

In a large skillet coated with nonstick cooking spray, sauté the garlic and onion over medium-high heat until tender. Add the ground meat, salt, pepper, basil, parsley, oregano, and carrots, cooking until the meat is done, about 7 minutes; drain excess liquid. Add the tomato paste and hot water; simmer for 5 minutes, and then set aside.

In a small bowl, blend the egg white and Ricotta cheese.

In a 13 x 9 x 2-inch baking dish coated with nonstick cooking spray, put a thin layer of the meat sauce, half the noodles, all of the Ricotta cheese mixture, and half the Mozzarella cheese. Repeat with half the remaining meat sauce, all of the remaining noodles, then the remainder of the meat sauce, and top with the remainder of the Mozzarella. Bake for 30 minutes, or until bubbly and well heated. Let sit for 10 minutes before serving.

Nutritional information per serving

Calories 380, Protein (g) 33, Carbohydrate (g) 37, Fat (g) 11, Calories from Fat (%) 26, Saturated Fat (g) 6, Dietary Fiber (g) 4, Cholesterol (mg) 74, Sodium (mg) 273
Diabetic Exchanges: *4 lean meat, 1.5 starch, 2 vegetable*

QUICK TIP

When layering lasagna, always spread a little sauce on the bottom of your lasagna dish so the pasta doesn't stick. End with sauce on top, as exposed noodles will turn dry and hard.

PASTA

❄ Quick Chicken Lasagna

Take the easy but delicious way out with this recipe from a good friend who doesn't have time to cook. It's made with commercial pasta sauce, rotisserie chicken, and no-boil noodles to create one of my very favorite lasagnas. Even more, this recipe is high in fiber and full of flavor. You can freeze this lasagna before baking it.

1 rotisserie chicken, skin removed and chicken cut into pieces (about 3 cups)

2 (26-ounce) jars red pasta sauce

1 (8-ounce) package no-boil lasagna noodles

2 cups shredded part-skim Mozzarella cheese

2 (10-ounce) packages chopped spinach, thawed and drained

1 (4-ounce) package crumbled goat cheese

MAKES 8 SERVINGS

Preheat the oven to 350°F.

Combine chicken pieces with both jars of the pasta sauce. In an oblong baking dish, spread a thin layer of the chicken sauce. Top with a layer of noodles, one-third of the chicken sauce, Mozzarella cheese, half the spinach, and one-third of the goat cheese. Repeat layering with noodles, chicken sauce, Mozzarella, the remaining spinach, and one-third of the goat cheese. Continue with the remaining noodles, chicken sauce, Mozzarella, and goat cheese. Bake, covered, for 50 minutes. Uncover and bake 5 minutes longer, or until bubbly. Serve immediately.

Nutritional information per serving
Calories 462, Protein (g) 36, Carbohydrate (g) 42,
Fat (g) 16, Calories from Fat (%) 32, Saturated Fat (g) 8,
Dietary Fiber (g) 7, Cholesterol (mg) 78, Sodium (mg) 1,107
Diabetic Exchanges: *4 lean meat, 1.5 starch, 1 vegetable, 1 other carbohydrate*

QUICK TIP

Try different flavored pasta sauces such as roasted garlic for bonus flavor.

PASTA

🥕 ❄ Vegetable Lasagna

This lasagna packed full of everyday veggies is so good that a local restaurant served my recipe at one time.

1 onion, chopped
1 teaspoon minced garlic
1 green bell pepper, seeded and chopped
1 (6-ounce) can tomato paste
1 (10-ounce) can diced tomatoes and green chilies
1 (10-ounce) can chopped tomatoes
1 (11.5-ounce) can tomato juice
1 teaspoon dried basil
1 teaspoon dried oregano
1 teaspoon dried thyme
1½ tablespoons red wine vinegar
1 bay leaf
½ pound fresh mushrooms, sliced
½ cup shredded peeled carrots
1 bunch broccoli cut into florets
½ pound lasagna noodles
Cheese Mixture (recipe follows)
1½ cups shredded part-skim Mozzarella cheese

MAKES 8 SERVINGS

Preheat the oven to 350°F.

Coat a large skillet with nonstick cooking spray, and add the onion, garlic, and green pepper; sauté over medium-high heat for 5 to 7 minutes, or until tender. Add the tomato paste, diced tomatoes and green chilies, chopped tomatoes, and tomato juice, bringing to a boil. Add the basil, oregano, thyme, vinegar, bay leaf, mushroom slices, carrot, and broccoli, lower the heat, and simmer 20 to 30 minutes, or until the vegetables are tender and the sauce has slightly thickened. Discard the bay leaf.

Cook the lasagna noodles according to the package directions, omitting any oil and salt; drain.

In a 13 x 9 x 2-inch baking dish, spoon a layer of vegetable sauce along the bottom. Layer one-third each of the lasagna noodles, Cheese Mixture (see recipe at right), vegetable sauce, and Mozzarella cheese. Repeat the layers. Bake, covered, for 30 minutes. Let stand 10 minutes before cutting.

Cheese Mixture (for Vegetable Lasagna)

2 cups fat-free cottage cheese

1 egg white

2 tablespoons chopped parsley

¼ cup Parmesan cheese

In a food processor, combine the cottage cheese, egg white, parsley, and cheese, blending well.

Nutritional information per serving

Calories 290, Protein (g) 22, Carbohydrate (g) 40, Fat (g) 5, Calories from Fat (%) 16, Saturated Fat (g) 3, Dietary Fiber (g) 5, Cholesterol (mg) 20 , Sodium (mg) 721
Diabetic Exchanges: 2 lean meat, 1.5 starch, 3 vegetable

❄ Seafood Lasagna

A divine creation. Sometimes I layer the Swiss cheese instead of putting it in the sauce, which is a delicious alternative method.

2 (14½-ounce) cans diced tomatoes, undrained

1 cup sliced fresh mushrooms

1 teaspoon dried oregano leaves

1 clove garlic, minced

Salt and pepper to taste

1 pound cooked, peeled small shrimp

1 tablespoon margarine

3 tablespoons all-purpose flour

1¾ cups skim milk

1 cup shredded reduced-fat Swiss cheese

1 pound white crabmeat, picked for shells

¼ cup dry white wine (optional)

8 lasagna noodles

MAKES 8 SERVINGS

Preheat the oven to 350°F.

In a large saucepan, combine the tomatoes, mushrooms, oregano, garlic, salt, and pepper. Bring to a boil. Reduce the heat, and simmer, uncovered, about 15 minutes, or until thickened. Stir in the shrimp. Set aside.

In another saucepan, melt the margarine and stir in the flour. Add the milk, and cook, stirring constantly, over medium heat until thickened and bubbly, 5 to 7 minutes. Stir in the Swiss cheese until melted. Add the crabmeat and wine, stirring carefully.

Cook the lasagna noodles according to the package directions, omitting any oil or salt; drain.

In a 13 x 9 x 2-inch pan coated with nonstick cooking spray, layer half the shrimp sauce, half the noodles, and half the cheese sauce. Repeat the layering. Bake for 25 minutes, or until heated. Let stand 10 minutes. Serve.

Nutritional information per serving

Calories 265, Protein (g) 33, Carbohydrate (g) 19, Fat (g) 6, Calories from Fat (%) 21, Saturated Fat (g) 2, Dietary Fiber (g) 2, Cholesterol (mg) 162, Sodium (mg) 608
Diabetic Exchanges: 4 lean meat, 1 starch, 1 vegetable

❄ Mediterranean Lasagna

This excellent Mediterranean, vegetarian version of a classic recipe is chock-full of fabulous ingredients and packed with intense flavor. I absolutely love this recipe and don't even miss the meat. I also prefer roasted red peppers and no boil lasagna.

1 large onion

1 teaspoon minced garlic

1 teaspoon dried mint flakes

2 (14-ounce) cans artichoke hearts, drained and coarsely chopped

½ cup chopped roasted red pepper, optional

1 (14-ounce) can Great Northern or navy beans, drained and rinsed

1 (10-ounce) package fresh spinach torn in pieces

5 tablespoons all-purpose flour

3 cups skim milk

½ pound lasagna noodles, either cooked or no-boil

¾ cup crumbled Feta cheese

¾ cup part-skim shredded Mozzarella cheese

MAKES 8 SERVINGS

Preheat the oven to 375°F.

In a skillet coated with nonstick cooking spray, sauté the onion, garlic, mint, artichoke hearts, red pepper, beans, and spinach over medium-high heat until tender; set aside.

In a large saucepan, mix the flour and milk to make a white sauce with a whisk, and cook over medium heat until thickened, 5 to 7 minutes.

In a 13 x 9 x 2-inch pan coated with nonstick cooking spray, spread a thin layer of the white sauce, half the noodles, half the spinach mixture, half the remaining white sauce, half the Feta, and half the Mozzarella. Repeat the layers. Cover, and bake 30 to 40 minutes, until bubbly and the noodles are done (if using no-boil noodles).

Nutritional information per serving

Calories 402, Protein (g) 24, Carbohydrate (g) 47,
Fat (g) 14, Calories from Fat (%) 30, Saturated Fat (g) 9,
Dietary Fiber (g) 6, Cholesterol (mg) 52, Sodium (mg) 948
Diabetic Exchanges: 2 lean meat, 2 starch, 0.5 skim milk, 1.5 vegetable, 1 fat

QUICK TIP

Purchase different flavored Feta cheese to enhance the flavors in this recipe.

❄ Jumbo Stuffed Shells

This dish, definitely a family favorite, is often requested when I'm out of town, since I make it ahead of time and freeze it for my family.

1 (12-ounce) package
   jumbo shells
1½ pounds ground sirloin
2 egg whites
¼ cup grated Parmesan
   cheese
¼ cup Italian bread
   crumbs
1 tablespoon chopped
   parsley
1 teaspoon dried basil
   leaves
½ teaspoon dried
   oregano leaves
Salt and pepper to taste
Tomato Sauce
   (recipe follows)
1 cup shredded
   part-skim Mozzarella
   cheese

MAKES 6 TO 8 SERVINGS

Preheat the oven to 350°F. Cook the pasta shells according to the package directions, omitting any oil and salt; drain and set aside.

In a skillet, cook the meat until done, 5 to 7 minutes over medium-high heat. Drain any excess fat. Add the egg whites, Parmesan cheese, bread crumbs, parsley, basil, oregano, salt, and pepper. Stuff the shells with the filling.

Pour half the Tomato Sauce (see recipe below) in a 2-quart baking dish. Arrange the stuffed shells on top, and cover with the remaining sauce. Bake for 20 minutes, or until well-heated. Sprinkle with the Mozzarella cheese, and continue baking for 10 minutes longer, or until cheese is melted. Serve immediately.

QUICK TIP

When you're in a hurry, purchase a jar of commercial red pasta sauce to use in this recipe instead of making the Tomato Sauce.

Tomato Sauce

1 medium onion,
   chopped
½ teaspoon minced garlic
3 cups tomato juice
1 (6-ounce) can tomato
   paste
½ teaspoon sugar
Salt and pepper to taste

In a large pot coated with nonstick cooking spray, sauté the onion over medium heat until tender, about 5 minutes. Add the garlic, tomato juice, tomato paste, sugar, salt, and pepper; simmer at least 10 minutes to allow the flavors to blend.

Nutritional information per serving
Calories 406, Protein (g) 33, Carbohydrate (g) 45,
Fat (g) 10, Calories from Fat (%) 23, Saturated Fat (g) 5,
Dietary Fiber (g) 3, Cholesterol (mg) 64, Sodium (mg) 776
Diabetic Exchanges: *3.5 lean meat, 2.5 starch, 1.5 vegetable*

PASTA

❄ Meaty Spinach Manicotti with Tomato Sauce

Sneak spinach into the meal with this creamy, meaty filling with a light tomato sauce. For a smooth sauce, substitute tomato sauce for tomatoes (some kids prefer it this way).

1 (8-ounce) package manicotti shells

1 pound ground sirloin

½ cup chopped onion

1 teaspoon minced garlic

1 cup reduced-fat Ricotta cheese

4 ounces reduced-fat cream cheese

1 (10-ounce) package frozen chopped spinach, thawed and squeezed dry

1 (28-ounce) can chopped tomatoes, with their juice

1 teaspoon dried oregano leaves

1 teaspoon dried basil leaves

Salt and pepper to taste

MAKES 8 SERVINGS

Preheat the oven to 350°F.

Cook the manicotti shells according to the package directions, omitting any oil and salt. Rinse, drain, and set aside.

In a large skillet coated with nonstick cooking spray, cook the meat, onion, and garlic over medium-high heat until the meat is done, about 7 minutes. Drain any excess grease. Mix in the Ricotta, cream cheese, and spinach. Stuff the shells with the meat mixture, and arrange in a 2- to 3-quart oblong baking dish coated with nonstick cooking spray.

In a large bowl, combine the tomatoes, oregano, basil, salt, and pepper. Pour the sauce over the shells. Cover, and bake for 15 minutes. Uncover, and bake for 10 minutes longer, or until bubbly and well heated.

Nutritional information per serving

Calories 270, Protein (g) 21, Carbohydrate (g) 30, Fat (g) 7, Calories from Fat (%) 29, Saturated Fat (g) 4, Dietary Fiber (g) 4, Cholesterol (mg) 48, Sodium (mg) 276
Diabetic Exchanges: *2 lean meat, 1.5 starch, 1.5 vegetable*

QUICK TIP

To prevent tomato based sauces (such as spaghetti sauce) from staining plastic storage containers, spray the containers liberally with nonstick cooking spray before adding the sauce.

PASTA

❄ Magnificent Meat Sauce with Spaghetti

Here's a fabulous classic meat sauce to satisfy all spaghetti-and-meat-sauce fans. It freezes well. Substitute one large jar spaghetti sauce for the tomatoes and seasonings, and add to the cooked ground meat for a fast meat sauce.

1 celery stalk with leaves, finely chopped

1 carrot, peeled and finely chopped

1 onion, finely chopped

½ teaspoon minced garlic

2 pounds ground sirloin

1 tablespoon dried oregano leaves

½ cup dry red wine

1 (28-ounce) can chopped tomatoes, in juice

2 tablespoons tomato paste

1 cup canned beef broth

1 teaspoon sugar

Salt and pepper to taste

1 (16-ounce) package pasta of your choice (spaghetti, spirals, bowties)

MAKES 6 TO 8 SERVINGS

In a heavy pot coated with nonstick cooking spray, sauté the celery, carrot, onion, and garlic over medium heat until tender, about 5 minutes. Add the meat and oregano. Cook, stirring, until the meat begins to brown, about 4 minutes. Add the wine, and simmer another 5 minutes or until meat is done. Then add the tomatoes, tomato paste, beef broth, and sugar. Simmer over medium heat for 20 minutes (it can simmer longer). Add the salt and pepper.

Meanwhile, cook the pasta according to the package directions, omitting any oil and salt. Drain, and serve with the meat sauce.

Nutritional information per serving
Calories 394, Protein (g) 31, Carbohydrate (g) 52, Fat (g) 6, Calories from Fat (%) 14, Saturated Fat (g) 2, Dietary Fiber (g) 4, Cholesterol (mg) 60, Sodium (mg) 332
Diabetic Exchanges: 3 very lean meat, 3 starch, 1.5 vegetable

QUICK TIP

Store leftover tomato paste in a zipper lock bag in the freezer. To reuse the paste, break off chunks or defrost it in the microwave.

PASTA

Chinese Pork Vermicelli

Chinese and pasta pair up, so there's no need for Chinese takeout. Marinate the pork early in the day to prepare when you're ready to eat.

⅓ cup reduced-sodium soy sauce

1 teaspoon ground ginger

¼ teaspoon crushed red pepper flakes

1 teaspoon minced garlic

1½ pounds pork tenderloin, trimmed of fat and cut into 1-inch cubes

1 (6-ounce) package frozen snow pea pods

1 cup (1½-inch) red bell pepper slices

1 (8-ounce) package vermicelli pasta

⅓ cup fat-free canned chicken broth

MAKES 6 SERVINGS

Combine the soy sauce, ginger, red pepper, and garlic in a large zipper-lock, heavy-duty plastic bag. Add the pork; seal the bag, shake it, and marinate in the refrigerator for at least 20 minutes to overnight.

Coat a large skillet with nonstick cooking spray, and heat over medium-high heat; add the pork mixture to the skillet, and stir-fry 3 minutes, or until the pork is browned. Add the snow peas and red bell pepper, sautéing until the vegetables are crisp-tender, 3 to 5 minutes.

Meanwhile, cook the pasta according to the package directions, omitting any oil and salt. Drain. Add the chicken broth and pasta to the skillet. Cook 1 minute longer, or until heated through. Serve immediately.

Nutritional information per serving
Calories 307, Protein (g) 31, Carbohydrate (g) 33,
Fat (g) 5, Calories from Fat (%) 14, Saturated Fat (g) 1,
Dietary Fiber (g) 2, Cholesterol (mg) 74, Sodium (mg) 634
Diabetic Exchanges: *3 very lean meat, 2 starch, 1 vegetable*

QUICK TIP

Stir-frying is a healthier method of cooking because the technique requires the ingredients to move constantly in the skillet, so very little oil is needed to prevent sticking.

No-Bake Cookies 365

Oatmeal Cookies 366

Chocolate Chip Cookies 366

Ultimate Chocolate Cookies 367

Peanut Butter Cookies 368

Holiday Cookies 369

Cookies and Cakes

Strudel 370

Lemon Sours 371

Lemon Squares 372

Apricot Oatmeal Bars 373

Heavenly Hash 374

Chocolate Chess Bars 375

Coffee Toffee Brownies 376

Chewy Chocolate Caramel Brownies 377

Gooey Chocolate Peanut Butter Brownies 378

Almost-Better-than-Sex Cake 379

Apple Cake with Broiled Topping 380

Apricot Cake 381

Banana Cake with Cream Cheese Frosting 382

Blueberry Pound Cake 383

Cream Cheese Coffee Cake 384

Coffee Cake with Streusel Filling 385

Cranberry Cake 386

Orange Cranberry Cake 387

Citrus Sensational Cake 388

Lemon Poppy Seed Cake 389

Boston Cream Pie 390

Sweet Potato Bundt Cake 391

Strawberry Custard Cake 392

Quick Pineapple Cake 394

Tropical Upside-Down Cake 395

Piña Colada Bundt Cake 396

Italian Cream Cake 397

Quick Italian Cream Cake 398

Wait Cake 399

Strawberry Angel Food Cake 400

Chocolate Pudding Cake 400

Coffee Angel Food Cake 401

Tiramisu Cake 402

Mocha Chocolate Bundt Cake 403

Triple Chocolate Cake 404

Red Velvet Cake 405

German Chocolate Bundt Cake 406

German Chocolate Sheet Cake 407

Old-Fashioned German Chocolate Layered Cake 408

Oatmeal Chocolate Cake 410

No-Bake Cookies

Keep these pantry ingredients available to make this popular, quick recipe at any time. It's so simple the kids will make these treats for you.

½ cup graham cracker crumbs

3 cups old-fashioned oatmeal

1½ cups sugar

¼ cup cocoa

½ cup skim milk

½ cup margarine

½ cup reduced-fat peanut butter

1 teaspoon vanilla extract

MAKES 48 COOKIES

In a medium bowl, combine the graham cracker crumbs and oatmeal; set aside.

In a large saucepan, stir the sugar, cocoa, milk, and margarine over medium heat until dissolved. Bring the mixture to a boil, and boil for 2 minutes—this is important. Remove from heat. Stir in the peanut butter and vanilla until well combined. Quickly blend in the oatmeal mixture. Beat by hand until thickened (a few minutes), if necessary.

Drop by teaspoonfuls onto waxed paper. Refrigerate until firm, and store in the refrigerator or another cool place.

Nutritional information per serving
Calories 82, Protein (g) 2, Carbohydrate (g) 12,
Fat (g) 3, Calories from Fat (%) 35, Saturated Fat (g) 1,
Dietary Fiber (g) 1, Cholesterol (mg) 0, Sodium (mg) 46
Diabetic Exchanges: *1 other carbohydrate, 0.5 fat*

QUICK TIP

Creamy or crunchy peanut butter will work equally well in the recipe.

COOKIES AND CAKES

Oatmeal Cookies

I tested many recipes to come up with this perfect oatmeal cookie: crispy, moist, and tasty.

⅓ cup canola oil
¾ cup light brown sugar
¾ cup sugar
1 egg
1 egg white
1 teaspoon vanilla extract
1½ cups all-purpose flour
1 teaspoon ground cinnamon
1 teaspoon baking soda
1½ cups old-fashioned oatmeal
½ cup chopped pecans

MAKES 36 TO 48 COOKIES

Preheat the oven to 350°F.

In a large bowl, stir together the oil, brown sugar, sugar, egg, egg white, and vanilla. In a small bowl, mix together the flour, cinnamon, and baking soda. Add the flour mixture to the sugar mixture. Stir in the oatmeal and pecans, mixing well. Drop by rounded teaspoonfuls onto a baking sheet coated with nonstick cooking spray. Bake for 10 to 12 minutes, or until lightly browned. Remove and let cool on wax paper.

Nutritional information per serving

Calories 73, Protein (g) 1, Carbohydrate (g) 11, Fat (g) 3, Calories from Fat (%) 33, Saturated Fat (g) 0, Dietary Fiber (g) 1, Cholesterol (mg) 4, Sodium (mg) 30
Diabetic Exchanges: *1 other carbohydrate, 0.5 fat*

Chocolate Chip Cookies

My daughters could make these cookies with their eyes closed—their friends all request them.

½ cup margarine
⅔ cup sugar
⅔ cup light brown sugar
1 egg
2 cups all-purpose flour
1 teaspoon baking soda
1 teaspoon vanilla extract
⅔ cup semisweet chocolate chips

MAKES 48 COOKIES

Preheat the oven to 375°F.

In a large mixing bowl, beat the margarine, sugar, and brown sugar until creamy. Add the egg, and beat well.

In another bowl, combine the flour and baking soda. Add to the margarine mixture, and beat just until blended. Add the vanilla. Stir in the chocolate chips. Drop spoonfuls of dough onto a baking sheet coated with nonstick cooking spray. Bake for 8 to 10 minutes or until lightly browned. Remove from the cookie sheet, and cool completely on a wire rack before serving.

Nutritional information per serving

Calories 71, Protein (g) 1, Carbohydrate (g) 11, Fat (g) 3, Calories from Fat (%) 34, Saturated Fat (g) 1, Dietary Fiber (g) 0, Cholesterol (mg) 4, Sodium (mg) 51
Diabetic Exchanges: *1 other carbohydrate, 0.5 fat*

Ultimate Chocolate Cookies

These chewy, rich, double-chocolate cookies are outstanding. The espresso powder enhances the chocolate flavor, and I personally love the toasted pecans in these. I store them in my freezer in zipper-lock bags to enjoy all the time.

½ cup margarine,
   softened

½ cup sugar

½ cup light brown sugar

1 egg

1 teaspoon vanilla extract

1 teaspoon instant
   espresso powder

1 teaspoon hot water

1¼ cups all-purpose flour

½ teaspoon baking soda

2 tablespoons cocoa

⅔ cup semisweet
   chocolate chips

⅓ cup chopped pecans,
   toasted, optional

MAKES 36 COOKIES

Preheat the oven to 350°F.

In a large mixing bowl, mix by hand the margarine, sugar, and brown sugar. Add the egg and vanilla, mixing until creamy. Dissolve the espresso powder in the hot water, and add to the sugar mixture.

In a medium bowl, combine the flour, baking soda, and cocoa; add to the sugar mixture, mixing well. Stir in the chocolate chips and pecans.

Drop by rounded spoonfuls onto a baking sheet coated with nonstick cooking spray. Bake for 8 to 10 minutes or until lightly browned. Don't overcook, as they harden as they cool. Remove from the baking sheet, and cool on wax paper or a wire rack.

Nutritional information per serving
Calories 79, Protein (g) 1, Carbohydrate (g) 11,
Fat (g) 4, Calories from Fat (%) 40, Saturated Fat (g) 1,
Dietary Fiber (g) 0, Cholesterol (mg) 6, Sodium (mg) 50
Diabetic Exchanges: *1 other carbohydrate, 1 fat*

QUICK TIP

You don't have to brew a pot of espresso coffee for this recipe. Look for instant espresso powder in the coffee section of the grocery store.

COOKIES AND CAKES

Peanut Butter Cookies

Nothing beats a rich, crumbly, nutty peanut butter cookie.

¼ cup margarine

½ cup light brown sugar

½ cup confectioners'
   sugar

1 egg

½ cup reduced-fat
   peanut butter

1 teaspoon vanilla extract

1½ cups all-purpose flour

½ teaspoon baking soda

⅓ cup chopped peanuts

MAKES 36 COOKIES

Preheat the oven to 375°F.

In a large mixing bowl, blend the margarine, brown sugar, and confectioners' sugar until fluffy. Add the egg, peanut butter, and vanilla. Mix until smooth.

In a medium bowl, combine the flour and baking soda. Add to the peanut butter mixture. Stir in the peanuts just until blended.

Drop the dough by rounded spoonfuls onto a baking sheet coated with nonstick cooking spray. Flatten each round with the back side of a fork two times (making a cross pattern). Bake for 10 to 12 minutes, or until lightly browned. Remove to a rack, and cool.

Nutritional information per serving

Calories 76, Protein (g) 2, Carbohydrate (g) 10,
Fat (g) 3, Calories from Fat (%) 38, Saturated Fat (g) 1,
Dietary Fiber (g) 0, Cholesterol (mg) 6, Sodium (mg) 55
Diabetic Exchanges: 0.5 other carbohydrate, 0.5 fat

QUICK TIP

Once a jar of peanut butter has been opened, it will stay fresh for about 3 months. After that, it should be refrigerated.

✏ ❄ Holiday Cookies

Tart cranberries team up with white chocolate for this cookie that is fabulous year-round.

½ cup margarine

1 cup sugar

1 egg

1 teaspoon vanilla extract

2 cups all-purpose flour

½ teaspoon baking powder

¼ cup cocoa

1 (7-ounce) jar marshmallow creme

½ cup chopped white chocolate chips

½ cup dried cranberries

½ cup chopped pecans

MAKES 48 COOKIES

Preheat the oven to 350°F.

In a large mixing bowl, cream the margarine and sugar. Add the egg and vanilla, mixing well.

In a medium bowl, combine the flour, baking powder, and cocoa; add to the margarine mixture. Add the marshmallow creme, stirring until combined. Stir in the white chocolate chips, cranberries, and pecans just until blended. The batter will be thick.

Drop by spoonfuls onto a baking sheet coated with nonstick cooking spray. Bake for 10 to 12 minutes, or until lightly browned. Remove to wire rack, and cool.

Nutritional information per serving

Calories 91, Protein (g) 1, Carbohydrate (g)14,
Fat (g) 4, Calories from Fat (%) 35, Saturated Fat (g) 1,
Dietary Fiber (g) 0, Cholesterol (mg) 5, Sodium (mg) 32
Diabetic Exchanges: *1 other carbohydrate, 1 fat*

QUICK TIP

Walnuts may be high in fat, but 70% of the fat is polyunsaturated, the healthier form of fat.

COOKIES AND CAKES

🥕 ❄️ Strudel

Here's an easy but delectable version of an involved recipe. Don't be afraid of this recipe if you are a person who gets nervous with dough—this is a workable dough with a sweet, nutty filling.

2¼ cups all-purpose flour

1 tablespoon sugar

½ teaspoon salt

½ cup margarine, melted

1 cup nonfat plain yogurt

1 (15.5-ounce) jar apricot spread or apricot preserves

½ cup light brown sugar

1 tablespoon ground cinnamon

⅔ cup chopped walnuts

½ cup golden raisins

2 tablespoons confectioners' sugar

MAKES 48 SLICES

In a large bowl, combine the flour, sugar, salt, margarine, and yogurt, and stir until the mixture forms a ball. Wrap the dough in waxed paper, and refrigerate for 1 hour.

Preheat the oven to 350°F.

Remove the dough from the refrigerator, and divide into four equal parts. Roll each piece of dough out on floured waxed paper to form a rectangle. Spread ¼ of the apricot spread over each entire rectangle.

Combine the brown sugar, cinnamon, walnuts, and raisins. Sprinkle one-fourth of the mixture over each rectangle. Roll each rectangle up lengthwise to form a roll. Place each roll on a baking sheet coated with non-stick cooking spray. Bake for 40 minutes to 1 hour. Sprinkle with confectioners' sugar. Let cool, and slice into 1-inch slices.

Nutritional information per serving
Calories 84, Protein (g) 1, Carbohydrate (g) 13,
Fat (g) 3, Calories from Fat (%) 32, Saturated Fat (g) 0,
Dietary Fiber (g) 1, Cholesterol (mg) 0, Sodium (mg) 53
Diabetic Exchanges: *1 other carbohydrate, 0.5 fat*

QUICK TIP

Walnuts are packed with omega 3's and add a wonderful flavor and crunch to this recipe.

COOKIES AND CAKES

Lemon Sours

These luscious lemon bars are great for any occasion.

1 cup all-purpose flour

2 tablespoons sugar

4 tablespoons margarine

2 eggs

1 cup light brown sugar

4 tablespoons lemon
  juice, divided

2 teaspoons grated
  lemon rind, divided

⅔ cup confectioners'
  sugar

MAKES 25 SQUARES

Preheat the oven to 350°F.

In a medium bowl, combine the flour and sugar. Cut in the margarine with a pastry blender or fork until the mixture resembles coarse meal. Press into an ungreased 9-inch square pan. Bake 13 to 15 minutes, or until light brown.

In a mixing bowl, beat together the eggs, brown sugar, 2 tablespoons lemon juice, and 1 teaspoon lemon rind until well mixed and light. Spread over the baked crust. Return to the oven, and bake for 20 minutes longer, or until the top is browned and puffed.

In a small bowl, mix together the remaining 2 tablespoons lemon juice, 1 teaspoon lemon rind, and the confectioners' sugar. Spread on the baked sours while warm. Cool, and slice into squares.

Nutritional information per serving

*Calories 90, Protein (g) 1, Carbohydrate (g) 17,
Fat (g) 2, Calories from Fat (%) 22, Saturated Fat (g) 0,
Dietary Fiber (g) 0, Cholesterol (mg) 17, Sodium (mg) 30*
Diabetic Exchanges: *1 other carbohydrate, 0.5 fat*

QUICK TIP

Room-temperature lemons will yield more juice than those that have been refrigerated.

COOKIES AND CAKES

✎ ❄ Lemon Squares

Here's the ultimate lemon bar recipe. Beware, lemon lovers, as you might find yourself eating lots of these lemon luxuries.

1¾ cups all-purpose flour, divided

⅓ cup plus 3 tablespoons confectioners' sugar

⅓ cup margarine

1⅓ cups sugar

1 tablespoon grated lemon rind

1 teaspoon baking powder

3 egg whites

1 egg

⅓ cup plus 1 tablespoon lemon juice

½ teaspoon butter extract

QUICK TIP

Purchase a jar of dried lemon rind in the spice section of the grocery store for those times when you don't have fresh lemons around.

MAKES 48 SQUARES

Preheat the oven to 350°F. Coat a 13 x 9 x 2-inch baking dish with nonstick cooking spray.

In a medium bowl, combine 1½ cups of the flour and ⅓ cup of the confectioners' sugar; cut in the margarine with a pastry blender or two knives until the mixture resembles coarse meal. Press the mixture firmly and evenly into the bottom of the baking pan. Bake for 20 minutes, or until lightly browned.

Combine the sugar, remaining ¼ cup flour, lemon rind, baking powder, egg whites, and egg in a medium bowl, and blend with a whisk. Stir in ⅓ cup lemon juice and the butter extract. Pour the mixture over the prepared crust. Bake for 20 minutes, or until set.

In a small dish, combine the remaining 3 tablespoons confectioners' sugar with the remaining 1 tablespoon lemon juice to make a glaze. Carefully spread the glaze over the hot lemon squares. Cool completely in the pan, and cut into squares.

Nutritional information per serving
Calories 58, Protein (g) 1, Carbohydrate (g) 11,
Fat (g) 1, Calories from Fat (%) 22, Saturated Fat (g) 0,
Dietary Fiber (g) 0, Cholesterol (mg) 4, Sodium (mg) 30
Diabetic Exchanges: *0.5 other carbohydrate*

Apricot Oatmeal Bars

This recipe has been a family favorite for years—we like to keep them in the freezer. The crumbly oatmeal topping with the tart apricot filling is a great combination.

½ cup margarine, melted
1½ cups old-fashioned oatmeal
1½ cups all-purpose flour
1 cup light brown sugar
1 teaspoon vanilla extract
1 teaspoon baking soda
¼ teaspoon ground cinnamon
⅓ cup chopped walnuts
1 (12-ounce) jar apricot preserves or spreadable fruit

MAKES 36 TO 48 BARS

Preheat the oven to 350°F.

In a large mixing bowl, mix together the margarine, oatmeal, flour, brown sugar, vanilla, baking soda, and cinnamon, mixing until it forms a crumbly dough. Stir in the walnuts. Press half the mixture into the bottom of a 13 x 9 x 2-inch baking pan coated with nonstick cooking spray. Spread the preserves over top. Crumble the other half of the oatmeal mixture over the preserves. Bake for 30 to 35 minutes, or until lightly browned. Cool, and cut into bars.

Nutritional information per serving

Calories 76, Protein (g) 1, Carbohydrate (g) 12, Fat (g) 3, Calories from Fat (%) 31, Saturated Fat (g) 0, Dietary Fiber (g) 1, Cholesterol (mg) 0, Sodium (mg) 52
Diabetic Exchanges: *1 other carbohydrate, 0.5 fat*

QUICK TIP

Try different preserves to create a new cookie.

COOKIES AND CAKES

Heavenly Hash

Simple and sensational! These addictive brownies are soooo good. Toss in some toasted pecans with the marshmallows for the height of indulgence.

2 cups all-purpose flour

1½ cups sugar

⅓ cup cocoa

1 cup water

⅓ cup canola oil

½ cup buttermilk

1 teaspoon baking soda

1 egg white, well beaten

1 (10-ounce) package miniature marshmallows

Chocolate Icing (recipe follows)

Chocolate Icing

6 tablespoons margarine

⅓ cup buttermilk

¼ cup cocoa

1 (16-ounce) box confectioners' sugar

1 teaspoon vanilla extract

MAKES 48 SERVINGS

Preheat the oven to 400°F.

Combine the flour, sugar, and cocoa in a mixing bowl. In a small saucepan, combine the water and oil; bring to a boil. Add the hot water to the flour mixture, and stir well.

In a small bowl, combine the buttermilk and baking soda, mixing well. Add the buttermilk mixture and the egg white to the batter; mix well. Spoon the batter into a 15 x 10 x 1-inch jelly-roll pan coated with nonstick cooking spray. Bake for 12 to 15 minutes. Remove from oven, and immediately top with the marshmallows. Slowly and evenly pour hot Chocolate Icing (see recipe below) on top of the marshmallows. Cool before cutting.

Combine the margarine, buttermilk, and cocoa in a medium saucepan; bring to a boil, and boil for 1 minute. Remove from the heat, and add the confectioners' sugar and vanilla. Blend until smooth.

Nutritional information per serving

Calories 131, Protein (g) 1, Carbohydrate (g) 25, Fat (g) 3, Calories from Fat (%) 21, Saturated Fat (g) 0, Dietary Fiber (g) 0, Cholesterol (mg) 0, Sodium (mg) 52
Diabetic Exchanges: *1.5 other carbohydrate, 0.5 fat*

FOOD FACT

If you don't have buttermilk, mix 1 tablespoon distilled vinegar or lemon juice with 1 cup milk.

COOKIES AND CAKES

Chocolate Chess Bars

These rich-tasting, easy-to-make brownies with a baked cream cheese topping get unbelievable praise every time I make them.

1 (18.25-ounce) package devil's food cake mix

1 egg

½ cup margarine, melted

1 tablespoon water

1 (8-ounce) package reduced-fat cream cheese

1 (16-ounce) box confectioners' sugar

3 egg whites

1 teaspoon vanilla extract

MAKES 48 SQUARES

Preheat the oven to 350°F.

In a large mixing bowl, combine the cake mix, egg, melted margarine, and water. Beat by hand until well blended. Pat the batter into the bottom of a 13 x 9 x 2-inch baking pan coated with nonstick cooking spray.

In a mixing bowl, beat the cream cheese, confectioners' sugar, and egg whites until the mixture is smooth and creamy. Add the vanilla. Pour over the batter in the pan. Bake for 45 minutes, or until the top is golden brown. Cool, and cut into squares.

Nutritional information per serving
Calories 114, Protein (g) 2, Carbohydrate (g) 17,
Fat (g) 4, Calories from Fat (%) 34, Saturated Fat (g) 1,
Dietary Fiber (g) 0, Cholesterol (mg) 15, Sodium (mg) 139
Diabetic Exchanges: *1 other carbohydrate, 1 fat*

QUICK TIP

Brownies and cookies freeze 2 to 3 months wrapped well in airtight wrapping or containers.

COOKIES AND CAKES

🥕 ❄️ Coffee Toffee Brownies

The rich caramel flavor with a hint of coffee and chocolate makes this a wonderful specialty brownie.

½ cup margarine

1 (16-ounce) box dark brown sugar

2 tablespoons instant coffee

1 tablespoon hot water

2 eggs

1 tablespoon vanilla extract

2 cups all-purpose flour

2 teaspoons baking soda

⅛ teaspoon salt

½ cup semisweet chocolate chips

MAKES 48 BROWNIES

Preheat the oven to 350°F. Coat a 13 x 9 x 2-inch baking pan with nonstick cooking spray.

In a small saucepan or in a microwave oven for 1 minute in a suitable container, melt the margarine and brown sugar over low heat. Combine the instant coffee with the hot water to dissolve, and combine with the brown sugar mixture in a mixing bowl. Stir and cool.

In a small bowl, whisk together the eggs and vanilla; mix into the brown sugar mixture. Combine the flour, baking soda, and salt, and stir into the brown sugar mixture. Stir in the chocolate chips. Pour the batter into the prepared pan, and bake for 30 to 35 minutes, or until a toothpick inserted in the middle comes out clean. Do not overcook. Cool in the pan, and cut into squares.

Nutritional information per serving
Calories 84, Protein (g) 1, Carbohydrate (g) 14,
Fat (g) 3, Calories from Fat (%) 28, Saturated Fat (g) 1,
Dietary Fiber (g) 0, Cholesterol (mg) 9, Sodium (mg) 87
Diabetic Exchanges: *1 other carbohydrate, 0.5 fat*

FOOD FACT

Brown sugar comes in light and dark granulated forms. The lighter the brown sugar, the more delicate the flavor. The very dark brown sugar has a pronounced molasses flavor.

🥕 ❄️ Chewy Chocolate Caramel Brownies

This sensational chocolate brownie with chewy caramel filling is a simple success. A kid favorite! These ingredients can be kept in the pantry for that quickly prepared "emergency" brownie. One time we even used a yellow cake mix for a not-so-chocolatey version.

8 ounces chewy caramels

⅔ cup evaporated skimmed milk, divided

1 (18.25-ounce) package German chocolate cake mix

½ cup margarine, softened

½ cup semisweet chocolate chips

MAKES 48 BROWNIES

Preheat the oven to 350°F.

In a microwave-safe dish, combine the caramels and ⅓ cup milk, and microwave until melted, about 2 minutes, stirring after 1 minute.

In a large mixing bowl, mix together the cake mix, the remaining ⅓ cup milk, and the margarine. Spread half the mixture in the bottom of a 13 x 9 x 2-inch pan coated with nonstick cooking spray. Bake for 6 minutes. Remove from the oven, and sprinkle with chocolate chips. Pour the caramel evenly over the chocolate chips, and drop the remaining cake mixture over the partially baked layer. Continue baking for 15 minutes, or until the sides pull away from the pan. Do not overbake; the brownie hardens as it cools. Cool before cutting.

Nutritional information per serving

*Calories 94, Protein (g) 1, Carbohydrate (g) 13,
Fat (g) 4, Calories from Fat (%) 39, Saturated Fat (g) 1,
Dietary Fiber (g) 0, Cholesterol (mg) 3, Sodium (mg) 116*
Diabetic Exchanges: *1 other carbohydrate, 1 fat*

COOKIES AND CAKES

✒ ❄ Gooey Chocolate Peanut Butter Brownies

Rich and gooey yet simple to make, these incredible brownies taste like a candy bar. I love the peanuts, but sometimes the young ones prefer their brownies without.

---

1 (18.25-ounce) package devil's food cake mix

1 (12-ounce) can fat-free sweetened condensed milk, divided

¼ cup margarine, melted

1 egg white

1 (7-ounce) jar marshmallow creme

½ cup peanut butter morsels

½ cup chopped peanuts, optional

MAKES 36 BROWNIES

Preheat the oven to 350°F. Coat a 13 x 9 x 2-inch baking pan with nonstick cooking spray.

In a mixing bowl, mix together the cake mix, ½ cup sweetened condensed milk, margarine, and egg white. Pat two-thirds of the batter into the bottom of the prepared pan (the batter will be stiff and sticky). Bake for 10 minutes.

In a mixing bowl, mix the remaining sweetened condensed milk and the marshmallow creme. Stir in the peanut butter morsels and peanuts. Carefully spread the mixture evenly over the partially baked brownie layer. Drop the remaining batter by spoonfuls over the marsh-mallow mixture. Bake for 25 to 30 minutes or until set. Cool completely before cutting.

Nutritional information per serving
Calories 138, Protein (g) 3, Carbohydrate (g) 23,
Fat (g) 4, Calories from Fat (%) 25, Saturated Fat (g) 1,
Dietary Fiber (g) 1, Cholesterol (mg) 10, Sodium (mg) 161
Diabetic Exchanges: *1.5 other carbohydrate, 1 fat*

Almost-Better-than-Sex Cake

Don't let the name scare you, as the recipe has been around for years. This is my lightened version of a highly requested recipe, but no one will ever be able to tell.

1 (18.25-ounce) package yellow cake mix

½ cup skim milk

¼ cup water

⅓ cup canola oil

2 eggs

2 egg whites

1 cup nonfat plain yogurt

1 (4-serving) box instant vanilla pudding and pie filling

1 (4-ounce) bar German chocolate, grated

⅓ cup semisweet chocolate chips

½ cup chopped pecans

MAKES 20 SERVINGS

Preheat the oven to 350°F. Coat a 10-inch Bundt pan with nonstick cooking spray.

In a large mixing bowl, combine the cake mix, milk, water, oil, eggs, egg whites, yogurt, and vanilla pudding. Beat slightly, only until the mixture is combined. Stir in the grated chocolate, chocolate chips, and pecans.

Pour the batter into the prepared pan. Bake for 45 to 55 minutes, or until an inserted toothpick comes out clean. Do not overbake. Cool 10 minutes, and invert onto a serving plate.

Nutritional information per serving

Calories 240, Protein (g) 4, Carbohydrate (g) 32, Fat (g) 12, Calories from Fat (%) 43, Saturated Fat (g) 2, Dietary Fiber (g) 1, Cholesterol (mg) 22, Sodium (mg) 263
Diabetic Exchanges: *2 other carbohydrate, 2.5 fat*

QUICK TIP

Grate chocolate in the food processor—break the chocolate into small chunks and chop with the metal blade using on/off pulses.

COOKIES AND CAKES

Apple Cake with Broiled Topping

This moist, chunky apple cake has the perfect amount of spice complemented by the toasty broiled topping. A winner!

6 tablespoons margarine

2 cups sugar

2 eggs

1 teaspoon vanilla extract

2 cups all-purpose flour

2 teaspoons ground cinnamon

1 teaspoon baking soda

½ cup buttermilk

4 cups diced peeled tart cooking apples

Broiled Brown Sugar Topping (recipe follows)

Broiled Brown Sugar Topping

2 tablespoons margarine

¼ cup evaporated skimmed milk

⅔ cup light brown sugar

1 teaspoon vanilla extract

½ cup chopped walnuts

MAKES 20 SERVINGS

Preheat the oven to 350°F. Coat a 13 x 9 x 2-inch baking pan with nonstick cooking spray.

In a large mixing bowl, beat together the margarine and sugar until creamy. Add the eggs and vanilla, mixing well.

In another bowl, combine the flour, cinnamon, and baking soda; add the flour mixture alternately with the buttermilk to the margarine mixture. Stir in the apples, and pour the batter into the prepared pan. Bake for 45 minutes, and cover with the Broiled Brown Sugar Topping (see recipe below).

FOOD FACT

Granny Smith apples are available year-round, and their tartness makes them a good cooking apple. Rome apples are primarily used for cooking, as their flavor grows richer when baked.

In a saucepan, heat the margarine, milk, and brown sugar until the mixture comes to a boil. Boil 2 minutes, and add the vanilla and walnuts. Spread on top of the cake, and broil in the oven for 2 minutes. Watch carefully.

Nutritional information per serving
Calories 237, Protein (g) 3, Carbohydrate (g) 41, Fat (g) 7, Calories from Fat (%) 27, Saturated Fat (g) 1, Dietary Fiber (g) 1, Cholesterol (mg) 22, Sodium (mg) 136
Diabetic Exchanges: *3 other carbohydrate, 1.5 fat*

Apricot Cake

Begin with a cake mix and add a few pantry ingredients to whip up an outstanding three-layer cake with a burst of flavor.

⅓ cup canola oil
1 (16-ounce) can light apricot halves, drained and chopped
½ cup apricot nectar
1 (18.25-ounce) package white cake mix
1 (3-ounce) box apricot gelatin
3 eggs
1 teaspoon vanilla extract
1 teaspoon butter extract
Apricot Frosting (recipe follows)

MAKES 16 SLICES

Preheat the oven to 350°F. Coat three 9-inch round cake pans with nonstick cooking spray.

In a mixing bowl, combine the oil, apricot, and apricot nectar. In another bowl, combine the cake mix and gelatin; add to the liquid mixture, and beat well. Add the eggs and extracts, beating well.

Pour the batter into the prepared cake pans, and bake for 20 to 25 minutes, or until the center springs back when touched. Cool for 10 minutes in the pans; then remove to wire racks. Frost the cooled layers with Apricot Frosting (see recipe below).

Apricot Frosting

6 tablespoons margarine
1 (16-ounce) box confectioners' sugar
¼ cup apricot nectar
1 teaspoon vanilla extract
½ teaspoon butter extract

In a medium mixing bowl, blend together the margarine, confectioners' sugar, nectar, and extracts until smooth.

Nutritional information per serving
Calories 374, Protein (g) 4, Carbohydrate (g) 62, Fat (g) 13, Calories from Fat (%) 31, Saturated Fat (g) 2, Dietary Fiber (g) 1, Cholesterol (mg) 42, Sodium (mg) 85
Diabetic Exchanges: *4 other carbohydrate, 2.5 fat*

COOKIES AND CAKES

Banana Cake with Cream Cheese Frosting

Nothing beats a good banana cake. For the ultimate version, add toasted walnuts and/or mini chocolate chips.

2½ cups all-purpose flour

1 teaspoon baking powder

1½ teaspoons baking soda

1 teaspoon ground cinnamon

¼ cup canola oil

1 cup dark brown sugar

1 egg

2 egg whites

2 cups mashed banana

2 teaspoons vanilla extract

1 cup buttermilk

Cream Cheese Frosting (recipe follows)

MAKES 16 SLICES

Preheat the oven to 350°F. Coat three 9-inch round cake pans with nonstick cooking spray.

In a medium bowl, combine the flour, baking powder, baking soda, and cinnamon; set aside.

In a large mixing bowl, beat the oil and brown sugar until light, add the egg and egg whites. Add the banana and vanilla, beating well. Add the mixed dry ingredients alternately with the buttermilk.

Pour the batter into the prepared pans, and bake for 15 to 20 minutes or until the center springs back when touched. Frost with the Cream Cheese Frosting (see recipe below).

QUICK TIP

When you have old bananas, peel and place them in zipper-lock bags in the freezer to pull out for banana cake and bread. Ripe bananas are the best for baking.

Cream Cheese Frosting

1 (8-ounce) package reduced-fat cream cheese, softened

3 tablespoons margarine, softened

1 (16-ounce) box confectioners' sugar

1 teaspoon vanilla extract

In a medium mixing bowl, beat the cream cheese and margarine until smooth. Add the confectioners' sugar, and beat until light. Blend in the vanilla.

Nutritional information per serving

Calories 359, Protein (g) 5, Carbohydrate (g) 65, Fat (g) 9, Calories from Fat (%) 23, Saturated Fat (g) 3, Dietary Fiber (g) 1, Cholesterol (mg) 24, Sodium (mg) 267
Diabetic Exchanges: *4.5 other carbohydrate, 2 fat*

COOKIES AND CAKES

Blueberry Pound Cake

This quick cake will impress anyone who takes a bite. If blueberries aren't in season, substitute frozen for fresh.

1 (18.25-ounce) package
  yellow cake mix
1 (8-ounce) package
  reduced-fat
  cream cheese
2 eggs
1⅓ cups water
1½ teaspoons vanilla
  extract
2 cups blueberries
½ cup chopped pecans
Confectioners' sugar,
  optional

MAKES 20 SERVINGS

Preheat the oven to 350°F. Coat a 10-inch Bundt pan with nonstick cooking spray.

In a large mixing bowl, mix the cake mix, cream cheese, eggs, water, and vanilla. Fold in the blueberries and pecans.

Pour the batter into the prepared pan. Bake for 40 minutes, or until inserted toothpick comes out clean. Do not overcook. Cool in the pan for 20 minutes, invert onto a serving plate, and sprinkle with confectioners' sugar, if desired.

Nutritional information per serving

Calories 172, Protein (g) 4, Carbohydrate (g) 23,
Fat (g) 8, Calories from Fat (%) 40, Saturated Fat (g) 3,
Dietary Fiber (g) 1, Cholesterol (mg) 31, Sodium (mg) 223
Diabetic Exchanges: 1.5 other carbohydrate, 1.5 fat

FOOD FACT

Deep red, purple, or blue foods like blueberries, cherries, strawberries, cranberries, and red grapes contain phytonutrients called anthocyanins. Studies have shown that these nutrients may reduce the risk of both heart disease and cancer.

COOKIES AND CAKES

✏️ ❄️ Cream Cheese Coffee Cake

Lovers of coffee cake and cheesecake will enjoy this rich, creamy cake.

2½ cups all-purpose flour

¾ cup sugar, divided

½ cup margarine

½ teaspoon baking powder

½ teaspoon baking soda

1 cup nonfat plain yogurt

1 teaspoon almond extract

4 egg whites, divided

1 (8-ounce) package reduced-fat cream cheese, softened

¼ cup sliced almonds

MAKES 12 SERVINGS

Preheat the oven to 350°F. Coat a 9-inch springform pan with nonstick cooking spray.

In a large bowl, combine the flour and ½ cup sugar. Cut in the margarine until the mixture resembles coarse crumbs. Reserve 1 cup of the crumb mixture.

To the remaining crumb mixture, add the baking powder, baking soda, yogurt, almond extract, and 2 egg whites. Spread the batter over the bottom and up the sides of the prepared pan.

In a small bowl, mix together the cream cheese, remaining ¼ cup sugar, and remaining 2 egg whites until creamy. Pour into the batter-lined pan. Sprinkle with the sliced almonds and the reserved crumb mixture. Bake for 45 minutes, or until the mixture is set and the crust is golden brown. Serve warm or cold. Refrigerate any leftovers.

Nutritional information per serving

Calories 271, Protein (g) 7, Carbohydrate (g) 31,
Fat (g) 13, Calories from Fat (%) 43, Saturated Fat (g) 4,
Dietary Fiber (g) 1, Cholesterol (mg) 14, Sodium (mg) 278
Diabetic Exchanges: 2 other carbohydrate, 2.5 fat

Coffee Cake with Streusel Filling

Sometimes a plain, rich coffee cake with a streusel filling hits the spot. Serve sliced for brunch or as a simple, yummy dessert.

½ cup margarine

1¼ cups sugar

2 cups nonfat plain yogurt

3 egg whites

1 teaspoon vanilla extract

1 teaspoon butter extract

3 cups all-purpose flour

1½ teaspoons baking powder

1 teaspoon baking soda

½ cup light brown sugar

1½ teaspoons ground cinnamon

½ cup chopped pecans

MAKES 24 SERVINGS

Preheat the oven to 350°F. Coat a 10-inch Bundt pan with nonstick cooking spray.

In a large mixing bowl, beat the margarine and sugar until fluffy. Add the yogurt, egg whites, and extracts, mixing well. In a medium bowl, combine the flour, baking powder, and baking soda. Gradually add to the yogurt mixture, mixing well.

Pour one-third of the batter into the prepared pan. Mix together the brown sugar, cinnamon, and pecans, and sprinkle half the mixture over the batter. Repeat the layers, ending with the batter. Bake for 55 minutes, or until a toothpick inserted in the center of the cake comes out clean. Cool in the pan 15 minutes, and invert onto a serving plate.

Nutritional information per serving

Calories 180, Protein (g) 4, Carbohydrate (g) 29, Fat (g) 6, Calories from Fat (%) 28, Saturated Fat (g) 1, Dietary Fiber (g) 1, Cholesterol (mg) 0, Sodium (mg) 152
***Diabetic Exchanges:** 2 other carbohydrate, 1 fat*

QUICK TIP

Nonfat sour cream can be substituted for yogurt.

COOKIES AND CAKES

Cranberry Cake

This heavenly white cake with a cranberry-and-almond topping can be enjoyed year-round using canned cranberry sauce.

½ cup margarine

1 cup sugar

1 egg

2 egg whites

½ teaspoon almond extract

2 cups all-purpose flour

1 tablespoon baking powder

1 cup nonfat plain yogurt

1 cup whole-berry cranberry sauce

½ cup sliced almonds

1 cup confectioners' sugar

2 tablespoons skim milk

½ teaspoon vanilla extract

MAKES 16 SERVINGS

Preheat the oven to 350°F. Coat a 13 x 9 x 2-inch baking pan with nonstick cooking spray.

In a large mixing bowl, cream the margarine and sugar until light and fluffy. Add the egg and egg whites, beating after each addition. Add the almond extract. In a small bowl, combine the flour and baking powder. Add to the sugar mixture alternately with the yogurt, beginning and ending with the flour mixture.

Pour the batter into the prepared pan. Spoon the cranberry sauce evenly over the batter; spread slightly, but do not try to cover the batter. Sprinkle with the almonds. Bake for 35 minutes, or until the cake slightly pulls away from the sides of pan.

In a small bowl, combine the confectioners' sugar, milk, and vanilla, stirring until smooth. Drizzle the glaze over the hot cake. Cool before serving.

Nutritional information per serving
Calories 247, Protein (g) 4, Carbohydrate (g) 41,
Fat (g) 8, Calories from Fat (%) 28, Saturated Fat (g) 1,
Dietary Fiber (g) 1, Cholesterol (mg) 14, Sodium (mg) 187
Diabetic Exchanges: 2.5 other carbohydrate, 1.5 fat

QUICK TIP

When measuring flour, don't use the measuring cup to scoop the flour out of the canister. Lightly spoon the flour into a dry measuring cup and level it with a knife for a more accurate measurement.

Orange Cranberry Cake

I always prepare this festive citrus cake during the holiday season, but now I also use dried cranberries year-round. The dates and cranberries provide a fruitcake personality.

½ cup margarine

1 cup sugar

1 egg

1 tablespoon grated orange rind

2¼ cups all-purpose flour

1 teaspoon baking soda

½ cup orange juice

½ cup skim milk

1½ cups chopped fresh or dried cranberries

⅔ cup chopped dates

½ cup confectioners' sugar

1½ tablespoons orange juice

MAKES 16 SERVINGS

Preheat the oven to 350°F. Coat a 10-inch Bundt pan with nonstick cooking spray.

In a large mixing bowl, cream the margarine and sugar until light and fluffy. Add the egg and orange rind, beating well. In a medium bowl, combine the flour and baking soda, and add to the creamed mixture alternately with the orange juice and milk. Stir in the cranberries and dates. Pour into the prepared pan, and bake for 40 minutes or until a toothpick inserted comes out clean. Cool 10 minutes. Invert the cake onto a serving platter.

Meanwhile, in a small saucepan, combine the confectioners' sugar and orange juice over low heat or in the microwave oven until smooth. Pour the orange glaze over the hot cake. Cool before serving.

Nutritional information per serving
Calories 215, Protein (g) 3, Carbohydrate (g) 38,
Fat (g) 6, Calories from Fat (%) 26, Saturated Fat (g) 1,
Dietary Fiber (g) 2, Cholesterol (mg) 13, Sodium (mg) 154
Diabetic Exchanges: *2.5 other carbohydrate, 1 fat*

QUICK TIP

Fresh cranberries can be stored in an airtight plastic bag for at least a month. They can be frozen for up to year, so stock up during cranberry season. There's no need to defrost cranberries before using them in a recipe.

Citrus Sensational Cake

If you're one that enjoys a plain yellow cake, then you'll love this citrus infused cake which has a simple flavor and is easy to make.

1 (18.25-ounce) box
yellow cake mix

3 eggs

2 tablespoons canola oil

1 (6-ounce) can orange
juice concentrate,
thawed, plus water to
equal 1 cup

⅓ cup peach nectar

1 teaspoon grated
orange rind

Citrus Frosting
(recipe follows)

MAKES 16 SERVINGS

Preheat the oven to 350°F. Coat two 9-inch round cake pans with nonstick cooking spray.

In a mixing bowl, beat together the cake mix, eggs, oil, and orange juice, mixing well. Add the peach nectar and orange rind. Pour the batter into the pans, and bake for 20 to 25 minutes, or until the center springs back when touched. Cool for 10 minutes; then remove to wire racks. Ice with Citrus Frosting (see recipe below).

Citrus Frosting

6 tablespoons margarine

1 (16-ounce) box
confectioners' sugar

4 tablespoons orange
juice

4 tablespoons orange
rind

In a medium mixing bowl, cream the margarine, confectioners' sugar, and orange juice and mix well. Add in the orange rind.

Nutritional information per serving

*Calories 224, Protein (g) 3, Carbohydrate (g) 51,
Fat (g) 10, Calories from Fat (%) 40, Saturated Fat (g) 2,
Dietary Fiber (g) 1, Cholesterol (mg) 40, Sodium (mg) 266*
Diabetic Exchanges: *4 other carbohydrate, 2 fat*

Lemon Poppy Seed Cake

Poppy seed cakes are popular bakery items, and this simple recipe is the best of both worlds—lemon, poppy seeds, and made with a cake mix.

1 (18.25-ounce) package yellow cake mix
¼ cup canola oil
¼ cup water
1⅓ cups nonfat plain yogurt
1 egg
3 egg whites
1 teaspoon almond extract
⅓ cup plus 3 tablespoons lemon juice
1 tablespoon poppy seeds
1 cup confectioners' sugar

MAKES 16 TO 20 SLICES

Preheat the oven to 350°F. Coat a 10-inch Bundt pan with nonstick cooking spray.

In a large mixing bowl, combine the cake mix, oil, water, yogurt, egg, egg whites, almond extract, and ⅓ cup lemon juice. Beat until creamy. Stir in the poppy seeds. Pour the batter into the Bundt pan, and bake for 40 minutes, or until a wooden toothpick inserted in the center of the cake comes out clean. Cool in the pan on a wire rack for 10 minutes.

Meanwhile, combine the confectioners' sugar and remaining 3 tablespoons lemon juice, stirring until smooth. Remove the cake from the pan onto a serving plate, and drizzle with the lemon glaze. Cool.

Nutritional information per serving
Calories 176, Protein (g) 3, Carbohydrate (g) 28,
Fat (g) 6, Calories from Fat (%) 28, Saturated Fat (g) 1,
Dietary Fiber (g) 1, Cholesterol (mg) 11, Sodium (mg) 187
Diabetic Exchanges: *2 other carbohydrate, 1 fat*

COOKIES AND CAKES

Boston Cream Pie

Cake, custard, and chocolate are three great tastes guaranteeing instant success.

2 egg yolks

½ cup sugar, divided

4 large egg whites

½ teaspoon cream
   of tartar

⅔ cup all-purpose flour

2 tablespoons margarine,
   melted

Custard Filling
   (recipe follows)

Glaze (recipe follows)

MAKES 10 TO 12 SERVINGS

Preheat the oven to 325°F. Line a 9-inch round cake pan with waxed paper and coat with nonstick cooking spray.

In a large bowl, combine the egg yolks and ¼ cup sugar. Beat with a mixer until thick and lemon colored. In a small bowl, beat the egg whites and cream of tartar with a mixer until foamy. Gradually add the remaining ¼ cup sugar, 1 tablespoon at time, beating until stiff peaks form. Gently fold the egg white mixture into the yolk mixture. Carefully fold the flour and margarine alternately into the egg mixture.

Spoon into the prepared pan. Bake for 25 minutes or until toothpick comes out clean. Cool in the pan 10 minutes; remove to a wire rack, and peel off the waxed paper. Cool.

Split the cake into 2 layers. Spread the Custard Filling (see recipe below) between the layers. Spread the Glaze (see recipe below) over the top. Refrigerate.

Custard Filling

3 tablespoons sugar

1 tablespoon cornstarch

1 cup skim milk

1 egg yolk, beaten

1 teaspoon vanilla extract

In a saucepan, combine the sugar and cornstarch. Gradually stir in the milk and egg yolk. Cook over medium heat, stirring constantly, until the mixture comes to a boil. Boil 1 minute, or until thickened. Remove from the heat; stir in the vanilla. Transfer to a medium bowl, cover with plastic wrap, and refrigerate until chilled, about 30 minutes.

Glaze

½ cup confectioners'
   sugar

3 tablespoons cocoa

2 tablespoons boiling
   water

1 tablespoon margarine

½ teaspoon vanilla extract

Combine the confectioners' sugar and cocoa; stir until well blended. Add the boiling water, margarine, and vanilla, stirring until smooth.

Nutritional information per serving

Calories 151, Protein (g) 4, Carbohydrate (g) 24, Fat (g) 4, Calories from Fat (%) 26, Saturated Fat (g) 1, Dietary Fiber (g) 1, Cholesterol (mg) 54, Sodium (mg) 64
Diabetic Exchanges: *1.5 other carbohydrate, 1 fat*

Sweet Potato Bundt Cake

Moist and spicy with a surprise streusel filling and almond glaze—this cake is a must to try!

⅓ cup canola oil

1½ cups sugar

1 cup light brown sugar

2 cups mashed sweet potato (yam) (canned or fresh)

½ cup skim milk

1 teaspoon vanilla extract

1 egg

3 egg whites

2 cups all-purpose flour

1 teaspoon baking powder

1 teaspoon baking soda

3 teaspoons cinnamon, divided

½ cup light brown sugar

½ teaspoon ground nutmeg

½ cup chopped pecans

2 tablespoons skim milk

1 cup confectioners' sugar

½ teaspoon almond extract

MAKES 16 SERVINGS

Preheat the oven to 350°F. Coat a 10-inch Bundt pan with nonstick cooking spray.

In a large mixing bowl, mix together the oil, sugar, brown sugar, sweet potato, milk, and vanilla. Add the egg and egg whites, one at a time, beating well with each addition.

In another bowl, mix together the flour, baking powder, baking soda, and 2 teaspoons cinnamon. Gradually add to the sugar mixture.

In a small bowl, combine the brown sugar, the remaining 1 teaspoon cinnamon, the nutmeg, and the pecans.

Sprinkle the bottom of the prepared pan with half the pecan mixture. Carefully cover with half of the batter, then the remaining the pecan mixture and remaining batter. Bake 40 to 45 minutes, or until a wooden toothpick inserted in the center comes out clean. Cool in the pan for 10 minutes; then invert on a serving plate. In a small bowl, mix the milk, confectioners' sugar, and almond to make a glaze. Spoon over the cake. Cool and serve.

Nutritional information per serving

Calories 299, Protein (g) 34, Carbohydrate (g) 54, Fat (g) 8, Calories from Fat (%) 23, Saturated Fat (g) 1, Dietary Fiber (g) 2, Cholesterol (mg) 14, Sodium (mg) 158
Diabetic Exchanges: 3.5 other carbohydrate, 1.5 fat

COOKIES AND CAKES

🥕 Strawberry Custard Cake

For a quicker version of this marvelous creation, just use a yellow cake mix layered with the fresh strawberries, custard, and whipped topping.

4 eggs, separated
2 tablespoons water
1 cup sugar
1 cup all-purpose flour
1 teaspoon baking
    powder
1½ tablespoons
    cornstarch
1 teaspoon vanilla extract
Strawberry Mixture
    (recipe follows)
Custard Filling
    (recipe follows)
1 (8-ounce) container
    fat-free whipped
    topping, thawed

MAKES 16 SLICES

Preheat the oven to 325°F. Coat two 9-inch round cake pans with nonstick cooking spray.

In a large mixing bowl, beat the egg yolks (reserving the whites) with 2 tablespoons water. Add the sugar gradually, and beat well. In a separate bowl, combine the flour, baking powder, and cornstarch, and add to the sugar mixture. Add the vanilla.

In another bowl, beat the egg whites until stiff, and fold into the batter. Pour batter into the prepared pans. Bake for 30 to 40 minutes, or until the top springs back when lightly touched. Remove from the pans, and cool on wire racks.

To assemble the cake, place the bottom layer on a serving plate. Top with the Strawberry Mixture (see recipe on following page). Spread all the Custard Filling (see recipe below) on top. Top with the second layer. Frost the sides and top with the whipped topping.

Strawberry Mixture

¼ cup water
¼ cup sugar
1 pint strawberries,
    hulled and cut in half

In a small saucepan, bring the water and sugar to a boil, boiling just until the sugar dissolves. Pour over the strawberries in a bowl, and refrigerate until chilled. Let the strawberries marinate in the syrup for 2 hours or for whatever length of time is available.

Custard Filling (for Strawberry Custard Cake)

3 tablespoons sugar

2 tablespoons cornstarch

⅛ teaspoon salt

1½ cups skim milk

1 egg

2 teaspoons vanilla
    extract

Combine the sugar, cornstarch, and salt in a saucepan. Gradually add the milk, stirring until blended. Cook over medium heat, stirring constantly, until the mixture thickens and comes to a boil. Boil 1 minute, stirring. Remove from heat.

In a small bowl, beat the egg at high speed until thick and lemon colored. Gradually stir one-fourth of the hot mixture into the beaten egg, then add to the remaining hot mixture. Cook, stirring constantly, for several minutes. Remove from heat; add the vanilla. Cover and refrigerate until chilled, about 20 minutes.

Nutritional information per serving
Calories 168, Protein (g) 4, Carbohydrate (g) 33,
Fat (g) 2, Calories from Fat (%) 10, Saturated Fat (g) 1,
Dietary Fiber (g) 1, Cholesterol (mg) 67, Sodium (mg) 89
Diabetic Exchanges: 2 other carbohydrate

FOOD FACT

Strawberries are rich in vitamin C. Store them in the refrigerator and wash just before using.

COOKIES AND CAKE

Quick Pineapple Cake

These few ingredients (that's right, there are no eggs!) make a melt-in-your-mouth cake.

1 (20-ounce) can crushed
   pineapple in its own
   juice (undrained)
2 cups all-purpose flour
1 cup sugar
1 teaspoon baking soda
Cream Cheese Frosting
   (recipe follows)

Cream Cheese Frosting

½ (8-ounce) package
   reduced-fat cream
   cheese
1 tablespoon margarine
1 teaspoon vanilla extract
1⅔ cups confectioners'
   sugar

MAKES 24 SERVINGS

Preheat the oven to 350°F. Coat a 13 x 9 x 2-inch baking pan with nonstick cooking spray.

In a large bowl, mix the pineapple, flour, sugar, and baking soda. Pour into the prepared pan. Bake for 30 to 40 minutes or until inserted toothpick comes out clean. Frost with the Cream Cheese Frosting (see recipe below) while the cake is hot. Cool and serve.

In a medium mixing bowl, combine the cream cheese and margarine until creamy. Add the vanilla and confectioners' sugar, mixing until well combined.

Nutritional information per serving

Calories 133, Protein (g) 2, Carbohydrate (g) 28, Fat (g) 2, Calories from Fat (%) 11, Saturated Fat (g) 1, Dietary Fiber (g) 1, Cholesterol (mg) 3, Sodium (mg) 81
Diabetic Exchanges: *2 other carbohydrate*

🥕 Tropical Upside-Down Cake

This tropical version of the fabulous picture-perfect cake will get big applause.

½ cup margarine, divided

1 cup dark brown sugar

1 (20-ounce) can
   pineapple chunks,
   undrained

2 tablespoons flaked
   coconut

¾ cup sugar

1 egg white

1 egg

1 teaspoon vanilla extract

1 teaspoon coconut
   extract

1 teaspoon butter extract

2 cups all-purpose flour

1½ teaspoons baking
   soda

½ cup fat-free sour cream

½ cup pineapple juice,
   reserved from the can

MAKES 24 SQUARES

Preheat the oven to 350°F.

Melt 4 tablespoons margarine, and pour into the bottom of a 13 x 9 x 2-inch baking pan. Press the brown sugar evenly over the margarine. Drain the pineapple chunks, reserving the juice, and arrange the pineapple chunks on top of the brown sugar. Sprinkle the coconut evenly over the pineapple.

In a large mixing bowl, cream together the remaining 4 tablespoons margarine and the sugar. Beat in the egg white, egg, and vanilla, coconut, and butter extracts.

In a separate bowl, combine the flour and baking soda. Gradually add to the creamed mixture, alternating with the sour cream and the reserved pineapple juice. Carefully spoon the batter into the pan, so as not to disturb the fruit. Bake for 30 minutes, or until a toothpick inserted in the center comes out clean. Invert the cake onto a serving platter, and cool before serving.

Nutritional information per serving

Calories 157, Protein (g) 2, Carbohydrate (g) 28,
Fat (g) 4, Calories from Fat (%) 24, Saturated Fat (g) 1,
Dietary Fiber (g) 1, Cholesterol (mg) 9, Sodium (mg) 139
Diabetic Exchanges: *2 other carbohydrate, 1 fat*

COOKIES AND CAKES

Piña Colada Bundt Cake

This tropical paradise of a moist, wonderful cake begins with a mix.

1 (18.25-ounce) package
yellow cake mix

1 (4-serving) package
instant vanilla pudding
and pie filling mix

1½ cups piña colada
drink mix, divided

⅓ cup canola oil

2 eggs

2 egg whites

⅓ cup flaked coconut

1 (8-ounce) can crushed
pineapple in its own
juice, undrained

1 cup confectioners' sugar

MAKES 16 SLICES

Preheat the oven to 350°F. Coat a 10-inch Bundt pan with nonstick cooking spray.

In a large mixing bowl, blend together the cake mix, pudding mix, 1 cup piña colada mix, oil, eggs, and egg whites until creamy. Stir in the coconut and pineapple, mixing well.

Pour the batter into the prepared pan. Bake for 45 minutes, or until a toothpick inserted in the center comes out clean. Cool in the pan 10 minutes, and then invert on a serving platter. Poke holes with a toothpick in the top of the cake.

In a small bowl, combine the remaining ½ cup piña colada mix and the confectioners' sugar, mixing well. Slowly drizzle over the cake. Cool before serving.

Nutritional information per serving

Calories 277, Protein (g) 3, Carbohydrate (g) 46,
Fat (g) 9, Calories from Fat (%) 29, Saturated Fat (g) 2,
Dietary Fiber (g) 1, Cholesterol (mg) 27, Sodium (mg) 309
Diabetic Exchanges: *3 other carbohydrate, 2 fat*

COOKIES AND CAKES

❄️Italian Cream Cake

This recipe was featured as the Cooking Light *magazine "Best Cake Ever" for their ten-year anniversary. I was thrilled when I created this lighter version of my very favorite cake. I include flaked coconut in the cake when I'm in the mood.*

½ cup margarine
¼ cup canola oil
2 cups sugar
2 eggs, separated
2 cups all-purpose flour
1 teaspoon baking soda
1 cup buttermilk
1 teaspoon vanilla extract
1 teaspoon butter extract
1 teaspoon coconut
   extract
½ cup chopped pecans
4 egg whites
Cream Cheese Frosting
   (recipe follows)

MAKES 16 TO 20 SLICES

Preheat the oven to 350°F. Coat three 9-inch round cake pans with nonstick cooking spray.

In a large mixing bowl, cream the margarine and oil. Gradually add the sugar, and beat until light and fluffy. Add the 2 egg yolks (reserving the egg whites), one at a time, beating well after each addition. In a small bowl, mix the flour and baking soda together. Add the flour to the sugar mixture, alternating with the buttermilk and ending with the flour. Beat after each addition. Add the vanilla, butter, and coconut extracts and the pecans.

In another mixing bowl, beat all 6 egg whites until stiff peaks form. Fold the beaten egg whites into the batter mixture. Pour the batter evenly into the prepared pans. Bake for 20 to 25 minutes, or until the tops spring back when lightly touched. Cool the cakes in the pans for 10 minutes; then turn them out onto racks to cool thoroughly. Frost the layers and sides with the Cream Cheese Frosting (see recipe below).

Cream Cheese Frosting

1 (8-ounce) package
   reduced-fat cream
   cheese, softened
3 tablespoons margarine
1 (16-ounce) box
   confectioners' sugar
1 teaspoon vanilla extract

In a medium mixing bowl, beat the cream cheese and margarine until smooth. Add the confectioners' sugar, and beat until light. Blend in the vanilla.

Nutritional information per serving
Calories 358, Protein (g) 5, Carbohydrate (g) 54,
Fat (g) 14, Calories from Fat (%) 35, Saturated Fat (g) 3,
Dietary Fiber (g) 1, Cholesterol (mg) 30, Sodium (mg) 216
Diabetic Exchanges: *3.5 other carbohydrate, 3 fat*

Quick Italian Cream Cake

This easy version of my favorite three-layer cake hits the spot for an indulgent quick dessert.

1 (18.25-ounce) package white cake mix
1 cup buttermilk
2 egg whites
1 egg
¼ cup canola oil
3 tablespoons light brown sugar
¼ cup flaked coconut
2 tablespoons chopped pecans
Cream Cheese Frosting (recipe follows)

Cream Cheese Frosting

1 (8-ounce) package reduced-fat cream cheese, softened
2 tablespoons margarine
1 (16-ounce) box confectioners' sugar
1 teaspoon vanilla extract

MAKES 28 SERVINGS

Preheat the oven to 350°F. Coat a 13 x 9 x 2-inch pan with nonstick cooking spray.

In a large mixing bowl, combine the cake mix, buttermilk, egg whites, egg, and oil, beating until well mixed.

In a small mixing bowl, combine the brown sugar, coconut, and pecans; set aside.

Spread half the batter in the bottom of the prepared pan, sprinkle with the brown sugar mixture, and carefully top with the remaining batter, spreading it out. Bake for 30 minutes, or until a toothpick inserted in the center comes out clean. Let cool, and spread with the Cream Cheese Frosting (see recipe below).

In a medium mixing bowl, beat the cream cheese and margarine together. Blend in the confectioners' sugar, mixing well. Add the vanilla, mixing well again.

Nutritional information per serving
Calories 206, Protein (g) 2, Carbohydrate (g) 33, Fat (g) 7, Calories from Fat (%) 31, Saturated Fat (g) 2, Dietary Fiber (g) 0, Cholesterol (mg) 14, Sodium (mg) 179
Diabetic Exchanges: *2 other carbohydrate, 1.5 fat*

Wait Cake

The hardest part of this cake is waiting to cut it per directions. (We have cheated and cut it after 24 hours, but it's best to wait for the moistest cake.) How such an easy cake can be so unbelievable is a secret to keep. For the deluxe version, I add coconut to the sour cream mixture in between the layers.

1 (18.25-ounce) package yellow cake mix
1 teaspoon baking powder
3 egg whites
1 egg
2 tablespoons canola oil
1⅓ cups water
2 cups light sour cream
1½ cups sugar
1 teaspoon almond extract
½ cup flaked coconut, optional
1½ cups fat-free frozen whipped topping, thawed

MAKES 16 TO 20 SLICES

Preheat the oven to 350°F. Coat two 9-inch round cake pans with nonstick cooking spray.

In a large mixing bowl, beat together the cake mix, baking powder, egg whites, egg, oil, and water until well mixed. Pour the batter into the prepared pans, and bake for 25 to 30 minutes or until the top springs back when touched. Cool the layers on wire racks in the pans for 10 minutes, then turn onto wire racks to cool.

Meanwhile, in a medium bowl, combine the sour cream, sugar, and almond extract, blending well. Add coconut, if desired. Chill in the refrigerator while the cake is baking.

When the cake has cooled, split each layer in half with a serrated knife. Spread the filling between the layers, reserving 1 cup for the frosting.

Combine the reserved 1 cup filling with the whipped topping, mixing until smooth. Spread the frosting on the sides and top of the cake. Seal the cake in an airtight container or cover tightly with plastic wrap; refrigerate for 36 to 48 hours before serving.

Nutritional information per serving
Calories 223, Protein (g) 3, Carbohydrate (g) 41,
Fat (g) 6, Calories from Fat (%) 22, Saturated Fat (g) 2,
Dietary Fiber (g) 1, Cholesterol (mg) 19, Sodium (mg) 225
***Diabetic Exchanges:** 2.5 other carbohydrate, 1 fat*

COOKIES AND CAKE

❄ Strawberry Angel Food Cake

When strawberries are in season, try this easy yet impressive dessert. This recipe is so simple that it makes a great emergency dessert.

1 (16-ounce) angel
   food cake
1 (8-ounce) package
   reduced-fat cream
   cheese, softened
½ cup sugar
¼ cup evaporated
   skimmed milk
2 pints strawberries,
   hulled and sliced

MAKES 10 TO 12 SLICES

With a serrated knife, slice the angel food cake horizontally into three equal layers. In a mixing bowl, beat together the cream cheese, sugar, and evaporated milk until creamy. Top the bottom cake layer with the filling and strawberries. Repeat the layers. Frost the top with the remaining filling. Refrigerate until serving.

Nutritional information per serving

Calories 196, Protein (g) 5, Carbohydrate (g) 35, Fat (g) 5, Calories from Fat (%) 21, Saturated Fat 3, Dietary Fiber (g) 1, Cholesterol (mg) 19, Sodium (mg) 225
***Diabetic Exchanges:** 2.5 other carbohydrate, 1 fat*

Chocolate Pudding Cake

A surprise chocolate pudding forms on the bottom of this cake, which is perfect for a family dessert.

½ cup sugar
1 cup all-purpose flour
2 teaspoons baking
   powder
2 tablespoons plus
   ¼ cup cocoa
½ cup skim milk
1 teaspoon vanilla extract
1 tablespoon margarine,
   melted
¾ cup light brown sugar
1½ cups boiling water

MAKES 12 TO 16 SERVINGS

Preheat the oven to 350°F. Coat a 9 x 9 x 2-inch baking pan with nonstick cooking spray.

In a bowl, combine the sugar, flour, baking powder, and 2 tablespoons cocoa. Stir in the milk, vanilla, and margarine. Spread the batter in the prepared pan.

Mix together the brown sugar and the remaining ¼ cup cocoa and sprinkle over the batter. Pour the boiling water over all; bake for 25 to 30 minutes. Serve hot.

Nutritional information per serving

Calories 109, Protein (g) 2, Carbohydrate (g) 24, Fat (g) 1, Calories from Fat (%) 8, Saturated Fat (g) 0, Dietary Fiber (g) 1, Cholesterol (mg) 0, Sodium (mg) 78
***Diabetic Exchanges:** 1.5 other carbohydrate*

Coffee Angel Food Cake

An angel food cake with a touch of coffee and almond makes for a heavenly indulgence. For an extra treat, top with toasted almond slices. This recipe is hard to beat if you're a fan of coffee.

1 (14½-ounce) package
  angel food cake mix
1 teaspoon vanilla extract
1 teaspoon almond
  extract
1 tablespoon instant
  coffee dissolved in
  1 tablespoon water
Coffee Icing
  (recipe follows)
⅓ cup sliced almonds,
  toasted

MAKES 16 SLICES

Mix the angel food cake according to the package directions, adding vanilla and almond extracts and coffee to the batter. Bake according to the package directions. Cool, and spread with the Coffee Icing (see recipe below). Sprinkle the almonds on the top and sides of the cake, and serve.

QUICK TIP

For a lighter version of any cake mix, combine the cake mix with 1 teaspoon baking powder, 3 egg whites, 1 whole egg, 2 tablespoons canola oil, and 1⅓ cups water. Bake according to the directions. Ice the cake with your favorite frosting.

Coffee Icing

6 tablespoons margarine
1 (16-ounce) box
  confectioners' sugar
2 tablespoons instant
  coffee dissolved in
  1 tablespoon water
3 to 4 tablespoons skim
  milk

In a mixing bowl, cream the margarine, confectioners' sugar, and dissolved coffee, adding milk as needed until the icing reaches good spreading consistency. Ice the top, sides, and center of the cake.

Nutritional information per serving
Calories 261, Protein (g) 3, Carbohydrate (g) 50, Fat (g) 5, Calories from Fat (%) 19, Saturated Fat (g) 1, Dietary Fiber (g) 0, Cholesterol (mg) 0, Sodium (mg) 276
Diabetic Exchanges: *3.5 other carbohydrate, 1 fat*

COOKIES AND CAKES

🥕 ❄️ Tiramisu Cake

A white cake mix is the base to this fabulous dessert made with everyday ingredients. If you like tiramisu, this recipe will excite your taste buds with the crunchy, candy-filled cake and Chocolate Cream Cheese Frosting.

1 (18.25-ounce) package
    white cake mix
1½ cups strongly brewed
    coffee, cooled, divided
4 egg whites
4 (1.4-ounce) bars toffee
    candy, finely chopped
1 tablespoon sugar
1 tablespoon cocoa
Chocolate Cream
    Cheese Frosting
    (recipe follows)

MAKES 16 SERVINGS

Preheat the oven to 350°F. Coat two 9-inch round cake pans with nonstick cooking spray.

In a large bowl, combine the cake mix, 1 cup coffee, and the egg whites. Beat until well mixed and creamy. Gently fold in the chopped candy. Spread the batter evenly into the prepared pans. Bake for 30 to 40 minutes, or until a toothpick inserted in the center comes out clean. Cool for 10 minutes; then remove from the pans and cool completely on wire racks.

In a small bowl, mix together the sugar, cocoa, and remaining ½ cup coffee. Lay the bottom cake layer on a serving plate, and spoon half the cocoa mixture evenly over the cake layer. Frost the bottom layer with the Chocolate Cream Cheese Frosting (see recipe below); then add the top layer. Spoon the remaining cocoa mixture onto the top layer, and ice the top and sides of the cake with the remaining frosting. Refrigerate until serving.

Chocolate Cream Cheese Frosting

¼ cup sugar
⅓ cup chocolate syrup
1 (8-ounce) package
    reduced-fat cream
    cheese
1 (8-ounce) container
    fat-free frozen whipped
    topping, thawed
1 teaspoon vanilla extract

In a mixing bowl, beat the sugar, chocolate syrup, and cream cheese until smooth. Fold in the whipped topping and vanilla until well combined.

Nutritional information per serving
Calories 290, Protein (g) 4, Carbohydrate (g) 45,
Fat (g) 10, Calories from Fat (%) 31, Saturated Fat (g) 5,
Dietary Fiber (g) 1, Cholesterol (mg) 15, Sodium (mg) 319
Diabetic Exchanges: 3 other carbohydrate, 2 fat

Mocha Chocolate Bundt Cake

I was testing a mocha chocolate cake from scratch and this recipe at the same time. This magnificent mocha cake won hands down, and it even begins with a mix! The hardest part about making this cake is to let it sit for 1 hour before serving.

1 (18.25-ounce) box devil's food cake mix
¼ cup canola oil
1 (4-serving) package instant chocolate pudding and pie filling
1 egg
3 egg whites
¾ cup strong brewed coffee
⅓ cup coffee liqueur
⅓ cup créme de cacao liqueur
Mocha Glaze (see recipe below)

MAKES 16 SLICES

Preheat the oven to 350°F. Coat a 10-inch Bundt pan with nonstick cooking spray.

In a large mixing bowl, combine the cake mix, oil, pudding mix, egg, egg whites, coffee, and liqueurs, blending very well.

Transfer the batter into the prepared pan. Bake for 40 to 45 minutes. Cool 15 minutes, and invert onto a serving platter. Using a fork or toothpick, pierce the cake every few inches; then spoon the Moha Glaze (see recipe below) over the cake. Let the cake absorb flavors for one hour before serving.

QUICK TIP

For a reduced-calorie version of this dessert, substitute milk for the liqueur in the cake and glaze.

Mocha Glaze

1 cup confectioners' sugar
2 tablespoons strongly brewed coffee
2 tablespoons créme de cacao liqueur

In a small bowl, mix the confectioners' sugar, coffee, and liqueur. Spoon the glaze over the cake according to the directions above.

Nutritional information per serving
Calories 272, Protein (g) 3, Carbohydrate (g) 44, Fat (g) 7, Calories from Fat (%) 23, Saturated Fat (g) 2, Dietary Fiber (g) 1, Cholesterol (mg) 13, Sodium (mg) 353
Diabetic Exchanges: 4 other carbohydrate, 2 fat

COOKIES AND CAKES

⬛❄️ Triple Chocolate Cake

I keep these pantry ingredients on hand to whip up this highly requested, fabulous cake. This is chocolate cake at its best and at its easiest to prepare—you will repeat this recipe very often.

Cocoa as needed

1 (18.25-ounce) package devil's food cake mix

1 (4-serving) box instant chocolate pudding and pie filling mix

1 cup fat-free sour cream

¼ cup canola oil

⅓ cup plus ¼ cup skim milk

1 egg

3 egg whites

⅓ cup almond liqueur (such as Amaretto)

2 teaspoons almond extract, divided

⅓ cup semisweet chocolate chips

1½ cups confectioners' sugar

MAKES 16 SLICES

Preheat the oven to 350°F. Coat a 10-inch Bundt pan with nonstick cooking spray and dust with cocoa.

In a large mixing bowl, combine the cake mix, pudding, sour cream, oil, ⅓ cup skim milk, egg, egg whites, liqueur, and 1 teaspoon almond extract. Beat with a mixer until well blended. Stir in the chocolate chips.

Pour batter into the prepared pan, and bake for 40 to 50 minutes, or until a toothpick inserted in the center comes out clean.

Meanwhile, mix the confectioners' sugar, remaining ¼ cup milk, and 1 teaspoon almond extract together in a small bowl. Cool the cake on a rack for 10 minutes before inverting onto a serving plate. Drizzle the glaze over the warm cake. Cool before serving.

Nutritional information per serving
Calories 296, Protein (g) 4, Carbohydrate (g) 49,
Fat (g) 8, Calories from Fat (%) 24, Saturated Fat (g) 2,
Dietary Fiber (g) 1, Cholesterol (mg) 14, Sodium (mg) 371
***Diabetic Exchanges:** 3.5 other carbohydrate, 1.5 fat*

QUICK TIP

When testing the cake for doneness, a toothpick might hit a chocolate chip, and you might think the cake isn't done. For an accurate reading, test it a few times.

🥕❄️ Red Velvet Cake

This lighter version of the popular recipe will fool even those who put red velvet cake on the top of their list of favorites. A great choice for the holidays.

1 (1-ounce) bottle red
  food coloring
¼ cup cocoa
½ cup margarine
2 cups sugar
2 eggs
2¼ cups all-purpose flour
1½ teaspoons baking
  soda
1 cup buttermilk
1½ teaspoons vanilla
  extract
1 teaspoon butter extract
1½ teaspoons vinegar
Cream Cheese Frosting
  (recipe follows)

Cream Cheese Frosting

1 (8-ounce) package
  reduced-fat cream
  cheese, softened
3 tablespoons margarine
1 (16-ounce) box
  confectioners' sugar
1 teaspoon vanilla extract

MAKES 16 SERVINGS

Preheat the oven to 350°F. Coat three 9-inch round cake pans with nonstick cooking spray.

In a small bowl, mix the red food coloring and cocoa with a fork; set aside.

In a large mixing bowl, cream the margarine and sugar until light and fluffy. Add the eggs, mixing well. Add the cocoa mixture to the margarine mixture, beating well. Combine the flour with the baking soda, and add alternately with the buttermilk to the creamed mixture, beginning and ending with the flour. Add the vanilla and butter extracts and the vinegar, mixing well.

Pour the batter into the prepared pans, and bake for 15 minutes, or until a toothpick inserted in the center comes out clean. Cool the layers on racks, and ice with the Cream Cheese Frosting (see recipe below).

In a mixing bowl, beat the cream cheese and margarine until smooth. Add the confectioners' sugar, and beat until light. Blend in the vanilla.

Nutritional information per serving
Calories 399, Protein (g) 5, Carbohydrate (g) 69, Fat (g) 12, Calories from Fat (%) 26, Saturated Fat (g) 4, Dietary Fiber (g) 1, Cholesterol (mg) 37, Sodium (mg) 295
Diabetic Exchanges: *4.5 other carbohydrate, 2.5 fat*

German Chocolate Bundt Cake

This healthier variation of a light chocolate cake with a streusel filling and a wonderful coconut-flavored glaze seems more like a piece of indulgence. One of our very favorites!

1 cup light brown sugar, divided

⅓ cup flaked coconut

⅓ cup chopped pecans

⅓ cup unsweetened cocoa

2 ounces German sweet baking chocolate

½ cup boiling water

1 cup sugar

⅓ cup margarine

2 teaspoons vanilla extract

1 egg

2 egg whites

2 cups all-purpose flour

2 teaspoons baking powder

½ teaspoon baking soda

1 cup buttermilk

Coconut Glaze (recipe follows)

MAKES 16 SERVINGS

Preheat the oven to 325°F. Coat a 10-inch Bundt pan with nonstick cooking spray.

Combine ½ cup brown sugar, the coconut, and pecans in a small bowl.

In a small bowl, combine the cocoa and baking chocolate; add the boiling water, stirring until the chocolate melts. Set aside.

In a large mixing bowl, beat the sugar, the remaining ½ cup brown sugar, and the margarine until creamy. Add the vanilla, egg, and egg whites, one at a time, beating well after each addition.

In another bowl, combine the flour, baking powder, and baking soda. Add the flour mixture to the sugar mixture alternately with the buttermilk, beginning and ending with the flour mixture. Stir in the cocoa mixture. Spoon half the batter into the prepared pan, and top with the coconut-pecan mixture. Spoon the remaining batter over the streusel. Bake 50 to 60 minutes, or until a wooden toothpick inserted in the center comes out clean. Cool in the pan on a wire rack 10 minutes; invert onto serving platter. Cool completely. Drizzle with the Coconut Glaze (see recipe below).

Coconut Glaze

1 cup confectioners' sugar

1 tablespoon margarine

½ teaspoon coconut extract

½ teaspoon vanilla extract

2 tablespoons skim milk

Combine the confectioners' sugar and margarine in a small bowl. Add the coconut and vanilla extracts and the milk, stirring well.

Nutritional information per serving

Calories 290, Protein (g) 4, Carbohydrate (g) 51, Fat (g) 9, Calories from Fat (%) 26, Saturated Fat (g) 2, Dietary Fiber (g) 1, Cholesterol (mg) 14, Sodium (mg) 191
Diabetic Exchanges: *3.5 other carbohydrate, 2 fat*

German Chocolate Sheet Cake

There will be lots of oohs *and* ahs *for this gooey one-layer version of an all-time favorite. When cut into small squares, it's great for party pickups and makes tons.*

1 (18.25-ounce) package German chocolate cake mix

1 egg

2 egg whites

1¾ cups water

1 (14-ounce) can fat-free sweetened condensed milk

⅓ cup flaked coconut

⅓ cup chopped pecans

¼ cup margarine

⅓ cup cocoa

1 (16-ounce) box confectioners' sugar

1 teaspoon vanilla extract

3 to 4 tablespoons skim milk

MAKES 48 SQUARES

Preheat the oven to 350°F. Coat a 15 x 11 x 1-inch baking pan with nonstick cooking spray.

In a large mixing bowl, beat together the cake mix, egg, egg whites, and water until creamy. Pour the batter into the prepared pan, and bake for 15 minutes.

Meanwhile, in a small bowl, combine the condensed milk, coconut, and pecans.

Preheat the broiler.

Pour the coconut mixture over the top of the cake, spreading it evenly. Broil for about 2 minutes, or until golden. Watch carefully. Remove from the oven, and let cool.

In a mixing bowl, beat together the margarine, cocoa, confectioners' sugar, and vanilla, adding the milk gradually until the frosting reaches spreading consistency. Spread over the cake. Cool before serving.

Nutritional information per serving
Calories 127, Protein (g) 2, Carbohydrate (g) 24, Fat (g) 3, Calories from Fat (%) 21, Saturated Fat (g) 1, Dietary Fiber (g) 0, Cholesterol (mg) 5, Sodium (mg) 93
Diabetic Exchanges: *1.5 other carbohydrate, 0.5 fat*

COOKIES AND CAKE

Old-Fashioned German Chocolate Layered Cake

German chocolate cake is one of my absolute favorites, so I created this lighter yet equally good version that both satisfies my craving and is kinder to my waistline.

2 tablespoons cocoa

2 ounces German sweet baking chocolate

½ cup boiling water

3 tablespoons margarine

2 tablespoons canola oil

2 cups sugar

1 egg yolk

1 tablespoon vanilla extract

½ teaspoon coconut extract

2 cups all-purpose flour

1 teaspoon baking soda

1 cup buttermilk

4 egg whites

Coconut Pecan Frosting (recipe follows)

MAKES 16 SERVINGS

Preheat the oven to 350°F. Coat three 9-inch round cake pans with nonstick cooking spray and dust with flour.

Add the cocoa and baking chocolate to the boiling water, and stir until melted; set aside to cool slightly.

In a large mixing bowl, beat together the margarine, oil, and sugar until creamy. Add the egg yolk, mixing well. Add the vanilla and coconut extracts. Gradually add the chocolate mixture. In a small bowl, mix together the flour and baking soda. Add the flour mixture to the creamed mixture alternately with the buttermilk, beginning and ending with the flour mixture.

In another mixing bowl, beat the egg whites until stiff peaks form. Gradually fold the egg whites into the chocolate mixture.

Pour the batter into the prepared pans. Bake for 20 minutes, or until a toothpick inserted in the center comes out clean. Cool in the pans 10 minutes, and remove to wire racks. Place a layer on a serving plate; spread with one-third of the Coconut Pecan Frosting (see recipe to right). Repeat with remaining layers and frosting.

QUICK TIP

To toast pecans or coconut: spread evenly on a baking sheet; bake, stirring occasionally, at 350°F for 7 to 10 minutes, or until lightly browned.

Coconut Pecan Frosting (for Old-Fashioned German Chocolate Layered Cake)

1 (12-ounce) can evaporated skimmed milk
1 (5-ounce) can evaporated skimmed milk
1 cup sugar
3 tablespoons cornstarch
1 egg yolk
2 teaspoons vanilla extract
½ teaspoon coconut extract
½ cup flaked coconut
½ cup chopped pecans, toasted

In a saucepan, combine both cans of evaporated milk and the sugar, cornstarch, and egg yolk. Bring to a boil over medium-high heat, stirring constantly until the mixture thickens and bubbles about 7 to 10 minutes. Remove from heat, and stir in the vanilla and coconut extracts, coconut, and pecans. Cool slightly, and frost the cake as directed.

Nutritional information per serving

Calories 343, Protein (g) 7, Carbohydrate (g) 59, Fat (g) 9, Calories from Fat (%) 24, Saturated Fat (g) 2, Dietary Fiber (g) 1, Cholesterol (mg) 28, Sodium (mg) 176
Diabetic Exchanges: 4 other carbohydrate, 2 fat

❄ Oatmeal Chocolate Cake

This not-too-sweet snack cake's oatmeal and chocolate are a great combination of flavors.

1½ cups boiling water

1 cup old-fashioned
   oatmeal

1 cup light brown sugar

½ cup sugar

½ cup margarine

1 egg

2 egg whites

1½ cups all-purpose flour

1 teaspoon baking soda

1 tablespoon cocoa

½ cup semisweet
   chocolate chips

MAKES 24 TO 28 SQUARES

Preheat the oven to 350°F. Coat a 13 x 9 x 2-inch baking pan with nonstick cooking spray.

In a large bowl, pour the boiling water over the oatmeal, and let stand for 10 minutes. Add the brown sugar, sugar, and margarine, stirring until the margarine melts. Add the egg and egg whites; mix well.

In a small bowl, mix together the flour, baking soda, and cocoa. Add the dry ingredients to the sugar mixture, mixing well. Stir in the chocolate chips. Pour into the prepared pan, and bake for about 40 minutes, or until a toothpick inserted in the center comes out clean. Don't overbake. Cool before serving.

Nutritional information per serving
Calories 127, Protein (g) 2, Carbohydrate (g) 20,
Fat (g) 5, Calories from Fat (%) 32, Saturated Fat (g) 1,
Dietary Fiber (g) 1, Cholesterol (mg) 8, Sodium (mg) 93
Diabetic Exchanges: *1.5 other carbohydrate, 1 fat*

QUICK TIP

Old-fashioned oats and quick-cooking oats can usually be interchanged in recipes.

Mock Chocolate Éclair 413

Chocolate Layered Dessert 414

Tropical Pizza 415

Bread Pudding 416

Cream Cheese Bread Pudding 417

Pineapple Bread Pudding with Lemon Apricot Sauce 418

Desserts and Pies

Sweet Potato Bread Pudding with Praline Sauce 419

Chocolate Bread Pudding with Caramel Sauce 420

Coffee Cheesecake 422

Cranberry Cheesecake 423

Sweet Potato Cheesecake 424

Chocolate Almond Cheesecake 425

Strawberry Custard Brûlée 426

Orange Caramel Flan 427

Fantastic Trifle 428

Chocolate Trifle 429

Fruit Trifle 430

Lemon Pineapple Trifle 431

Pineapple Trifle 432

Glazed Bananas 432

Ice Cream Pie 433

Coffee Toffee Dessert 434

Mocha Fudge Mousse Pie 435

Tiramisu 436

Chocolate Fondue 437

Banana Éclair 438

Peach Crisp 440

Berry Crisp 441

Nectarine and Raspberry Crumble 442

Blueberry Pineapple Crunch 443

Apple Peanut Crumble 444

Chocolate Chip Pie 444

Chocolate Chess Pie 445

Custard Pie 445

Apple Crumble Pie 446

Banana Cream Pie 447

Peanut Butter Banana Pie 448

Blueberry Meringue Pie 449

Lemon Meringue Pie 450

Sweet Potato Pecan Crumble Pie 452

German Chocolate Angel Pie 453

Strawberry Margarita Pie 454

Vanilla Sauce 454

Mock Chocolate Éclair

Layers of pudding and graham crackers topped with a chocolate sauce make this a simple but indulgent dessert. It can be the made the night before and refrigerated until ready to serve.

2 wrapped packages
  graham crackers from
  16-ounce box
2 (4-serving) packages
  vanilla instant pudding
  and pie filling mix
3 cups skim milk
4 ounces fat-free frozen
  whipped topping,
  thawed
Chocolate Topping
  (recipe follows)

Chocolate Topping

¼ cup cocoa
⅔ cup sugar
¼ cup skim milk
1 tablespoon vanilla
  extract
1 tablespoon margarine

MAKES 15 TO 20 SERVINGS

Layer the bottom of a 13 x 9 x 2-inch baking dish with one-third of the graham crackers.

In a mixing bowl, beat the pudding mix with the milk until it thickens; set aside for several minutes. Fold in the whipped topping. Spread half of the pudding mixture over the graham crackers. Repeat the layers, ending with the graham crackers on top (three layers of graham crackers). Spread with the Chocolate Topping (see recipe below).

Combine the cocoa, sugar, and milk in a saucepan. Bring to a boil for 1 minute. Remove from heat, and add the vanilla and margarine. Cool slightly, and pour over top the graham cracker layer.

Nutritional information per serving
Calories 156, Protein (g) 3, Carbohydrate (g) 31,
Fat (g) 2, Calories from Fat (%) 13, Saturated Fat (g) 0,
Dietary Fiber (g) 1, Cholesterol (mg) 1, Sodium (mg) 250
Diabetic Exchanges: *2 other carbohydrate*

🥕 Chocolate Layered Dessert

Because it's simple to make and everyone's favorite, I continually make this recipe for family and friends and still get wonderful remarks. This is a great make-ahead dessert that appeals to all ages.

1 cup all-purpose flour

7 tablespoons margarine

½ cup chopped pecans

1 (8-ounce) package reduced-fat cream cheese

⅔ cup confectioners' sugar

2 cups fat-free frozen whipped topping, thawed, divided

Pudding Layer (recipe follows)

Pudding Layer

2 (4-serving) packages instant chocolate pudding and pie filling mix

3 cups skim milk

1 teaspoon vanilla extract

MAKES 16 SERVINGS

Preheat the oven to 350°F.

With a fork, mix together the flour and margarine until crumbly. Stir in the pecans, and press into an ungreased 13 x 9 x 2-inch pan. Bake for 20 minutes or until lightly browned. Cool completely.

In a mixer, blend the cream cheese and confectioners' sugar until creamy. Fold in the whipped topping. Spread on top of the first layer. Top with the Pudding Layer (see recipe below). Cover with the remaining 1¼ cup whipped topping. Refrigerate.

Mix the pudding mix with the milk, and prepare according to package directions. Add the vanilla.

Nutritional information per serving
Calories 223, Protein (g) 4, Carbohydrate (g) 27,
Fat (g) 11, Calories from Fat (%) 44, Saturated Fat (g) 3,
Dietary Fiber (g) 1, Cholesterol (mg) 11, Sodium (mg) 305
Diabetic Exchanges: 2 other carbohydrate, 2 fat

QUICK TIP

For variety, use different flavored puddings in this recipe, from white chocolate to pistachio.

Tropical Pizza

Every time I make this tropical decadence, everyone wants the recipe. Easy and picture-perfect, it's a great way to enjoy fruit, especially when the fruit is in season. Be creative and substitute your favorite fruits.

1 (18-ounce) roll refrigerated ready-to-slice sugar cookie dough

⅓ cup sugar

1 (8-ounce) package fat-free cream cheese

1 teaspoon coconut extract

1½ teaspoons grated orange rind

1 cup fat-free frozen whipped topping, thawed

1 (26-ounce) jar mango slices, drained, or 1 fresh mango, sliced

1 (16-ounce) can pineapple slices, drained, or 1 fresh pineapple, sliced

1 (11-ounce) can mandarin orange segments, drained

¼ cup apricot preserves

1 tablespoon orange liqueur or orange juice

2 tablespoons coconut, toasted, optional

MAKES 12 SERVINGS

Preheat the oven to 350°F.

Press the cookie dough into a 12- to 14-inch pizza pan coated with nonstick cooking spray. Bake for 12 minutes, and cool completely.

In a medium mixing bowl, blend together the sugar, cream cheese, and coconut extract until well mixed. Stir in the orange rind and whipped topping, mixing until smooth. Spread the cream cheese mixture on top of the cooled crust. Arrange the mango slices around the edge of the iced pizza. Then, arrange a roll of the pineapple slices around the edge. Next, arrange the mandarin orange slices in another ring to fill the center of the pizza.

In a small saucepan or in the microwave, heat the apricot preserves and orange liqueur just until melted. Spoon the glaze over the fruit. Sprinkle with the toasted coconut, if desired. Refrigerate until serving.

Nutritional information per serving

Calories 269, Protein (g) 4, Carbohydrate (g) 48, Fat (g) 6, Calories from Fat (%) 21, Saturated Fat (g) 2, Dietary Fiber (g) 0, Cholesterol (mg) 5, Sodium (mg) 253
Diabetic Exchanges: *1 fruit, 2 other carbohydrate, 1 fat*

QUICK TIP

Go ahead and grate more orange rind than you'll need for the recipe—you can grate a whole orange or lemon and freeze the rind until needed.

DESSERTS AND PIES

🥕 Bread Pudding

Here's a low-fat version of a Southern delight. Serve warm with the Rum Sauce.

8 cups French bread,
  cut into small pieces
½ cup raisins
¼ cup light brown sugar
½ cup sugar
½ teaspoon ground
  cinnamon
1½ cups skim milk
1 (12-ounce) can
  evaporated skimmed
  milk
1 teaspoon vanilla extract
1 teaspoon butter extract
1 egg yolk
4 egg whites
Rum Sauce
  (recipe follows)

MAKES 10 TO 12 SERVINGS

Preheat the oven to 350°F.

Spread the French bread in a 3-quart baking dish. Sprinkle the raisins over the bread.

In a medium bowl, combine the brown sugar, sugar, cinnamon, milk, evaporated milk, vanilla and butter extracts, and the egg yolk.

In a mixing bowl, beat the egg whites until stiff peaks form; fold into the sugar mixture. Pour over the bread and raisins in the pan. Let sit 5 minutes. Bake for 30 to 40 minutes or until set, and serve hot with Rum Sauce (see recipe below).

QUICK TIP

Folding egg whites into a mixture means combining ingredients lightly while preventing loss of air by using two motions. To fold whites, first lighten the mixture by stirring a small portion of the beaten whites into it. Then gently fold in the rest of the egg whites, scooping under the mixture and smoothing over the top.

Rum Sauce

2 tablespoons all-purpose
  flour
2 tablespoons margarine
½ cup sugar
1 cup skim milk
1 tablespoon dark rum
  or 1 teaspoon rum
  extract

In a small saucepan over medium heat, combine the flour, margarine, and sugar. Gradually add the milk, stirring constantly. Cook until the mixture comes to a boil and thickens, 10 to 12 minutes. Remove from heat, and stir in the rum. Serve over the hot bread pudding.

Nutritional information per serving

Calories 251, Protein (g) 8, Carbohydrate (g) 46, Fat (g) 3, Calories from Fat (%) 12, Saturated Fat (g) 1, Dietary Fiber (g) 1, Cholesterol (mg) 20, Sodium (mg) 251
Diabetic Exchanges: *0.5 skim milk, 0.5 fruit, 2 other carbohydrate*

THE HOLLY CLEGG TRIM & TERRIFIC COOKBOOK

Cream Cheese Bread Pudding

Baked cream cheese topping over bread pudding takes this favorite dessert to a new level.

1 (16-ounce) loaf
  French bread
2 eggs, divided
4 egg whites, divided
1 cup sugar, divided
1 teaspoon vanilla extract
1 teaspoon butter extract
3 cups skim milk
1 teaspoon ground
  cinnamon
1 (8-ounce) package
  fat-free cream cheese,
  softened

MAKES 10 TO 12 SERVINGS

Preheat the oven to 350°F. Cut the French bread into 1-inch squares. Place the bread in a 13 x 9 x 2-inch baking dish coated with nonstick cooking spray.

In a large bowl, lightly beat together 1 egg and 3 egg whites. Add ½ cup of the sugar and the vanilla and butter extracts; mix well. Slowly add the milk to the egg mixture, mixing well. Pour over the bread squares. Sprinkle the mixture with the cinnamon.

In a large mixing bowl, beat the cream cheese with the remaining ½ cup sugar. Add the remaining egg and egg white, blending until smooth. Spread the mixture evenly over the soaked bread. Bake, uncovered, for 45 minutes, or until firm. Let cool slightly before serving.

Nutritional information per serving

Calories 227, Protein (g) 10, Carbohydrate (g) 41, Fat (g) 2, Calories from Fat (%) 8, Saturated Fat (g) 1, Dietary Fiber (g) 1, Cholesterol (mg) 38, Sodium (mg) 382
Diabetic Exchanges: *1 very lean meat, 2.5 other carbohydrate*

QUICK TIP

When preparing bread pudding, use bread that is slightly hard to ensure the proper texture after it's baked. Bread pudding originated in New Orleans as a means of using up French bread that goes stale so quickly.

DESSERTS AND PIES

Pineapple Bread Pudding with Lemon Apricot Sauce

With the fabulous Lemon Apricot Sauce, this incredible bread pudding will melt in your mouth. The sauce is good with ice cream, pound cake, or just a spoon.

1 (16-ounce) loaf French bread, sliced

1 (20-ounce) can crushed pineapple with juice

2 eggs

1 egg white

1 cup skim milk

¾ cup sugar

1 teaspoon vanilla extract

1 teaspoon butter extract

1 teaspoon ground cinnamon

Lemon Apricot Sauce (recipe follows)

MAKES 10 TO 12 SERVINGS

Preheat the oven to 350°F. Lay the French bread slices in a 2-quart oblong dish coated with nonstick cooking spray. Spread the crushed pineapple with juice evenly over the bread.

In a large bowl, beat together the eggs and egg white with the milk, sugar, vanilla extract, butter extract, and cinnamon. Pour evenly over the pineapple. Bake for 45 minutes, or until set. Serve the hot bread pudding with the Lemon Apricot Sauce (see recipe below).

Lemon Apricot Sauce

⅓ cup sugar

⅓ cup apricot nectar

1 teaspoon cornstarch

1 (5-ounce) can evaporated skimmed milk

1 tablespoon lemon juice

In a small saucepan, combine the sugar and nectar; bring to a boil. In a small bowl, combine the cornstarch and evaporated milk, and add to the nectar mixture. Return to a boil, and cook for 1 minute, or until thickened, stirring constantly. Remove from the heat; add the lemon juice.

Nutritional information per serving

Calories 240, Protein (g) 6, Carbohydrate (g) 48, Fat (g) 2, Calories from Fat (%) 8, Saturated Fat (g) 1, Dietary Fiber (g) 2, Cholesterol (mg) 36, Sodium (mg) 276
Diabetic Exchanges: *3 other carbohydrate*

🥕 Sweet Potato Bread Pudding with Praline Sauce

If you enjoy sweet potatoes and cinnamon, "incredible," "fabulous," and "unbelievable" are adjectives you'll to describe this melt-in-your-mouth dessert. The Praline Sauce is so delicious you'll want to spoon it up and eat it by itself.

1 (16-ounce) loaf French bread, cut into squares

1 (15-ounce) can sweet potatoes (yams), drained and mashed

1 (12-ounce) can evaporated skimmed milk

1½ cups skim milk

2 eggs

2 egg whites

2 tablespoons molasses

1 teaspoon cinnamon

½ teaspoon nutmeg

2 teaspoons vanilla extract

Praline Sauce (recipe follows)

MAKES 10 TO 12 SERVINGS

Preheat the oven to 350°F.

Place the French bread squares in a 2-quart oblong casserole dish coated with nonstick cooking spray.

In a mixing bowl, beat the sweet potato, evaporated milk, milk, eggs, egg whites, molasses, cinnamon, nutmeg, and vanilla. Pour evenly over the bread, and press with your hands to submerge the bread in the liquid mixture. Bake 35 to 45 minutes, or until the pudding is set. Top each serving with the Praline Sauce (see recipe below), and serve immediately.

Praline Sauce

2 cups sugar

3 tablespoons margarine

½ teaspoon baking soda

1 cup buttermilk

In a very large pot (mixture foams up while cooking), cook the sugar, margarine, baking soda, and buttermilk over medium heat, stirring frequently, until the sugar is dissolved. The mixture will foam; stir to beat down the foaming. The color will begin to caramelize. Cook until a slight brown color, about 20 to 30 minutes.

Nutritional information per serving
Calories 361, Protein (g) 10, Carbohydrate (g) 69, Fat (g) 5, Calories from Fat (%) 13, Saturated Fat (g) 1, Dietary Fiber (g) 2, Cholesterol (mg) 38, Sodium (mg) 430
Diabetic Exchanges: *0.5 skim milk, 4 other carbohydrate*

Chocolate Bread Pudding with Caramel Sauce

The light chocolate bread pudding with the rich caramel sauce makes this an irresistible dessert to be enjoyed right out of the oven. There is never a bite left over.

1 cup skim milk

2 cups evaporated skimmed milk

1¼ cups sugar

¼ cup cocoa

3 eggs

3 egg whites

1 tablespoon vanilla extract

1 (16-ounce) loaf egg, challah, Hawaiian, or sweet bread, cut into cubes

1 cup semisweet chocolate chips

Caramel Sauce (recipe follows)

MAKES 10 TO 12 SERVINGS

In a heavy saucepan over medium-high heat, combine the milk, evaporated milk, sugar, and cocoa . Stir until the sugar dissolves and the mixture comes to a boil. Remove from heat and cool slightly.

In a large bowl, beat the eggs, egg whites, and vanilla until blended. Gradually whisk in the chocolate mixture, and add the bread cubes and chocolate chips. Transfer to a 3-quart casserole dish coated with nonstick cooking spray. Let stand, mashing occasionally, until the bread absorbs some of the custard, about 30 minutes.

Preheat the oven to 350°F.

Cover the dish with foil. Bake about 30 to 40 minutes, or until set in the center. Serve warm or at room temperature with the warm Caramel Sauce (see recipe on the following page).

Caramel Sauce (for Chocolate Bread Pudding with Caramel Sauce)

1¼ cups sugar

½ cup water

¼ cup light corn syrup

1 tablespoon lemon juice

1 cup evaporated skimmed milk

½ cup chopped pecans, toasted, optional

Stir the sugar and water in a large heavy saucepan over medium heat until the sugar dissolves. Mix in the corn syrup and lemon juice. Increase the heat, and boil without stirring until the syrup turns deep amber, about 10 to 15 minutes. Remove from heat. Pour in the milk (the mixture will bubble up). Stir over low heat until the caramel is melted and smooth. Increase the heat, and boil about 4 minutes longer. Remove from heat. Cover and chill, if not serving immediately. Stir in the pecans, if desired.

Nutritional information per serving
Calories 446, Protein (g) 13, Carbohydrate (g) 83,
Fat (g) 8, Calories from Fat (%) 16, Saturated Fat (g) 4,
Dietary Fiber (g) 2, Cholesterol (mg) 75, Sodium (mg) 310
Diabetic Exchanges: *0.5 skim milk, 5 other carbohydrate, 1 fat*

QUICK TIP

Sometimes I spoon the Praline Sauce directly on the hot Bread Pudding right out of the oven so that it's easier to serve and store.

Coffee Cheesecake

A rich, creamy cheesecake with a touch of coffee. Leave out the coffee and you have a traditional cheesecake for purists. Cheesecakes freeze well.

¾ cup graham cracker crumbs

1 tablespoon cocoa

¾ cup plus 2 tablespoons sugar, divided

2 tablespoons margarine, melted

1 (8-ounce) package reduced-fat cream cheese

1 (8-ounce) package fat-free cream cheese, softened

⅓ cup all-purpose flour

1 tablespoon cornstarch

1 egg

2 tablespoons instant coffee dissolved in 1 teaspoon vanilla extract

⅓ cup fat-free sour cream

½ cup skim milk

4 egg whites

MAKES 10 TO 12 SERVINGS

Preheat the oven to 325°F.

In a small bowl, combine the graham cracker crumbs, cocoa, 2 tablespoons sugar, and melted margarine. Press into the bottom of a 9-inch springform pan.

In a large mixing bowl, combine the cream cheeses, flour, cornstarch, ½ cup sugar, egg, and the coffee dissolved in vanilla, beating until well combined. Add the sour cream and milk, mixing well.

In a separate bowl, beat the egg whites until stiff, gradually adding the remaining ¼ cup sugar. Fold into the cream cheese mixture, and pour the mixture over the crust in the springform pan. Bake for 1 hour. Leave in the oven with the door slightly open for 1 more hour. Refrigerate for at least 2 hours before serving.

Nutritional information per serving
Calories 212, Protein (g) 8, Carbohydrate (g) 28,
Fat (g) 7, Calories from Fat (%) 31, Saturated Fat (g) 3,
Dietary Fiber (g) 0, Cholesterol (mg) 33, Sodium (mg) 275
***Diabetic Exchanges:** 2 other carbohydrate, 1.5 fat*

QUICK TIP

When mixing cheesecake, use room temperature ingredients, don't overbeat, and mix at low speed to avoid whipping in excess air that will cause the cheesecake to rise and fall during baking. Do not overbake: cheesecake is done when the center is still wobbly and the edges are brown.

DESSERTS AND PIES

✏️ ❄️ Cranberry Cheesecake

Everyone always loves cheesecake, and this recipe laced and topped with cranberries is a real holiday treat. Bake prepared in graham cracker crusts in foil-lined pans to give as gifts.

½ cup graham cracker crumbs

1 tablespoon margarine, melted

1 (8-ounce) package reduced-fat cream cheese, softened

1 (8-ounce) container part-skim Ricotta cheese

½ cup sugar

½ teaspoon almond extract

3 egg whites

Cranberry Topping (recipe follows)

Cranberry Topping

1 (16-ounce) can whole-berry cranberry sauce

¼ cup sugar

1 tablespoon cornstarch

¼ cup water

MAKES 8 TO 10 SERVINGS

Preheat the oven to 350°F. Coat a 9-inch pie plate with nonstick cooking spray.

In a small bowl, combine the graham crackers and margarine. Pat the mixture into the bottom of the pie plate.

In a large mixing bowl, combine the cream cheese and Ricotta until well blended. Add the sugar and almond extract, mixing well.

In another mixing bowl, beat the egg whites until soft peaks form. Fold the egg whites gradually into the cheese mixture until well combined. Pour half of the batter into the pie plate. Spread with ¾ cup of the Cranberry Topping (see recipe below), and cover with the remaining cheesecake batter. Bake for 40 to 45 minutes, or until set. Remove from the oven, and cool on a rack. When cool, spread with the remaining Cranberry Topping. Refrigerate until chilled, about 2 hours.

In a medium saucepan, cook the cranberry sauce and sugar over medium-low heat until the mixture is smooth, about 3 minutes. In a small bowl, combine the cornstarch and water; add to the saucepan. Cook over medium heat, stirring constantly, until the mixture thickens. Refrigerate until lukewarm, 15 to 20 minutes, stirring in the refrigerator every 10 minutes. Remove ¾ cup cranberry topping for the inside of the cheesecake. Refrigerate the remaining topping until well chilled.

Nutritional information per serving

Calories 261, Protein (g) 6, Carbohydrate (g) 38, Fat (g) 9, Calories from Fat (%) 31, Saturated Fat (g) 6, Dietary Fiber (g) 1, Cholesterol (mg) 27, Sodium (mg) 261
Diabetic Exchanges: 2.5 other carbohydrate, 2 fat

DESSERTS AND PIES

❄ Sweet Potato Cheesecake

This incredibly rich and velvety sweet potato cheesecake with a spiced crust is cheesecake at its best. For a shortcut, purchase a prepared reduced-fat 9-inch graham cracker crust. This is a wonderful fall dessert.

1 cup graham cracker crumbs

2 tablespoons sugar

1 teaspoon ground cinnamon, divided

½ teaspoon ground allspice, divided

2 tablespoons margarine, melted

2 (8-ounce) packages reduced-fat cream cheese

1 cup nonfat plain yogurt

1 (15-ounce) can sweet potatoes (yams), drained and mashed, or 1 cup fresh, cooked and mashed

1⅓ cups dark brown sugar

1 egg

1 egg white

2 teaspoons vanilla extract

MAKES 10 TO 12 SERVINGS

Preheat the oven to 350°F.

In a small bowl, combine the cracker crumbs, sugar, ½ teaspoon cinnamon, ¼ teaspoon allspice, and the margarine. Pat into the bottom and up the sides of a 9-inch springform pan.

In a large bowl, beat together the cream cheese and yogurt until creamy. Add the sweet potatoes, brown sugar, remaining ½ teaspoon cinnamon, and remaining ¼ teaspoon allspice, beating until smooth. Add the egg and egg white one at a time, beating after each addition. Add the vanilla.

Spoon the mixture into the crust. Bake 50 to 60 minutes, or until set. Remove from the oven to cool. Refrigerate until chilled, about 2 hours.

Nutritional information per serving

Calories 308, Protein (g) 7, Carbohydrate (g) 44,
Fat (g) 12, Calories from Fat (%) 34, Saturated Fat (g) 6,
Dietary Fiber (g) 1, Cholesterol (mg) 45, Sodium (mg) 299
Diabetic Exchanges: *3 other carbohydrate, 2.5 fat*

FOOD FACT

Sweet potatoes (yams) are rich in beta carotene and a good source of Vitamins C and E.

✎ ❄ Chocolate Almond Cheesecake

Cheesecake lovers can indulge themselves with this rich-tasting version of an all-time favorite.

½ cup chocolate wafer
   crumbs

1 (8-ounce) package
   fat-free cream cheese

1 (8-ounce) package
   reduced-fat cream
   cheese

1 cup sugar

1½ cups fat-free cottage
   cheese, pureéd in food
   processor until smooth

1 egg

1 teaspoon vanilla extract

¼ cup all-purpose flour

¼ cup cocoa

⅓ cup almond liqueur

MAKES 10 TO 12 SERVINGS

Preheat the oven to 325°F. Spread the chocolate crumbs on the bottom of a 9-inch springform pan; set aside.

In a large mixing bowl, beat together the cream cheeses, sugar, cottage cheese, egg, and vanilla. In a small bowl, mix together the flour and cocoa; gradually add to the cream cheese mixture. Add the almond liqueur.

Pour the batter into the pan, and bake for 1 hour, or until set. Remove from the oven, cool to room temperature, and refrigerate until well chilled. Remove the sides of the pan, and serve.

Nutritional information per serving

Calories 216, Protein (g) 10, Carbohydrate (g) 29,
Fat (g) 5, Calories from Fat (%) 22, Saturated Fat (g) 3,
Dietary Fiber (g) 1, Cholesterol (mg) 36, Sodium (mg) 307
Diabetic Exchanges: *2 other carbohydrate, 1 fat*

QUICK TIP

A cheesecake shrinks in the pan as it cools, which can sometimes cause it to crack if the cheesecake sticks to the side of the pan. To help to prevent it from cracking, run a knife around the edge of the pan after removing it from the oven.

Strawberry Custard Brûlée

Restaurant quality in the comfort of your own home. Raspberries can be substituted for strawberries.

1½ cups fresh
   strawberries, rinsed
   and sliced
2 tablespoons sugar
1½ tablespoons
   cornstarch
1 egg, lightly beaten
1 cup skim milk
2 tablespoons nonfat
   plain yogurt
½ teaspoon vanilla extract
2 tablespoons light
   brown sugar

MAKES 5 SERVINGS

Divide the strawberries among five 4- to 6-ounce ramekins or custard cups; set aside.

In a saucepan, combine the sugar and cornstarch; stir well. Add the egg, and gradually stir in the milk. Cook over low heat for 7 to 10 minutes or until thickened, stirring constantly. Remove from heat; cool 5 minutes. Fold in the yogurt and vanilla, mixing well.

Spoon the custard mixture evenly over the strawberries. Place the ramekins on a baking sheet. Sprinkle the top with the brown sugar. Broil 4 inches from heat for about 2 minutes, or until the sugar melts, or brown the tops with a miniature kitchen torch. Serve immediately, or refrigerate.

Nutritional information per serving
Calories 101, Protein (g) 4, Carbohydrate (g) 19,
Fat (g) 1, Calories from Fat (%) 11, Saturated Fat (g) 0,
Dietary Fiber (g) 1, Cholesterol (mg) 43, Sodium (mg) 45
Diabetic Exchanges: *1.5 other carbohydrate*

FOOD FACT

Brûlée is "burnt cream," a rich custard topped with a hard sugar crust.

Orange Caramel Flan

This orange-flavored, creamy custard is light yet very satisfying. If you enjoy flan, this recipe is a wonderful choice.

½ cup sugar, divided

1 tablespoon water

3 eggs

¼ cup frozen orange juice concentrate, thawed

1 (12-ounce) can evaporated skimmed milk

½ cup skim milk

2 teaspoons vanilla extract

⅛ teaspoon almond extract

MAKES 6 SERVINGS

Preheat the oven to 300°F.

In a heavy, small saucepan, mix ¼ cup sugar with the water. Cook over medium-low heat until the sugar dissolves, stirring frequently. Increase the heat, and boil without stirring until the sugar turns deep golden brown, swirling the pan occasionally. Immediately pour the caramel into six 6-ounce custard cups. Carefully tilt the cups slightly, covering as much of the bottoms (but not the sides) as possible. Set the cups aside.

In a large bowl, whisk the eggs, orange juice concentrate, and remaining ¼ cup sugar. Gradually whisk in both the milks and the extracts. Divide the custard among the prepared cups.

Place the cups in a large baking pan. Add enough hot water to the pan to come halfway up the sides of the cups. Bake until the custards are set, about 80 minutes. Remove the cups from the water. Cover, and refrigerate overnight. Run a small, sharp knife around the custard sides to loosen. Invert a custard onto each plate, or eat inside the cup.

Nutritional information per serving

*Calories 182, Protein (g) 9, Carbohydrate (g) 30,
Fat (g) 3, Calories from Fat (%) 13, Saturated Fat (g) 1,
Dietary Fiber (g) 0, Cholesterol (mg) 109, Sodium (mg) 116*
Diabetic Exchanges: *0.5 skim milk, 0.5 fruit, 1 other carbohydrate*

DESSERTS AND PIES

Fantastic Trifle

Trifles serve a crowd and make a nice presentation. Of all my trifles, this is the one for which people always request the recipe. It's easy to make and a guaranteed winner.

1 (16-ounce) angel food cake
⅔ cup sugar
3 tablespoons cocoa
1 tablespoon cornstarch
1 (5-ounce) can evaporated skimmed milk
¼ cup coffee liqueur
3 (1.4-ounce) chocolate-covered toffee candy bars, crushed
3 (4-serving) packages instant vanilla pudding and pie filling mix
3 cups skim milk
2 bananas, peeled and sliced
1 (12-ounce) container fat-free frozen whipped topping, thawed

MAKES 16 SERVINGS

Cube the cake and place in a large bowl.

To make the chocolate sauce: In a small pot, combine the sugar, cocoa, cornstarch, and evaporated milk. Cook over low heat until thickened, 7 to 10 minutes. Remove from heat; add the coffee liqueur, and cool. Pour the chocolate mixture over the cake in the bowl. Add the crushed candy to the cake mixture.

In a mixer, beat or whisk the pudding mix and 3 cups skim milk until thick. Pour over the angel food cake mixture.

In a trifle dish, layer the cake mixture, banana, and whipped topping. Repeat the layers, ending with the whipped topping. Refrigerate until serving.

Nutritional information per serving
Calories 299, Protein (g) 5, Carbohydrate (g) 61,
Fat (g) 3, Calories from Fat (%) 9, Saturated Fat (g) 2,
Dietary Fiber (g) 1, Cholesterol (mg) 5, Sodium (mg) 505
Diabetic Exchanges: *4 other carbohydrate, 0.5 fat*

QUICK TIP

Crush any extra toffee candy bars to sprinkle on top of the Trifle. It can also be garnished with strawberries.

Chocolate Trifle

When you need a show-stopping quick dessert to serve a crowd, here's your answer. No one can resist this dazzling series of chocolate layers. Make ahead of time, and refrigerate until ready to serve.

1 (18.25-ounce) package devil's food cake mix

1⅓ cups water

1 egg

2 egg whites

1 (4-serving) package instant chocolate pudding and pie filling mix

3 cups cold skim milk

⅓ cup coffee liqueur

½ cup chopped chocolate-covered toffee candy bars, (2 1.4-ounce bars)

1 (8-ounce) container fat-free frozen whipped topping, thawed

MAKES 16 SERVINGS

Preheat the oven to 350°F. Coat two 9-inch round baking pans with nonstick cooking spray.

Combine the cake mix, water, egg, and egg whites in a mixing bowl, and beat for 2 minutes. Pour the batter evenly into the prepared pans. Bake for 25 to 30 minutes, or until a toothpick inserted in the center comes out clean. Let cool on a wire rack, and remove from the pans.

In a medium mixing bowl, combine the pudding mix and milk, and prepare according to the package directions. Chill in the refrigerator.

To assemble, place a cake layer in the bottom of a trifle dish or large glass bowl, then sprinkle with half the coffee liqueur, half the toffee candy, half the pudding, and half the whipped topping. Repeat the layers. Refrigerate until serving.

Nutritional information per serving
Calories 248, Protein (g) 5, Carbohydrate (g) 40,
Fat (g) 6, Calories from Fat (%) 23, Saturated Fat (g) 3,
Dietary Fiber (g) 1, Cholesterol (mg) 37, Sodium (mg) 411
Diabetic Exchanges: *2 other carbohydrate, 1 fat*

QUICK TIP

Try using chocolate fudge pudding in this recipe for more chocolate flavor, or milk chocolate pudding for a lighter version.

DESSERTS AND PIES

🥕 Fruit Trifle

When summer fruit is in season, here's an outstanding choice—homemade custard layered with fresh fruit is hard to beat. Use whatever fruit you enjoy, and prepare this quick-to-fix luscious creation. For the speedy approach, instant vanilla pudding may be substituted for custard.

½ cup sugar

⅓ cup cornstarch

3 cups skim milk

2 egg yolks, slightly beaten

1 teaspoon vanilla extract

1 (16-ounce) angel food cake, cut into ½-inch slices

½ cup sherry, divided

1 pound fresh strawberries, stemmed and sliced

2 bananas, peeled and sliced

1 pint fresh blueberries

2 kiwis, peeled and sliced

1 (12-ounce) container fat-free frozen whipped topping, thawed

MAKES 16 SERVINGS

In a 2-quart saucepan, stir together the sugar and cornstarch. Gradually add the milk, stirring until smooth. Stir in the beaten egg yolks. Cook over medium heat, stirring constantly, until the mixture comes to a boil. Boil for 2 minutes, and remove from the heat. Stir in the vanilla. Transfer to a large bowl, cover with waxed paper, and refrigerate until chilled, about 30 minutes.

Arrange half the angel food cake slices in a single layer in a trifle dish or a deep glass bowl. Drizzle with ¼ cup of the sherry. Layer with half the fruit, half the custard, and half the whipped topping. Repeat the layers with the remaining ingredients, beginning with angel food cake and sherry and ending with the whipped topping. Refrigerate until ready to serve.

Nutritional information per serving
Calories 211, Protein (g) 4, Carbohydrate (g) 44, Fat (g) 1, Calories from Fat (%) 5, Saturated Fat (g) 0, Dietary Fiber (g) 2, Cholesterol (mg) 27, Sodium (mg) 251
Diabetic Exchanges: *3 other carbohydrate*

FOOD FACT

Low-fat dairy products are rich in calcium, which is important for building strong bones, teeth, and muscles.

Lemon Pineapple Trifle

When tart lemon custard is combined with pineapple-lemon filling, lemon lovers will not be able to contain themselves. Ladyfingers are available in most grocery stores in the bakery or frozen foods section.

¼ cup cornstarch

1 cup sugar

⅓ cup cold water

1 cup hot water

⅔ cup lemon juice

1 egg yolk, lightly beaten

½ (8-ounce) package reduced-fat cream cheese, softened (4 ounces)

1 (8-ounce) can crushed pineapple, drained

1 (8-ounce) container fat-free frozen whipped topping, thawed, divided

24 ladyfingers

MAKES 10 SERVINGS

In a medium saucepan, mix the cornstarch and sugar. Gradually add the cold water, stirring to mix. Add the hot water and lemon juice, and bring to a boil over medium heat, stirring constantly. Cook until thickened, 7 to 10 minutes, then gradually pour 1 cup of the hot mixture into the egg yolk in a small bowl, stirring constantly. Return that mixture to the saucepan, and continue cooking for 1 minute. Transfer the custard to a large bowl, cover, and refrigerate until chilled.

Divide the custard in half; using a fork or whisk, blend half the custard with the cream cheese. Mix in the pineapple. Fold half the container of whipped topping into the pineapple custard mixture; set aside.

In a trifle bowl or a deep glass bowl, place a layer of the ladyfingers along the bottom and around the side of the dish. Next, spread the bottom with half the plain lemon custard. Spread with half the pineapple-lemon filling. Top with the remaining ladyfingers. Spread with the remaining plain lemon custard, and top with the rest of the pineapple-lemon filling. Top this with the remaining whipped topping. Refrigerate for at least 2 hours before serving.

Nutritional information per serving
Calories 273, Protein (g) 4, Carbohydrate (g) 51, Fat (g) 5, Calories from Fat (%) 18, Saturated Fat (g) 3, Dietary Fiber (g) 1, Cholesterol (mg) 126, Sodium (mg) 103
Diabetic Exchanges: *3.5 other carbohydrate, 1 fat*

DESSERTS AND PIES

🥕 Pineapple Trifle

This effortless, elegant dessert will make a statement. Pineapple, cream cheese layers, and whipped topping will entice even the chocoholics. For the height of indulgence, add fresh berries.

1½ (8-ounce) packages
   reduced-fat cream
   cheese
   (12 ounces total)
⅔ cup sugar
1 (5-ounce) can
   evaporated
   skimmed milk
1 (16-ounce) angel food
   cake, cubed
1 (20-ounce) can crushed
   pineapple, with juice
2 tablespoons cornstarch
1 (8-ounce) container
   fat-free frozen whipped
   topping, thawed

MAKES 8 TO 10 SERVINGS

In a mixing bowl, beat the cream cheese, sugar, and evaporated milk until creamy. Fold in the cubed angel food cake.

In a small saucepan, combine the pineapple and cornstarch. Cook over low heat until thick, stirring constantly; set aside to cool 5 to 7 minutes.

In a trifle dish or a deep glass bowl, layer half the angel food cake mixture, half the pineapple mixture, and half the whipped topping. Repeat again, ending with whipped topping. Refrigerate until ready to serve.

Nutritional information per serving
Calories 343, Protein (g) 8, Carbohydrate (g) 59,
Fat (g) 8, Calories from Fat (%) 21, Saturated Fat (g) 5,
Dietary Fiber (g) 1, Cholesterol (mg) 25, Sodium (mg) 521
Diabetic Exchanges: *4 other carbohydrate, 1.5 fat*

🥕 Glazed Bananas

Everyday ingredients turn into a dessert that makes a fabulous ending to a meal or a great anytime dessert snack. Serve over frozen vanilla yogurt or ice cream.

2 tablespoons margarine
¼ cup light brown sugar
⅛ teaspoon ground
   cinnamon
¼ cup fresh orange juice
3 firm bananas, peeled,
   split lengthwise, and
   halved

MAKES 6 SERVINGS

In a pan, heat the margarine, brown sugar, cinnamon, and orange juice until bubbly. Add the banana slices, and cook for 5 minutes, turning as needed. Serve immediately.

Nutritional information per serving
Calories 127, Protein (g) 1, Carbohydrate (g) 24,
Fat (g) 4, Calories from Fat (%) 27, Saturated Fat (g) 1,
Dietary Fiber (g) 1, Cholesterol (mg) 0, Sodium (mg) 49
Diabetic Exchanges: *1 fruit, 0.5 other carbohydrate, 1 fat*

Ice Cream Pie

Looking for a simple ice cream dessert that all ages will request? You came to the right recipe. Keep it easy by using whatever chocolate cookies you have lying around for the crust—crush the cookies in a food processor or by hand.

1 cup chocolate wafer crumbs
1 cup graham cracker crumbs
¼ cup margarine, melted
½ gallon nonfat vanilla frozen yogurt
Chocolate Sauce (recipe follows)

Chocolate Sauce

⅔ cup sugar
3 tablespoons cocoa
1 tablespoon cornstarch
1 (5-ounce) can evaporated skimmed milk
1 tablespoon margarine
1 teaspoon vanilla extract

MAKES 16 SERVINGS

In a medium bowl, combine the chocolate wafer crumbs and graham cracker crumbs with the melted margarine, stirring until combined. Pat into the bottom of a 13 x 9 x 2-inch pan, and chill until firm.

Soften the vanilla frozen yogurt, and spread on top of the crust. Chill in the freezer for 20 to 30 minutes. Top with the Chocolate Sauce (see recipe below), and return to the freezer until ready to serve.

In a small saucepan, combine the sugar, cocoa, and cornstarch. Gradually add the evaporated milk. Cook over low heat, stirring, until the mixture thickens and boils, 7 to 10 minutes. Remove from heat. Add the margarine and vanilla. Cool slightly before spreading on top of the frozen pie.

Nutritional information per serving
Calories 238, Protein (g) 7, Carbohydrate (g) 41,
Fat (g) 6, Calories from Fat (%) 21, Saturated Fat (g) 1,
Dietary Fiber (g) 1, Cholesterol (mg) 3, Sodium (mg) 217
Diabetic Exchanges: 3.5 other carbohydrate, 1 fat

QUICK TIP

Use your imagination with this recipe, and try different flavored frozen yogurts or low fat ice creams to satisfy taste buds. Heavenly Hash low-fat ice cream was sooo good!

Coffee Toffee Dessert

This impressive, simple, make-ahead ice cream dessert is a perfect ending to any meal. The coffee liqueur can be omitted if you prefer.

1 (10-ounce)
   angel food cake
1 tablespoon instant
   coffee
1 tablespoon hot water
1 teaspoon vanilla extract
4 (1.4-ounce) bars
   chocolate-covered
   toffee candy bars
1 quart nonfat vanilla
   frozen yogurt, softened
1 (8-ounce) container fat-
   free frozen whipped
   topping, thawed
2 tablespoons coffee
   liqueur

MAKES 16 SERVINGS

Slice the angel food cake, and lay it along the bottom of a 9-inch springform pan coated with nonstick cooking spray.

Dissolve the coffee in the hot water; cool. Add the vanilla to the coffee.

Crush the candy bars in a food processor or by pounding with a mallet. In a large bowl, combine the crushed candy and the dissolved coffee mixture with the softened frozen yogurt. Quickly spoon the mixture on top of the angel food cake.

Mix the whipped topping with the coffee liqueur, and spread over the yogurt layer. Freeze overnight, or until firm enough to cut.

Nutritional information per serving
Calories 180, Protein (g) 4, Carbohydrate (g) 31,
Fat (g) 4, Calories from Fat (%) 18, Saturated Fat (g) 2,
Dietary Fiber (g) 0, Cholesterol (mg) 6, Sodium (mg) 200
Diabetic Exchanges: 2 other carbohydrate, 1 fat

QUICK TIP

Try substituting with different flavors of frozen yogurt, ice cream, or liqueurs to create different versions of this dessert.

Mocha Fudge Mousse Pie

This recipe I created was a cover recipe for Cooking Light *magazine and was selected as one of their ten best recipes on their ten-year anniversary. A brownie mix and a pudding mix make this brownie decadence effortless to prepare. For flair, garnish with shaved chocolate.*

⅓ cup warm water
1 teaspoon instant coffee
1 (19.85-ounce) box
  reduced-fat or regular
  fudge brownie mix
2 egg whites
1 teaspoon vanilla extract
⅓ cup chopped pecans
Mousse (recipe follows)

MAKES 8 TO 10 SERVINGS

Preheat the oven to 350°F. Coat a 9-inch pie plate with nonstick cooking spray.

In a small cup, stir together the water and the coffee until dissolved.

In a large bowl, combine the brownie mix, coffee mixture, egg whites, and vanilla, stirring with a spoon until well mixed. Stir in the pecans. Pour the batter into the prepared pie plate. Bake for 25 minutes, or until the cake is set in the pan. Do not overbake.

Cool on a wire rack. Spread with the Chocolate Mousse (see recipe below), and top with the coffee-flavored whipped topping. Refrigerate until serving.

Chocolate Mousse

¾ cup skim milk
2 tablespoons coffee
  liqueur, divided
1 teaspoon instant coffee
1 (4-serving) package
  chocolate-flavored
  instant pudding and
  pie filling mix
1 (8-ounce) container
  fat-free frozen whipped
  topping, thawed,
  divided

In a large bowl, stir together the milk, 1 tablespoon coffee liqueur, and coffee until the coffee is dissolved. Add the pudding mix, and beat at the high speed of a mixer for 1 minute, or until thick. Gently fold in half of the whipped topping. Spread the mixture evenly over the cooled brownie crust.

Combine the remaining 1 tablespoon coffee liqueur with the remaining half of the whipped topping, mixing gently. Spread over the pudding mixture in the pie.

Nutritional information per serving
Calories 348, Protein (g) 5, Carbohydrate (g) 66,
Fat (g) 7, Calories from Fat (%) 19, Saturated Fat (g) 2,
Dietary Fiber (g) 2, Cholesterol (mg) 0, Sodium (mg) 361
Diabetic Exchanges: *4.5 other carbohydrate, 1.5 fat*

Tiramisu

Another cover recipe for Cooking Light *magazine, this personal creation was the most requested recipe of the magazine's ten-year anniversary. Try it and you will see why! Espresso powder can be used to make the coffee.*

½ cup espresso or
   very strong coffee
¼ cup plus 1 tablespoon
   sugar
3 tablespoons coffee
   liqueur
1 (8-ounce) package
   reduced-fat cream
   cheese, softened
¾ cup confectioners'
   sugar
1½ cups fat-free frozen
   whipped topping,
   thawed and divided
3 egg whites
20 ladyfingers, split
Cocoa, for sprinkling

MAKES 16 SERVINGS

In a small bowl, combine the espresso coffee, 1 tablespoon sugar, and the coffee liqueur; set aside.

In a large mixing bowl, combine the cream cheese with the confectioners' sugar, beating until well blended. Fold in 1 cup of the whipped topping.

In another large mixing bowl, beat the egg whites until soft peaks form; add the remaining ¼ cup sugar, and continue beating until stiff peaks form. Fold into the cream cheese mixture.

In a 9 x 9 x 2-inch dish, place a layer of the split ladyfingers across the bottom of the dish. Drizzle with half the espresso mixture and half the cream cheese mixture; and repeat the layers, beginning with the split ladyfingers and ending with the cream cheese mixture. Spread the remaining ½ cup whipped topping in a thin layer on the top, and sprinkle with cocoa. Refrigerate until well chilled.

Nutritional information per serving
Calories 149, Protein (g) 4, Carbohydrate (g) 22,
Fat (g) 4, Calories from Fat (%) 27, Saturated Fat (g) 3,
Dietary Fiber (g) 0, Cholesterol (mg) 60, Sodium (mg) 96
Diabetic Exchanges: *1.5 other carbohydrate, 1 fat*

QUICK TIP

Instant espresso powder can be used interchangeably with instant coffee. The espresso powder has a more concentrated flavor, and it dissolves in cold liquid more easily than coffee crystals. It is available in the coffee section at most grocery stores.

Chocolate Fondue

This is great for cocktail parties. Serve with fresh fruit, including strawberries, for an eye-appealing presentation.

2 cups sugar

¾ cup unsweetened cocoa

2 tablespoons cornstarch

¼ teaspoon salt

4 cups cold skim milk

3 tablespoons margarine

1 teaspoon vanilla extract

¼ teaspoon butter extract

MAKES 40 (2-TABLESPOON) SERVINGS

Mix the sugar, cocoa, cornstarch, and salt together in a saucepan. Add skim milk, stirring well. Over medium heat, bring to a boil. Lower the heat, and simmer 20 minutes. Remove from heat. Add the margarine, vanilla, and butter extract. For dipping, use angel food cake cut into squares, marshmallows, or fresh fruit.

Nutritional information per serving

Calories 63, Protein (g) 1, Carbohydrate (g) 12, Fat (g) 1, Calories from Fat (%) 15, Saturated Fat (g) 0, Dietary Fiber (g) 0, Cholesterol (mg) 0, Sodium (mg) 37
Diabetic Exchanges: 1 other carbohydrate

QUICK TIP

Reheat chocolate fondue in the microwave. Microwave for 1 minute, stir, and repeat until melted.

DESSERTS AND PIES

🥕 Banana Éclair

When I want an indulgent dessert with a spectacular presentation, this is my first choice. This showpiece-quality dessert is a little time-consuming, but it's worth the effort. Make the shell ahead, and fill on the day of serving. Slice the éclair in half lengthwise, and then cut in slices down the middle to serve to a crowd.

1 cup water
½ cup margarine
1 cup all-purpose flour
2 tablespoons sugar
2 eggs
3 egg whites
Banana Cream Filling
   (recipe follows)
Chocolate Glaze
   (recipe follows)

MAKES 16 TO 18 SERVINGS

Preheat the oven to 400°F.

In a large saucepan over medium heat, bring the water and margarine to a boil, cooking until the margarine is melted. In a small bowl, combine the flour with the sugar, and add to the margarine mixture all at once, stirring vigorously with a spoon until the dough forms a ball and leaves the sides of the pan. Remove the pan from the heat. Beat in the eggs and egg whites with a spoon, one at a time, and continue beating until the dough is stiff and glossy.

On a 15 x 10 x 1-inch jelly roll pan coated with non-stick cooking spray, form about two-thirds of the dough into one long oblong about 7 inches wide. Reserve a little extra dough to spoon into mounds along the top of the oblong. Bake for 20 to 25 minutes, or until golden brown. Remove from the oven, and with a sharp knife, make slits along the sides of the éclair about 2 inches apart to let the steam escape. Return to the oven, and continue baking for 10 minutes longer. Remove to a cooling rack.

Carefully slice off the top of the éclair. It may come off in pieces. Remove, and scoop out any soft dough inside the shell. Cool thoroughly.

Place the bottom on a serving platter. Fill the bottom éclair shell with half the Banana Cream Filling (see recipe at right). Slice the remaining bananas over the topping. Cover with the remaining filling. Cover with the baked shell top (or pieces to form the top if not in a whole piece), and drizzle with the Chocolate Glaze (see recipe at right). Refrigerate until serving time.

Banana Cream Filling

2 envelopes whipped topping mix
1 cup cold skim milk
6 to 8 bananas, divided
¼ cup banana liqueur

In a large mixing bowl, combine both envelopes of the whipped topping with the milk, beating until the topping is very thick and forms a peak.

Mash enough bananas to make 2 cups, and mix with the banana liqueur. Fold the banana mixture into the whipped topping.

Chocolate Glaze

1 tablespoon margarine, melted
2 tablespoons cocoa
1 teaspoon vanilla extract
⅔ cup confectioners' sugar
3 tablespoons boiling water

In a small bowl, combine the melted margarine, cocoa, vanilla, and confectioners' sugar. Stir in the boiling water to make a thin glaze. Refrigerate.

Nutritional information per serving
Calories 187, Protein (g) 3, Carbohydrate (g) 26, Fat (g) 8, Calories from Fat (%) 36, Saturated Fat (g) 2, Dietary Fiber (g) 1, Cholesterol (mg) 24, Sodium (mg) 96
Diabetic Exchanges: 1.5 other carbohydrate, 1.5 fat

QUICK TIP

The banana liqueur may be omitted—just add 1 teaspoon vanilla to mixture.

DESSERTS AND PIES

Peach Crisp

Using frozen peaches makes it possible to enjoy this dessert year-round. I admit I'm partial to the oatmeal crumbly topping, and it's likely you will be, too.

2 (16-ounce) packages frozen peaches, thawed

2 tablespoons cornstarch

⅓ cup sugar

2 tablespoons lemon juice

5 tablespoons margarine

⅓ cup light brown sugar

1 tablespoon vanilla extract

¾ cup all-purpose flour

¼ teaspoon baking soda

1½ cups old-fashioned oatmeal

MAKES 10 TO 12 SERVINGS

Preheat the oven to 350°F.

Lay the fruit in an oblong 2-quart casserole dish. In a small bowl, mix together the cornstarch and sugar. Toss the cornstarch mixture and lemon juice with the peaches in the casserole dish.

In a medium bowl, mix together the margarine, brown sugar, and vanilla. In a small bowl, stir together the flour and baking soda, and mix with the oatmeal and margarine mixture until crumbly. Sprinkle on top of the peaches.

Bake for 45 minutes, or until the topping is brown and the mixture is bubbly. Serve immediately.

Nutritional information per serving

Calories 195, Protein (g) 3, Carbohydrate (g) 32, Fat (g) 6, Calories from Fat (%) 27, Saturated Fat (g) 1, Dietary Fiber (g) 3, Cholesterol (mg) 0, Sodium (mg) 85
Diabetic Exchanges: 2 other carbohydrate, 1 fat

Berry Crisp

Yummy! I had some frozen raspberries and whipped up this dessert to serve over frozen vanilla yogurt. It works well substituting other berries, too.

1 quart fresh raspberries or blueberries, or 1 (16-ounce) package frozen berries

3 tablespoons sugar

¼ cup margarine, softened

⅓ cup all-purpose flour

⅓ cup light brown sugar

¾ cup old-fashioned oatmeal

MAKES 4 TO 6 SERVINGS

Preheat the oven to 350°F.

Place the fruit in the bottom of a 9-inch square baking pan coated with nonstick cooking spray. Sprinkle the sugar over the fruit.

In a medium bowl, blend together the margarine, flour, brown sugar, and oatmeal until the mixture resembles a coarse meal. Sprinkle over the fruit. Bake for 30 minutes, or until lightly browned. Serve hot.

Nutritional information per serving

Calories 242, Protein (g) 3, Carbohydrate (g) 40, Fat (g) 9, Calories from Fat (%) 31, Saturated Fat (g) 1, Dietary Fiber (g) 7, Cholesterol (mg) 0, Sodium (mg) 94

Diabetic Exchanges: 0.5 fruit, 2 other carbohydrate, 2 fat

QUICK TIP

Don't let winter months keep you from enjoying fruit. Fresh or frozen is best, but canned fruit works fine, too.

Nectarine and Raspberry Crumble

Nectarines and raspberries are two of my favorites, so this recipe that mixes the two together with a crumbly oatmeal topping is at the top of my list. Frozen fruit may also be used; defrost first.

6 tablespoons light
   brown sugar, divided

3 tablespoons all-purpose
   flour, divided

½ teaspoon ground
   cinnamon

4 ripe nectarines, peeled
   and sliced 2 inches thick

½ pint fresh raspberries

1 cup old-fashioned
   oatmeal

2 tablespoons margarine

2 tablespoons fresh
   orange juice

MAKES 6 TO 8 SERVINGS

Preheat the oven to 425°F. Coat a 9-inch pie plate with nonstick cooking spray.

In a small bowl, combine 2 tablespoons brown sugar, 2 tablespoons flour, and the cinnamon. Toss with the nectarines. Gently toss in the raspberries. Place the fruit mixture in the prepared pie plate.

Combine the remaining 4 tablespoons brown sugar, the oatmeal, and the remaining 1 tablespoon flour with the margarine and orange juice, mixing until crumbly. Crumble over the fruit.

Bake for 25 to 30 minutes, or until the fruit is bubbly. If the topping begins to brown too quickly, cover loosely with foil. Serve hot or reheated.

Nutritional information per serving
Calories 158, Protein (g) 3, Carbohydrate (g) 29,
Fat (g) 4, Calories from Fat (%) 21, Saturated Fat (g) 1,
Dietary Fiber (g) 3, Cholesterol (mg) 0, Sodium (mg) 38
Diabetic Exchanges: *2 other carbohydrate, 1 fat*

QUICK TIP

Just wash nectarines before using—they don't require peeling. Store ripe nectarines in the refrigerator for up to five days.

✏️ ❄️ Blueberry Pineapple Crunch

So quick and easy, but unbelievably good. Lemon lovers will have a big smile while enjoying this cobbler-type dessert. It's great just out of the oven with frozen vanilla yogurt.

1 (20-ounce) can crushed pineapple in juice, undrained

2 cups fresh or frozen blueberries

1 (18.25-ounce) box lemon cake mix

⅔ cup light brown sugar

½ cup margarine, melted

MAKES 16 SERVINGS

Preheat the oven to 350°F.

In a 13 x 9 x 2-inch baking pan coated with nonstick cooking spray, spread the pineapple and blueberries along the bottom of the pan. Sprinkle evenly with the cake mix and brown sugar. Drizzle with the margarine. Bake for 45 to 50 minutes, or until bubbly. Serve hot.

Nutritional information per serving

Calories 246, Protein (g) 1, Carbohydrate (g) 43, Fat (g) 8, Calories from Fat (%) 30, Saturated Fat (g) 2, Dietary Fiber (g) 1, Cholesterol (mg) 0, Sodium (mg) 279
Diabetic Exchanges: *3 other carbohydrate, 1.5 fat*

FOOD FACT

Blueberries are a good source of fiber and the photochemical anthocyanosides that serve as antioxidants to fight cancer.

DESSERTS AND PIES

Apple Peanut Crumble

Baked apples with a peanut crumble topping hot out of the oven—sinfully good!

5 cooking apples, peeled,
  cored, and sliced
  (7 to 8 cups)
⅔ cup light brown sugar
½ cup all-purpose flour
½ cup old-fashioned
  oatmeal
½ teaspoon ground
  cinnamon
½ teaspoon ground
  nutmeg
⅓ cup margarine
2 tablespoons reduced-
  fat peanut butter

MAKES 8 SERVINGS

Preheat the oven to 350°F.

Coat a 2-quart oblong casserole dish with nonstick cooking spray. Lay the apples in the dish.

In a mixing bowl, combine the brown sugar, flour, oatmeal, cinnamon, nutmeg, margarine, and peanut butter. Mix until the consistency is crumblike. Sprinkle over the top of the apples. Bake for 30 minutes, or until the apples are tender and the mixture is bubbly. Serve hot.

Nutritional information per serving

Calories 251, Protein (g) 3, Carbohydrate (g) 41, Fat (g) 10, Calories from Fat (%) 33, Saturated Fat (g) 2, Dietary Fiber (g) 3, Cholesterol (mg) 0, Sodium (mg) 118
Diabetic Exchanges: *1 fruit, 1.5 other carbohydrate, 2 fat*

Chocolate Chip Pie

This fast-to-fix crustless pie is like eating a thick chocolate chip cookie.

2 cups all-purpose flour
1 teaspoon baking
  powder
½ teaspoon baking soda
1¼ cups light brown
  sugar
4 tablespoons margarine,
  melted
2 eggs
1 tablespoon vanilla
  extract
⅔ cup semisweet
  chocolate chips

MAKES 8 SERVINGS

Preheat the oven to 350°F. Coat a 9-inch pie plate with nonstick cooking spray.

In a medium bowl, combine the flour, baking powder, and baking soda; set aside.

In a large bowl, combine the brown sugar, margarine, eggs, and vanilla. Stir in the dry mixture and the chocolate chips. Spoon into the prepared pie plate. Bake for 30 minutes, or until a knife inserted in the center comes out clean. Don't overbake. Let cool on a wire rack before serving.

Nutritional information per serving

Calories 307, Protein (g) 4, Carbohydrate (g) 53, Fat (g) 9, Calories from Fat (%) 26, Saturated Fat (g) 3, Dietary Fiber (g) 1, Cholesterol (mg) 43, Sodium (mg) 190
Diabetic Exchanges: *3.5 other carbohydrate, 2 fat*

Chocolate Chess Pie

This effortless pie is truly outstanding—simple, sweet, and an indulgence to eat. Everyone always wants seconds.

2 tablespoons margarine, melted

1 cup sugar

1 tablespoon all-purpose flour

3 tablespoons cocoa

1 (5-ounce) can evaporated skimmed milk

2 eggs, beaten

1 teaspoon vanilla extract

1 unbaked (9-inch) pie shell

MAKES 8 SERVINGS

Preheat the oven to 350°F.

In a large mixing bowl, mix together the margarine, sugar, flour, cocoa, evaporated milk, eggs, and vanilla, beating well.

Pour the mixture into the pie shell. Bake for 30 minutes, or until firm. Cool and serve.

Nutritional information per serving

Calories 289, Protein (g) 5, Carbohydrate (g) 42, Fat (g) 11, Calories from Fat (%) 35, Saturated Fat (g) 4, Dietary Fiber (g) 1, Cholesterol (mg) 59, Sodium (mg) 173
Diabetic Exchanges: *3 other carbohydrate, 2 fat*

Custard Pie

A true custard lovers' delight—plain but palate-pleasing. To trim fat, use the crust recipe for the Apple Crumble Pie, page 446.

3 cups skim milk

1 cup sugar

½ cup all-purpose flour

2 eggs

1 teaspoon vanilla extract

1 unbaked (9-inch) pie shell

MAKES 8 SERVINGS

Preheat the oven to 350°F.

In a medium saucepan, heat the milk over low heat.

In a medium bowl, mix the sugar, flour, and eggs. Beat well and pour into the heated milk. Cook over medium heat until the mixture boils and thickens, 10 to 12 minutes. Remove from heat and add the vanilla. Pour the custard filling into the pie shell. Bake for 20 to 30 minutes, or until set. Cool and serve.

Nutritional information per serving

Calories 297, Protein (g) 7, Carbohydrate (g) 49, Fat (g) 8, Calories from Fat (%) 26, Saturated Fat (g) 4, Dietary Fiber (g) 0, Cholesterol (mg) 60, Sodium (mg) 164
Diabetic Exchanges: *3 other carbohydrate, 1.5 fat*

DESSERTS AND PIES

❄ Apple Crumble Pie

Nothing beats a good apple pie, and this is the best—you'll love the crumbly topping with a light lemon glaze. For convenience, use a 9-inch unbaked pie crust from your grocery store.

1 cup plus 1 tablespoon all-purpose flour, divided

2 tablespoons cold water

2 tablespoons canola oil

1 teaspoon vanilla extract

1 teaspoon ground cinnamon

1 tablespoon water

⅓ cup sugar

4 cups peeled, sliced tart baking apples

Topping (recipe follows)

½ cup confectioners' sugar

2 tablespoons lemon juice

Topping

½ teaspoon ground cinnamon

½ cup crushed nonfat pretzels

¼ cup light brown sugar

¾ cup all-purpose flour

5 tablespoons margarine, chilled and cut into pieces

MAKES 8 SLICES

Preheat the oven to 350°F.

In a small bowl, mix 1 cup flour and the cold water and oil together; press into a 9-inch pie plate.

In a large bowl, combine the vanilla, cinnamon, 1 tablespoon water, 1 tablespoon flour, sugar, and apples. Fill the crust with the filling. Sprinkle the filling with the Topping (see recipe below).

Bake for 1 hour, or until the apples are done and the pie is bubbly. In a measuring cup mix the confectioners' sugar and lemon juice. Drizzle the glaze over the hot pie. Serve hot.

In a small bowl, combine the cinnamon, pretzels, brown sugar, and flour. Cut in the margarine until the mixture is crumbly.

Nutritional information per serving
Calories 341, Protein (g) 4, Carbohydrate (g) 58, Fat (g) 11, Calories from Fat (%) 29, Saturated Fat (g) 1, Dietary Fiber (g) 2, Cholesterol (mg) 0, Sodium (mg) 165
Diabetic Exchanges: *4 other carbohydrate, 2 fat*

DESSERTS AND PIES

Banana Cream Pie

Here's the ultimate combination for banana pudding fans. For a short cut, purchase a prepared graham cracker crust.

1 cup reduced-fat vanilla wafer crumbs

2 tablespoons margarine, melted

¼ cup plus ⅓ cup sugar

2 tablespoons cornstarch

1½ cups skim milk

1 egg, beaten

1 tablespoon vanilla extract

3 bananas, sliced

3 egg whites

QUICK TIP

If a pie crust browns too quickly, cover the edges with strips of foil and continue baking.

MAKES 8 SERVINGS

Preheat the oven to 375°F.

In a pie plate, mix the vanilla wafer crumbs and margarine. Press the mixture into the bottom and up the sides of the pie plate, and bake for 5 to 7 minutes; set aside.

Increase the oven temperature to 400°F. In a medium saucepan, combine ¼ cup of the sugar and the cornstarch. Gradually add the milk, stirring until blended. Cook over medium heat, stirring constantly, until the mixture thickens and comes to a boil, 10 to 15 minutes. Boil 1 minute longer, stirring constantly.

In a small bowl, gradually stir one-third of the hot mixture into the beaten egg. Return this to the remaining hot mixture, stirring constantly. Cook for another 2 minutes, stirring constantly. Remove from the heat, and add the vanilla. Spread the banana slices on the baked pie crust, and then cover with the custard.

With a mixer, beat the egg whites until soft peaks form. Gradually add the remaining ⅓ cup sugar, beating until stiff peaks form. Spread the meringue over the filled pie, and bake for 4 to 5 minutes, until the meringue begins to turn golden. Watch closely. Serve immediately.

Nutritional information per serving
Calories 228, Protein (g) 5, Carbohydrate (g) 42, Fat (g) 5, Calories from Fat (%) 19, Saturated Fat (g) 1, Dietary Fiber (g) 1, Cholesterol (mg) 27, Sodium (mg) 141
Diabetic Exchanges: 3 other carbohydrate, 1 fat

Peanut Butter Banana Pie

A good old-fashioned banana pie with a touch of peanut butter is a hard combination to beat. Sprinkle with the chopped peanuts, if desired.

1¼ cups reduced-fat vanilla wafer crumbs

2 tablespoons margarine, melted

⅔ cup sugar

3 tablespoons cornstarch

1½ cups skim milk

2 eggs, lightly beaten

2 tablespoons reduced-fat crunchy peanut butter

1 teaspoon vanilla extract

3 cups sliced banana

1½ cups fat-free frozen whipped topping, thawed

MAKES 8 SERVINGS

In a pie plate, mix together the vanilla wafer crumbs and margarine. Press into a 9-inch pie plate; set aside.

In a small, heavy saucepan, combine the sugar and cornstarch. Gradually add the milk, stirring with a whisk until well blended. Cook over medium heat until the mixture comes to a boil; then cook for 1 minute more, stirring with a whisk. In a small bowl, gradually add about ⅓ cup hot custard to the beaten eggs, stirring constantly with a whisk. Return the egg mixture to the pot. Cook over medium heat until thick (about 1 minute), stirring constantly. Remove from heat, and stir in the peanut butter and vanilla. Cool slightly.

Arrange the banana slices in the bottom of the prepared crust; spoon the filling over the banana slices. Press plastic wrap onto the surface of the filling; chill 4 hours. Remove the plastic wrap. Spread the whipped topping evenly over the filling. Refrigerate until well chilled, and serve.

Nutritional information per serving

Calories 310, Protein (g) 5, Carbohydrate (g) 56, Fat (g) 7, Calories from Fat (%) 20, Saturated Fat (g) 1, Dietary Fiber (g) 2, Cholesterol (mg) 54, Sodium (mg) 171
Diabetic Exchanges: *4 other carbohydrate, 1.5 fat*

Blueberry Meringue Pie

Use this easy, terrific crust with any pie. No rolling necessary—just pat into a pie dish.

1 cup all-purpose flour

1 tablespoon light brown sugar

3 tablespoons canola oil

2 tablespoons cold water

½ cup water

½ cup plus 3 tablespoons sugar, divided

2 tablespoons cornstarch

¼ teaspoon ground cinnamon

4 cups blueberries

1 tablespoon lemon juice

2 egg whites

QUICK TIP

Never freeze custard or cream pies with meringue topping, but baked fruit pies freeze fine. Well-wrapped frozen baked fruit pies keep up to four months in the freezer.

MAKES 8 SERVINGS

Preheat the oven to 350°F.

In a medium bowl, combine the flour and brown sugar. Add the oil, stirring with a fork until crumbly. Add 2 tablespoons cold water, and stir until the ingredients are moistened. Press the dough evenly over the bottom and up the sides of a 9-inch pie plate. Bake for 10 to 15 minutes, or until lightly browned.

In a large saucepan, combine ½ cup water, ½ cup sugar, and the cornstarch, stirring well. Cook over medium heat, stirring constantly, until smooth, thickened, and transparent, about 3 minutes. Add the cinnamon and blueberries, and continue cooking over low heat for about 15 minutes. Remove from the heat; add the lemon juice. Pour the mixture into the baked crust.

In a mixer, beat the egg whites until stiff. Gradually add 3 tablespoons sugar, and continue beating until stiff, glossy peaks form. Spread the meringue over the blueberries in the pie. Bake for 10 to 12 minutes, or until well browned. Watch carefully. Cool and serve. Refrigerate the leftovers.

Nutritional information per serving

Calories 228, Protein (g) 3, Carbohydrate (g) 43, Fat (g) 6, Calories from Fat (%) 21, Saturated Fat (g) 0, Dietary Fiber (g) 2, Cholesterol (mg) 0, Sodium (mg) 19
Diabetic Exchanges: *3 other carbohydrate, 1 fat*

DESSERTS AND PIES

Lemon Meringue Pie

Someone always requests an old-fashioned lemon meringue pie, especially one that's easy on the figure. It's best served on the day it's made, or the pie tends to get "weepy." Cheat by using an already prepared pie crust to save time.

1 cup all-purpose flour
1 tablespoon sugar
⅛ teaspoon baking
　powder
3 tablespoons margarine
2 tablespoons water
½ teaspoon vanilla
　extract
Lemon Filling
　(recipe follows)
Meringue
　(recipe follows)

MAKES 8 SERVINGS

Preheat the oven to 375°F.

In a medium bowl, combine the flour, sugar, and baking powder. Cut in the margarine until coarse crumbs form. Stir in the water and vanilla with a fork. Gather the dough into a small, flattened ball; on a floured surface, roll out to fit a 9-inch pie plate. If the dough is too stiff, add more water.

Transfer the dough to the pie plate, and pierce with a fork. Bake for 10 to 15 minutes, or until lightly browned. Remove from the oven and cool the pie crust slightly.

Lower the oven temperature to 350°F. Fill the baked crust with the Lemon Filling (see recipe below). Spread the Meringue (see recipe below) over the pie filling, spreading it all the way to the edges. Bake the pie for 10 to 12 minutes, or until lightly brown. Cool, and then refrigerate until well chilled. Serve.

Lemon Filling

¼ cup cornstarch
1 cup sugar
⅓ cup cold water
1 cup hot water
½ cup lemon juice
1 teaspoon grated
　lemon rind
2 egg yolks,
　slightly beaten

In a large saucepan, combine the cornstarch and sugar. Blend in the cold water and then the hot water. Cook over medium-high heat, stirring constantly, until the mixture is thick and clear, about 10 minutes. Remove from the heat, and add the lemon juice and lemon rind. Return to the stove, and continue cooking for 2 minutes. In a small bowl, blend about ½ cup of the hot mixture into the egg yolks. Return the yolk mixture to the saucepan, and continue cooking for 2 more minutes, stirring constantly.

Meringue (for Lemon Meringue Pie)

3 egg whites

¼ teaspoon cream of tartar

¼ cup sugar

½ teaspoon vanilla extract

In a mixing bowl, beat the egg whites with the cream of tartar at high speed until soft peaks form. Gradually add the sugar, beating well after each addition. Add the vanilla. Continue beating until the meringue again forms soft peaks.

Nutritional information per serving

Calories 264, Protein (g) 4, Carbohydrate (g) 50, Fat (g) 6, Calories from Fat (%) 19, Saturated Fat (g) 1, Dietary Fiber (g) 1, Cholesterol (mg) 53, Sodium (mg) 81
Diabetic Exchanges: *3.5 other carbohydrate, 1 fat*

QUICK TIP

To beat egg whites: Place the egg whites in a clean glass or metal (not plastic) bowl. Beat with a mixer until peaks form. Any bit of fat, oil, or yolk in the bowl will prevent the whites from whipping.

DESSERTS AND PIES

Sweet Potato Pecan Crumble Pie

The ultimate pie! The crumbly topping with the crunchy bottom and the rich filling make this the most outstanding sweet potato pie you will ever eat! For a lower-fat version, use the crust from the Blueberry Meringue Pie on page 463.

¼ cup plus ⅓ cup light brown sugar

½ cup chopped pecans, divided

1 unbaked (9-inch) pie shell

1 (15-ounce) can sweet potatoes (yams), drained

⅓ cup sugar

2 eggs

1½ teaspoons ground cinnamon, divided

¼ teaspoon ground allspice

1 (12-ounce) can evaporated skimmed milk

2 teaspoons vanilla extract, divided

½ cup all-purpose flour

3 tablespoons margarine

MAKES 8 TO 10 SERVINGS

Preheat the oven to 425°F.

In a small bowl, mix together ¼ cup brown sugar and ¼ cup pecans. Sprinkle on the bottom of the pie shell.

In a mixing bowl, mix together the sweet potato, sugar, eggs, 1 teaspoon cinnamon, allspice, milk, and 1 teaspoon vanilla until creamy. Pour into the pie shell, and bake for 15 minutes. Reduce the oven temperature to 350°F, and continue baking for another 25 minutes.

Meanwhile, in a small bowl, mix together the remaining ⅓ cup brown sugar, remaining 1 teaspoon vanilla, flour, and the margarine with a fork until crumbly. Stir in the remaining ¼ cup pecans. Sprinkle over the pie, and continue baking for another 20 minutes, or until done. Cool for 15 minutes, and serve.

Nutritional information per serving

Calories 351, Protein (g) 7, Carbohydrate (g) 49, Fat (g) 15, Calories from Fat (%) 37, Saturated Fat (g) 4, Dietary Fiber (g) 2, Cholesterol (mg) 48, Sodium (mg) 205
Diabetic Exchanges: *3.5 other carbohydrate, 3 fat*

German Chocolate Angel Pie

A light meringue is filled with a heavenly chocolate mixture for a cool dessert that can be made several days ahead and stored in the freezer for later serving. An all-age pleaser.

3 egg whites, room temperature

¼ teaspoon salt

¼ teaspoon cream of tartar

¾ cup sugar

1 tablespoon plus 1 teaspoon vanilla extract, divided

1 (4-ounce) bar German sweet chocolate

3 tablespoons water

1 (8-ounce) container fat-free frozen whipped topping, thawed

MAKES 8 SERVINGS

Preheat the oven to 300°F.

In a medium bowl, beat the egg whites with the salt and cream of tartar until foamy. Add the sugar, 2 tablespoons at a time, beating well after each addition. Continue beating until stiff peaks form. Fold in 1 tablespoon vanilla. Spoon into a 9-inch glass pie plate coated with nonstick cooking spray, forming a nestlike shell. Bake for 45 minutes or until set. Cool.

In a microwave-safe bowl, melt the chocolate in the water for 30 seconds, stirring in the microwave until melted; cool. Add 1 teaspoon vanilla. Fold the cooled chocolate into the whipped topping. Spoon into the baked meringue shell. Freeze. Thaw slightly to serve.

Nutritional information per serving

Calories 198, Protein (g) 2, Carbohydrate (g) 37, Fat (g) 4, Calories from Fat (%) 17, Saturated Fat (g) 2, Dietary Fiber (g) 1, Cholesterol (mg) 0, Sodium (mg) 109
Diabetic Exchanges: *2.5 other carbohydrate, 1 fat*

DESSERTS AND PIES

⭐ ❄️ Strawberry Margarita Pie

By combining a margarita cocktail with vanilla ice cream, you have a rich, easily made, creamy and refreshing dessert.

2 pints fresh
  strawberries, sliced
½ cup frozen lemonade
  concentrate, thawed
¼ cup tequila
2 tablespoons Triple Sec
1 quart fat-free vanilla ice
  cream, softened
1 (9-inch) prepared
  reduced-fat graham
  cracker crust

MAKES 8 SERVINGS

In a large bowl, mix together the strawberries, lemonade, tequila, and Triple Sec. Quickly fold in the vanilla ice cream until the mixture is combined and creamy. Immediately spoon the mixture carefully into the pie shell, and freeze until firm.

Nutritional information per serving

Calories 288, Protein (g) 6, Carbohydrate (g) 55, Fat (g) 3, Calories from Fat (%) 10, Saturated Fat (g) 1, Dietary Fiber (g) 2, Cholesterol (mg) 0, Sodium (mg) 163
Diabetic Exchanges: *3.5 other carbohydrate, 0.5 fat*

⭐ Vanilla Sauce

This sauce is the perfect companion to fresh fruit. Layer fresh berries with the sauce, or fill crêpes with berries and top with the sauce.

1½ cups skim milk
¼ cup sugar
1 tablespoon cornstarch
1 tablespoon cold water
1 egg yolk
1 tablespoon vanilla
  extract

MAKES 12 (2-TABLESPOON) SERVINGS

In a medium saucepan over medium heat scald the milk and sugar. In a measuring cup, dissolve the cornstarch in the water; add to the hot milk, stirring in gradually. In a small bowl, pour some of the hot milk mixture into the egg yolk, and transfer back to the saucepan. Cook, stirring constantly, for 5 minutes, or until the mixture thickens slightly and comes to a boil. Remove from the heat, and add the vanilla. Cool and refrigerate.

Nutritional information per serving

Calories 37, Protein (g) 1, Carbohydrate (g) 6, Fat (g) 1, Calories from Fat (%) 12, Saturated Fat (g) 0, Dietary Fiber (g) 0, Cholesterol (mg) 18, Sodium (mg) 17
Diabetic Exchanges: *0.5 other carbohydrate*

Surprise Rolls 457

Cinnamon Rolls 458

Sticky Honey Buns 459

Easy Bunny Biscuits 459

Egg in the Bread 460

Ham and Cheese Breakfast Bake 461

Kids in the Kitchen

Funny Faces 462

Rah-Rahs 463

Friendly Dog Salad 463

Special Apple Salad 464

Burger Soup 464

Cheesy Broccoli Soup 465

Pizza Rice 465

Creepy Crawlers 466

Open-Face Tic-Tac-Toe Sandwiches 466

Jack-O'-Lantern Sandwiches 467

Reindeer Sandwiches 467

Cheese Quesadillas 468

Mini Cheese Pizzas 468

Mexican Pizza 469

Sweet Potato Pizza 469

Meatballs and Spaghetti 470

Sloppy Joes 471

Baby Burgers 471

Popcorn Cake 472

Ice Cream Cone Cupcakes 473

Clowns 474

Double Chocolate Candy Pizza 475

Ooey Gooey Squares 476

Double Chocolate Box Cookies 476

Simple Sensational Chocolate Cake 477

Chocolate Mint Brownies 478

All-American Crunch 479

Strawberry Heart Cake 480

Ghost Suckers 481

Munch Mix 481

Strawberry Smoothie 482

Fruit Dip 482

🥕 Surprise Rolls

My youngest daughter makes these for breakfast, and whenever friends are over these rolls are always requested. I keep these ingredients on hand to be ready at any time.

---

3 tablespoons light
   brown sugar
½ teaspoon ground
   cinnamon
8 large marshmallows
2 tablespoons margarine,
   melted
1 (8-ounce) can reduced-
   fat crescent dinner rolls

MAKES 8 ROLLS

Preheat the oven to 375°F. Coat 8 muffin cups in a muffin tin with nonstick cooking spray or paper liners.

Mix the brown sugar and cinnamon together in a small bowl. Dip each marshmallow in the melted margarine, and roll in the sugar mixture.

Separate the crescent dough into triangles. Wrap one triangle around each marshmallow, and pinch the dough together. Place each one in a muffin tin. If there is any extra margarine, drizzle over the top of the rolls. Bake for 8 to 12 minutes or until lightly browned. Serve immediately.

Nutritional information per serving
Calories 168, Protein (g) 2, Carbohydrate (g) 23,
Fat (g) 7, Calories from Fat (%) 40, Saturated Fat (g) 1,
Dietary Fiber (g) 0, Cholesterol (mg) 0, Sodium (mg) 276
Diabetic Exchanges: *1 starch, 0.5 other carbohydrate, 1 fat*

❄ Cinnamon Rolls

When you have the urge for a wonderful cinnamon roll, make this quick recipe using canned biscuits and common pantry ingredients. These are as good as those found in a bakery.

1 (10-biscuit) can
   refrigerated biscuits
4 tablespoons margarine,
   softened
2 tablespoons sugar
1 teaspoon ground
   cinnamon
¼ cup raisins, optional
¼ cup chopped pecans,
   optional

MAKES 10 ROLLS

Preheat the oven to 425°F.

Flatten each biscuit with your hand or a rolling pin, and spread with margarine.

In a small bowl, combine the sugar and cinnamon. Sprinkle the cinnamon mixture on top of the margarine. Sprinkle with the raisins and pecans, if desired. Roll up each biscuit from one side to the other. On an ungreased 15 x 10 x 1-inch baking sheet, arrange each biscuit roll to form an individual circle, touching one end of the roll to the other. Bake for 8 to 10 minutes or until lightly browned. Serve hot.

Nutritional information per serving
Calories 101, Protein (g) 1, Carbohydrate (g) 12,
Fat (g) 5, Calories from Fat (%) 46, Saturated Fat (g) 1,
Dietary Fiber (g) 0, Cholesterol (mg) 0, Sodium (mg) 233
Diabetic Exchanges: *1 starch, 1 fat*

🥕❄️🎲 Sticky Honey Buns

Easy to make, excellent, and a family favorite.

1 (10-biscuit) can
   refrigerated biscuits
½ cup honey
1 cup flaked coconut
⅓ cup chopped pecans,
   optional

MAKES 10 BUNS

Preheat the oven to 400°F. Coat 10 muffin cups in a muffin tin with nonstick cooking spray or paper liners.

Cut each biscuit round into three pieces. Pour the honey into a small bowl; in another small bowl or on a plate, mix together the coconut and pecans. Dip each biscuit piece into the honey; then coat lightly (roll) with the coconut-pecan mixture. Place three coated biscuit pieces into each muffin cup. Bake for 15 minutes, or until the biscuits are golden brown and done.

Nutritional information per serving

Calories 137, Protein (g) 2, Carbohydrate (g) 27, Fat (g) 3, Calories from Fat (%) 19, Saturated Fat (g) 2, Dietary Fiber (g) 1, Cholesterol (mg) 0, Sodium (mg) 200
Diabetic Exchanges: *1 starch, 1 other carbohydrate, 0.5 fat*

🥕 Easy Bunny Biscuits

Lots of fun to make and to eat. Turns breakfast into an exciting meal. Great for Easter.

1 (10-biscuit) can
   refrigerated biscuits
10 raisins
5 maraschino cherry
   halves
20 slivered almonds

MAKES 5 BISCUITS

Preheat the oven to 450°F. Place five biscuits on an ungreased 15 x 10 x 1-inch baking sheet.

To assemble the bunny biscuits: Cut the remaining 5 biscuits in half, and pull a little to form ears. Press 2 biscuit halves (ears) under the top of each whole biscuit to form the bunny head. In each whole biscuit, press in two raisins for the eyes, a cherry half for the nose and two slivered almonds on each side of cherry half for the whiskers. Bake for 10 minutes, or until the biscuits are done. Serve immediately.

Nutritional information per serving

Calories 116, Protein (g) 3, Carbohydrate (g) 21, Fat (g) 2, Calories from Fat (%) 16, Saturated Fat (g) 0, Dietary Fiber (g) 1, Cholesterol (mg) 0, Sodium (mg) 360
Diabetic Exchanges: *1.5 fruit*

🥕 Egg in the Bread

This timeless recipe has been referred to by a dozen different names. It's a great way to start the day.

1 slice white or whole
    wheat bread
1 teaspoon margarine
1 egg
Salt and pepper to taste

MAKES 1 EGG IN THE BREAD

Cut a 2-inch-square hole in the center of the bread.

In a small skillet coated with nonstick cooking spray, heat the margarine until melted and sizzling, and place the bread in the skillet. Break the egg into the hole. Place the cut square of bread in the pan, and cook it, too. Cook over a medium heat until the egg white is set, about 3 minutes. Turn over with a spatula, and cook on the other side until the egg is done and set. Add the salt and pepper to taste.

Nutritional information per serving
Calories 188, Protein (g) 9, Carbohydrate (g) 16,
Fat (g) 10, Calories from Fat (%) 48, Saturated Fat (g) 2,
Dietary Fiber (g) 1, Cholesterol (mg) 213, Sodium (mg) 269
Diabetic Exchanges: *1 medium-fat egg, 1 starch, 1 fat*

Ham and Cheese Breakfast Bake

For those slumber parties, here's a simple breakfast casserole that feeds a group. Prepare ahead, and pop in the oven the morning after.

12 slices white or whole
    wheat bread
6 slices reduced-fat
    American cheese
4 ounces lean sliced ham,
    cut into pieces
3 eggs
4 egg whites
2½ cups skim milk
1 teaspoon prepared
    mustard
1 teaspoon
    Worcestershire sauce
Salt and pepper to taste

MAKES 8 TO 10 SERVINGS

Preheat the oven to 350°F. Coat a 3-quart oblong baking dish with nonstick cooking spray.

Trim the crusts off the slices of bread and throw away; line the bottom of the dish with six slices of bread. Place a slice of cheese on top of each slice of bread. Sprinkle with the pieces of ham. Top with the remaining six slices of bread.

In a large bowl, blend together the eggs, egg whites, milk, mustard, Worcestershire sauce, salt, and pepper until well mixed. Pour the egg mixture evenly over the layered bread. Cover with plastic wrap, and refrigerate overnight or leave out at room temperature for 1 hour. Bake for 45 minutes to 1 hour, or until puffed up, lightly browned, and the egg is cooked inside. Serve immediately.

Nutritional information per serving
Calories 191, Protein (g) 13, Carbohydrate (g) 22,
Fat (g) 5, Calories from Fat (%) 25, Saturated Fat (g) 2,
Dietary Fiber (g) 1, Cholesterol (mg) 76, Sodium (mg) 620
Diabetic Exchanges: *1 lean meat, 1.5 starch*

QUICK TIP

Use whatever cheese you desire in this recipe—reduced fat shredded Cheddar works great, too. This dish is the perfect way to start the day with calcium and protein.

KIDS IN THE KITCHEN

Funny Faces

This fun recipe makes one face. A 16-ounce can of peaches contains about six peach halves, so adjust the ingredients accordingly. If you're serving at a party, have several bowls of different-colored coconut available for different colored hair.

1 canned peach half
2 raisins
1 maraschino cherry half
2 tablespoons flaked
   coconut
Few drops of food
   coloring

MAKES 1 FUNNY FACE

Place 1 peach half on a small plate. With a toothpick, scoop out two tiny holes in the peach half, and push in the raisins for eyes. Place a cherry half on the lower part of the peach for the mouth.

In a small bowl, toss the coconut with a few drops of food coloring to make the hair the color you want. Arrange the colored coconut on the top and sides of the peach to complete the funny face.

Nutritional information per serving
Calories 93, Protein (g) 1, Carbohydrate (g) 17,
Fat (g) 3, Calories from Fat (%) 28, Saturated Fat (g) 3,
Dietary Fiber (g) 1, Cholesterol (mg) 0, Sodium (mg) 29
Diabetic Exchanges: 1 fruit, 0.5 fat

🥕 Rah-Rahs

Lots of little girls want to be a cheerleader, and this recipe allows you to create one of your own. Kids are more willing to try all these foods when they're prepared in this creative way.

1 canned peach half
½ hard-boiled egg
4 raisins
¼ maraschino cherry
Ruffled lettuce leaf,
    washed and drained
2 (2- to 3-inch) carrot
    sticks
2 (2- to 3-inch) celery
    sticks
2 tablespoons shredded
    reduced-fat Cheddar
    cheese

MAKES 1 RAH-RAH

Place the peach half, cut side down, on a plate to form the body of your Rah-Rah. Place the hard-boiled egg half, cut side down, on top of the peach half to form the head. Make two tiny holes in the egg for the eyes; push in 2 raisins. Place the ¼ cherry piece under the raisins for the mouth. Place the lettuce leaf on the bottom of the peach, tucking the leaf under a little, for the skirt. Place a carrot stick on each side of the peach for arms, and place two celery sticks below the lettuce leaf for legs. Place the shredded cheese around the top and sides of the egg for the hair, and place 2 more raisins on the peach for buttons.

Nutritional information per serving
Calories 133, Protein (g) 8, Carbohydrate (g) 15, Fat (g) 5, Calories from Fat (%) 34, Saturated Fat (g) 3, Dietary Fiber (g) 1, Cholesterol (mg) 114, Sodium (mg) 136
Diabetic Exchanges: *1 medium-fat meat, 1 fruit*

🥕 Friendly Dog Salad

A good choice for animal lovers. Name your salad after your dog.

5 canned pear halves
    (about one 16-ounce
    can)
5 ruffled lettuce leaves,
    washed and drained
10 large pitted prunes
10 raisins
5 maraschino cherry
    halves

MAKES 5 FRIENDLY DOG SALADS

Place one pear half, cut side down, on each lettuce leaf. Place a pitted prune on each side of the large end of the pear half for the ears. (Use 2 prunes for each pear half.) Scoop out two tiny holes in each pear half for the eyes, and place 1 raisin in each hole. Place a cherry half at the top of the narrow end of the pear half for the nose.

Nutritional information per serving
Calories 85, Protein (g) 1, Carbohydrate (g) 22, Fat (g) 0, Calories from Fat (%) 0, Saturated Fat (g) 0, Dietary Fiber (g) 3, Cholesterol (mg) 0, Sodium (mg) 3
Diabetic Exchanges: *1.5 fruit*

KIDS IN THE KITCHEN

Special Apple Salad

Use a combination of red and green apples to enjoy this delicious salad. Remember, an apple a day keeps the doctor away!

6 cups chopped apples
   (peel left on)
2 tablespoons lemon juice
½ cup chopped celery
⅓ cup raisins
1 cup miniature
   marshmallows
¼ cup light mayonnaise

MAKES 8 SERVINGS

In a bowl, toss the apples with the lemon juice to coat evenly. Mix in the celery, raisins, and marshmallows. Stir in the mayonnaise until all is well coated, and store, covered, in the refrigerator until serving.

Nutritional information per serving

Calories 113, Protein (g) 1, Carbohydrate (g) 24, Fat (g) 3, Calories from Fat (%) 21, Saturated Fat (g) 0, Dietary Fiber (g) 2, Cholesterol (mg) 3, Sodium (mg) 71
Diabetic Exchanges: *1 starch, 0.5 other carbohydrate, 0.5 fat*

Burger Soup

Years ago we made this for a house full of kids, and everyone raved about it—it's a great way to get veggies into their diets.

1 pound ground sirloin
1 onion, chopped
1 teaspoon minced garlic
1 (15-ounce) can tomato
   sauce
1 (14½-ounce) can
   chopped tomatoes
4 cups water
Salt and pepper to taste
1 tablespoon
   Worcestershire sauce
1 bay leaf
1 cup sliced peeled
   carrots (in rings)
1 (11-ounce) can corn
   niblets, drained
⅓ cup rice, uncooked

MAKES 8 SERVINGS

In a large pot, cook the meat, onion, and garlic until the meat is done. Drain any excess liquid. Add the tomato sauce, tomatoes, water, salt, pepper, Worcestershire sauce, bay leaf, and carrots. Bring to a boil, lower heat, and cook for 10 minutes. Add the corn and rice, and continue cooking over medium heat until the rice is done and the carrots are tender, about 30 to 40 minutes. Add more water if too thick. Serve.

Nutritional information per serving

Calories 160, Protein (g) 14, Carbohydrate (g) 21, Fat (g) 3, Calories from Fat (%) 16, Saturated Fat (g) 1, Dietary Fiber (g) 3, Cholesterol (mg) 30, Sodium (mg) 482
Diabetic Exchanges: *1.5 very lean meat, 1 starch, 1 vegetable*

🥕 ❄️ Cheesy Broccoli Soup

Broccoli is disguised in this nutritious soup. If you want a cheesier soup, add more cheese.

1 tablespoon margarine
1 onion, chopped
½ cup all-purpose flour
3 cups fat-free canned
  chicken broth
2 (10-ounce) packages
  frozen chopped
  broccoli, thawed and
  drained
1½ cups skim milk
4 ounces reduced-fat
  pasteurized processed
  cheese spread, cut
  into cubes
Salt and pepper to taste

MAKES 6 TO 8 SERVINGS

In a large saucepan, melt the margarine and sauté the onion over medium heat until tender, about 5 minutes. Blend in the flour, stirring. Gradually add the chicken broth, mixing until blended with the flour. Add the broccoli, stirring to combine. Bring the mixture to a boil, stirring, and reduce the heat to low. Cover and cook for 15 to 20 minutes, or until the broccoli is done and the soup thickens. Add the milk, stirring until heated and thickened. Add the cheese cubes to the soup, stirring and cooking over low heat until the cheese is melted and smooth. Season with the salt and pepper. Serve immediately.

Nutritional information per serving

Calories 120, Protein (g) 9, Carbohydrate (g) 15, Fat (g) 3, Calories from Fat (%) 24, Saturated Fat (g) 1, Dietary Fiber (g) 3, Cholesterol (mg) 7, Sodium (mg) 515
Diabetic Exchanges: *1 lean meat, 0.5 starch, 1 vegetable*

🥕 ❄️ Pizza Rice

Rice and pizza team up to make a child's dream team. Use for a main or a side dish; either way, it's a hit. Omit the green pepper if desired

1 small green bell
  pepper, seeded and
  chopped, optional
1 (14½-ounce) can diced
  tomatoes, with juice
1 (.7-ounce) package
  Italian salad dressing
  mix
4 cups cooked rice
1 cup shredded part-skim
  Mozzarella cheese

MAKES 4 TO 6 SERVINGS

In a small skillet coated with nonstick cooking spray, sauté the green pepper until tender. Set aside.

In a large pot, combine the tomatoes with the Italian dressing, mixing over a low heat. Stir in the cooked rice, green pepper, and cheese. Cook over a low heat until well heated and the cheese is melted, 3 to 5 minutes. Serve.

Nutritional information per serving

Calories 205, Protein (g) 8, Carbohydrate (g) 35, Fat (g) 3, Calories from Fat (%) 15, Saturated Fat (g) 2, Dietary Fiber (g) 2, Cholesterol (mg) 11, Sodium (mg) 599
Diabetic Exchanges: *0.5 lean meat, 2 starch, 1 vegetable*

Creepy Crawlers

Kids will have lots of fun making these sandwiches. They will even eat the carrot strip "legs."

2 slices bread

2 teaspoons peanut
 butter or enough to
 cover bread

1 carrot, peeled and
 sliced into 8 sticks

2 raisins

MAKES 1 SANDWICH

To make a sandwich, cut circles out of 2 slices of bread with a round cookie cutter or glass. Spread the peanut butter on top of one circle. Place 8 carrot sticks for "legs" on the edge of the circle, sticking out on both sides. Top with the other circle of the bread, and put two raisins on top for the eyes.

Nutritional information per serving

*Calories 217, Protein (g) 7, Carbohydrate (g) 32,
Fat (g) 7, Calories from Fat (%) 29, Saturated Fat (g) 1,
Dietary Fiber (g) 4, Cholesterol (mg) 0, Sodium (mg) 317*
Diabetic Exchanges: *0.5 high-fat meat, 1.5 starch, 1.5 vegetable*

Open-Face Tic-Tac-Toe Sandwiches

Definitely more exciting than a ham and cheese sandwich, this will appeal to kids who like to play games. With this tic-tac-toe board, you're sure to be a winner.

1 slice reduced-fat
 American cheese

1 slice bread

½ slice reduced-fat
 processed Swiss cheese

½ slice extra lean ham

Circular carrot slices

MAKES 1 SANDWICH

To make an open-face sandwich, place the slice of American cheese on top of the slice of bread. Cut the piece of Swiss cheese into four narrow strips. Arrange the Swiss cheese strips on top of the American cheese to form a tic-tac-toe board. Cut the strips of ham to form X's, and put on the tic-tac-toe board in the pattern you wish. Use the carrot circles for the O's. Toast in a toaster oven or broil under a hot broiler until the cheese bubbles. Serve immediately.

Nutritional information per serving

*Calories 173, Protein (g) 13, Carbohydrate (g) 18,
Fat (g) 6, Calories from Fat (%) 31, Saturated Fat (g) 3,
Dietary Fiber (g) 1, Cholesterol (mg) 22, Sodium (mg) 854*
Diabetic Exchanges: *1.5 lean meat, 1 starch*

Jack-O'-Lantern Sandwiches

Year-round this can be a grilled cheese "face" sandwich, and in the fall it becomes the ideal Halloween sandwich.

2 slices dark bread
  (pumpernickel or dark
  whole wheat)
1 slice reduced-fat
  American cheese

MAKES 1 JACK-O'-LANTERN SANDWICH

On one slice of bread, cut out a jack-o'-lantern face. Place a slice of cheese on an uncut slice of bread. Broil or toast in the oven until the cheese is melted. Remove from the oven, and top with the cut slice of bread.

Nutritional information per serving
Calories 181, Protein (g) 10, Carbohydrate (g) 27,
Fat (g) 5, Calories from Fat (%) 22, Saturated Fat (g) 2,
Dietary Fiber (g) 3, Cholesterol (mg) 10, Sodium (mg) 683
Diabetic Exchanges: *1 lean meat, 2 starch*

Reindeer Sandwiches

Year after year, each of my children volunteered me to make their favorite reindeer sandwiches for their school Christmas party. Get the kids to help make ahead; cover with damp paper towels, refrigerate, and you're ready in a flash.

1 tablespoon creamy
  peanut butter or
  enough to cover bread
2 slices bread
2 twisted pretzels
2 raisins
1 maraschino cherry,
  halved

MAKES 1 REINDEER SANDWICH

Spread the peanut butter on one slice of bread, and top with the other slice. Cut a triangular shape in the sandwich, discarding the ends and remainder of the sandwich. Place a twisted pretzel between the two slices of bread on two points of the triangle to form the reindeer's antlers. Place two raisins for the eyes and a cherry half on the remaining point for the nose.

Nutritional information per serving
Calories 297, Protein (g) 10, Carbohydrate (g) 41,
Fat (g) 11, Calories from Fat (%) 32, Saturated Fat (g) 2,
Dietary Fiber (g) 3, Cholesterol (mg) 1, Sodium (mg) 629
Diabetic Exchanges: *0.5 high-fat meat, 2.5 starch, 1 fat*

Cheese Quesadillas

These make a great snack or dinner. If you have leftover chicken, add with the cheese. Of course, include whatever ingredients you prefer.

2 (6- or 8-inch) flour
  tortillas
½ cup reduced-fat
  Cheddar or Monterey
  Jack cheese
Taco sauce, as desired

MAKES 3 SERVINGS

In a pan coated with nonstick cooking spray, on low heat, place one flour tortilla. Sprinkle with the cheese, and top with the other flour tortilla. Cook about 1 to 1½ minutes on each side, turning with a spatula. Coat the pan again with nonstick cooking spray, and use a spatula to turn, cooking until the cheese is melted and the tortillas are light brown. Watch carefully. Cut into six wedges, and serve with taco sauce.

Nutritional information per serving

Calories 110, Protein (g) 7, Carbohydrate (g) 12, Fat (g) 3, Calories from Fat (%) 28, Saturated Fat (g) 2, Dietary Fiber (g) 1, Cholesterol (mg) 10, Sodium (mg) 294
Diabetic Exchanges: *0.5 lean meat, 1 starch*

Mini Cheese Pizzas

Keep these ingredients around for a quick snack or lunch. Add pepperoni, if desired.

1 (10-biscuit) can flaky
  refrigerated biscuits
⅓ cup tomato sauce
½ teaspoon dried
  oregano leaves
½ cup shredded part-
  skim mozzarella cheese

MAKES 10 PIZZAS

Preheat the oven to 450°F. Pat each biscuit into a 4-inch circle on a baking sheet coated with nonstick cooking spray.

  In a small bowl, mix together the tomato sauce and oregano, and spoon the sauce on each biscuit round. Sprinkle the cheese over the tomato sauce, and bake for 8 to 10 minutes, or until the cheese is melted. Serve immediately.

Nutritional information per serving

Calories 67, Protein (g) 3, Carbohydrate (g) 10, Fat (g) 2, Calories from Fat (%) 21, Saturated Fat (g) 1, Dietary Fiber (g) 0, Cholesterol (mg) 3, Sodium (mg) 252
Diabetic Exchanges: *0.5 starch*

❄ Mexican Pizza

My daughter Haley loves to have her friends over for parties, and their standard request is my homemade pizza. I tried this Mexican version, and not a piece was left.

½ pound ground sirloin
1 tablespoon chili
    powder
1 teaspoon ground cumin
1 (10-ounce) Boboli crust
    or pizza crust
1 cup salsa
1½ cups reduced-fat
    Monterey Jack cheese

MAKES 8 SERVINGS

Preheat the oven to 450°F.

In a small skillet, cook the meat until browned. Drain any excess grease. Add the chili powder and cumin. Cover the pizza crust with the salsa, cheese, and seasoned meat. Bake for 8 minutes, or until crisp. Slice, and serve.

Nutritional information per serving

Calories 201, Protein (g) 16, Carbohydrate (g) 17, Fat (g) 7, Calories from Fat (%) 33, Saturated Fat (g) 3, Dietary Fiber (g) 1, Cholesterol (mg) 27, Sodium (mg) 486
Diabetic Exchanges: *2 lean meat, 1 starch*

🥕 Sweet Potato Pizza

Here's a fun way to introduce this nutritious veggie to the kids. A pizza always gets their attention. For a variation, sprinkle with marshmallows and cinnamon instead of sugar.

4 to 5 cups thinly sliced
    fresh sweet potatoes
    (yams), peeled
¼ cup light brown sugar
1 teaspoon ground
    cinnamon
¼ teaspoon ground
    nutmeg

MAKES 6 TO 8 SERVINGS

Preheat the oven to 400°F. Coat a 12-inch pizza pan with nonstick cooking spray.

Arrange the sweet potato slices to cover the pizza pan, overlapping the slices. Spray the slices with nonstick cooking spray. Bake 15 minutes or until tender.

In a small bowl, mix together the brown sugar, cinnamon, and nutmeg, and sprinkle evenly over the potato slices. Return to the oven, and continue baking until the potato slices are crispy, 5 to 10 minutes more. Slice, and serve immediately.

Nutritional information per serving

Calories 97, Protein (g) 1, Carbohydrate (g) 23, Fat (g) 0, Calories from Fat (%) 0, Saturated Fat (g) 0, Dietary Fiber (g) 2, Cholesterol (mg) 0, Sodium (mg) 11
Diabetic Exchanges: *1 starch, 0.5 other carbohydrate*

KIDS IN THE KITCHEN

❄ Meatballs and Spaghetti

Believe it or not, my mother turns to this basic but simple and delicious recipe for her meatballs and spaghetti. The younger ones will like the smooth sauce with no "green things" in it, yet grown-ups find there's plenty of flavor.

2 pounds ground sirloin
½ cup Italian bread crumbs
2 tablespoons grated Parmesan cheese
2 egg whites
1 tablespoon chopped parsley
½ teaspoon garlic powder
1 teaspoon dried oregano leaves
1 teaspoon dried basil leaves
Sauce (recipe follows)
1 (16-ounce) package spaghetti

MAKES 8 SERVINGS

Preheat the oven to broil.

In a large bowl, combine the meat, bread crumbs, Parmesan cheese, egg whites, parsley, garlic powder, oregano, and basil, mixing well to combine. With moistened hands, shape the meat mixture into balls. Place the meatballs on a baking sheet coated with nonstick cooking spray. Broil the meatballs for 5 to 7 minutes on each side; remove from the oven and add to the sauce (see recipe below). Bring to a boil, reduce the heat, and continue cooking for about 30 minutes.

Meanwhile, prepare the spaghetti according to the package directions; drain. Serve the cooked spaghetti with the meatballs.

Sauce

1 (28-ounce) can tomato purée
1 (8-ounce) can tomato sauce
1 teaspoon dried oregano leaves
1 teaspoon dried basil leaves

In a large pot, combine the tomato purée, tomato sauce, oregano, and basil. Cook over medium heat, stirring occasionally, until thoroughly heated, 4 to 6 minutes.

Nutritional information per serving

Calories 431, Protein (g) 34, Carbohydrate (g) 59, Fat (g) 7, Calories from Fat (%) 14, Saturated Fat (g) 2, Dietary Fiber (g) 4, Cholesterol (mg) 61, Sodium (mg) 774
Diabetic Exchanges: *3 lean meat, 3 starch, 2 vegetable*

❄ Sloppy Joes

This oldie-but-goodie is easy to throw together for a quick dinner—corn is a great addition.

1 pound ground sirloin
1 small onion, chopped
1 (8-ounce) can tomato
  sauce
2 tablespoons light
  brown sugar
½ teaspoon paprika
Salt and pepper to taste
1 (7-ounce) can whole
  kernel corn, drained
4 hamburger buns, toasted

MAKES 4 SLOPPY JOES

In a large skillet, cook the meat and onion until done, about 5 minutes; drain any excess liquid. Add the tomato sauce, brown sugar, paprika, salt, pepper, and corn. Cook over medium-low heat about 10 minutes, or until well heated and combined. To serve, spoon the meat mixture over the toasted buns.

Nutritional information per serving

Calories 335, Protein (g) 28, Carbohydrate (g) 42, Fat (g) 7, Calories from Fat (%) 19, Saturated Fat (g) 3, Dietary Fiber (g) 3, Cholesterol (mg) 60, Sodium (mg) 724
Diabetic Exchanges: *3 lean meat, 2.5 starch, 1 vegetable*

Baby Burgers

Fun to make, and they look like real burgers. Mint lovers will love these.

Few drops water
Few drops green food
  coloring
¼ cup flaked coconut
48 reduced-fat vanilla
  wafers
24 chocolate-covered
  peppermint patties,
  unwrapped
Water
½ to 1 teaspoon sesame
  seeds

MAKES 24 BURGERS

Preheat the oven to 350°F.

In a small bowl, combine the few drops water and the green food coloring. Add the coconut, and toss until all of the coconut is tinted green; set aside.

Place half the vanilla wafers, flat side up, on an ungreased baking sheet. Place one mint patty on each of the vanilla wafers. Place in the oven for about 1 minute, or just until the chocolate begins to soften. Remove from the oven, and sprinkle each with ½ teaspoon tinted coconut. Top with another vanilla wafer, flat side down, and press gently. Using your finger, dab the top of each vanilla wafer with just enough water to moisten, and sprinkle with a few sesame seeds.

Nutritional information per serving

Calories 89, Protein (g) 1, Carbohydrate (g) 18, Fat (g) 2, Calories from Fat (%) 18, Saturated Fat (g) 1, Dietary Fiber (g) 0, Cholesterol (mg) 0, Sodium (mg) 32
Diabetic Exchanges: *0.5 starch, 0.5 other carbohydrate*

KIDS IN THE KITCHEN

Popcorn Cake

This colorful treat will tantalize your taste buds with sweet and salty in one bite.

½ cup unpopped plain popcorn

Dash salt, optional

4 cups miniature marshmallows

½ cup margarine

⅔ cup miniature candy-coated milk chocolate candies

MAKES ABOUT 20 POPCORN CAKES

Pop the popcorn according to the package directions. Add salt if desired; set aside to cool.

In a medium pot, melt the marshmallows and margarine over low heat, stirring constantly, until smooth. Combine the candy-coated milk chocolate candies with the popcorn. Remove the marshmallow mixture from the heat, and pour over the popcorn and candies. Mix gently. Spoon the mixture into a 13 x 9 x 2-inch pan or a 2-quart oblong pan coated with nonstick cooking spray. Refrigerate until the mixture until it hardens, so it's easier to cut.

Nutritional information per serving

Calories 126, Protein (g) 1, Carbohydrate (g) 16, Fat (g) 7, Calories from Fat (%) 46, Saturated Fat (g) 2, Dietary Fiber (g) 1, Cholesterol (mg) 1, Sodium (mg) 63
Diabetic Exchanges: *1 other carbohydrate, 1 fat*

Ice Cream Cone Cupcakes

Be creative: use different-flavored cake mixes, and top the icing with sprinkles. For a time-saver, use reduced-fat canned frosting.

1 (18.25-ounce) box
  yellow cake mix
24 flat-bottomed wafer
  ice cream cones
6 tablespoons margarine
1 (16-ounce) box
  confectioners' sugar
3 to 4 tablespoons
  skim milk
1 teaspoon vanilla extract

MAKES 18 TO 24 CONE CUPCAKES

Preheat the oven to 350°F. Prepare the cake mix batter according to the package directions.

Spoon the batter into the cones, filling three-quarters full, and place the cones in muffin pans. Bake according to the package directions for cupcakes. Cool.

To prepare the icing, in a mixing bowl, beat together the margarine and confectioners' sugar, adding enough milk to reach spreading consistency. Add the vanilla. Ice each cone cupcake.

Nutritional information per serving

Calories 207, Protein (g) 1, Carbohydrate (g) 39,
Fat (g) 5, Calories from Fat (%) 22, Saturated Fat (g) 1,
Dietary Fiber (g) 1, Cholesterol (mg) 0, Sodium (mg) 176
Diabetic Exchanges: 2.5 other carbohydrate, 1 fat

KIDS IN THE KITCHEN

🥕 Clowns

Turn the crispy rice treats into the head of your clown. Use different candies and colors to individualize your own clown.

4 cups miniature
marshmallows

3 tablespoons margarine

6 cups crispy rice cereal

20 muffin paper cups

Reduced-fat creamy
peanut butter,
as needed

10 sugar ice cream cones

Small assorted gum
drops, sliced crosswise
in half

5 red jelly beans, sliced
lengthwise in half

MAKES 10 CLOWNS

In a large, heavy pot, mix together the marshmallows and margarine over low heat, stirring constantly, until the marshmallows are melted and the mixture is smooth. Remove from the heat. Add the cereal, and stir gently to coat evenly. Cool the mixture about 5 minutes, or until it can be handled easily. Shape into ten balls (put margarine on your hands to keep the mixture from sticking to them). Place the balls on waxed paper, and let stand until firm (about 30 minutes).

Flatten 2 paper muffin cups for the base, and place a cereal ball on top for the head. For the hat, spread peanut butter (as your glue) on the edge of the open end of a sugar cone, and attach the cereal ball. Spread a tiny bit of peanut butter on 2 gum drop halves to make them stick to the cereal ball for the eyes. Spread a tiny bit of peanut butter on 3 gum drop halves to make them stick on the cone hat for the pom-poms. Spread peanut butter on a jelly bean half for the mouth on the cereal ball. Repeat with remaining cereal bars.

Nutritional information per serving
Calories 198, Protein (g) 2, Carbohydrate (g) 39,
Fat (g) 4, Calories from Fat (%) 18, Saturated Fat (g) 1,
Dietary Fiber (g) 0, Cholesterol (mg) 0, Sodium (mg) 204
Diabetic Exchanges: *1 starch, 1.5 other carbohydrate, 0.5 fat*

❄ Double Chocolate Candy Pizza

This recipe has made me the most popular mom throughout all three of my kids' younger years of school. Now my teenage daughters make it themselves, and it's requested by all their friends. Every time I make this for the kids, the adults are the first to grab a piece. Cut into small squares to please a crowd.

½ cup margarine

1 cup sugar

1 egg

1 teaspoon vanilla extract

1½ cups all-purpose flour

¼ cup cocoa

½ teaspoon baking soda

1 cup candy-coated milk chocolate candies, divided

¼ cup flaked coconut

1½ cups miniature marshmallows

½ cup chopped pecans, optional

MAKES 12 TO 16 SLICES

Preheat the oven to 350°F. Coat a 12- to 14-inch pizza pan with nonstick cooking spray.

In a large mixing bowl, beat together the margarine and sugar until fluffy. Add the egg and vanilla, blending well.

In a small bowl, combine the flour, cocoa, and baking soda. Gradually add to the sugar mixture, blending until well mixed.

Spread the dough on the prepared pan, spreading the dough to within 1 inch of the edge of the pan. Sprinkle the dough with the candies, coconut, marshmallows, and pecans. Bake 18 to 20 minutes, or until the edges are set. Don't overbake. Cool, and cut into slices.

Nutritional information per serving
Calories 235, Protein (g) 3, Carbohydrate (g) 36,
Fat (g) 9, Calories from Fat (%) 35, Saturated Fat (g) 3,
Dietary Fiber (g) 1, Cholesterol (mg) 15, Sodium (mg) 123
Diabetic Exchanges: *2.5 other carbohydrate, 2 fat*

QUICK TIP

Use seasonal candies to keep in the holiday spirit on Halloween, Christmas, Valentine's Day, and Easter.

KIDS IN THE KITCHEN

Ooey Gooey Squares

My daughter Haley whips up these most requested squares for parties and friends all the time.

1 (18.25-ounce) package
  yellow cake mix
½ cup margarine, melted
1 egg
1 tablespoon water
1 (8-ounce) package
  fat-free or reduced-fat
  cream cheese
1 (16-ounce) box
  confectioners' sugar
2 egg whites
1 teaspoon vanilla extract
1 cup semisweet
  chocolate chips

MAKES 48 SQUARES

Preheat the oven to 350°F. Coat a 13 x 9 x 2-inch baking pan with nonstick cooking spray.

In a mixing bowl, beat together the cake mix, margarine, egg, and water until well mixed. Spread the batter into the bottom of the prepared pan.

In a mixing bowl, beat together the cream cheese, confectioners' sugar, egg whites, and vanilla. Stir in the chocolate chips. Pour this mixture over the batter in the pan. Bake for 40 to 50 minutes, or until the top is golden brown. Cool and cut into squares.

Nutritional information per serving

Calories 122, Protein (g) 2, Carbohydrate (g) 21, Fat (g) 4, Calories from Fat (%) 29, Saturated Fat (g) 1, Dietary Fiber (g) 0, Cholesterol (mg) 5, Sodium (mg) 117
Diabetic Exchanges: 1.5 other carbohydrate, 1 fat

Double Chocolate Box Cookies

Start with a cake mix to make these outstanding cookies—even the finest baker won't suspect.

1 (18.25-ounce) box
  devil's food cake mix
3 tablespoons canola oil
1 egg
2 egg whites
¾ cup semisweet
  chocolate chips

MAKES 36 TO 48 COOKIES

Preheat the oven to 350°F. Coat a baking sheet with non-stick cooking spray.

In a mixing bowl, beat together the cake mix, oil, egg, and egg whites until creamy. Stir in the chocolate chips. Drop by rounded teaspoons onto the prepared baking sheet. Bake for 10 minutes, or until lightly browned. Cool on a wire rack or waxed paper.

Nutritional information per serving

Calories 67, Protein (g) 1, Carbohydrate (g) 10, Fat (g) 3, Calories from Fat (%) 36, Saturated Fat (g) 1, Dietary Fiber (g) 0, Cholesterol (mg) 4, Sodium (mg) 87
Diabetic Exchanges: 0.5 other carbohydrate, 0.5 fat

Simple Sensational Chocolate Cake

This perfect beginner's cake uses four simple ingredients, with simple instructions, to create a mouthwatering chocolate cake with a moist, puddinglike texture.

1 (4-serving) package cook-and-serve chocolate pudding mix

2 cups skim milk

1 (18.25-ounce) package devil's food cake mix

⅔ cup semisweet chocolate chips

MAKES 36 SERVINGS

Coat a 13 x 9 x 2-inch baking pan with nonstick cooking spray.

Prepare the pudding mix according to the package directions, using the skim milk; cool to room temperature.

Preheat the oven to 350°F.

In a bowl, stir together the cake mix and the prepared chocolate pudding. Spread into the prepared pan. Sprinkle with the chocolate chips. Bake for 25 to 30 minutes, or until a toothpick inserted in the center comes out clean. Don't overbake. Cool, and cut into squares.

Nutritional information per serving

Calories 89, Protein (g) 1, Carbohydrate (g) 16, Fat (g) 2, Calories from Fat (%) 23, Saturated Fat (g) 1, Dietary Fiber (g) 1, Cholesterol (mg) 0, Sodium (mg) 129
Diabetic Exchanges: *1 other carbohydrate*

KIDS IN THE KITCHEN

Chocolate Mint Brownies

This easy brownie recipe with mint filling and bitter chocolate glaze is impressive. With your eyes closed, you will think you are eating a delicious chocolate mint. This is a great holiday recipe, and you can even use food coloring.

1 (22.5-ounce)
   box reduced-fat or
   regular brownie mix
¾ teaspoon peppermint
   extract, divided
3 tablespoons reduced-
   fat cream cheese
3 tablespoons margarine,
   melted, divided
2 cups confectioners'
   sugar
Few drops green food
   coloring
1 tablespoon cocoa
1 tablespoon water

MAKES 48 BROWNIES

Preheat the oven to 350°F. Coat a 13 x 9 x 2-inch baking pan with nonstick cooking spray.

Prepare the brownie mix according to package directions, adding ¼ teaspoon of the peppermint extract. Pour the batter into the prepared pan. Bake according to the package directions. Do not overbake. Remove from the oven, and cool completely to room temperature.

In a mixing bowl, beat together the cream cheese, 1 tablespoon margarine, the confectioners' sugar, and ½ teaspoon peppermint extract until smooth. Add a few drops of green food coloring, mixing. Spread on the baked brownie layer.

In a small bowl, mix together the remaining 2 tablespoons margarine, cocoa, and water. Spread carefully over the cream cheese layer, and cool. Cut into squares.

Nutritional information per serving
*Calories 83, Protein (g) 1, Carbohydrate (g) 16,
Fat (g) 2, Calories from Fat (%) 20, Saturated Fat (g) 1,
Dietary Fiber (g) 0, Cholesterol (mg) 1, Sodium (mg) 60*
Diabetic Exchanges: *1 other carbohydrate, 0.5 fat*

QUICK TIP

If you're in a hurry to cool the brownie layer, place it in the refrigerator to cool it quickly. Make sure that you don't put the hot pan next to something that will be affected by its heat.

🥕 ❄️ All-American Crunch

Shhh! Cake mix and canned fillings are key ingredients for this rich tasting dessert.

1 (21-ounce) can cherry
  pie filling
1 (21-ounce) can
  blueberry pie filling
1 (18.25-ounce) package
  white cake mix
⅓ cup chopped pecans
⅓ cup flaked coconut
½ cup margarine, melted

MAKES 16 SERVINGS

Preheat the oven to 350°F.

In the bottom of a 13 x 9 x 2-inch baking pan, spread the cherry pie filling and blueberry pie filling in a pattern, making sure the bottom of the pan is completely covered. Keep each pie filling separate to form a design on the bottom. Sprinkle the dry cake mix evenly over the filling. *Do not stir.* Sprinkle the top with the pecans and coconut, and pour the melted margarine evenly over the top.

Bake for 30 minutes, or until browned. Serve immediately or at room temperature.

Nutritional information per serving
Calories 286, Protein (g) 2, Carbohydrate (g) 45,
Fat (g) 11, Calories from Fat (%) 35, Saturated Fat (g) 2,
Dietary Fiber (g) 1, Cholesterol (mg) 0, Sodium (mg) 276
Diabetic Exchanges: *3 other carbohydrate, 2 fat*

KIDS IN THE KITCHEN

🥕 ❄ Strawberry Heart Cake

This awesome cake is too good to save for only Valentine's Day. Turn into a round layered cake year-round with 9-inch round pans. It begins with a cake mix and is easy to make.

1 (18.25-ounce) box
   white cake mix
¼ cup canola oil
2 eggs
2 egg whites
1 (3-ounce) package
   strawberry gelatin
½ (10-ounce) package
   frozen sliced
   strawberries (½ cup)
   (reserve extra for
   frosting)
½ cup skim milk
Strawberry Frosting
   (recipe follows)

MAKES 16 SERVINGS

Preheat the oven to 350°F. Coat one 9 x 9 x 2-inch square pan and one 9-inch round cake pan with nonstick cooking spray.

In a mixing bowl, combine the cake mix, oil, eggs, egg whites, strawberry gelatin, ½ cup strawberries, and milk, mixing until well blended. Divide the batter, and pour into the prepared pans. Bake for 25 to 30 minutes, or until a wooden toothpick inserted in the center comes out clean. Remove from the pans, and cool completely.

To form the heart: Place the square cake on a large platter. Cut the round cake in half, and place each half with the cut side next to the square side. You may need to trim corners. This now makes a heart. Turn the cakes so the square cake's pointed end is down and the round halves are at the top. Frost the heart cake with Strawberry Frosting (see recipe below).

Strawberry Frosting

3 tablespoons margarine
1 (16-ounce) box
   confectioners' sugar
½ (10-ounce) package
   frozen sliced
   strawberries (½ cup)

In a medium mixing bowl, mix together the margarine, confectioners' sugar, and remaining strawberries until well blended.

Nutritional information per serving
Calories 336, Protein (g) 3, Carbohydrate (g) 60,
Fat (g) 9, Calories from Fat (%) 25, Saturated Fat (g) 2,
Dietary Fiber (g) 1, Cholesterol (mg) 27, Sodium (mg) 262
Diabetic Exchanges: *4 other carbohydrate, 2 fat*

Ghost Suckers

I can't even count the times I made these for Halloween favors at my kids' school parties when they were younger.

Sheet of white tissue
    paper
Round lollipop suckers
Black string licorice
Black marker

MAKES AS MANY AS YOU WANT

Place a sheet of white tissue paper over the top of each sucker. Gather under the candy, and tie the tissue with the black string licorice. With the black marker, make two dots on your ghost for eyes.

Nutritional information per serving
Calories 59, Protein (g) 0, Carbohydrate (g) 14,
Fat (g) 0, Calories from Fat (%) 0, Saturated Fat (g) 0,
Dietary Fiber (g) 0, Cholesterol (mg) 0, Sodium (mg) 17
Diabetic Exchanges: *1 other carbohydrate*

Munch Mix

Chocolate and peanut butter, sweet and salty, make this a favorite in my home. I often find my girls in the kitchen whipping up this easy, irresistible treat. Sometimes I also toss in pretzels or raisins.

1¼ cups reduced-fat
    peanut butter
1¼ cups semisweet
    chocolate chips
1 (15.2-ounce) box honey
    nut oven-toasted rice
    and corn cereal squares
1 cup confectioner's
    sugar

MAKES 32 (¼-CUP) SERVINGS

In a microwave-safe bowl or in a pan on the stovetop, melt together the peanut butter and chocolate chips. Mix with the cereal.

    In a large, shallow container with a lid, place half the confectioners' sugar and all of the cereal mixture, then the remaining confectioner's sugar. Shake until evenly coated.

Nutritional information per serving
Calories 149, Protein (g) 4, Carbohydrate (g) 23,
Fat (g) 6, Calories from Fat (%) 32, Saturated Fat (g) 2,
Dietary Fiber (g) 1, Cholesterol (mg) 0, Sodium (mg) 157
Diabetic Exchanges: *1 starch, 0.5 other carbohydrate, 1 fat*

KIDS IN THE KITCHEN

Strawberry Smoothie

This makes a great snack, and my girls can whip these up themselves in the blender (or food processor). Refreshing, soothing, and delicious.

2 cups strawberries,
   fresh or frozen
2 tablespoons sugar
1 teaspoon lemon juice
1 cup low-fat vanilla
   yogurt

MAKES 3 SERVINGS

In a food processor or blender, mix together at high speed the strawberries, sugar, lemon juice, and yogurt until well blended. Serve immediately or refrigerate.

Nutritional information per serving
Calories 131, Protein (g) 5, Carbohydrate (g) 26, Fat (g) 1, Calories from Fat (%) 9, Saturated Fat (g) 1, Dietary Fiber (g) 2, Cholesterol (mg) 4, Sodium (mg) 55
Diabetic Exchanges: *1 skim milk, 0.5 fruit, 0.5 other carbohydrate*

Fruit Dip

All kids love to dip, so here's a super way to serve assorted fresh fruit. Store the dip in your fridge with cut-up fruit for a ready-made snack.

1 (7-ounce) jar
   marshmallow creme
1 (8-ounce) package
   reduced-fat cream
   cheese
1 tablespoon grated
   orange rind
2 tablespoons orange
   juice
Few drops of food
   coloring, optional
Fresh fruit of your choice

MAKES 16 (2-TABLESPOON) SERVINGS

In a mixing bowl, beat together the marshmallow creme and cream cheese until smooth. Stir in the orange rind and orange juice. Stir in the food coloring of your choice, if you want a colored dip. Refrigerate until time to serve, and serve with your fruit of choice.

Nutritional information per serving
Calories 78, Protein (g) 2, Carbohydrate (g) 11, Fat (g) 3, Calories from Fat (%) 36, Saturated Fat (g) 2, Dietary Fiber (g) 0, Cholesterol (mg) 10, Sodium (mg) 71
Diabetic Exchanges: *0.5 other carbohydrate, 0.5 fat*

Suggested Menus

Stock Your Pantry with Cooking Supplies

Back to Basics

Reference

Roasting Chart

Tips & Tricks

Cooking Terms

SUGGESTED MENUS

Brunch

Breakfast Buffet
Crabmeat Egg Casserole, page 76 or
    Bread Pudding Florentine, page 75
Hot Fruit Casserole, page 81
Quick Cheese Grits, page 80
Chunky Whole Wheat Apple Muffins,
    page 71
Coffee Cake with Streusel Filling, page 385

Southwestern Brunch
Egg and Green Chile Casserole, page 77
Mexican Brunch Biscuit Bake, page 56
Nectarine and Raspberry Crumble,
    page 442

Easy Kids Group
Baked French Toast, page 82
Ham and Cheese Breakfast Bake, page 461

Hearty Dish
Steak Creole with Cheese Grits, page 79

Make-Ahead Muffin Batter
Bran Muffins, page 74

Sweet Rolls
Surprise Rolls, page 457
Cinnamon Crescents, page 69
Cinnamon Rolls, page 458
Sticky Honey Buns, page 459
Cream Cheese Coffee Cake, page 384

Lunch

Soup & Salad 1
Peach Soup, page 91
Curried Chicken Salad, page 146
Beer Bread, page 53
Oatmeal Cookies, page 366 or Ultimate
    Chocolate Cookies, page 367

Soup & Salad 2
Corn Soup, page 100
Deluxe Tuna Salad, page 151
Lemon Raspberry Muffins, page 72
Mocha Fudge Mousse Pie, page 435

Hot Lunch
Caesar Salad, page 123
Crêpes Florentine, page 196
Orange Glazed Carrots, page 172
Pretzel Strawberry Gelatin, page 160
Mock Chocolate Éclair, page 413

Lunch with a Twist
Artichoke Soup, page 113
Salmon Patties with Horseradish Caper
    Sauce, page 295
Mediterranean Couscous Salad, page 135
Chocolate Bread Pudding with
    Caramel Sauce, page 320

Grilled Tuna Salad with Wasabi
    Ginger Vinaigrette, page 154
Oriental Cabbage Salad, page 129

Herb Biscuits, page 57
Lemon Pineapple Trifle, page 431

Salad Trio
Marinated Italian Tuna Salad, page 150
Waldorf Pasta Salad, page 138
Cucumber and Tomato Salad, page 129
Lemon Poppy Seed Cake, page 389

Mandarin Chicken Salad, page 148
Pasta Salad with Herb Dijon Vinaigrette,
    page 140
Mango Salad with Citrus Sauce, page 162
Italian Puffs, page 55
Chocolate Chess Pie, page 445

Main Dish Salads
Taco Rice Salad, page 157
Paella Salad, page 159
Salad Niçoise, page 153
Wild Rice and Pork Salad, page 156
Greek Chicken Salad Bowl, page 147
Greek Seafood Pasta Bowl, page 145

Dinners

Barbecue
Barbecued Brisket, page 245
Baked Beans, page 166
Macaroni, Tomato, and Corn Salad,
    page 132
Chocolate Chess Pie, page 495

Seven-Layer Salad, page 130
Barbecued Pork Roast, page 267
Sweet Potato Oven Fries, page 186

Green Bean Casserole, page 177
Apple Cake with Broiled Topping,
    page 380

Family Pleasers
Skillet Pizza Chicken, page 217
Perfect Pasta, page 323
Sicilian Broccoli, page 169
Ice Cream Pie, page 433

Simple Baked Crusty Chicken, page 212
One-Step Macaroni and Cheese, page 179
Green Beans (your choice)
Chocolate Chip Pie, page 444

Smothered Round Steak, page 250
Garlic Smashed Potatoes, page 181
Dijon Glazed Carrots, page 172
Herbed Biscuits, page 57
Berry Crisp, page 441

Sirloin Steak Strips, page 249
Easy Potato Casserole, page 184
Dijon Glazed Carrots, page 172
Chocolate Chess Pie, page 445

Tossed Green Salad (your choice)
Jumbo Stuffed Shells, page 359
Cheesy Spicy Spinach, page 197
Herbed French Bread, page 54
German Chocolate Angel Pie, page 453

Spicy Baked Fish, page 286
Parmesan Potato Sticks, page 190
Broccoli Casserole, page 170
Banana Cream Pie, page 447

Oven-Fried Parmesan Chicken, page 211
Pizza Rice, page 465
Ooey Gooey Squares, page 476
Special Apple Salad, page 464
Burger Soup, page 464

Chicken and Linguine, page 337
Italian Spinach Pie, page 199
Beer Bread, page 53
Chocolate Bread Pudding with
    Caramel Sauce, page 320

Southwestern
Shrimp Tacos with Tropical Salsa, page 306
Black Bean and Corn Salad, page 131
Guacamole, page 17
Chocolate Chess Pie, page 445

One-Dish Meals
Mexican Chicken Casserole, page 237
Chicken and Dumplings, page 250
Meatball Stew, page 119
Traditional Meat-and-Macaroni-Casserole,
    page 252
Chicken and Sausage Gumbo, page 93
Shrimp, Corn, and Sweet Potato Soup,
    page 104
Southwestern Shrimp and Black Bean
    Chili, page 117
Italian Soup, page 110
Lasagnas—Southwestern, page 255,
    Mediterranean, page 358

New Year's Day
Black-Eyed Pea Dip, page 31
Mixed Greens with Citrus Vinaigrette
    and Sugared Pecans, page 125

Mock Cabbage Rolls, page 262
Chocolate Almond Cheesecake, page 425

Glazed Pork Tenderloin, page 270
Black-Eyed Pea and Rice Salad, page 134
Spinach Oriental, page 200
Strawberry Margarita Pie, page 454

Holiday Dinners
Cornish Hens with Wild Rice Stuffing,
    page 239
Sweet Potato Casserole with
    Praline Topping, page 188
Green Bean Casserole, page 177
Cranberry Cheesecake, page 423

Honey-Glazed Turkey Breast or Turkey,
    page 241
Yam Corn Bread Stuffing, page 205
Squash Casserole, page 202
Cranberry Mold, page 161
Sweet Potato Pecan Pie, page 452

Cranberry Chicken with Wild Rice,
    page 229
Broccoli Casserole, page 170
Carrot Soufflé, page 171
Sweet Potato Bread Pudding with
    Praline Sauce, page 319

Elegance with Ease
Cream of Brie and Spinach Soup, page 107
Company Chicken, page 214
Rice and Noodles, page 192
Almond Asparagus, page 165
Pull-Apart Biscuit Bake, page 57
Strawberry Custard Brûlée, page 426

Raspberry Spinach Salad, page 123
Veal Saltimbocca, page 276
Wild Rice and Peppers, page 191
Italian Puffs, page 55
Tiramisu Cake, page 402

Green Salad with Oriental Vinaigrette,
    page 127
Asian Meat Marinade, page 282
Wasabi Mashed Potatoes, page 183
Broccoli with Lemon Ginger Sauce,
    page 169
Apple Peanut Crumble, page 444

Spinach Salad, page 124
Tenderloin Mexicana, page 247
Southwestern Stuffed Potatoes, page 185
Orange Caramel Flan, page 427

Orange Almond Mixed Green Salad,
    page 127
Glazed Salmon, page 294
Penne with Spinach, Sun-Dried Tomatoes
    and Goat Cheese, page 325
Pull-Apart Biscuit Bake, page 57
Cream Cheese Coffee Cake, page 384

Easy Crab Soup, page 94
Veal Marengo, page 277
Green Bean and Artichoke Casserole,
    page 176
Perfect Pasta, page 323
Tiramisu, page 436

Pork Florentine Wellington with Green
    Peppercorn Sauce, page 268

Roasted Sweet and White Potatoes,
    page 187
Broccoli with Mustard Vinaigrette,
    page 168
Herbed Biscuits, page 57
Peanut Butter Banana Pie, page 448

Louisiana Legend Dinner
Easy Shrimp and Corn Soup, page 103
Marinated Crabmeat Salad, page 139
Italian Shrimp, page 301
Baked Italian Oysters, page 320
Perfect Pasta, page 323
Herb French Bread, page 54
Strawberry Custard Brûleé, page 426

Chinese Takeout
Shrimp Fried Rice, page 300
Chinese Chicken and Broccoli Stir Fry,
    page 227
Chinese Pork Vermicelli, page 362
Fortune Cookies

Buffets

Cocktail Party
Shrimp, Avocado, and Artichoke, page 20
Salmon Mousse with Dill Sauce,
    Crackers, page 37
Sweet-and-Spicy Chicken Strips, page 31
Glazed Brie, Fruit and Crackers, page 47
Artichoke Squares, page 45
Stuffed Flank Steak, sliced, Miniature
    Rolls, page 247
Chocolate Fondue and Fruit, page 437
Angel Food Cake Squares

Football Fever Buffet
Hamburger Dip, Chips, page 33 or
    Tex-Mex Dip, Chips, page 18
White Chicken Chili, page 115 or
    Speedy Chili, page 116
Cheesy Corn Muffins, page 74
Almost-Better-than-Sex Cake, page 379
Chocolate Chess Bars, page 375

Mexican Buffet
Tortillas Shrimp Bites, page 39
Fiesta Salsa, page 26
Southwestern Grilled Beef Fajitas, page 253
Crabmeat Enchiladas, page 298
Coffee Toffee Brownies, page 434

Caribbean Buffet
Sweet Cheese Ball, page 27
Beef and Chicken Shish Kabobs, page 254
Black Bean and Corn Salad, page 131
Loaded Couscous Salad, page 136
Tropical Pizza, page 415

Louisiana Buffet
Marinated Crab Fingers, page 35
Corn Salad, page 131
Oyster Rockefeller Dip, page 29
Turkey Jambalaya, page 242
Grilled Shrimp, page 307
Sweet Potato Cheesecake, page 424

Kids Buffet
Mini Taco Cups, page 43
Cheese Quesadillas, page 468
Fruit Dip, Fresh Fruit, page 26
Oven Fried Parmesan Chicken Strips,
    page 211

Chocolate Chip Cookies, page 366
Peanut Butter Cookies, page 368 or
    Double Chocolate Candy Pizza,
    page 475

Dessert Buffet
Banana Éclair, page 438
Fantastic Trifle, page 428
Italian Cream Cake, page 397
Blueberry Pound Cake, page 383
Pickups: Strudel, page 370 and
    Heavenly Hash, page 374
Flavored Coffees and Champagne

Friend's Freezer-Friendly Casseroles
Crawfish and Rice Casserole, page 315
Crawfish Fettuccine, page 352
Seafood Casserole, page 318
Cheesy Shrimp Rice Casserole, page 311
One-Dish Chicken Casserole, page 231
Mexican Chicken Casserole, page 237
Chicken Vermicelli, page 342
Crispy Southwestern Lasagna, page 255
Traditional Meat-and-Macaroni
    Casserole, page 252
Lasagna: Mediterranean, Old-Fashioned,
    page 358, 354
Mock Cabbage Rolls, page 262

Snacks–Grab and Go
Cereal Mixture, page 83
Snack Mix, page 83
Granola, page 84
Munch Mix, page 481

STOCK YOUR PANTRY
WITH COOKING SUPPLIES

One way to encourage nutritional meals and ease preparation is to have a stocked pantry. Many of the recipes in this book call for the following simple ingredients—keep these foods on hand, and you can have a quick and healthy meal every day!

Refrigerator Staples

Biscuits, refrigerated
Cheese (varieties or reduced-fat)
Eggs
Fruit
Garlic, chopped in jar
Garlic, fresh
Horseradish
Lemon juice
Lime juice
Margarine
Mixed greens
Onion, green
Onion, yellow
Peppers, green
Skim milk
Sour cream (fat-free or light)
Yogurt (fat-free or light)

Pantry Staples

Barley
Bread (whole wheat or white)
Bread crumbs (Italian or plain)
Broth (cubed or granules)
Bulgur (yes, try using it!)
Couscous
Evaporated skimmed milk
Oil, canola
Oil, olive

Oil, peanut
Pasta, assorted shapes and flavors
Pizza crusts (focaccia bread or Boboli)
Rice, brown
Rice, white
Salsa or flavored salsa
Tuna fish, white or salmon (canned)
Vinegar, balsamic
Vinegar, rice
Vinegar, wine

Baking Staples

Almond extract
Baking powder
Baking soda
Butter extract
Cake mix, chocolate
Cake mix, white
Cake mix, yellow
Chocolate chips, semisweet
Cocoa
Coconut extract
Cornstarch
Dried fruit (assorted)
Evaporated skimmed milk
Flour, all purpose
Flour, self-rising
Flour, whole wheat
Instant pudding

Nonstick cooking spray
Nuts (assorted)
Oatmeal
Oil, canola
Sugar, brown
Sugar, confectioners'
Sugar, granulated
Sweetened condensed milk (fat-free or
    reduced-fat)
Vanilla extract

Condiment Staples
Capers
Honey
Hot sauce
Ketchup
Mayonnaise (light or low-fat)
Mustard (Dijon or yellow)
Roasted red peppers bottled in liquid in jars
Salad dressing (fat-free or reduced-fat)
Salsa
Soy sauce
Spaghetti pasta sauces (in jars)
Vinegar, balsamic
Vinegar, cider
Vinegar, distilled
Worcestershire sauce

Spice Pantry Staples
Basil leaves
Bay leaves
Chili powder
Cilantro
Cinnamon (ground)
Cumin (ground)
Curry
Dill weed

Garlic powder
Ginger (ground)
Nutmeg
Oregano leaves
Paprika
Parsley flakes (dried)
Pepper, black
Pepper, coarsely ground
Red pepper flakes
Rosemary leaves
Tarragon leaves
Thyme leaves

Canned Goods
Beans (assorted)
Black olives
Broth, beef
Broth, chicken
Broth, vegetable
Corn
Creamed soups (reduced-fat)
Green chilies (diced)
Tomato sauce
Tomatoes and green chilies, diced
Tomatoes, diced
Tuna and salmon

Frozen Pantry Staples
Chicken breasts
Pork tenders
Fish
Frozen veggies (spinach, corn, broccoli etc.)
Frozen yogurt
Ice cream (reduced-fat or fat-free)
Shrimp
Sirloin (ground, roast)
Turkey breast

BACK TO BASICS

Common Cooking Methods

Microwave

- Advantages are a short cooking time, few nutrients lost, and colors and flavors stay brighter.
- Put a small amount of water in the dish; cover to create steam for cooking.
- Cook at 100 percent power. Halfway through their cooking time, stir and rearrange the veggies or food.
- Use a microwave-safe baking dish.

Boiling

- Easy, but it can leach out nutrients.
- Immerse the veggies in enough water to cover.
- Boiling is now unfashionable: the vegetables don't stay crisp-tender (exceptions include potatoes, sweet potatoes, and corn).
- Good for tough vegetables.

Roasting

- To prepare, peel vegetables, cut into large chunks, and toss with a little olive oil.
- Sprinkle with herbs, salt, and pepper.
- Roast in oven at 350 to 400 degrees until tender.
- Good for thick-skinned vegetables, such as potatoes and winter squash.

Steaming

- Quick, and vegetables aren't waterlogged—a gentle way of cooking.
- Watch closely, so the pot doesn't boil dry (no water).
- You need a steamer basket or platform to lift veggies out of the water—bring to a boil, add veggies, cover, and reduce heat to cook until tender.
- The liquid should not touch the food; the steam has to circulate.

Stir-Frying

- Vegetables are cut into small, even pieces and stirred over intensely high heat, with a minimum of fat and liquid, in the fastest cooking time possible.
- Reduces the amount of fat needed to cook dense veggies and brings out great flavor.
- Efficient cooking method, as pieces have room to move in the pan, allowing surfaces constant exposure to the heat.

Herbs

Common Herbs

Basil: Minty, clovelike flavor, and a key ingredient in Mediterranean and Italian cooking (pesto and tomato sauces), salads, stews, meats, and eggs. Basil is a summer herb, but during the winter it can be grown successfully inside in a sunny window. Available dried.

Bay leaf: This pungent, woodsy herb from the evergreen bay laurel tree, native to the Mediterranean, is mostly available dried. Bay leaves are used to flavor soups, stews, sauces, vegetables, and meats. They are removed before serving. Fresh bay leaves are seldom used in cooking.

Bouquet garni: A bunch of herbs (usually parsley, thyme, and bay leaf) that are tied together or placed in a cheesecloth bag and used to flavor soups, stews, and broths. The tied bag is easily removed before the dish is served.

Chervil: A mild-flavored member of the parsley family with a distinctive anise tarragon flavor. Chervil can be used like parsley and is best fresh, when available. Used in eggs, fish, salads, sauces, soups, and stuffing.

Chives: Mild onion flavor; available fresh year-round. Fresh chives can be snipped with scissors and will grow back after cutting. Best to add at the end of the cooking, to retain their flavor. Chives are used to flavor appetizers, soups, eggs, and salads. Dried chives don't have the same flavor.

Cilantro: Also known as fresh coriander or Chinese parsley, cilantro has a distinct aromatic flavor used in Asian, Caribbean, and Latin American cooking. Cilantro is available year-round in grocery stores and is sold in bunches. Season to taste—a little goes a long way.

Dill weed: A delicate, tangy, lemony taste. Use with fish, seafood, salads, egg dishes, breads, sauces, and vegetables. Fresh dill leaves are available in late summer and early fall. Available dried.

Marjoram (sweet marjoram): Belonging to the mint family, marjoram has a mild, sweet, oreganolike flavor. Most often found dried. Used to flavor lamb, veal, poultry, fish, stews, soups, and vegetables. Available dried.

Mint: Peppermint has a sharp pungent flavor; spearmint is more delicate. Both have a sweet, refreshing flavor and a cool aftertaste. Mint is available year-round but is more plentiful in the summer months; dried mint flakes retain their flavor well. Mint is used in both sweet and savory dishes (like Mediterranean cooking) to flavor sauces, vegetables, jellies, fruit, alcoholic beverages, and as a garnish for desserts.

Oregano: Belongs to the mint family and is related to marjoram and thyme. Oregano has a robust, pungent flavor and aroma. Makes an attractive small plant, an easy perennial to grow. Great with pizza or any Italian dish, soups, tomato-based dishes, sauces, vegetables, and chicken. Available dried.

Parsley: A slightly peppery-fresh-flavored herb, parsley is used as a garnish and a mild flavoring. The two varieties are curly leaf, which is used more in garnishing, and flat leaf or Italian, more strongly flavored and used in cooking. Fresh curly parsley is available year-round, while Italian parsley is not always to be found.

Rosemary: Belonging to the mint family, this silver-green, needle-shaped leaf is highly aromatic and has a bold flavor with hints of both lemon and pine. Delicious sprinkled over any roasted meat, poultry, tomato-based dishes, seafood, stuffing, and soups. Easy to grow outside in hot, mild areas. Dried leaves are available.

Sage: Slightly bitter with a musty mint taste, sage is the primary herb in poultry seasoning. Dried sage (whole leaves or ground) is available, and this powerful, assertive herb requires care in its use. Used in stuffing, sausages, and dressings, and complements most vegetables.

Tarragon: Has a spicy, sharp flavor with licorice overtones and is essential to classic French cooking. Tarragon is available fresh in the summer and early fall. Use sparingly because of its dominant flavor. Available dried.

Thyme: Has a minty yet lemony aroma. It is the basic herb in French cuisine and integral to bouquet garni (see page 493). Thyme is used to season poultry, meat, vegetables, fish dishes, and soups. Fresh thyme is easily grown outdoors in pots. Available dried either ground or as leaves—I prefer leaves.

Dry Herb Tips

■ Dried or ground herbs begin to lose their flavor about six months after the container has been opened. (Mark the purchase date on the bottom of the container).

■ Dried herbs can be added early in the cooking process of recipes, as they require longer exposure to heat and moisture to release their flavor.

■ Store dried herbs in a tightly covered container in a cool, dark cupboard to maximize their shelf life.

■ Crush dried herbs in your hand. This breaks down the leaves to better release their flavor.

■ Dry herbs for fresh herbs: 1 teaspoon dried is equivalent to 1 tablespoon of fresh.

Fresh Herb Tips

■ Most fresh herbs are added to a dish at the end of the cooking time (basil, for example) so that the heat does not destroy their fresh flavor and aroma.

■ To store fresh herbs such as basil, chives, cilantro, parsley, and rosemary, snip off the stem ends and place in a glass or jar with the stems in about one inch of water. Seal with a plastic bag, and refrigerate for up to a week.

■ Oregano, tarragon, and thyme should last in a dry plastic bag in the refrigerator for four to six days.

Salad Greens

■ 1 pound salad greens = about 6 cups torn pieces

■ To renew wilted greens, place them in ice water with 2 tablespoons lemon juice; cover and refrigerate for 1 hour. Time permitting, wrap the dried greens in dry paper towels, and refrigerate up to 4 hours.

Common Salad Greens

Arugula: Intensely flavored and spicy. Best used as an accent with milder greens. Choose smaller leaves for less distinctive flavor. Use soon after purchase.

Bibb lettuce: Delicate, mild flavor and

tender, pliable leaves similar to those of Boston.

Butter or Boston lettuce: A tender, mild, and sweet staple lettuce. Delicious as a main green.

Curly endive (chicory): Slightly bitter, and with a fresh, crisp texture.

Escarole: Slightly bitter, mild flavor with pleasant, nutty undertones. Part of the endive family. Good as an accent green.

Green leaf and red leaf lettuce: Distinctive, buttery, fairly sweet. A versatile lettuce, good alone or in mixes. A staple lettuce.

Iceberg lettuce: Bland and mild flavor, crunchy taste. A cheap, quick, and easy salad. Keeps in refrigerator for 1 week. Choose solid, compact heads with tight leaves that range from medium green outer leaves to pale green inner leaves.

Mesclun: Not a type of lettuce or green. The name refers to a "chic" mix of greens of various textures and flavors (sweet, spicy, bitter, almost always including arugula and a bit of herbs). A year-round staple that is more expensive than other mixes.

Radicchio: Strong, bittersweet, and crunchy, this red-leafed green adds color to mixtures. A member of the endive family, it lasts only a few days in the refrigerator and is expensive.

Romaine lettuce: Crisp, strongly flavored, somewhat bittersweet staple green. Mild enough as the main element of a salad or adds crunch and flavor to mixed green salads. Choice of lettuce for Caesar salad. Keeps in refrigerator up to 1 week.

Spinach: Not a lettuce, but used for salad. Strong, somewhat bitter. Great alone or mixed with other greens. Wash leaves thoroughly, as fresh spinach is usually sandy and dirty.

Watercress: With a strong, peppery flavor, watercress adds pep to other green mixtures. Also used as a garnish. Use soon after purchase.

Cooking Oils

When stored in a cool, dark, place, most oils will keep for 1 year. If you live in a warm climate or want to keep oils for a longer time, refrigerate them.

Canola oil: Light, mildly flavored, monounsaturated oil. Its high smoke point makes it great for high-heat cooking such as deep frying. All purpose: good for baking, cooking, and stir-frying and will not dominate the food.

Extra-virgin olive oil: Strong, slightly fruity flavor and good for salads, stir-frys, and most cooking. Monounsaturated.

Peanut oil: Slightly heavy, nutty flavor, monounsaturated, with a high smoke point for high-heat cooking such as deep frying. Good for salads and stir-fries.

Safflower oil: With its light, bland flavor, safflower is an all-purpose oil, good for baking.

Sesame oil: For Asian cooking and for drizzling on stir-fries. The toasted varieties are rich in flavor, and the untoasted are lighter in taste. Polyunsaturated.

ROASTING CHART

Beef	Weight (lbs.)	Oven Temp.	Minutes per Pound	Doneness
Eye Round	2 to 3	325ºF	20 to 22	medium rare
Rib Eye	4 to 6	350ºF	18 to 20	medium rare
			20 to 22	medium
Sirloin Tip	4 to 6	325ºF	25 to 30	medium rare
			30 to 35	medium
	8 to 10	325ºF	18 to 22	medium rare
			23 to 25	medium
Tenderloin (whole)	4 to 6	425ºF	45 to 60 (total cooking time)	medium rare
(half)	2 to 3	425ºF	35 to 45 (total cooking time)	medium rare

Pork	Weight (lbs.)	Oven Temp.	Minutes per Pound
Crown Roast	6 to 8	350ºF	20 to 22
Ham, bone-in or boneless, fully cooked	10 to 16	350ºF	10 to 12
Loin, bone-in	3 to 12	350ºF	20 to 22
Tenderloin	½ to 1	350ºF	20 to 22

Poultry	Weight (lbs.)	Oven Temp.	Minutes per Pound
Chicken			
Whole, unstuffed	3 to 3½	350ºF	20 to 22
	4 to 10	350ºF	20
Duckling, unstuffed	4 to 5	400ºF for 30 min. then 350ºF	15 to 18
Capon, unstuffed	8 to 10	350ºF	20 to 22
Rock Cornish Hen, unstuffed	¾ to 1¼	350ºF	45 to 75 (total cooking time)

Turkey*			Total Cooking Time (hours)
Unstuffed	6 to 8	325ºF	2¼ to 3¼
	8 to 12	325ºF	3 to 3½
	12 to 16	325ºF	3½ to 4½
	16 to 20	325ºF	4 to 5
	20 to 24	325ºF	4½ to 5½
Stuffed	6 to 8	325ºF	3 to 3½
	8 to 12	325ºF	3½ to 4½
	12 to 16	325ºF	4 to 5
	16 to 20	325ºF	4½ to 5½
	20 to 24	325ºF	5 to 6½

*A turkey is done when it reaches 180ºF at the inner thigh and juices are clear, not reddish pink, when the thigh muscle is deeply pierced. If the turkey is stuffed, the temperature at the center of the stuffing should be 160ºF. Begin checking turkey about 1 hour before the end of the recommended roasting time.

THE HOLLY CLEGG TRIM & TERRIFIC COOKBOO

TIPS & TRICKS

Soups

■ If a soup or stew is too salty, add 1 cup potatoes. Discard them after they have cooked. The potatoes will absorb the salt.

■ If a stew or soup is too sweet, gradually add salt to fix the flavor.

■ If a stew or soup is slightly burnt, milk will take out the burnt taste.

■ Remove fat from soups and stews by dropping ice cubes into the pot. The fat will cling to the cubes as you stir. Take the cubes out before they melt. Fat also clings to lettuce leaves.

■ For too sweet a main dish or vegetable, add 1 teaspoon cider vinegar.

■ To save leftover canned tomato paste: Place level tablespoonfuls on a foil- or plastic wrap–lined pan; freeze until solid. Transfer the frozen paste to a self-sealing freezer bag, label, and date. The frozen paste can be added directly to hot sauces, soups, and stews.

■ When pasta or rice is added to soups, they expand to two or three times their original size.

■ To thicken soups, add 1 tablespoon cornstarch to 1 cup liquid.

■ Don't boil soups with dairy products, as they might separate; after adding milk, heat soup softly.

Eggs

■ If you can't remember whether an egg is hard cooked or fresh, spin it. If it wobbles, it is raw. If it spins easily, it is hard cooked.

■ A fresh egg will sink in water, but a stale one will float.

Produce

■ To perk up soggy lettuce, add lemon juice to a bowl of cold water and soak the lettuce in the bowl for 1 hour in the refrigerator.

■ Store celery and lettuce in paper bags, not plastic. Leave the outside leaves and stalks alone until ready to use.

■ Sunlight doesn't ripen tomatoes; warmth does. Store tomatoes with their stems pointed down, and they will stay fresh longer.

■ To get the most juice out of fresh lemons or limes, bring them to room temperature or microwave them on high for 30 seconds. Then roll them on the counter to burst the juice cells; slice and juice.

■ To keep cut fruit from browning, gently mix the fruit with a small amount of honey to coat the fruit. Honey's acidity prevents fruit from turning brown.

■ Prepare (slice, peel, or dice) veggies just before cooking—never let them sit in water. When they're exposed to air or soaked in water, veggies quickly lose much of their vitamin content and flavor.

- Never add baking soda when you're cooking green vegetables: it will keep them green, but it destroys their vitamin content and makes them mushy.
- To preserve nutrients, cook vegetables as quickly as possible in a covered pot.
- When buying veggies, look for firmness, lots of green or primary color of the veggie, and lack of damage with no soft spots or bruises.
- Vegetables are at the point of being fully cooked when you start smelling their aroma.

Sweets
- To soften rock-hard brown sugar, simply add a slice of soft bread to the package and close the bag tightly. In a few hours, the sugar will be soft again.
- Marshmallows won't dry out when frozen.
- To keep sticky ingredients such as corn syrup, honey, and molasses from sticking to a measuring cup, lightly oil the inside of the measuring cup before using, or coat with nonstick cooking spray.
- If a cake is stuck to the pan, try dipping the bottom of the pan in hot water to soften the ingredients (fat or sugar) causing the cake to adhere to the pan.

Hate those cracks in cheesecakes?
- Don't over beat ingredients, because then you beat excess air into the cheesecake and it may puff up in the oven, then collapse toward the end of the baking period.
- Try running a knife between the edge of the cheesecake and the side of the pan

as soon as you remove the cake from the oven. This allows the cake to pull away cleanly from the sides of the pan as it contracts while cooling.
- Longer cooking with lower temperatures minimizes cracks.

Freezing Tips
- Food should be in an airtight container to retain maximum freshness.
- Liquids expand when frozen, so leave space in the container for expansion.
- Freeze in gallon-size freezer bags, squash out the air, and stack flat.
- Refreezing: the general rule is that if food still has ice crystals, it can be refrozen.
- Label frozen food containers with contents, number of servings, and the date.
- Cream and custard fillings are not satisfactory for freezing.
- Most baked goods, cakes, pies, and cookies freeze well.
- All soups can be frozen. Those that contain vegetable chunks that might get mushy can be puréed after thawing, then reheated with broth or milk.

General Tips
- If you overbrown garlic, throw it away and begin again.
- Begin your sautéing with a hot pan. If using a nonstick pan, put fat in before heating.
- Toasting nuts intensifies their flavor, so you can use less.
- Pat chicken breasts dry before sautéing them.

- Freeze boneless, skinless chicken breasts, beef, and pork for 10 minutes before slicing for stir-fry: they'll slice more evenly and quickly.
- To remove skin from chicken easier, use a paper towel to grab the skin.
- After cutting onions or garlic, get rid of the odor on your hands by rubbing them on a stainless-steel utensil (a spoon is the easiest) under cold running water.
- To peel garlic quickly, snip the pointy ends off individual cloves and microwave them for 10 to 15 seconds.
- When sour cream or yogurt is added to a recipe, don't let it come to a boil: boiling will cause separation in the sauce. To prevent separation, the recipe should include about 2 tablespoons flour or 1 tablespoon cornstarch for every cup of broth plus sour cream to be thickened. If the sauce does begin to separate, push the meat to one side and whisk the sauce vigorously to bring it back together.
- To keep fruit rinds from getting stuck in the grater, cover the grater with plastic wrap. If you don't have time to grate, buy the dried version in the spice section of your grocery.
- When you burn something in a pan, add baking soda and water, and the burn residue will come out.
- For easy food removal from a mold, spray with nonstick cooking spray.
- To counteract the acid in tomato and other acidic sauces, always add a pinch of sugar.

- If available, use fresh ingredients, then frozen, and then canned. Most importantly, use what is most convenient.

Thickeners
- Flour is most often used to thicken saucy mixtures.
- Cornstarch produces a more translucent mixture than flour and has twice the thickening power.
- Before adding either of them, mix with a small amount of cold water first, mixing well to prevent lumps in your sauce or gravy.

COOKING TERMS

Bake: To cook food, covered or uncovered, using the indirect, dry heat of an oven. The term usually refers to cooking cakes, cookies, desserts, and casseroles.

Baste: To moisten foods during cooking with pan drippings or sauce to enhance flavor and prevent the food's drying.

Beat: To smooth a mixture by whipping in a mixer or briskly with a wire whisk.

Blanch: To plunge food into boiling water for a brief time to preserve color and nutritional value, to loosen skins of tomatoes or peaches, or to achieve crisp, tender vegetables.

Blend: To combine, using a mixer or by hand, two or more ingredients until smooth and uniform in texture, flavor, and color.

Boil: To heat a liquid until bubbles form continuously, rise in a steady pattern, and break the liquid's surface.

Bouquet garni: A grouping of herbs tied together or wrapped in cheesecloth (thyme, parsley, bay leaf) used to flavor soups, stews, and stocks.

Braise: To cook food slowly in a small amount of liquid in a tightly covered pan on the stove top. Recommended for less tender cuts of meat.

Broil: To cook food a certain distance directly under dry heat. The indoor version of grilling.

Caramelize: To melt sugar slowly over low heat in a pot until it becomes a golden brown, caramel-flavored syrup.

Chop: To cut into coarse or fine irregular pieces, using a knife or food processor.

Coat: To cover food evenly with crumbs or sauce.

Cream: To beat a mixture consisting usually of margarine and sugar to a light fluffy consistency. This process incorporates air into the mixture so baked products have a lighter texture.

Cube: To cut food into uniform pieces, usually half an inch or larger, using a knife.

Cut in: To work a solid fat (margarine) into dry ingredients, usually with a pastry blender or two knives in a crisscross motion, until coarse crumbs form.

Dash: Less than one-eighth teaspoon of an ingredient.

Dice: To cut food into squares smaller than half an inch, using a knife.

Dissolve: To stir a dry ingredient into a liquid ingredient until the dry ingredient disappears.

Drizzle: To pour topping in thin lines in an uneven pattern over food.

Flake: To gently break a food into small pieces using a fork (used in cooking fish).

Fold: To gently combine, using a spatula, a lighter mixture with a heavier mixture by using a circular motion bringing the contents of a bowl to the top.

Glaze: A thin, glossy coating on a food.

Grate: To rub a hard-textured food (such as cheese) against the small, rough, sharp-edged holes of a grater.

Grease: To coat a surface with a thin layer of fat or oil. Nonstick cooking spray may be substituted.

Julienne: To cut food into thin, matchlike sticks about two inches long.

Knead: To work dough with the heels of your hands in a pressing and folding motion until it becomes smooth and elastic.

Marinade: A savory liquid in which food is placed to add flavor and tenderize. "Marinate" refers to the process.

Mash: To press or beat a food to remove lumps and create a smooth mixture.

Mince: To cut food into very fine pieces, smaller than "chopped."

Pare: To cut off the skin or outer covering of a fruit or vegetable using a small knife or vegetable peeler.

Partially set: A mixture is chilled to a consistency of unbeaten egg whites. Other ingredients are added at this stage so they will stay evenly distributed and not sink to the bottom or float.

Peel: To cut off the outer covering or skin of a vegetable or fruit.

Poach: To cook in simmering liquid just below the boiling point.

Preheat: To heat an oven to a specific temperature before using it.

Purée: To change a solid food into a liquid or heavy paste, usually by using a blender or food processor.

Reconstitute: To bring a concentrate or condensed food to its original strength by adding water or another specified liquid.

Reduce: To boil liquid rapidly, uncovered, so some of the liquid evaporates, intensifying its flavor and cutting the amount of liquid.

Rind: The skin or outer coating of a food (citrus fruits, watermelon, cheese).

Roast: To cook with a dry-heat cooking method (no liquid and uncovered in an oven). Used for meats, poultry, and vegetables.

Roux: A French term that refers to a mixture of flour and a fat (oil) cooked to a golden or rich brown color and used for thickening in sauces, soups, and gumbos.

Sauté: To cook or brown food in a small amount of hot fat with a frequent tossing or turning motion.

Scald: To heat a liquid to just below the boiling point. Tiny bubbles will form at the edge, and a thin skin will form on top of milk.

Score: To cut narrow grooves or slits partway through the outer surface of a food to tenderize or for appearance.

Sear: To brown a food quickly on all sides, using a high heat to seal in the juices.

Shred: To cut into long, thin pieces using the round smooth, holes of a shredder.

Simmer: To cook a food in liquid that is kept just below the boiling point. Bubbles will rise slowly and break just below the surface.

Skim: To remove a substance such as fat or foam from the surface of a liquid.

Slice: To cut food into uniform-size, flat, thin pieces.

Soft peaks: To beat egg whites until peaks are rounded or curled when beaters are lifted from the bowl while the whites are still moist and glossy.

Soften: To let cold food stand at room temperature before using (margarine, cream cheese).

Steam: To cook food by placing on a rack or in a steamer basket over a small amount of boiling water so that the vapor given off by the boiling water cooks the food. Steaming helps to retain flavor, shape, color, texture, and nutritional value.

Stew: To cook food in liquid in a covered pot for a long time until tender.

Stir: To mix ingredients with a spoon or utensil to combine them, to prevent food from sticking during cooking, or to cool food after cooking.

Stiff peaks: To beat egg whites until peaks stand up straight when the beaters are lifted from the bowl while the whites are still moist and glossy.

Stir-fry: An Oriental method of quickly cooking small pieces of food in hot oil over high heat, stirring constantly. Have all ingredients cut before beginning.

Strain: To pour a mixture or liquid through a fine sieve or strainer to remove larger pieces.

Toss: To mix ingredients lightly by lifting and dropping them with two utensils (salad greens).

Whip: To beat a food lightly and rapidly using a wire whisk or mixer, to incorporate air into the mixture and increase its volume.

Zest: The colored outer portion of citrus fruit peel that is often used as a flavoring in recipes. Zest can be purchased dried in the spice section in the form of lemon or orange peel.

Index

A

Almond(s)
Asparagus, 165
Cabbage Salad, Oriental, 129
Chocolate Cheesecake, 425
Orange Mixed Green Salad, 127
Angel Food Cake
Coffee, 401
Strawberry, 400
Angel Hair (Capellini)
Chicken, Greek Lemon, over, 339
with Crabmeat, 350
Mediterranean, 333
Perfect Pasta, 323
Shrimp, and Salsa Casserole, 349
Shrimp and, 343
Appetizers
Artichoke Bites, 44
Artichoke Squares, 45
Artichokes, Stuffed, Hearty, 46
Brie, Glazed, 47
Caponata, 32
Caviar Mold, 36
Cheese Ball, Sweet, 27
Chicken, Strips, Sweet-and-Spicy, 31
Crab Fingers, Marinated, 35
Crabmeat Mold, 35
Mushrooms, Stuffed, Seafood-, 40
Mushrooms, Stuffed, Portabello, with Goat
    Cheese and Roasted Red Peppers, 41
Pizza, Artichoke and Red Pepper, 48
Pizza, Asparagus and Brie, 50
Pizza, Tortilla, Spinach-and-Cheese, 49
Salmon, Cold Poached, with
    Dill Dijon Sauce, 38
Salmon Mousse with Dill Sauce, 37
Shrimp, Avocado, and Artichoke, 20
Shrimp, Marinated, 34
Shrimp Spread, 21
Shrimp Cocktail Spread, 22
Spinach Balls with Jezebel Sauce, 42
Taco Cups, Mini, 43

Tortilla Pinwheels, Smoked Salmon, 39
Tortilla Pizza, Spinach-and-Cheese, 49
Tortilla Shrimp Bites, 39
See also Dips
Apple(s)
Cake, with Broiled Topping, 380
Crumble, Peanut, 444
Muffins, Chunky Whole Wheat, 71
Pasta Salad, Waldorf, 138
Pie, Crumble, 446
Salad, Special, 464
Apricot(s)
Bread, 66
Cake, 381
Frosting, 381
Jezebel Sauce, Spinach Balls with, 42
Lemon Sauce, Pineapple Bread
    Pudding with, 418
Oatmeal Bars, 373
Strudel, 370
Artichoke(s)
Bites, 44
Chicken Breasts with Mushrooms and, 222
Dip, 44
Dip, Spinach, 28
and Green Bean Casserole, 176
Lasagna, Mediterranean, 358
Pizza, and Red Pepper, 48
Shrimp, and Avocado, 20
Soup, 113
Squares, 45
Stuffed, Hearty, 46
Tuna Salad, Deluxe, 151
Asian(-Style)
Coleslaw, 128
Meat Marinade, 282
Asparagus
Almond, 165
and Brie Pizza, 50
Chicken Roll-Ups, 232
Ziti Primavera, Shrimp, 347
Avocado(s)
Guacamole, 17

Guacamole, Wasabi, 18
Salsa, Fiesta, 26
Shrimp, and Artichoke, 20
Soup, Cucumber and, 90

B

Banana(s)
  Bread, Butterscotch, 67
  Bread, Cranberry, 63
  Cake with Cream Cheese Frosting, 382
  Cream Pie, 447
  Éclair, 438–439
  Fruit Casserole, Hot, 81
  Glazed, 432
  Peanut Butter Pie, 448
  Trifle, Fantastic, 428
  Trifle, Fruit, 430
Barbecue(d)
  Beef Brisket, 245
  Chicken, Indoor, 224
  Pork Roast, 267
  Shrimp (Italian), 301
Bar Cookies
  Apricot Oatmeal, 373
  Chocolate Chess Bars, 375
  Lemon Sours, 371
  Lemon Squares, 372
  Ooey Gooey Squares, 476
  See also Brownies
Barley
  Casserole, 193
  Chicken, and Bowtie Soup, 98
  and Vegetable Soup, Beefy, 109
  and Wild Rice Pilaf, 192
Basil
  Cherry Tomatoes with, Sautéed, 203
  Shrimp with Fettuccine, 348
Bean(s)
  Baked, 166
  Chicken Fiesta Salad, 149
  Chili
    Black Bean, Shrimp and, Southwestern, 117

Chicken, White, 115
  Speedy, 116
  Vegetarian, Quick, 114
Couscous Salad, Mediterranean, 135
Dip
  Black Bean, 16
  Black-Eyed Pea, 31
  Mexican, 33
  Pizza, Shrimp Southwestern, 23
  Tex-Mex, 18
Lasagna, Mediterranean, 358
Salad
  Black-eyed Pea and Rice, 134
  Corn and Black Bean, 131
  Tuna and White Bean, 152
Sauce, Chicken with, Southwestern, 236
Soup
  Black Bean, 97
  Three Bean, 96
  White Bean, Shrimp, and Pasta, 102
See also Black Bean(s); Black-Eyed Pea(s);
  Garbanzo Bean(s); Green Bean(s);
  White Bean(s)
Beef
  Artichokes, Stuffed, Hearty, 46
  Beans, Baked, 166
  Brisket, Barbecued, 245
  Burger Soup, 464
  Cabbage Rolls, Mock, 262
  Cabbage, Stuffed, 263
  Chili, Speedy, 116
  Dirty Rice, 194
  Eggplant, and Rice, Italian, 259
  Fajitas, Grilled, Southwestern, 253
  Hamburger Dip, 33
  Lasagna, Crispy Southwestern, 255
  Lasagna, Mexican, 256
  and Macaroni Casserole, Traditional, 252
  Manicotti, Meaty Spinach, with
    Tomato Sauce, 360
  Marinade, Asian, 282
  Meatballs for a Crowd, 261
  Meatball Stew, 119

Meat Loaf, Italian, 258
Meat Sauce, 264
Meat Sauce with Spaghetti, 361
Moussaka, 264–265
Peppers, Stuffed, 260
Pizza, Mexican, 469
Pot Roast, Italian-Style, 246
Rice Salad, Taco, 157
Shells, Jumbo, Stuffed, 359
Shish Kabobs, and Chicken, 254
Sloppy Joes, 471
Steak
    Creole with Cheese Grits, 79
    Flank, Grilled, 247
    Flank, Stuffed, 248
    Round, Smothered, 250
    Sirloin Strips, 249
Stew, Quick, 120
Stir-Fry, 251
Taco, Cups, Mini, 43
Tamale Pie, 257
Tenderloin Mexicana, 247
Vegetable and Barley Soup, 109
Beer
    Beef Stew, Quick, 120
    Bread, 53
Bell Pepper(s)
    Caponata, 32
    Chili, Black Bean, Shrimp and,
        Southwestern, 117
    Chili, Vegetarian, Quick, 114
    Fettuccine, Crawfish, 352
    Flank Steak, Stuffed, 248
    Pasta Salad, Italian, 141
    Pasta Toss, Scallop and, 353
    roasting, 15, 248
    Stuffed, 260
    Wild Rice and, 191
    See also Red Bell Pepper(s)
Berry(ies)
    Bread, Lemon, 60
    Crisp, 441
    See also names of berries

Biscuits, 56
    Brunch Bake, Mexican, 56
    Easy Bunny, 459
    Herbed, 57
    Pull-Apart, Bake, 57
    Yam, 58
Bisque
    Potato, Double, 105
    Salmon, 94
Black Bean(s)
    Chicken, Ginger, and, 226
    Chili, Shrimp and, Southwestern, 117
    and Corn Salad, 131
    Dip, 16
    Dip, Pizza, Shrimp Southwestern, 23
    Enchiladas, Chicken and, 238
    Enchiladas, Spinach and, 195
    Pasta, Spicy Southwestern, 326
    Rice Salad, Southwestern, 158
    Soup, 97
    Soup, Three Bean, 96
    Tortellini Salad, Southwestern, 143
    Veggie Wraps, Yam, 208
Black-Eyed Pea(s)
    Dip, 31
    and Rice Salad, 134
Blueberry(ies)
    Bread, Lemon, 60
    Crisp, 441
    Crunch, All-American, 479
    frozen, baking with, 60
    Meringue Pie, 449
    Pineapple Crunch, 443
    Pound Cake, 383
    Trifle, Fruit, 430
Boston Cream Pie, 390
Bowtie, Chicken, and Barley Soup, 98
Brandy Sauce, Pork Medallions with, 272
Bran Muffins, 74
Bread
    Egg Casserole, Crabmeat, 76
    Egg in the, 460
    French, Herbed, 54

French Toast, Baked, 82
Ham and Cheese Breakfast Bake, 461
See also Breads; Rolls
Bread Pudding, 416
  Chocolate, with Caramel Sauce, 420–421
  Cream Cheese, 417
  Florentine, 75
  Pineapple, with Lemon Apricot Sauce, 418
  Sweet Potato, with Praline Sauce, 419
Breads
  Apricot, 66
  Banana Cranberry, 63
  Beer, 53
  Buns, Sticky Honey, 459
  Butterscotch Banana, 67
  Chocolate Zucchini, 68
  Corn Bread, Surprise, 73
  Cranberry Orange, 59, 61
  Cranberry Yam, Easy, 62
  Crescents, Cinnamon, 69
  Lemon Berry, 60
  Mango, 65
  Zucchini, 64
  See also Biscuits; Muffins; Rolls
Brie
  and Asparagus Pizza, 50
  Glazed, 47
  in pizza, 310
  Shrimp, with Oranges and Pasta, 346
  and Spinach Soup, Cream of, 107
Broccoli
  Casserole, 170
  Chicken Divan, 219
  and Chicken Stir-Fry, Chinese, 227
  Lasagna, Vegetable, 356–357
  with Lemon Ginger Sauce, 169
  with Mustard Vinaigrette, 168
  Pasta Salad with Herb Dijon Vinaigrette, 140
  Salad, Sweet-and-Sour, 133
  Sicilian, 169
  Soup, 95
  Soup, Cheesy, 465

Brownies
  Chocolate Caramel, Chewy, 377
  Chocolate Chess Bars, 375
  Chocolate Mint, 478
  Chocolate Peanut Butter, Gooey, 378
  Coffee Toffee, 376
  Heavenly Hash, 374
Brown Sugar Topping, Broiled, 380
Bundt Cake
  German Chocolate, 406
  Mocha Chocolate, 403
  Piña Colada, 396
  Sweet Potato, 391
Bunny Biscuits, Easy, 459
Burger(s)
  Baby, 471
  Soup, 464
Butterscotch Banana Bread, 67

C

Cabbage
  Coleslaw, Asian-Style, 128
  Rolls, Mock, 262
  Salad, Oriental, 129
  Stuffed, 263
Caesar Salad, 123
Cakes
  Almost-Better-than-Sex, 379
  Angel Food, Coffee, 401
  Angel Food, Strawberry, 400
  Apple with Broiled Topping, 380
  Apricot, 381
  Banana with Cream Cheese Frosting, 382
  Blueberry Pound, 383
  Boston Cream Pie, 390
  Citrus, 388
  Coffee Cake, Cream Cheese, 384
  Coffee Cake with Streusel Filling, 385
  Cranberry, 386
  Cream, Italian, 397
  Cream, Italian, Quick, 398
  Cupcakes, Ice Cream Cone, 473
  Lemon Poppy Seed, 389

Orange Cranberry, 387
Red Velvet, 405
Strawberry Custard, 392–393
Strawberry Heart, 480
Tiramisu, 402
Upside-Down, Tropical, 395
Wait, 399
See also Bundt Cake; Cheesecake;
    Chocolate, Cake
Candy(ies)
  Burgers, Baby, 471
  Clowns, 474
  Ghost Suckers, 481
  Pizza, Double Chocolate, 475
  Popcorn Cake, 472
Cannelloni, Chicken and Spinach, 341
Capellini. See Angel Hair
Caper
  Clam Sauce, Shrimp with, 303
  Horseradish Sauce, 295
Caponata, 32
Caramel
  Chocolate Brownies, Chewy, 377
  Flan, Orange, 427
  Sauce, Chocolate Bread Pudding
      with, 420–421
Carrot(s)
  Beef Stew, Quick, 120
  Dijon Glazed, 172
  Lasagna, Vegetable, 356–357
  Orange Glazed, 171
  Pot Roast, Italian-Style, 246
  Soufflé, 171
Casseroles
  Barley, 193
  Broccoli, 170
  Chicken, Mexican, 237
  Chicken, One-Dish, 231
  Chicken Vermicelli, 342
  Corn, Creamy, 173
  Crabmeat Egg, 76
  Egg and Green Chile, 77
  Fruit, Hot, 81

Green Bean, 177
Green Bean and Artichoke, 176
Ham and Cheese Breakfast Bake, 461
Meat-and-Macaroni, Traditional, 252
Pork Chop, 266
Potato, Easy, 184
Rice, Cheesy Shrimp, 311
Rice, and Crawfish, 315
Seafood, 318
Seafood and Wild Rice, 319
Shrimp, Salsa, and Pasta, 349
Spinach Mushroom, 198
Squash, 202
Sweet Potato, with Praline Topping, 188
Tortellini and Eggplant, 334
Cauliflower Supreme, 173
Caviar Mold, 36
Celery
  Caponata, 32
  Pasta Salad, Waldorf, 138
Cereal
  Mixture, 83
  in Munch Mix, 481
  in Snack Mix, 83
Cheese
  adding to sauces, 318
  Ball, Sweet, 27
  Broccoli Casserole, 170
  Broccoli Soups, 95, 465
  Cauliflower Supreme, 173
  Corn Muffins, 74
  freezing, 199
  grating, 233
  Grits, Quick, 80
  Grits with Steak Creole, 79
  and Ham Breakfast Bake, 461
  Macaroni and, One-Step, 179
  Manicotti, Eggplant with
      Cheesy Spinach Filling, 335
  Manicotti, Meaty Spinach, with
      Tomato Sauce, 360
  Quesadillas, 468
  Sandwiches, Jack-O'-Lantern, 467

Sandwiches, Open-Face Tic-Tac-Toe, 466
Shrimp Rice Casserole, 311
Spinach, Spicy, 197
Spinach Pie, Italian, 199
See also Brie; Cream Cheese;
    Enchiladas; Feta; Goat Cheese;
    Lasagna; Parmesan; Pizza; Pizza-Style
Cheesecake
  Chocolate Almond, 425
  Coffee, 422
  cracking, prevention of, 425
  Cranberry, 423
  Sweet Potato, 424
Cherry(ies)
  Chicken, Jubilee, 220
  Crunch, All-American, 479
  Fruit Casserole, Hot, 81
Cherry Tomato(es)
  Salsa, Fiesta, 26
  Sautéed, with Basil, 203
  Tuna Salad, Marinated Italian, 150
Chicken
  Barbecued, Indoor, 224
  with Bean Sauce, Southwestern, 236
  Breasts with Artichokes and Mushrooms, 222
  Breasts Diane, 215
  Breasts Florentine, 221
  Cannelloni, and Spinach, 341
  Casserole, Mexican, 237
  Casserole, One-Dish, 231
  Cherry Jubilee, 220
  Chili, White, 115
  Company, 214
  Cranberry, with Wild Rice, 229
  Crusty, Simple Baked, 212
  Dijon Rosemary, 212
  Divan, 219
  and Dumplings, 230
  Enchiladas, and Black Bean, 238
  Fajita Pizza, 235
  Full-of-Flavor, 228
  Ginger, and Black Beans, 226
  Greek Lemon, over Pasta, 339

Gumbo, and Sausage, 93
Honey Pecan, 213
Italian, 218
Lasagna, Quick, 355
Lemon Feta, 223
and Linguine, 337
Marinated, Easy, 216
Paprika, 223
Parmesan, Oven-Fried, 211
Pasta, Mediterranean, 340
Peanut, 225
Pizza, Skillet, 217
Primavera, 338
Roll-Ups, 232
Salad
  Bowl, Greek, 147
  Curried, 146
  Fiesta, 149
  Mandarin, 148
Salsa, 233
Shish Kabobs, Beef and, 254
Soup, Barley, Bowtie and, 98
Soup, Tortilla, 99
Stir-Fry, and Broccoli, Chinese, 227
Strips, Sweet-and-Spicy, 31
Tequilla, 234
Vermicelli, 342
Chick Pea(s). *See* Garbanzo Bean(s)
Chiles
  Green, and Egg Casserole, 77
  Salsa, Fiesta, 26
Chili
  Chicken, White, 115
  Speedy, 116
  Vegetarian, Quick, 114
Chinese
  Chicken and Broccoli Stir-Fry, 227
  Pork Vermicelli, 362
Chips, Tortilla, Homemade, Salsa with, 25
Chocolate
  Bread Pudding with Caramel Sauce, 420–421
  Cake
    Bundt, German Chocolate, 406

Bundt, Mocha, 403
Layered, German Chocolate,
   Old-Fashioned, 408–409
Oatmeal, 410
Pudding, 400
Sheet, German Chocolate, 407
Simple, 477
Triple, 404
candy-coated, in Snack Mix, 83
Cheesecake, Almond, 425
Cookies, 367
Cookies, Box, Double Chocolate, 476
Cookies, Holiday, 369
Éclair, Mock, 413
Fondue, 437
Frosting, Cream Cheese, 402
Glaze, 439
Icing, 374
Layered Dessert, 414
Pie
   Angel, German Chocolate, 453
   Chess, 445
   Mousse, Mocha Fudge, 435
Pizza, Double Chocolate Candy, 475
Sauce, 433
Zucchini Bread, 68
See also Brownies
Chocolate Chip(s)
Cookies, 366
in Munch Mix, 481
Pie, 444
Chowder, Squash, and Corn, Spicy, 101
Cilantro, Salsa with Tortilla Chips, 25
Cinnamon
Crescents, 69
Granola, 84
Rolls, 458
Citrus
Cake, 388
Frosting, 388
Sauce, Mango Salad with, 162
Vinaigrette, Mixed Greens with
   Sugared Pecans and, 125

Clam Caper Sauce, Shrimp with, 303
Coconut
Frosting, Pecan, 409
Funny Faces, 462
Glaze, 406
Coffee
Angel Food Cake, 401
Cheesecake, 422
Icing, 401
Tiramisu, 436
Tiramisu Cake, 402
Toffee Brownies, 376
Toffee Dessert, 434
See also Espresso
Coffee Cake
Cream Cheese, 384
with Streusel Filling, 385
Coleslaw, Asian-Style, 128
Collards, cooking method, 195
Cookies
Box, Double Chocolate, 476
Chocolate, 367
Chocolate Chip, 366
Holiday, 369
No-Bake, 365
Oatmeal, 366
Peanut Butter, 368
See also Bar Cookies; Brownies
Corn
Bean Dip, Mexican, 33
and Black Bean Salad, 131
Casserole, Creamy, 173
Casserole, Tamale and, 174
Chicken Salad, Fiesta, 149
Chili, Black Bean, Shrimp and,
   Southwestern, 117
Chili, Speedy, 116
Chowder, and Squash, Spicy, 101
Dip, 19
Macaroni, and Tomato Salad, 132
Muffins, Cheesy, 74
Okra and, 181
Pasta, Spicy Southwestern, 326

Pasta and Veggies, Marinated, 142
Pork Stew, Southwestern, 118
Salad, 131
Salsa Chicken, 233
Salsa, Fiesta, 26
Scallop, Pepper, and Pasta Toss, 353
Shrimp Tacos with Tropical Salsa, 306
Soup, 100
Soup, Shrimp and, Easy, 103
Soup, Shrimp, Sweet Potato and, 104
Squash Casserole, 202
Tamale Pie, 257
Tortellini Salad, Southwestern, 143
Corn Bread
    Dressing, 204
    Stuffing, Yam, 205
    Surprise, 73
Cornish Hens with Wild Rice Stuffing, 239
Corn Muffins, Cheesy, 74
Couscous
    Salad, Loaded, 136
    Salad, Mediterranean, 135
Crab(meat)
    Angel Hair with, 350
    Cakes, 299
    Egg Casserole, 76
    Enchiladas, 298
    Fingers, Marinated, 35
    au Gratin, 297
    Lasagna, Seafood, 357
    Mold, 35
    Salad, Marinated, 139
    Seafood Casserole, 318
    Soup, Easy, 94
    Wild Rice Casserole, Seafood and, 319
Cranberry(ies)
    Bread, Banana, 63
    Bread, Orange, 61
    Bread, Yam, Easy, 62
    Cake, 386
    Cake, Orange, 387
    Cheese Ball, Sweet, 27
    Cheesecake, 423

Chicken with Wild Rice, 229
Cookies, Holiday, 369
Granola, 84
Green Salad, Mixed with
    Sunflower Seeds and, 126
Mold, 161
Muffins, Pineapple, 70
Scones, Orange, 59
Crawfish
    Dip, 30
    Elegante, 313
    Étouffée, 314
    Fettuccine, 352
    Mushrooms, Seafood-Stuffed, 40
    and Rice Casserole, 315
Cream Cake
    Italian, 397
    Italian, Quick, 398
Cream Cheese
    Bread Pudding, 417
    Cheese Ball, Sweet, 27
    Coffee Cake, 384
    Frosting, 382, 394, 397, 398, 405
    Frosting, Chocolate, 402
    Shrimp Cocktail Spread, 22
    Shrimp Spread, 21
    Tortilla Pinwheels, Smoked Salmon, 39
    See also Cheesecake
Creepy Crawlers, 466
Creole Steak with Cheese Grits, 79
Crêpes Florentine, 196
Crescents, Cinnamon, 69
Crisps
    Berry, 441
    Peach, 440
Crumble
    Apple Peanut, 444
    Apple Pie, 446
    Nectarine and Raspberry, 442
    Pie, Sweet Potato Pecan, 452
Crunch, All-American, 479
Cucumber(s)
    and Avocado Soup, 90

Dill Sauce, Salmon Mousse with, 37
Dip, Zesty, 24
Gazpacho, White, 88
Pasta and Veggies, Marinated, 142
and Tomato Salad, 129
Cupcakes, Ice Cream Cone, 473
Curried Chicken Salad, 146
Custard
Boston Cream Pie, 390
Brûlée, Strawberry, 426
Cake, Strawberry, 392–393
Orange Caramel Flan, 427
Pie, 445
Trifle, Fruit, 430
Trifle, Lemon Pineapple, 431

D

Date(s), Cheese Ball, Sweet, 27
Dessert Sauces
Caramel, Chocolate Bread
Pudding with, 420–421
Chocolate, 433
Lemon Apricot, Pineapple Bread
Pudding with, 418
Praline, Sweet Potato Bread
Pudding with, 419
Rum, 416
Vanilla, 454
Dijon. *See* Mustard
Dill
Dressing, 145
Sauce, Salmon Mousse with, 37
Dips
Artichoke, 44
Bean, Mexican, 33
Black Bean, 16
Black-Eyed Pea, 31
Corn, 19
Crawfish, 30
Cucumber, Zesty, 24
Fruit, 26, 482
Guacamole, 17
Guacamole, Wasabi, 18

Hamburger, 33
Hummus, 24
Oyster Rockefeller, 29
Red Bell Pepper, Roasted, 15
Salsa, Fiesta, 26
Salsa with Tortilla Chips, 25
Shrimp
Rémoulade, 19
Shrimp Cocktail Spread, 22
Southwestern Pizza, 23
Spread, 21
Spinach, 16
Spinach Artichoke, 28
in taco cups, mini, 43
Tex-Mex, 18
Dirty Rice, 194
Dog Salad, Friendly, 463
Dressing
Corn Bread, 204
Wild Rice and Oyster, 206
See also Stuffing
Dumplings, Chicken and, 230

E

Éclair
Banana, 438–439
Chocolate, Mock, 413
Egg(s)
Bread, in the, 460
Crabmeat Casserole, 76
folding whites, 416
French Toast, Baked, 82
and Green Chile Casserole, 77
Ham and Cheese Breakfast Bake, 461
Hard-Boiled
Caviar Mold, 36
Niçoise Salad, 153
Rah-Rahs, 463
Meringue Pie, Blueberry, 449
Meringue Pie, Lemon, 450–451
Soufflé, Carrot, 171
Tex-Mex, 78
See also Custard

Eggplant
  Caponata, 32
  Manicotti with Cheesy Spinach Filling, 335
  Meat, and Rice, Italian, 259
  Moussaka, 264–265
  Parmesan, 175
  Parmesan, Trout, 291
  Pasta, 331
  Spinach, and Pasta, 332
  Stuffing, Basic, 207
  and Tortellini Casserole, 334
Enchiladas
  Chicken and Black Bean, 238
  Crabmeat, 298
  Spinach and Black Bean, 195
Espresso
  Chocolate Cookies, 367
  powder, 436
  See also Coffee

F

Fajitas
  Beef, Grilled, Southwestern, 253
  Chicken, Pizza, 235
Feta
  Chicken, Lemon, 223
  and Shrimp with Pasta, 345
Fettuccine
  Crawfish, 352
  Scallop, Pepper, and Pasta Toss, 353
  Shrimp, 344
  Shrimp, Basil, with, 348
  Shrimp, and Feta with, 345
Fish
  Florentine, 287
  Fry, 292
  Gumbo, Seafood, 92
  Mediterranean Catch, 288
  Pizza Baked, 289
  with Shrimp Stuffing, Baked, 290
  Spicy Baked, 286
  thawing, 292
  See also Salmon; Shellfish; Trout; Tuna

Flan, Orange Caramel, 427
Flank Steak
  Grilled, 247
  Stuffed, 248
Fondue, Chocolate, 437
French Bread, Herbed, 54
French Toast, Baked, 82
Fries, Oven
  Potato Sticks, Parmesan, 190
  Sweet Potato, 186
Frosting
  Apricot, 381
  Citrus, 388
  Coconut Pecan, 409
  Cream Cheese, 382, 394, 397, 398, 405
  Cream Cheese, Chocolate, 402
  Strawberry, 480
  See also Icing
Fruit(s)
  Casserole, Hot, 81
  Dips, 26, 482
  Dried, Granola, 84
  Pizza, Tropical, 415
  Trifle, 430
  See also names of fruits
Funny Faces, 462

G

Garbanzo Bean(s)
  Hummus, 24
  Pasta and Veggies, Marinated, 142
Garlic, Potatoes, Smashed, 181
Gazpacho
  with Shrimp, 87
  White, 88
Ginger
  Cabbage, Stuffed, 263
  Chicken and Black Beans, 226
  Lemon Sauce, Broccoli with, 169
  -Wasabi Vinaigrette, Grilled
    Tuna Salad with, 154
Glaze(d)
  Bananas, 432

Boston Cream Pie, 390
Brie, 47
Chocolate, 439
Cinnamon Crescents, 69
Coconut, 406
Dijon, Carrots, 172
Honey-, Turkey Breast, 241
Mocha, 403
Orange, Carrots, 171
Pork Tenderloin, 270
Salmon, 294
Goat Cheese
 Penne with Spinach, Sun-Dried
   Tomatoes and, 325
 Portabello Mushrooms Stuffed with
   Roasted Red Peppers and, 41
Granola, 84
Green Bean(s)
 and Artichoke Casserole, 176
 Casserole, 177
 Marinated, 133
 Salad Niçoise, 153
Green Salad, Mixed
 with Citrus Vinaigrette and
   Sugared Pecans, 125
 with Cranberries and Sunflower Seeds, 126
 mesclun, 126
 Orange Almond, 127
 with Oriental Vinaigrette, 127
Grits
 Cheese, with Steak Creole, 79
 Cheese, Quick, 80
 variations, 80
Guacamole, 17
 Wasabi, 18
Gumbo
 Chicken and Sausage, 93
 Seafood, 92

H

Ham, and Cheese Breakfast Bake, 461
Hamburger Dip, 33
Heavenly Hash, 374

Herb(s), Herbed
 Biscuits, 57
 French Bread, 54
 substituting fresh, 155
 Vinaigrette, Dijon, Pasta Salad with, 140
 See also names of herbs
Honey
 Cereal Mixture, 83
 Granola, 84
 Mustard Lamb Chops, 280
 Pecan Chicken, 213
 Pork Tenderloin, Glazed, 270
 Snack Mix, 83
 Sticky Buns, 459
 Turkey Breast, -Glazed, 241
Hors d'Oeuvres. *See* Appetizers; Dips
Horseradish
 Mashed Potatoes, 182
 Sauce, Caper, Salmon Patties with, 295
 Sauce, Tuna Steaks with, 296
Hummus, 24

I

Ice Cream
 Coffee Toffee Dessert, 434
 Pie, 433
 Pie, Strawberry Margarita, 454
Ice Cream Cone Cupcakes, 473
Icing
 Chocolate, 374
 Coffee, 401
 See also Frosting
Italian(-Style)
 Chicken, 218
 Cream Cake, 397
 Cream Cake, Quick, 398
 Eggplant, Meat, and Rice, 259
 Meat Loaf, 258
 Oysters, Baked, 320
 Pasta Salad, 141
 Pot Roast, 246
 Puffs, 55
 Scampi, 308

Shrimp, 301
Soup, 110
Spinach Pie, 199
Tuna Salad, Marinated, 150

J

Jack-O'-Lantern Sandwiches, 467
Jambalaya
Shrimp, Speedy, 312
Turkey, 242
Jezebel Sauce, Spinach Balls with, 42

K

Kale, cooking method, 195
Kugel, Pineapple Noodle, 178

L

Lamb
Chops, Honey Mustard, 280
Chops, Loin with Mint Sauce, 281
Lasagna
Chicken, Quick, 355
Crispy Southwestern (Tortilla), 255
Mediterranean, 358
Mexican (Tortilla), 256
Old-Fashioned, 354
Seafood, 357
Vegetable, 356–357
Lemon
Apricot Sauce, Pineapple Bread
Pudding with, 418
Bread, Berry, 60
Cake, Poppyseed, 389
Chicken, Feta, 223
Chicken, Greek, over Pasta, 339
Citrus Sauce, Mango Salad with, 162
Citrus Vinaigrette, Mixed Greens
with Sugared Pecans and, 125
Ginger Sauce, Broccoli with, 169
Meringue Pie, 450–451
Muffins, Raspberry, 72
Shrimp, Marinated, 34
Shrimp, Marinated, Broiled, 302

Sours, 371
Squares, 372
Trifle, Pineapple, 431
Linguine
Chicken and, 337
Chicken Mediterranean, 340
Chicken Primavera, 338

M

Macaroni
-and-Meat Casserole, Traditional, 252
and Cheese, One-Step, 179
Tomato, and Corn Salad, 132
Mandarin Chicken Salad, 148
Mango
Bread, 65
Pizza, Tropical, 415
Salad with Citrus Sauce, 162
Salsa, Shrimp with, 305
Manicotti, Eggplant, with Cheesy
Spinach Filling, 335
Maple Syrup, French Toast, Baked, 82
Marinade, Marinated
Asian Meat, 282
Chicken, Easy, 216
Crabmeat Salad, 139
Green Beans, 133
Lamb Loin Chops with Mint Sauce, 281
Orange and Wine, 254
Pasta and Veggies, 142
Pork Tenderloin Oriental, Grilled, 271
Shrimp, 34
Shrimp, Broiled, 302
Tuna Salad, Italian, 150
Marshmallows
Apple Salad, Special, 464
Chocolate Candy Pizza, Double
Chocolate, 475
Clowns, 474
Popcorn Cake, 472
Rolls, Surprise, 457
Meatball(s)
for a Crowd, 261

and Spaghetti, 470
  Stew, 119
Meat Loaf, Italian, 258
Meat Sauce, 264
  with Spaghetti, 361
Mediterranean
  Capellini, 333
  Chicken Pasta, 340
  Couscous Salad, 135
  Lasagna, 358
Meringue Pie
  Blueberry, 449
  German Chocolate Angel, 453
  Lemon, 450–451
Mexican
  Bean Dip, 33
  Beef Tenderloin, 247
  Brunch Biscuit Bake, 56
  Chicken Casserole, 237
  Lasagna, 256
  Pizza, 469
Mint
  Burgers, Baby, 471
  Chocolate Brownies, 478
  Sauce, Lamb Loin Chops with, 281
Mocha
  Chocolate Bundt Cake, 403
  Fudge Mousse Pie, 435
Molds
  Caviar, 36
  Crabmeat, 35
  Cranberry, 161
Moussaka, 264–265
Mousse
  Pie, Mocha Fudge, 435
  Salmon, with Dill Sauce, 37
Muffins
  Apple, Chunky Whole Wheat, 71
  Bran, 74
  Corn, Cheesy, 74
  Cranberry Pineapple, 70
  Lemon Raspberry, 72
  Tropical, 73

Munch Mix, 481
Mushroom(s)
  Angel Hair with Crabmeat, 350
  Beef Stew, Quick, 120
  Chicken Breasts with Artichokes and, 222
  Chicken, Full-of-Flavor, 228
  Chicken Primavera, 338
  Eggplant Pasta, 331
  Jambalaya, Turkey, 242
  Lasagna, Vegetable, 356–357
  Pot Roast, Italian-Style, 246
  Scallop Stir-Fry with
    Crispy Noodle Pancakes, 316–317
  Seven-Layer Salad, 130
  Shrimp, Clemanceau, 304
  Shrimp Fettuccine, 344
  Spaghetti Sauce, Meatless, 329
  Spinach Casserole, 198
  Spinach Oriental, 200
  Stuffed, Portabello, with Goat Cheese
    and Roasted Red Peppers, 41
  Stuffed, Seafood-, 40
  Tuna Salad, Deluxe, 151
  Ziti Primavera, Shrimp, 347
Mustard
  Dijon, Carrots, Glazed, 172
  Dijon Herb Vinaigrette, Pasta Salad with, 140
  Dijon Rosemary, Chicken, 212
  Dijon Sauce, Dill, Cold
    Poached Salmon with, 38
  Dijon Sauce, Pecan Trout with, 285
  Honey Lamb Chops, 280
  Sauce, Pork Tenderloin, with, 273
  Vinaigrette, Broccoli with, 168

N
Nectarine and Raspberry Crumble, 442
Niçoise Salad, 153
Noodle(s)
  Kugel, Pineapple, 178
  Pancakes, Crispy, Scallop Stir-Fry with,
    316–317
  Pudding, 180

Ramen, Coleslaw, Oriental, 129
and Rice, 192
Nut(s)
Brie, Glazed, 47
Cheese Ball, Sweet, 27
Snack Mix, 83
toasting, 408
See also names of nuts

O

Oatmeal
Apricot Bars, 373
Chocolate Cake, 410
Cookies, 366
Cookies, No-Bake, 365
Granola, 84
Okra, and Corn, 181
Olive(s)
Caponata, 32
Dip, Tex-Mex, 18
Onion Soup, 112
Ooey Gooey Squares, 476
Orange(s)
Almond Mixed Green Salad, 127
Bread, Cranberry, 61
Caramel Flan, 427
Carrots, Glazed, 171
Cranberry Cake, 387
Fruit Dip, 26
Mandarin Chicken Salad, 148
Sauce, Citrus, Mango Salad with, 162
Scones, Cranberry, 59
Shrimp, with Pasta and, 346
Vinaigrette, Citrus, Mixed Greens
with Sugared Pecans and, 125
and Wine Marinade, 254
Oriental
Cabbage Salad, 129
Pork Tenderloin, Grilled, 271
Spinach, 200
Vinaigrette, Mixed Green Salad with, 127

Oyster(s)
Italian, Baked, 320
Rockefeller Dip, 29
and Wild Rice Dressing, 206

P

Paella Salad, 159
Pancakes
Basic, 82
Noodle, Crispy, Scallop Stir-Fry with, 316–317
Paprika Chicken, 223
Parmesan
Chicken, Oven-Fried, 211
Eggplant, 175
Eggplant, Trout, 291
Potato Sticks, 190
Pasta
Bowtie, Chicken, and Barley Soup, 98
Cannelloni, Chicken and Spinach, 341
Chicken Vermicelli, 342
cooking liquid, reserved, 343
cooking method, 323
Eggplant, 331
Eggplant, Spinach and, 332
Manicotti, Eggplant, with
Cheesy Spinach Filling, 335
Meatballs and Spaghetti, 470
Meat Sauce with, 361
Penne with Spinach, Sun-Dried
Tomatoes, and Goat Cheese, 325
Pork Vermicelli, Chinese, 362
Rigatoni with Roasted Tomato Sauce, 330
Shells, Jumbo, Stuffed, 359
Shrimp, and White Bean Soup, 102
Shrimp with Oranges and, 346
Smoked Salmon, Snap Peas and, 351
Spaghetti Sauce, Meatless, 329
Spicy Southwestern, 326
Squash, Double, Pasta Toss, 336
Thai, 327
Tomatoes, Fresh, Vermicelli with, 324
Vodka, 228

Ziti Primavera, Shrimp, 347
See also Angel Hair; Fettuccine; Lasagna;
     Linguine; Macaroni; Noodle(s);
     Tortellini Pasta Salads
Pasta Salad
  with Herb Dijon Vinaigrette, 140
  Italian, 141
  Macaroni, Tomato, and Corn, 132
  Salmon, 155
  Seafood, Greek, 145
  Tortellini Shrimp, 144
  Tortellini, Southwestern, 143
  and Veggies, Marinated, 142
  Waldorf, 138
Pea(s)
  Chicken, Casserole, One-Dish, 231
  Chicken Primavera, 338
  Paella Salad, 159
  Seafood and Wild Rice Casserole, 319
  Shrimp Clemanceau, 304
  Snap, Smoked Salmon, and Pasta, 351
  Soup, Split, 111
  See also Snow Peas
Peach(es)
  Crisp, 440
  Fruit Casserole, Hot, 81
  Funny Faces, 462
  Rah-Rahs, 463
  Soup, 91
Peanut(s)
  Chicken, 225
  Coleslaw, Asian-Style, 128
  Thai Pasta Dish, 327
Peanut Butter
  Apple Crumble, 444
  Banana Pie, 448
  Chocolate Brownies, Gooey, 378
  Cookies, 368
  Cookies, No-Bake, 365
  Munch Mix, 481
  Sandwiches, Creepy Crawlers, 466
  Sandwiches, Reindeer, 467
Pears, in Friendly Dog Salad, 463

Pecan(s)
  Caramel Sauce, 421
  Cheese Ball, Sweet, 27
  Chicken, Honey, 213
  Chocolate Cookies, 367
  Coconut Frosting, 409
  Pasta Salad, Waldorf, 138
  Praline, Sweet Potatoes, Stuffed, 189
  Praline Topping, Sweet Potato
       Casserole with, 188
  Sugared, Mixed Greens with
       Citrus Vinaigrette and, 125
  Sweet Potato Crumble Pie, 452
  Trout, with Dijon Sauce, 285
Penne, with Spinach, Sun-Dried
     Tomatoes, and Goat Cheese, 325
Peppercorn, Green, Sauce, Pork
     Florentine Wellington with, 268
Pepper(s). *See* Bell Pepper(s); Chiles;
     Red Bell Pepper(s)
Pies
  Apple Crumble, 446
  Banana Cream, 447
  Blueberry Meringue, 449
  Chocolate Chess, 445
  Chocolate Chip, 444
  Custard, 445
  freezing, 449
  German Chocolate Angel, 453
  Ice Cream, 433
  Lemon Meringue, 450–451
  Mousse, Mocha Fudge, 435
  Peanut Butter Banana, 448
  Spinach, Italian, 199
  Strawberry Margarita, 454
  Sweet Potato Pecan Crumble, 452
Pilaf, Wild Rice and Barley, 192
Piña Colada Bundt Cake, 396
Pineapple
  Blueberry Crunch, 443
  Bread Pudding with Lemon Apricot Sauce,
     418

Cake
  Bundt, Piña Colada, 396
    Quick, 394
    Upside-Down, Tropical, 395
  Cranberry Mold, 161
  Fruit Casserole, Hot, 81
  Muffins, Cranberry, 70
  Muffins, Tropical, 73
  Noodle Kugel, 178
  Pizza, Tropical, 415
  Pork, Sweet-and-Sour, 274
  Salsa, Tropical, Shrimp Tacos with, 306
  Trifle, 432
  Trifle, Lemon, 431
  Zucchini Bread, 64
Pinwheels, Smoked Salmon Tortilla, 39
Pizza
  Artichoke and Red Pepper, 48
  Asparagus and Brie, 50
  Chicken Fajita, 235
  Chocolate, Double, Candy, 475
  Mexican, 469
  Mini Cheese, 468
  Sweet Potato, 469
  Tortilla, Spinach-and-Cheese, 49
  Tropical, 415
  White, Shrimp-and-Spinach, 310
Pizza-Style
  Chicken, Skillet, 217
  Dip, Shrimp Southwestern, 23
  Fish, Baked, 289
  Rice, 465
Popcorn Cake, 472
Poppyseed Cake, Lemon, 389
Pork
  Chop Casserole, 266
  Florentine Wellington with
    Green Peppercorn Sauce, 268
  Ham and Cheese Breakfast Bake, 461
  Medallions with Brandy Sauce, 272
  Roast, Barbecued, 267
  Squash, and Tomatoes, Italian, 275
  Stew, Southwestern, 118

  Sweet-and-Sour, 274
  Tenderloin
    Diane with Wild Rice, 269
    Glazed, 270
    with Mustard Sauce, 273
    Oriental, Grilled, 271
  Vermicelli, Chinese, 362
  and Wild Rice Salad, 156
  See also Sausage
Portabello Mushrooms, Stuffed with Goat
    Cheese and Roasted Red Peppers, 41
Potato(es)
  Beef Stew, Quick, 120
  Bisque, Double Potato, 105
  Casserole, Easy, 184
  Mashed, Horseradish, 182
  Mashed, Wasabi, 183
  Niçoise Salad, 153
  Roasted, Sweet Potatoes and White, 187
  Salad, 137
  Shrimp Clemanceau, 304
  Smashed, Garlic, 181
  Soup, Creamy, 106
  Sticks, Parmesan, 190
  Stuffed, Southwestern, 185
  types of, 185
  Vichyssoise, 89
Pot Roast, Italian-Style, 246
Pound Cake, Blueberry, 383
Praline
  Sauce, Sweet Potato Bread Pudding with, 419
  Sweet Potatoes, Stuffed, 189
  Topping, Sweet Potato Casserole with, 188
Pretzel(s)
  Snack Mix, 83
  Strawberry Gelatin, 160
Prosciutto
  Turkey Steaks with, 240
  Veal, Saltimbocca, 276
Pudding
  Cake, Chocolate, 400
  Chocolate Layered Dessert, 414

Noodle, 180
Noodle Kugel, Pineapple, 178
See also Bread Pudding; Trifle
Pumpkin Soup, 107

Q

Quesadillas, Cheese, 468

R

Rah-Rahs, 463
Raspberry(ies)
  Crisp, 441
  Crumble, Nectarine and, 442
  Muffins, Lemon, 72
  Salmon Framboise, 294
  Spinach Salad, 123
Red Bell Pepper(s)
  Dip, Roasted, 15
  Pizza, Artichoke and, 48
  Roasted, Portabello Mushrooms Stuffed
    with Goat Cheese and, 41
  roasting, 15, 248
  See also Bell Pepper(s)
Red Velvet Cake, 405
Reindeer Sandwiches, 467
Rémoulade, Shrimp, 19
Rice
  Cabbage Rolls, Mock, 262
  Cabbage, Stuffed, 263
  Cheesy Shrimp Casserole, 311
  Chicken Casserole, One-Dish, 231
  Chicken, Italian, 218
  and Crawfish Casserole, 315
  Dirty, 194
  Eggplant, and Meat, Italian, 259
  Fried, Shrimp, 300
  Jambalaya, Turkey, 242
  and Noodles, 192
  Peppers, Stuffed, 260
  Pizza, 465
  Pork Chop Casserole, 266
  Salad
    Black-Eyed Pea and, 134

Paella, 159
Southwestern, 158
Taco, 157
Wild, and Pork, 156
Southwestern, 190
Summer, 191
yields, 134
See also Wild Rice
Rigatoni, with Roasted Tomato Sauce, 330
Rolls
  Cinnamon, 458
  Crescents, Cinnamon, 69
  Italian Puffs, 55
  Surprise, 457
Rosemary, Chicken, Dijon, 212
Rum Sauce, 416

S

Salads
  Apple, Special, 464
  Black Bean and Corn, 131
  Black-Eyed Pea and Rice, 134
  Broccoli, Sweet-and-Sour, 133
  Cabbage, Oriental, 129
  Caesar, 123
  Coleslaw, 128
  Corn, 131
  Couscous, Loaded, 136
  Couscous, Mediterranean, 135
  Crabmeat, Marinated, 139
  Cranberry Mold, 161
  Cucumber and Tomato, 129
  Friendly Dog, 463
  Green Beans, Marinated, 133
  Mango, with Citrus Sauce, 162
  Niçoise, 153
  Potato, 137
  Seven-Layer, 130
  Spinach, 124
  Spinach, Raspberry, 123
  Strawberry Gelatin, Pretzel, 160
  See also Chicken, Salad; Green Salad, Mixed;
    Pasta Salad; Rice, Salad; Tuna, Salad

Salmon
  Bisque, 94
  Framboise, 294
  Glazed, 294
  Mousse with Dill Sauce, 37
  Pasta Salad, 155
  Patties with Horseradish Caper Sauce, 295
  Poached, Cold, with Dill Dijon Sauce, 38
  Smoked, Snap Peas, and Pasta, 351
  Smoked, Tortilla Pinwheels, 39
  Steaks, Superb, 293
Salsa
  Chicken, 233
  Fiesta, 26
  Mango, Shrimp with, 305
  Shrimp, and Pasta Casserole, 349
  with Tortilla Chips, 25
  Tropical, Shrimp Tacos with, 306
Sandwiches (Kids)
  Creepy Crawlers, 466
  Jack-O'-Lantern, 467
  Reindeer, 467
  Sloppy Joes, 471
  Tic-Tac-Toe, Open-Face, 466
Sauces
  Bean, Chicken with, Southwestern, 236
  Brandy, Pork Medallions with, 272
  Caper Clam, Shrimp with, 303
  Citrus, Mango Salad with, 162
  Dijon, Pecan Trout with, 285
  Dill, Salmon Mousse with, 37
  Dill Dijon, Cold Poached Salmon with, 38
  Green Peppercorn, Pork
      Florentine Wellington with, 268
  Horseradish Caper, Salmon Pattties with, 295
  Horseradish, Tuna Steaks with, 296
  Jezebel, Spinach Balls with, 42
  Lemon Ginger, Broccoli with, 169
  Meat, 264
  Meat, with Spaghetti, 361
  Mint, Lamb Loin Chops with, 281
  Mustard, Pork Tenderloin, with, 273
  Spaghetti, Meatless, 329

Tomato, 261, 335, 359, 470
Tomato, Meaty Spinach Manicotti with, 361
Tomato, Roasted, Rigatoni with, 330
White, 265, 298
See also Dessert Sauces
Sausage
  Corn Bread Stuffing, 204
  Eggplant, Meat, and Rice Italian, 259
  Gumbo, Chicken and, 93
  Jambalaya, Speedy, 312
  Jambalaya, Turkey, 242
Scallop(s)
  Broiled, 317
  cooking method, 316
  Pasta Salad, Greek Seafood, 145
  Pepper, and Pasta Toss, 353
  Stir-Fry with Crispy Noodle Pancakes,
      316–317
Scampi, Italian Style, 308
Scones, Cranberry Orange, 59
Seafood. See Fish; Shellfish
Seeds
  Granola, 84
  Sunflower, Green Salad, Mixed
      with Cranberries and, 126
Seven-Layer Salad, 130
Shellfish
  Casserole, 318
  Gumbo, 92
  Lasagna, 357
  Mushroom(s), -Stuffed, 40
  Pasta Salad, Greek, 145
  and Wild Rice Casserole, 319
  See also Crab(meat); Crawfish;
      Oyster(s); Scallop(s); Shrimp
Shells, Jumbo, Stuffed, 359
Shish Kabobs, Beef and Chicken, 254
Shrimp
  and Angel Hair, 343
  Avocado, and Artichoke, 20
  and Black Bean Chili, Southwestern, 117
  with Caper Clam Sauce, 303
  Clemanceau, 304

THE HOLLY CLEGG TRIM & TERRIFIC COOKBO

and Feta with Pasta, 345
Fettuccine, 344
with Fettuccine, Basil, 348
Grilled, 307
Italian (Barbecue), 301
Jambalaya, Speedy, 312
Lasagna, Seafood, 357
with Mango Salsa, 305
Marinated, 34
Marinated, Broiled, 302
Mushrooms, Seafood-Stuffed, 40
with Oranges and Pasta, 346
Paella Salad, 159
Pasta Salad, Greek Seafood, 145
Pizza, White, -and-Spinach, 310
Rémoulade, 19
Rice Casserole, Cheesy, 311
Rice, Fried, 300
Salsa, and Pasta Casserole, 349
Sauté, 307
Scampi, Italian Style, 308
Seafood Casserole, 318
Soups
    Corn, Sweet Potato and, 104
    Corn and, Easy, 103
    Gazpacho with, 87
    White Bean, Pasta and, 102
and Spinach Skillet Surprise, 309
Spread, 21
Spread, Shrimp Cocktail, 22
Stuffing, Fish with, Baked, 290
Tortellini Salad, 144
Tortilla Bites, 39
Wild Rice Casserole, Seafood and, 319
Ziti Primavera, 347
Sicilian Broccoli, 169
Sirloin Steak Strips, 249
Sloppy Joes, 471
Smoked Salmon. *See* Salmon
Smoothie, Strawberry, 482
Snack Mix, 83
Snow Peas
    Pasta Salad with Herb Dijon Vinaigrette, 140

Pork Vermicelli, Chinese, 362
Scallop Stir-Fry with Crispy
        Noodle Pancakes, 316–317
Shrimp Fettuccine, 344
Wild Rice and Pork Salad, 156
Soufflé, Carrot, 171
Soups
    Artichoke, 113
    Bean, Three Bean, 96
    Black Bean, 97
    Broccoli, 95
    Broccoli, Cheesy, 465
    Burger, 464
    Chicken, Barley, and Bowtie, 98
    Chicken and Sausage Gumbo, 93
    Chicken Tortilla, 99
    cooking time, 109
    Corn, 100
    Corn and Squash Chowder, Spicy, 101
    Crab, Easy, 94
    Cucumber and Avocado, 90
    flour thickening, 93
    Gazpacho with Shrimp, 87
    Gazpacho, White, 88
    Italian, 110
    Onion, 112
    Pea, Split, 111
    Peach, 91
    Potato Bisque, Double Potato, 105
    Pumpkin, 107
    Salmon Bisque, 94
    Seafood Gumbo, 92
    Shrimp and Corn, Easy, 103
    Shrimp, Corn, and Sweet Potato, 104
    Shrimp, White Bean, and Pasta, 102
    soy milk substitute in, 89
    Spinach and Brie, Cream of, 107
    Strawberry, 91
    Vegetable and Barley, Beefy, 109
    Vegetable, Southwestern, 108
    Vichyssoise, 89
    Wild Rice, 113
    See also Chili

Southwestern
  Chicken with Bean Sauce, 236
  Fajitas, Beef, Grilled, 253
  Lasagna, Crispy, 255
  Pasta, Spicy, 326
  Pork Stew, 118
  Potatoes, Stuffed, 185
  Rice, 190
  Rice Salad, 158
  Shrimp and Black Bean Chili, 117
  Shrimp Pizza Dip, 23
  Tortellini Salad, 143
  Vegetable Soup, 108
  Vodka Pasta, 328
Soy protein, sources of, 89, 124
Spaghetti
  Meatballs and, 470
  Sauce, Meat, 361
  Sauce, Meatless, 329
Spinach
  Balls with Jezebel Sauce, 42
  and Black Bean Enchiladas, 195
  Bread Pudding, Florentine, 75
  and Brie Soup, Cream of, 107
  Cannelloni, Chicken and, 341
  Cheesy, Spicy, 197
  Chicken Breasts, Florentine, 221
  Chicken Lasagna, Quick, 355
  Chicken Salad Bowl, Greek, 147
  Chicken Salad Mandarin, 148
  Crêpes Florentine, 196
  Dip, 16
    Artichoke, 28
    Oyster Rockefeller, 29
  Eggplant, and Pasta, 332
  Filling, Cheesy, Eggplant Manicotti with, 335
  Fish Florentine, 287
  Lasagna, Mediterranean, 358
  Manicotti, Meaty, with Tomato Sauce, 360
  Mushroom Casserole, 198
  Oriental, 200
  Penne with Sun-Dried Tomatoes,
    Goat Cheese and, 325

Pie, Italian, 199
Pork Florentine Wellington
    with Green Peppercorn Sauce, 268
Salad, 124
Salad, Raspberry, 123
and Shrimp Skillet Surprise, 309
Squash, Rockefeller, 201
Tortilla Pizza, -and-Cheese, 49
White Pizza, Shrimp-and-, 310
Spreads
  Cheese Ball, Sweet, 27
  Shrimp, 21
  Shrimp, Avocado, and Artichoke, 20
  Shrimp Cocktail, 22
Squash
  Casserole, 202
  and Corn Chowder, Spicy, 101
  Pasta Toss, 336
  Pork, and Tomatoes, Italian, 275
  Rockefeller, 201
  summer, 336
Steak. See Beef, Steak
Stews
  Beef, Quick, 120
  flour thickening, 93
  Meatball, 119
  Pork, Southwestern, 118
Stir-Fry
  Beef, 251
  Chicken, Peanut, 225
  Chicken and Broccoli, Chinese, 227
  Pork Vermicelli, Chinese, 362
  Scallop, with Crispy Noodle Pancakes,
    316–317
Strawberry(ies)
  Angel Food Cake, 400
  Custard Brûlée, 426
  Custard Cake, 392–393
  Frosting, 480
  Gelatin, Pretzel, 160
  Heart Cake, 480
  Pie, Margarita, 454

Smoothie, 482
Soup, 91
Trifle, Fruit, 430
Strudel, 370
Stuffed
   Artichokes, Hearty, 46
   Cabbage, 263
   Flank Steak, 248
   Mushrooms, Portabello, with Goat Cheese
      and Roasted Red Peppers, 41
   Mushrooms, Seafood-, 40
   Peppers, 260
   Potatoes, Southwestern, 185
   Shells, Jumbo, 359
   Sweet Potatoes, Praline, 189
Stuffing
   Corn Bread, Yam, 205
   Eggplant, Basic, 207
   Shrimp, Fish with, Baked, 290
   Wild Rice, Cornish Hens with, 239
   See also Dressing
Suckers, Ghost, 481
Sunflower Seeds, Green Salad,
   Mixed with Cranberries and, 126
Sweet-and-Sour
   Broccoli Salad, 133
   Pork, 274
Sweet Potato(es) (Yams)
   Biscuits, 58
   Bisque, Double Potato, 105
   Bread, Cranberry, Easy, 62
   Bread Pudding with Praline Sauce, 419
   Bundt Cake, 391
   Casserole Praline Topping, 188
   Cheesecake, 424
   Corn Bread Stuffing, 205
   Oven Fries, 186
   Pie, Pecan Crumble, 452
   Pizza, 469
   Pork Stew, Southwestern, 118
   Praline Stuffed, 189
   Roasted, and White Potatoes, 187

Shrimp, and Corn Soup, 104
Veggie Wraps, 208
Swiss Chard, cooking method, 198

T
Taco(s)
   Cups, Mini, 43
   Rice Salad, 157
   Shrimp, with Tropical Salsa, 306
Tamale and Corn Casserole, 174
Tequilla Chicken, 234
Tex-Mex
   Dip, 18
   Eggs, 78
Thai Pasta Dish, 327
Three Bean Soup, 96
Tic-Tac-Toe Sandwiches, Open-Face, 466
Tiramisu, 436
   Cake, 402
Toffee
   Coffee Brownies, 376
   Coffee Dessert, 434
Tofu, as cream cheese substitute, 22
Tomato(es)
   Chili
      Black Bean, Shrimp and, Southwestern, 117
      Chicken, White, 115
      Vegetarian, Quick, 114
   Eggplant, Spinach, and Pasta, 332
   Eggplant Parmesan, 175
   Gazpacho with Shrimp, 87
   Lasagna, Vegetable, 356–357
   Meat Sauce with Spaghetti, 361
   Niçoise Salad, 153
   Pasta, Spicy Southwestern, 326
   Pork, and Squash, Italian, 275
   Pot Roast, Italian-Style, 246
   Salads
      and Cucumber, 129
      Macaroni, Corn and, 132
      Seven-Layer, 130
   Salsa, Fiesta, 26
   Salsa with Tortilla Chips, 25

Sauce, 261, 335, 359, 470
Sauce, Meaty Spinach Manicotti with, 361
Sauce, Roasted, Rigatoni with, 330
Spaghetti Sauce, Meatless, 329
Sun-Dried, Penne with Spinach,
    Goat Cheese and, 325
Tex-Mex Dip, 18
Veal with, 279
Vermicelli with Fresh Tomatoes, 324
Vodka Pasta, 328
See also Cherry Tomato(es)
Tortellini
  and Eggplant Casserole, 334
  Pasta Salad with Herb Dijon Vinaigrette, 140
  Salad, Southwestern, 143
  Salad, Shrimp, 144
  Seven-Layer Salad, 130
Tortilla(s)
  Chicken Casserole, Mexican, 237
  Chicken Soup, 99
  Chips, Homemade, Salsa with, 25
  Eggs, Tex-Mex, 78
  heating, 306
  Lasagna, Crispy Southwestern, 255
  Lasagna, Mexican, 256
  Pinwheels, Smoked Salmon, 39
  Pizza, Spinach-and-Cheese, 49
  Quesadillas, Cheese, 468
  Shrimp Bites, 39
  Shrimp Tacos with Tropical Salsa, 306
  Tamale Pie, 257
  Wraps, Yam Veggie, 208
  See also Enchiladas
Trifle
  Chocolate, 429
  Fantastic, 428
  Fruit, 430
  Lemon Pineapple, 431
Trout
  Eggplant Parmesan, 291
  Pecan, with Dijon Sauce, 285

Tuna
  albacore, 151
  Salad
    Deluxe, 151
    Grilled, with Wasabi-Ginger
      Vinaigrette, 154
    Italian, Marinated, 150
    Niçoise, 153
    and White Bean, 152
  Steaks with Horseradish Sauce, 296
Turkey
  Breast, Honey-Glazed, 241
  Jambalaya, 242
  Steaks with Prosciutto, 240

U

Upside-Down Cake, Tropical, 395

V

Vanilla Sauce, 454
Veal
  Elegante, 278
  Marengo, 277
  Saltimbocca, 276
  with Tomatoes, 279
Vegetable(s)
  Caponata, 32
  Chicken Primavera, 338
  Lasagna, 356–357
  nutrients in, 128
  and Pasta, Marinated, 142
  Rice, Summer, 191
  Soup
    and Barley, Beefy, 109
    Italian, 110
    Southwestern, 108
  Ziti Primavera, Shrimp, 347
  See also names of vegetables
Vegetarian Chili, Quick, 114
Vermicelli
  Chicken, 342
  Eggplant Pasta, 331

with Fresh Tomatoes, 324
Pork, Chinese, 362
Thai Pasta Dish, 327
Vinaigrette
  Citrus, Mixed Greens with
      Sugared Pecans and, 125
  Dill Dressing, 145
  Herb Dijon, Pasta Salad with, 140
  Mustard, Broccoli with, 168
  Niçoise Salad, 153
  Oriental, Mixed Green Salad with, 127
  Wasabi-Ginger, Grilled Tuna Salad
      with, 154
Vodka Pasta, 228

W

Wait Cake, 399
Waldorf Pasta Salad, 138
Wasabi
  about, 183
  Guacamole, 18
  Mashed Potatoes, 183
  Vinaigrette, Ginger, Grilled
      Tuna Salad with, 154
White Bean(s), 167
  Chicken Chili, 115
  Shrimp, and Pasta Soup, 102
  and Tuna Salad, 152
White Sauce, 265, 298
  Pizza, Shrimp and Spinach, 310
Wild Rice
  and Barley Pilaf, 192
  Chicken, Cranberry, with, 229
  and Oyster Dressing, 206
  and Peppers, 191
  and Pork Salad, 156
  Pork Tenderloin Diane with, 269
  and Seafood Casserole, 319
  Soup, 113
  Stuffing, Cornish Hens with, 239
Wraps, Yam Veggie, 208

Y

Yams. *See* Sweet Potato(es)

Z

Ziti Primavera, Shrimp, 347
Zucchini
  Bread, 64
  Bread, Chocolate, 68
  Chili, Vegetarian, Quick, 114
  Pasta Toss, 336

Substitutions

If You Don't Have	Amount	Substitute
Balsamic vinegar	1 tablespoon	1 tablespoon sherry or cider vinegar or ¼ cup red wine
Buttermilk	1 cup	1 tablespoon lemon juice or vinegar plus milk to make 1 cup or 1 cup plain fat-free or low-fat yogurt
Chocolate		
unsweetened chocolate	1 ounce block	3 tablespoons cocoa plus 1 tablespoon margarine
semisweet chocolate	1 ounce	1 ounce unsweetened chocolate plus 1 tablespoon sugar
semisweet chocolate chips	6 ounces	½ cup plus 1 tablespoon cocoa plus ¼ cup plus 3 tablespoons sugar plus 3 tablespoons margarine
semisweet chocolate chips	1 cup	6 ounces semisweet baking chocolate, chopped
Cornstarch	1 tablespoon	2 tablespoons all-purpose flour
Flour		
all-purpose	1 cup	1 cup self-rising flour, but omit any salt and baking powder from the recipe
self-rising	1 cup	1 cup all-purpose flour plus 1½ teaspoons baking powder plus ½ teaspoon salt
Pumpkin or apple pie spice	1 teaspoon	½ teaspoon ground cinnamon, ¼ teaspoon ground ginger, ⅛ teaspoon ground allspice, and ⅛ teaspoon ground nutmeg
Baking powder	1 teaspoon	1 teaspoon baking soda plus ½ teaspoon cream of tartar
Garlic	1 medium clove	⅛ teaspoon garlic powder or ¼ teaspoon instant minced garlic
Milk	1 cup	½ cup evaporated milk plus ½ cup water
Mustard, prepared	1 tablespoon	1 teaspoon dry ground mustard
Poultry seasoning	1 teaspoon	¼ teaspoon ground thyme plus ¾ teaspoon ground sage
Ricotta cheese	1 cup	1 cup cottage cheese
Sour cream	1 cup	1 cup plain fat-free yogurt
Tomato juice	1 cup	½ cup tomato sauce plus ½ cup water
Tomato paste	½ cup	1 cup tomato sauce cooked, uncovered, until reduced to ½ cup
Tomato sauce	2 cups	¾ cup tomato paste plus 1 cup water
Wine		
red	1 cup	1 cup apple cider, beef broth, tomato juice, or water
white	1 cup	1 cup apple juice, chicken broth, or water
Yogurt, plain	1 cup	1 cup sour cream